Roots of Contemporary Human Experiences

Published by AFRICAN SUN MeDIA under the SUN PReSS imprint
Place of publication: Stellenbosch, South Africa

Copyright © 2025 AFRICAN SUN MeDIA and the editors

This publication was subjected to an independent double-blind peer evaluation by the publisher.

The editor and the publisher have made every effort to obtain permission for and acknowledge the use of copyrighted material. Refer all enquiries to the publisher.

Views reflected in this publication are not necessarily those of the publisher.

First edition 2025

ISBN 978-0-6398893-4-4
ISBN 978-0-6398893-5-1 (e-book)
https://doi.org/10.52779/9780639889351

Set in Alegreya Sans 11.5/16
Cover design, typesetting and production by AFRICAN SUN MeDIA
Cover image: © Natasha Raubenheimer

SUN PReSS is an imprint of AFRICAN SUN MeDIA. Scholarly, professional and reference works are published under this imprint in print and electronic formats.

Our publications can be ordered from:
orders@africansunmedia.co.za
Takealot: bit.ly/2monsfl
Google Books: bit.ly/2k1Uilm
africansunmedia.store.it.si (e-books)
Amazon: amzn.to/2ktL.pkL
JSTOR: https://bit.ly/3udc057

Visit africansunmedia.co.za for more information.

Roots

of

Contemporary Human Experiences

A Journey Through Everyday Emotions

Melanie Moen and
Yolandi-Eloise Janse van Rensburg (eds.)

SUN PRESS

CONTENTS

ACKNOWLEDGMENT

Herewith, we would like to thank the Faculty of Military Science, Stellenbosch University for providing the financial means to make the publication of this book possible.

I

Never have I witnessed emotions as deep and powerful as those a father holds for his children. Tom, Léna, and Zoé Fontaine, whether near or far, each of you leaves a profound emotional imprint on your dad. Our stories may look different, but our connection is found in the underlying emotion. We love you deeply, unconditionally, always.

Yolandi

I

I dedicate this book to my family, who I unconditionally love.

Melanie

PREFACE

Yolandi-Eloïse Janse van Rensburg
Melanie Moen

The ability to understand emotions and emotional experiences has always been important to function effectively in society. Emotional experiences are reactions in response to events or situations that are influenced by a subjective internal feeling, how the body responds to a specific emotion, and how one then reacts to or behaves toward the outer world.

Developing an understanding of the interplay among social, cognitive, and biological processes in emotion is important. A group of international researchers combined their collective expertise to write this book on daily experiences, which are rooted in basic emotions. The overarching theme of the book concerns the understanding of basic emotions. Each chapter commences with a vignette that plays off in a small coastal town called

Riverside, where a close-knit group of friends (Eric, Mel, Ophelia, Tim, Isabelle, Oscar, and Nicky) go through daily experiences that elicit different emotions. The reader can use the vignette from the beginning of each chapter to relate to the experience of basic emotions (i.e., reported in literature as basic emotions theory, which are happiness, sadness, disgust, anger, fear and surprise) and blended, more self-conscious emotional experiences (e.g., shame, guilt, pride, hubris, aggression, trauma, courage, awe and hope).

By demonstrating a particular emotion in each chapter, we address various themes of several important emotions that shape our lives. Our approach to this book is to define and describe these emotions by referring to the origin of each emotion (e.g., biological, social, situational and learnt), describing different theoretical lenses regarding an emotion and to highlight the valence or opposite of a specific emotion (i.e., the subjective positive or negative character of paired emotions, e.g., hope vs despair, humility vs pride). The term *opposite emotion* is used as a metaphorical tool to understand the emotional landscape and not as an actual fact about emotions having opposite relationships with other emotions. For example, stating that the opposite of happiness is sadness, or that the opposite of salt is pepper – this is not necessarily true, as these two different emotions are like the two different substances. Finally, each chapter also concludes with an application section, which provides some suggestions on enhancing or reducing the experience of specific emotions. In the final chapter, a broad overview of emotional intelligence is provided.

Given that this book is compiled for both academic and public audiences, it is written using colloquial language, while being scientifically grounded. Reading this book may improve one's self-awareness about emotions (i.e., recognising emotions in the self and others), enhance decision-making (e.g., avoiding impulsive reactions by showing emotional control), build better relations by developing compassion and empathy, and improve effective communication (i.e., by expressing one's own emotions more appropriately).

CHAPTER SUMMARIES

Chapter 1 / Mapping the Route: Understanding the Roots of
Emotional Experiences

Yolandi-Eloïse Janse van Rensburg
Melanie Moen

Have you ever wondered where emotions come from, how they can be defined, how long they last, or how many there are? This chapter sets the landscape for a basic understanding of emotions. Although there are many different theories, numerous empirical research studies, and countless books and reviews on each of the themes discussed in this chapter, each section provides a summary to provide a general and theoretical basis from which the remaining chapters can be understood.

Chapter 2 / Happiness is a Balancing Act

Linda Bosman

This chapter delves into the intricate landscape of two fundamental human emotions, happiness and sadness. Drawing upon an array of interdisciplinary research, it seeks to provide a comprehensive understanding of the nuanced facets of these emotions. This review explores the diverse dimensions of happiness and sadness, shedding light on their impact on individual wellbeing and societal dynamics. This piece aims to contribute to a deeper appreciation of the complexity of human emotional experiences by analysing the biological underpinnings, psychological determinants, and cultural and social influences.

Chapter 3 / Rotten Roots: The Physical, Psychological and Moral
Intricacies of Disgust

Melanie Moen

Disgust is not an easy emotion to define, the diversity and multifaceted characteristics of disgust complicates the definition. Disgust is recognised as a basic and universal emotion that is often described as a feeling of revulsion towards something that is perceived as offensive, unpleasant or dirty. Besides pathogen avoidance, disgust is also described from moral, social and cultural perspectives, which can sometimes also include dehumanisation of the subject of disgust. However, this complicated emotion can also be associated with both sexual disgust and self-disgust. Although disgust is mostly described as a negative emotion, it also serves an important means of protecting humans. Humour and elevation are often used as therapeutic interventions as solutions to social disgust.

Chapter 4 / A Kaleidoscope of Self-conscious Emotions: Shame, Guilt, Embarrassment, and Pride

Yolandi-Eloïse Janse van Rensburg

This chapter provides a better understanding of self-conscious emotions by disentangling 'sister emotions', which are all related in some way. More specifically, shame, guilt, embarrassment, pride, and hubris are briefly described. Research shows that shame and hubristic pride are both negatively-valenced emotions, and that neither of these emotions are necessarily helpful, as they have been found to significantly relate to mental health problems. Additionally, embarrassment, which is a less intense form of shame, is experienced in public, is physical and short-lived. Finally, legitimate guilt and authentic pride are positively-valenced emotions, as both these emotions significantly relate to prosocial behaviour. The chapter provides a roadmap to move from shame to enhancing authentic pride.

Chapter 5 / Human Anger and Aggression: Nature versus Nurture

Christiaan Bezuidenhout

Anger and aggressive acts are complex emotions and difficult to define. Several theories consider nature versus nurture when defining anger and aggression. Nature, nurture and all the interlinking variables cannot be viewed independently, as they influence and complement one another. The earlier contributions about specific drives in humans, learning processes, as well as biology and psychology, set the stage for the many efforts that have developed over time to explain anger and aggression. Some scholars believe aggression can be utilised in a positive way, and that everyone needs a bit of aggression to lead a healthy, productive life. In this chapter, we will also contemplate that one should never forget free choice. Every person has a choice as to how they will react to aggressive stimuli or when and why they need to display aggression.

Chapter 6 / The Thin Line that Cuts Through Every Heart: Fear
and Courage

Yolandi-Eloïse Janse van Rensburg

Palesa Luzipo

Lindiwe Masole

Feelings of fear may originate from various sources, such as events, bodily injuries or death, encountering dangerous animals, or agoraphobic situations. New research shows that prolonged feelings of fear can lead to permanent damage to one's physical health and may even affect one's future offspring. This chapter briefly presents scientific findings on the sources and processes of fear, and how one may respond. We propose courage, and while it is not necessarily the opposite of fear, it is one way to deal with situations where one might experience fear. In this chapter, we provide a brief discussion on what courage entails.

Chapter 7 / Tainted Roots: Trauma and its Impact on Emotions

Tyler I. Counsil

In this chapter, readers will delve into the widespread occurrence of trauma and its profound impacts on various aspects of wellbeing, including emotional, cognitive, and physical health, as well as resilience. Readers will examine different types of trauma, and consider cultural influences on its manifestation and effects across its lifespan. Trauma, stemming from shocking or devastating events, can manifest as either acute or chronic, depending on an individual's perception. Although its recognition dates to ancient times, the formal term emerged in the 19th century. Since then, research has linked trauma to disruptions in physical and cognitive functioning, emotional dysregulation, and conditions like post-traumatic stress disorder (or PTSD). Biologically, trauma triggers responses from the amygdala. Societal, genetic and cultural factors, including sexual identity, socio-economic status, and religious beliefs, also play significant roles in trauma development. Various forms of trauma exist, such as bullying, interpersonal violence, and abuse, each carrying profound emotional consequences like anxiety and social isolation. Despite its pervasive nature, evidence-based interventions like cognitive behavioural therapy offer avenues for managing trauma's emotional toll. Prevention efforts target individual, relational, and societal factors to foster resilience and reduce traumatic experiences.

Chapter 8 / Passion: The Known Unknown
Sifiso Shabangu

This chapter explores the origins of passion and how we have come to understand it. Originally regarded as an overwhelming and meaningless bundle of human emotions, passion has evolved to be understood as purposeful, precise, and a contributor to identity creation and a meaningful existence. The physiological roots of passion within the brain systems will be discussed. The relationship of passion and romantic love will also be explored. Passion propels us to initiate romantic relationships and fuels our desire to be with another person beyond sexual gratification, as an evolutionary tool for continued existence of humanity. Further, the relationship between passion and addiction reveals that obsessive passion is a conduit to addiction. This is sometimes evident in passionate love, where the 'addicted partner' compulsively, uncontrollably, and increasingly desires the other. This chapter will also explore lust, the desire for sexual gratification, and how lustful paraphilias can sometimes result in aggression and loss of life. The absence of passion (apathy), pleasure (anhedonia), and the inability to identify and express emotion (alexithymia) will be discussed to highlight what could be understood as the 'opposite' of passion. Finally, we will describe emotion regulation strategies to help enhance passionate engagement.

Chapter 9 / Looking at You to See Me: Exploring Empathy
and Compassion

Elsa Etokabeka

Melanie Moen

Most of us will, at some stage in our life, experience challenges of a severe or lesser degree. Therefore, it is important to have supportive people in our lives who can listen empathetically. The benefits of being heard by others creates an opportunity to note one's own feelings, express them, as well as make sense of what has transpired. Compassion demonstrated both towards oneself and others, creates a space of acceptance and care. In this chapter, the value of empathy and compassion will be highlighted. More specifically, we will illuminate the definitions of empathy and compassion, while attempting to provide a broad description of the origins of these emotions. The positive side of both emotions will also be discussed, while the consequences of the absence of these emotions will be outlined. Different ways of enhancing these emotions will also be described in this chapter.

Chapter 10 / Trust: Taking Risks Until Scepticism is Trounced

Judite Ferreira-Prévost

In this chapter, we aim to present trust as a vibrant, complex, interactive and dynamic construct, forming the basis of our relationships, and indeed necessary for our very social survival. We will come to understand that trust can be found in our emotions, thoughts and actions, and that, although we can at times consciously manage it, we find that sometimes it appears spontaneously. We will also appreciate how our previous experiences, disposition, expectations, sense of control and values, as well as our perceptions of the ability, goodwill and integrity of the person or situation awaiting our trust, influence the trajectory of the trust process. We will come to realise that ultimately, trust calls for us to become vulnerable, take a risk and act. This chapter will attempt to bring a deeper appreciation of trust in its various facets, and offer strategies and ideas on which to ponder, which may empower one to trust more wisely, but to also become a more trusting – and hopefully trustworthy – human being.

Chapter 11 / Awe: Vastly Beyond Surprise

Mathieu Gagnon

After the brief story illustrating the awe experienced by the character Nicky, we explore the nature and many nuances of this emotion. This chapter begins by explaining how awe differs from surprise, and why this distinction matters to better understand Nicky's experience. Next, we will explore the kind of emotion that awe is, and the different forms it can take. Further, the conditions under which one can experience awe and the diverse ways in which it manifests itself will be revealed. The origins and functions of awe are explained, and we explore what is currently known concerning the development of this emotion during childhood and beyond. Having delt with such fundamental questions, we will move on to how awe influences our mental health and wellbeing, as well as our prosocial and consumption behaviours. Lastly, we recommend ways in which one can deliberately experience awe in daily life. In the end, we hope to leave a sense of appreciation for this important human emotion, and a curiosity as to how to find more of it in everyday things.

Chapter 12 / The Superpower of Hope

Melissa Greenberg

Palesa Luzipo

Lobna Chérif

Yolandi-Eloïse Janse van Rensburg

This chapter briefly presents the theoretical frameworks underpinning hope as a cogitative process and an emotion. Cultivating hope fosters personal success and performance, and enhances overall life satisfaction. Therefore, this chapter also briefly addresses how one can best harness hope, using it as a psychological buffer and coping mechanism to foster improved health and wellbeing. Finally, hope's antithetical counterpart, despair, is briefly discussed, as measures to manage hopelessness are proposed.

Chapter 13 / Emotional Intelligence Research Over Four Decades: Implications for Researchers and Practitioners in \ Basic Emotions

Gina Görgens-Ekermans

This chapter will provide a brief overview of emotional intelligence (EI) research over the last four decades, by focusing on unpacking the foundational role of emotions in EI, providing an overview of prominent approaches to the conceptualisation and operationalisation of EI, exploring whether emotional intelligence can be developed, and review the known benefits of such training interventions, as well as briefly discussing practical recommendations and best practice guidelines for EI interventions, set within the unifying framework of social and emotional learning programmes.

CHAPTER 1

Mapping the Route: Understanding the Roots of Emotional Experiences

Yolandi-Eloïse Janse van Rensburg
Melanie Moen

Friday the 13th – Just another night at the movies

In a quaint little coastal town called Riverside, Eric, Mel, Ophelia, Tim, Isabelle, Oscar and Nicky have shared the most intimate parts of their lives with each other. Since becoming friends in high school, they have remained friends for 20 years. And whenever a Friday falls on the 13th of any calendar month, it has become a tradition, or more of a ritual, for the group of friends to meet for supper and watch a movie together.

On this specific Friday evening, the movie ends with a majestic scene: blue-grey mountains, a red sky, and sentimental music in the background. After two intense, nail-biting hours, all the movie characters get their happy ending, with the exception of the main character, who dies. The movie evokes intense emotions in each of the friends. As they all glare in silence at the big screen for the last few minutes, each reflects on the movie, and for a moment, on their own life. Nicky is left in awe; this was a real jaw-dropper – she could not even imagine the story ending like it did; Oscar is pumped for action – scary horror scenes always get him excited. Mel is sobbing, because the main character, the good-hearted sister, dies in the movie – which reminds her of her own recent loss; Eric is angry because the thug in the movie is never caught and literally gets away with murder; Tim feels that his passion is rekindled by hearing the music in the movie – he is ready to write his next masterpiece; and Isabelle is left feeling both sad (because the main character dies), but also hopeful – perhaps, like the character in the movie, she too might find the love of her life.

Who knew how their lives would change over the next few weeks? Life in Riverside would never be the same...

Introduction

As humans, we all experience emotions and most of us think we know what emotions are. However, defining emotions can be difficult. For instance, most of us know what a pear looks and tastes like, but explaining the experience and sensation of eating a pear to someone else might be challenging. Similarly, the ability to understand and to teach others about emotions may also be difficult. When one considers the vignette at the beginning of this chapter, we can acknowledge that every person experiences, interprets and reacts differently to a shared or similar situation. What complicates the understanding of emotions is that emotions have different features, which involve feelings and experiences, and are often represented from cognitive, behavioural, physiological, expressive, and neurological perspectives (Mordka, 2016; Ortony et al., 2022). In addition to this, emotions can also be experienced with different intensities and can oscillate between positive or negative experiences; emotions might be used to appraise situations, and may assist people to allocate resources and prioritise daily life. Emotions are one of the most central and pervasive aspects of human experiences and life, and they are instrumental in tailoring cognitive style to situational demands, they facilitate decision-making, they prepare one for rapid motor responses (e.g., fear prior to fight, flight, freeze), and they also assist in learning. Some theorists believe that emotions are functional, in that they help people deal with concerns, by enabling them to adapt, and therefore to cope in certain situations. Additionally, emotions are linked to our deepest values (i.e., who and what we love, what we dislike, or what we despise), and help us form and engage in relationships (Keltner et al., 2014). Emotions not only colour, deepen, and enrich human experiences, but they also cause dramatic disruptions in life (Ortony, 2022).

Therefore, understanding the interplay amongst social, cognitive, and biological processes in experiencing emotions is important, and critical for the effective functioning in society (Satpute et al., 2016). To make sense of the complex processes involved in understanding emotions, one must be able to understand the origins thereof.

Distinguishing between affect, mood, emotion and feeling

Affect, mood, feeling, and emotion are often used interchangeably, but researchers agree that these constructs are conceptually and empirically different (Amstadter, 2008). To understand emotions better, it is important to differentiate between these concepts from the outset. The best way to explain these concepts is to use a metaphor: 'emotion' is lighting a match to make a fire (i.e., the spark), 'feeling' is the warmth the fire brings, 'mood' is the surrounding atmosphere (being outside in the wilderness at night), and 'affect' is the general (pleasant/unpleasant) experience of the evening. These concepts are explained in more detail next.

Affect refers to the superordinate class for all valenced conditions, and is used as an umbrella term to encompass emotion, mood, and feeling (Amstadter, 2008). Where an emotion follows a specific eliciting event and is intense (but limited in duration), affective feelings refer to the subjective experiences of emotions or moods. Affective feelings can be distinguished from those that are nonaffective in nature, for instance hunger. Affect is also embedded in social, cultural, and historical context and the meaning of affective practices is constructed in relation to context (Schall, 2011). Similarly, affect refers to a combination of positive and negative emotions or moods, with 'positive affect' referring to several positive states (e.g., enjoyment), and 'negative affect' consisting of various negative states (Reinhard-Pekrun & Linnenbrink-Garcia, 2014). The functionality of affect is evident – *directly*, in the way people deal with certain stimuli in the environment, and *indirectly*, in the way people cognitively process information about the environment (Schall, 2011).

Mood is described as a short-lived emotional state, usually low in intensity. Moods differ from emotions because they lack stimuli and have no clear starting point; therefore, moods are of lower intensity and lack specific reference (Pekrun & Linnenbrink-Garcia, 2014). Mood refers to a state that typically lasts for hours, days, or weeks, and may linger as a subtle background presence. Exactly when a mood begins or ends may be unclear. Episodes of emotion are typically directed at an object, whereas moods are often objectless and free-floating. Moods are different, compared to emotions, because emotions are more specific. For instance, one can become angry if someone swears at them, but one cannot always determine why one is feeling irritable or a specific way (Keltner et al., 2014).

Feeling is emotion that has been rendered conscious. Although emotions develop as biological processes, they culminate as personal mental experiences. The contrast here is between the outer and visible aspects of an emotion and its inner, intimate experience. The former is a collection of biological responses – from alterations in behaviour and hormonal levels, to changes in facial expression – that can in many cases be scientifically measured. The latter is the private awareness of a specific emotion and what one is feeling. That is why one can describe your own feelings fairly accurately, but one may struggle to describe others' with the same degree of confidence. Thus, one may be able to describe other people's outer expressions, but only theorise about their inner feelings (Frazetto, 2013).

Emotions are "flexible response sequences elicited by internal or external events appraised as relevant to an organism's well-being" (Amstadter, 2008, p. 211). Emotions serve as a communicative function in humans, and their expression constitutes an outward communication of an inner state (Reinhard-Pekrun & Linnenbrink-Garcia, 2014). Emotional states are experiences at specific moments in time (Van Steelandt et al., 2005). It is a common assumption that emotion is a conscious experience; however, there are theorists who propose that emotional processes can also take place outside of conscious awareness (Schall, 2011). Emotions are often defined as part of a complex reaction pattern, involving experiential, behavioural and physiological elements. Emotions indicate how individuals deal with matters or situations they find personally significant. Emotions can, therefore, be described as multifaceted, involving sets of coordinated physiological processes. For example, fear before undergoing an operation can include feelings of *what if I die?* (affective); worries about the operation itself, and whether the surgeons are competent to follow the correct procedures (cognitive); physical responses such as an increased heart rate as the day for the operations draws closer (physiological); impulses to cancel the operation (motivation), and the tangible appearance of fear on the face when being pushed into theatre for the operation (expression) (Pekrun & Linnenbrink-Garcia, 2014).

Core affect is often translated as the everyday feeling. In its primitive form, core affect is free-floating – in other words it lacks an object. For instance, one can feel anxious without knowing why the feeling is present. Core affect thus fits the ontological requirements for a primitive and simple emotional ingredient. Core affect is that neurophysiological state consciously accessible as the simplest raw feelings evident in moods and emotions, such as feeling pleasant versus feeling unpleasant. Core affect consists of all possible combinations of arousal and valence (i.e., high versus low energy and pleasure versus displeasure), and, therefore, it includes states that would not be called emotions, for example fatigue (low arousal and negatively-valenced) or excited (high arousal and positively-valenced). Therefore, a person is always in some state of core affect, which can be neutral, mild, or extreme, and is part of most physiological processes (Millon et al., 2003). One might best understand core affect as the 'raw material' from which emotions are made.

Basic and complex emotions

Many emotion theorists hold that there exists a small set of discrete, primary and basic emotions. Basic emotions are associated with recognisable facial expressions and tend to happen instinctually. Although basic emotion theory (BET) has been criticised (e.g., Ortony, 2022; Smith & Schneider, 2009), some researchers still believe that the BET holds true (Hutto, 2018). After much reading and debate, we mostly identified with Ekman (1992), who acknowledges six basic emotions namely happiness, sadness, fear, anger, disgust and surprise. In fact, Ekman (1992) provides nine criteria, which distinguish basic emotions: (1) universal facial expressions, (2) presence in other primates, (3) specific physiology, (4) distinct antecedent events, (5) a coherent response pattern, (6) quick onset, (7) brief duration, (8) accompanying a distinct appraisal pattern, and (9) an unbidden occurrence. Other theorists have suggested additional defining characteristics to add to this criteria, such as distinct ways that basic emotions influence perceptions, or subsequent behavioural actions (Izard, 1992; Selenski & Larsen, 2000). Following these criteria, Eckman (1993) later added to the list of six basic emotions (to include guilt, pride, and shame to name a few).

However, researchers have reported different accounts of what qualify as basic emotions and how many of these basic emotions in fact exist. For example, Mowrer (1960) identified only pleasure versus pain, while Cowan and Keltner (as cited in Ortony, 2022) identified as many as 18 basic emotions, namely, amusement, anger, anxiety, awe, confusion, contentment, desire, disgust, elation, embarrassment, fear, interest, love, pain, relief, sadness, surprise, and triumph. Overall, there is an acceptance of the general idea of having what is referred to as either basic or primary emotions (Hutto et al., 2018). Adding to basic emotions theory are secondary emotions or *blends* of these basic emotions. In fact, much like the colour wheel, Plutchik (1980) developed the nuanced idea of using the six basic emotions as building blocks, so that more complex emotions can emanate from them when they are mixed (e.g., surprise and happiness might lead to awe; fear and disgust together may cause shame).

Mixed emotions

Earlier theorists, such as Brehm and Miron (2006) challenged the view that opposite emotions are experienced simultaneously. These authors posited that negative and positive affects are independent and cannot occur simultaneously, and that 'mixed emotion' is best described as a rapid shift between opposing states. However, current theories seem to characterise mixed emotions as the simultaneous experience of both positive and negative feelings. These mixed emotions are a type of emotion blend, defined as the simultaneous occurrence of two or more emotions, with similar or opposing valences. For instance, when people appear to be midway between experiencing two emotions, such as pleasure and pain, they might be experiencing 'mixed emotions' (Zheng et al., 2021; Larson & MacGraw, 2014). Positively-valenced emotions encompass various discrete forms, such as excitement, hope, and happiness, while negatively-valenced emotions, like fear, sadness, and disgust, also exhibit diverse manifestations. Consequently, it is plausible that mixed emotions can manifest in numerous forms, depending on the combination of different emotions (Larson & McGraw, 2014).

Zheng et al. (2021) believe that mixed emotions can have a positive impact on a person's wellbeing, and that it might buffer the negative effect of stressful events on an individual's health. The experience of mixed emotions is also influenced by one's openness to experience, their resilience, as well as their age. In various situations, individuals can experience a blend of positive and negative emotions simultaneously. Such mixed emotions often arise in more complex scenarios, like winning a disappointing prize, or reminiscing about a lost love with both warmth and sadness. As described in the vignette, Isabelle felt sad because the main character in the movie died. However, she also felt hope to find her possible true love. Compared to singular-valanced emotions, experiencing mixed emotions appears to offer a more appropriate response to emotionally intricate events, accurately mirroring both coexisting positive and negative aspects.

This mixed emotional experience proves particularly advantageous in stressful circumstances, where it becomes challenging to evade the negative effects of distressing events. A dash of positive emotion might aid in alleviating an overall feeling of negativity. The adaptive nature of mixed emotions becomes apparent in how they can mitigate the intensity of negativity associated with adverse situations: the presence of positive emotions alters the perception of negative emotions by reducing their physiological arousal, while still acknowledging their presence. Hence, experiencing mixed emotions facilitates a reduction in distress, without compromising the informative aspect of emotions (Braniecka et al., 2014). According to Larsen and McGraw (2014), embracing both the positive and negative aspects of situations can be beneficial during challenging times, as it enables individuals to confront adversity and eventually derive meaning from life's trials, leading to a sense of emotional wellbeing. Braniecka et al. (2014) provide empirical evidence, indicating that experiencing both positive and negative affects concurrently may assist in coping with difficult situations. More recently, scientists used magnetic resonance imaging (MRI) to show that mixed emotions are, in fact, experienced in very specific areas of the brain, and are not simply a blend of purely positive and negative emotions (Vaccaro, 2024). More research should be conducted to fully understand mixed emotions.

Defining emotion

The concept of *emotion* presents a particularly difficult one, and describing it rarely generates the same answer. The lack of an agreed-upon definition of the term emotion has led to serious misunderstandings about this topic. We, therefore, need to address this issue and mark our position. To present a comprehensive overview and definition of *emotion*, several perspectives are highlighted to elucidate the concept, whereafter a summarised definition that guides the remaining chapters of this book is provided.

First, the word emotion comprises two elements: *e* (denoting *from*) and *movere* (meaning *to move*). The *e* signifies something that is outside or external, which is also connected to moving out from one place to another, and, therefore, refers to an action (Mordka, 2016). Merriam-Webster (n.d.) defines emotion as, "[a] conscious mental reaction (as anger or fear) subjectively experienced as [a] strong feeling usually directed toward a specific object and typically accompanied by physiological and behavioural changes in the body." Adding to this, Keltner and Gross (1999, p. 468) define emotion as "episodic, relatively short-term, biologically based patterns of perception, experience, physiology, action, and communication that occur in response to specific physical and social challenges and opportunities," while Keltner et al. (2014) define emotion as a psychological state or process that mediates between our concerns (or goals) and events in the world. These authors state that emotions can be defined by using three different facets: the first facet is *behavioural* – we often express emotion through facial and vocal expressions, posture and gestures. The second facet is *physiological* – emotions involve activations in the brain, the autonomic nervous system, as well as other systems in the body. In other words, bodily aspects help to prepare us for actions of a particular kind, for instance, preparing ourselves to escape. The third aspect is the *experiential* aspect – we often become conscious of our emotions so that we can represent our experience of emotions in language, for instance, when we discuss emotions we experienced with or amongst other people. For example, emotional experiences can give rise to inspiring forms of fiction, poetry, music, art and dance (Keltner et al., 2014).

Given these three definitions of emotion, we also add the definition of Ortony (2022), which reports that for a mental state to be labelled as an emotion, it must possess the following three features: first, it must be *intentional* (i.e., *about* something). For instance, one can be ashamed or proud of something that was done in the past, or show fear in a scary situation. However, emotions are different compared to affective conditions, such as moods, pathologies, and core affect, as these are not experienced about anything in particular (e.g., one might be in a bad mood, but not for any singular reason). Second, the mental state must be *valenced* (i.e., positive, negative, or mixed assessment). Third, for a mental state to be called an emotion, it must be *conscious*; thus, moving away from the idea that emotions are implicit and unconscious (i.e., one experiences an emotion, becomes aware of it, and, therefore, can discuss the emotion felt).

Taking these definitions together in this book, we define emotions as a conscious, relatively short-term reaction, which is accompanied by physiological and behavioural changes in the body, which is intentionally experienced because of some form of stimuli that is either mixed, positively, or negatively valanced. We add to this notion that emotions are functional, in that they help us deal adaptively with concerns specific to a context or situation. We also agree that emotions are linked to our *deepest values* and/ or *goals*, who and what we love, what we dislike or what we despise, and what we wish to achieve. Further, emotions also help form and engage in interpersonal relationships (Keltner et al., 2014) and that emotions serve a communicative function (Mackenzie & Alba-Juez, 2019). Additionally, we agree with the neuroscientific perspective, which considers emotions as instruments and motivators for culture, arguing that intellect is embedded in affect.

Theoretical contributions that explain emotion

Emotions and emotional interplay have been studied from various angles, including cognitive, developmental, clinical, social and neuroscience perspectives (Cacioppo & Gardner, 1999). Whilst some researchers have described emotions as feelings of bodily events (i.e., emotions arise because of physical arousal in the body, such as a racing heart, sweat, and heavy breathing indicates the experience of fear), others believe that emotions involve a cognitive appraisal of the body's physiological response, in light of a specific situation. However, many theorists agree that emotions are a subset of the broader class of affective phenomena (Cacioppo & Gardner, 1999). Although emotion is an extremely complex and mysterious experience encountered daily, we provide a summary of different theories of emotion. Many of these broad theories have been supported with empirical evidence, but they have also been criticised by researchers. Although there are more than 150 theories of emotion, we provide a summary of the nine broad categories. These clusters of theories should not be seen as being in opposition to each other, but rather as a means of enhancing a holistic understanding of emotional experiences (i.e., and are somewhat in line with the ideas of Strongman, 2003).

Evolutionary. These theories of emotion are related to Darwin's (1872) evolutionary theory, where emotions are linked to human behavioural repertoire and motivation, and allow humans (and animals) to survive and reproduce. Darwin proposed that emotional expressions are largely derived from habits that, in our evolutionary or individual past, had once been useful. Darwin believed that emotional expressions are based on reflex-like mechanisms and may continue to occur, whether they are still useful or not. Darwin further believed that our emotions are linked to our past and built strong arguments for the universality of facial expressions (Keltner et al., 2014).

Physiological. In addition to evolutionary theories, some researchers have allowed us to think broadly about the role of bodily systems in emotion (physiological, neurological, biological). These theories build on historical theory of emotion to include bodily reactions. *Physiological theories* suggest that responses within the body are responsible for emotions. One well-known theory in this cluster is the *James-Lange theory*, suggesting that an external stimulus (arousal) leads to a physiological reaction (causing the autonomic nervous system to react), which in turn causes an emotion (e.g., whilst Oscar is watching the movie scene where the thief enters the house, it causes him to have heart palpitations, causing his emotion, e.g., excitement or fear). Although criticised by many, researchers continue to find contemporary evidence that supports this theory (Barrett, 2012). However, the *Cannon-Bard theory*, which is also supported by neurobiological science, differs somewhat from the James-Lang theory, claiming that bodily reactions and emotions occur simultaneously instead of sequentially (e.g., watching the scene where the thief enters the house, Oscar's heart pounds, his hands sweat, and he experiences excitement or fear, all at once). The *facial-feedback hypothesis* suggests that facial expressions are necessary to experience emotion (thus encouraging facial expressions, such as forcing oneself to smile when one's inclination is to frown) may impact emotions (i.e., forcing a smile will lead to happiness; Folk & Dunn, 2024). On the other hand, the *Schacter-Singer two-factor theory* states that, because physiological arousal is very similar across the different types of emotions, the cognitive appraisal of a situation is linked to the emotion experienced. In this instance, Oscar watches the scene where the thief enters the house, he experiences that his heart is pounding, and simultaneously, a cognitive label is created (i.e., *I am scared*); therefore, the emotion of fear emerges.

Biological and neurological theories propose that activity within the brain leads to emotional responses. There is both a *somatic* component (i.e., comprising physiological and peripheral activity, both inside and outside of the brain), and a gross *motor* component (comprising facial and vocal expressions, and physical behaviour, e.g., fight, flight, freeze when experiencing fear, or showing pulled-up eyebrows, wide-open eyes, and a gasping mouth when surprised). Using magnetic resonance imaging (MRI) and positron emission tomography (PET), scientists have begun to make great progress in understanding the areas of the brain involved in different types of emotion. In fact, with neuroimaging meta-analyses, scientists have found that emotion is related to a group of structures in the centre of the brain, called the limbic system, which includes various parts of the brain (e.g., the hypothalamus, thalamus, amygdala, and the hippocampus, all of which are relevant in mediating emotional responses). Additionally, neurochemicals (e.g., dopamine, noradrenaline, and serotonin) may impact the brain's activity level. Some theorists believe that basic emotions, such as anger, disgust, fear, happiness, sadness, or surprise (and secondary, or blends of these basic emotions), are biologically basic, inherited, and that each is associated with very different parts of the brain (Lindquist et al., 2012). However, other academics interested in a brain-based view of emotion may not necessarily share this view. For more information on emotions and the brain, we recommend reading Barrett (2017).

Developmental. Emotional development occurs throughout life; however, infant attachment plays a vital role in emotional development. According to *differential emotions theory*, emotions retain their adaptive functions across a person's lifespan. Although different sets of emotions may become more prominent at different stages of a person's life, there are four specific emotional developmental milestones across life, which are recorded (e.g., Abe & Izard, 1999). These milestones include *infancy* (i.e., emotions are used to signal needs, desires, distress to caregivers); *toddler and preschool* (2–5 years), which is associated with an increase in anger (e.g., commonly referred to as the terrible twos), but also an increased capacity for experiencing empathy, and (for example) embarrassment, which fosters prosocial behaviour. Next, *middle and late childhood* (6–12 years) is associated with increased social comparison and the ability to conceptualise self-evaluative emotions, such as enhanced shame and pride. Further, *adolescence* is characterised with changes in cognitive (i.e., enhanced capacity for abstract thinking), biological (e.g., puberty), and social (e.g., heightened self-consciousness and competition amongst peers) elements of emotion. These social-cognitive changes may result in emotional conflict and distress. Additionally, although literature on children's emotional development is well documented, aspects of differential emotions theory in *adulthood* only progressed much later.

To give some examples, empirical cross-sectional and longitudinal studies have revealed that *anger* may decrease across a lifetime while *disgust* may increase; the intensity of negative affect may decrease (until around 60 years, but increasing again after 85 years); general positive affect (e.g., happiness) may generally increase until around 70–80 years, and emotional *expressivity*, *complexity* of emotional experiences, and the *intensity* of felt emotions may also vary across different ages (see Consedine & Magai, 2006, for more explicit examples). Furthermore, as one grows older, one may experience emotions as more complex, which might be caused by becoming more reflective when ageing. Current conversations on development include the intertwine between biology and environmental processes that produce a specific outcome. For instance, epigenetics has revealed the mechanisms by which nature and nurture work together to impact behaviour, for example, when particular experiences or events suppress or trigger a genetic predisposition (it might be that the tendency to be anxious is a genetic predisposition which is triggered by a particular stressful situation) (Miller, 2022).

Cognitive and appraisal. These theories argue that thoughts and other mental activities play an essential role in forming emotions. Theorists have had different ideas as to how emotions are generated in cognitive theories. For example, Lazarus (1982) views cognition and emotion being almost instantaneous. Thus, in this instance, one first experiences a stimulus, then thinks about it, and then simultaneously experiences a physiological response and an emotion (e.g., a thief enters someone's house; they *think* he might have a gun and the person realises they might therefore be injured or even be killed; they then experience heart palpitations and the emotion, fear, simultaneously). Contrary to this, Zajonc (as cited in Frijda, 1993) argues emotion precedes cognition; that emotion and cognition are independent, and that memory and beliefs play an important role in experiencing emotion. Additionally, the *cognitive appraisal theory* is used to understand the emotion-cognition link (e.g., danger is related to fear, or loss is linked to sadness). In appraisal theories of emotion, the core concept is, that what elicits an emotion, is not only an event per se, but rather the cognitive interpretation or appraisal of that event (Ellsworth & Scherer, 1988). Current debates concur that people's first-person emotional experiences are dependent on not only the situation itself, but also their subjective evaluation or appraisal of that situation (Doan, 2025).

Social. Emotions are not only predetermined biological reactions, but are also shaped by interpersonal relationships and social norms. For example, what one society considers appropriate emotional expressions or reactions, may differ vastly from another. For this reason, emotions are also constructed as a social phenomenon. Van Kleef and Côté (2022) highlight various phenomena, which may influence our emotions when we interact with others, for example: *primitive emotional contagion* (i.e., when one comes to feel the same emotions that others express; for instance, when someone smiles at you, you smile back and because you smiled, you feel happier). This phenomenon might be accounted for by the process of empathy or the activation of autobiographical memories (i.e., taking the perspective of someone, or acquired through socialisation, or from one's own experiences; Niedenthal, 2004). Next, on how we express and perceive emotions amongst others, *expressive modality* refers to the way in which emotions are displayed to others (e.g., facial expressions, voice, body, language, and symbols like emojis), and e*motion perception ability* is the capability to identify others' emotions with accuracy. Further, *affective reaction* is about how we feel in response to a particular event, person, or stimulus (e.g., when Eric shares his frustration he experienced during the day with Tim – by listening to Eric's story, Tim might also experience the same emotions of frustration and anger); *reciprocal emotional reaction* refers to the dynamic interplay of emotions between individuals (e.g., the emotional reaction of a mother when her toddler has a tantrum will have a direct influence on how the child will emotionally react). Additionally, emotional responses may be, more or less, appropriate within certain contexts (i.e., social learning theory; Bandura & Walters, 1977). Furthermore, the *functional equivalence hypothesis* posits that there is some overlap between expressions of emotion and certain trait markers (which may influence emotion). For example, in an experiment, Hess et al. (2007) found that angry expressions on dominant male faces are perceived as more threatening, compared to the same expressions on more affiliative female faces. Finally, the *emotions as social information theory*, is a broad, integrative theoretical framework, which further elaborates on the interpersonal effects of emotions (see Van Kleef & Côté, 2022).

The essence of human experience lies in the interactions one has with others (Jang & Elfenbein, 2015). Beyond mere words, the exchange of emotions serves as a swift and effective way to synchronise social actions by conveying insights into others' internal states. Chung et al. (2024) found that shared emotional experiences, like the friends of Riverside who get together to watch movies, increase social bonding and the feeling of connectedness. Humans possess a remarkable ability to express emotions through various means, such as facial expressions, vocal tones, body language, and mediums like written communication, music, and art, making emotional experiences multimodal. Similarly, humans are adept at perceiving these emotional cues, and those who can do so skilfully, gain an edge in both their social and professional endeavours.

Environment, culture, language, and gender. Emotions encompass subjective human experiences that involve the interpretation of emotional meaning, which can originate from within an individual or from the immediate surrounding environment. Environmental stimuli can evoke feelings of pleasantness, aesthetic appreciation, and physiological restoration, thereby serving as motivators for behaviour, as observed by Ulrich (1983). This theme also explores the spiritual dimensions of emotion, such as experiences of awe, which may evoke a sense of connection to something greater than oneself, often associated with encounters in natural wilderness settings. Adding to this, the initial conceptualisation of emotions can be traced back to religious narratives. Eastern religious philosophies, like Buddhism, offer insights into the collective consciousness and spiritual dimensions of emotion, suggesting a view of emotion as transcending individual experience and connecting to a broader spiritual realm. Finally, although we recognise that the broader environment exerts a significant emotional influence on individuals, with emotions serving adaptive functions, theoretical advancement in this area remains to be further explored.

Furthermore, emotions are largely shaped by both *language* and *culture*, and are often intertwined. In fact, emotional labels are heavily tainted by language and culture, and the more one expands their vocabulary and knowledge about different cultures, the more nuanced emotions one might be able to experience (and express). To give one example, the German word *schadenfreude* is a word used to describe having excitement or pleasure in seeing someone suffer harm or misfortune. For more examples of emotional labels used across different parts of the world, see Smith (2016), who provides a further 154 classic examples.

Additionally, how emotions are understood, expressed, and regulated across different cultures, may be influenced by various factors, such as *display rules* (i.e., which emotions may be expressed openly, for instance, a father who scolds and smacks his son every time he cries by saying "big boys do not cry"); *regulation* (e.g., some cultures may emphasise emotional suppression, while others may encourage seeking social support); *recognition* (i.e., having distinct vocabularies for describing specific emotions), and *valence* (e.g., perceiving a smile as being positive, negative, or neutral). For a greater understanding of culture and emotion, see the work of Matsumoto (e.g., Hwang & Matsumoto, 2016).

Finally, in terms of gender differences, men and women's emotional expressions are not perceived in the same way, as their emotions may be influenced by biological, social, cultural, and psychological factors. Adding to this, given the differential socialisation of boys versus girls in upbringing, different social roles might be linked to men (e.g., provider, protector, dominant, power-related) and women (childrearing, domestic work, caring) (Niedenthal, 2004). Therefore, emotions might also be experienced differently in terms of how they are *expressed* (e.g., women tend to express emotions more openly and frequently compared to men); their *intensity* (e.g., women may experience emotions more intensely, as opposed to men), and how emotions are *regulated* (e.g., women are often more inclined to seek social support, while men are more likely to suppress their emotions) (Deng et al., 2016). In addition, gender differences may be perceived in terms of the *types* of emotions experienced. For instance, anger is perceived more readily when displayed by men, whereas happiness is perceived more instantly by women (Doan, 2025; Becker et al., 2007).

Duration of emotions

Emotional states are experiences at particular moments in time. Such experiences are usually assumed to be mutually exclusive, implying that people may not experience different emotions at the same time. In terms of correlations, at the within-subject level, emotions should not be significantly related (irrespective of their valence) (Vansteelandt et al., 2004). Additionally, emotions are distinct from affective traits. Emotions are brief and typically about personally meaningful circumstances, whereas *affect* is more long-lasting, often free-floating, or objectless, and at a level of subjective experience (Frederickson, 2001).

Emotions are often viewed as episodes that are evoked by a variety of stimuli. Neurophysiological changes can also cause changes in emotions; for instance, some people take drugs to increase their positive affect or to reduce their negative affect. A defining characteristic of emotions is that they are about something; therefore, they are event-focused, for instance a teacher who is happy when teaching. Therefore, one can assume that emotions are commonly short-lived and linked to an event (Pekrun & Linnenbrink-Garcia, 2014).

The duration of an emotion can be determined relatively easily, because in contrast to moods, emotions start with the occurrence of an external event, and end when the intensity of the emotional response returns to a baseline. The duration of emotions is highly variable, ranging from a few seconds to several hours, and sometimes even longer. For instance, sadness can last much longer than surprise or disgust (Verduyn & Lavrijsen, 2014). Researchers report that an episode of fear can last fewer than 15 seconds, while anger and joy can last anything between 15 to 60 minutes (Pekrun & Linnenbrink-Garcia, 2014). The reason why some emotions may last longer, as compared to others, is because one might ruminate over the event, making it feel as though an emotion is lasting longer.

Theoretical discussions often outline several factors that could potentially influence the length of emotional experiences. First, there are certain trait predictors, which remain consistent (both within and across emotional episodes), for example, being a generally 'happy person' throughout life. Second, episode predictors are factors that remain constant within a specific emotional episode, but may vary across different episodes, such as the significance of the triggering situation. Third, moment predictors are variables that fluctuate within a single emotional episode, like the intermittent reappearance of the person who initially caused the emotional experience (Verduyn et al., 2009). Furthermore, it should be noted that rumination plays an important role in determining the variability in duration between emotions. *Rumination* refers to the chronic activation of the cognitive component of an emotional response (e.g., thinking about extremely embarrassing moments for extended periods of time may lead to other negative emotions). Emotions characterised by high levels of rumination can persist over an extended period. Given that rumination is a typically repetitive and passive process, one might assume that rumination prolongs emotions by sustaining or even strengthening the original affective meaning of the emotional event (Verduyn & Lavrijsen, 2014). Rumination is considered effortful, controlled, and conscious, which is often aimed at reducing depressive feelings. However, the actual effect of rumination is the opposite (Gross, 2010), and elevated levels of rumination contribute to the prolonged experience of sadness (Verduyn & Lavrijsen, 2014), which, when extended for long periods, may lead to depression (Gross, 2010).

Emotional regulation

Defining and conceptualising emotional regulation is complex. Emotion regulation refers to how individuals consciously and unconsciously adjust the intensity and duration of their positive and/or negative emotional states to achieve a specific goal (Kraiss et al., 2020). Emotion regulation is also related to the processes by which individuals modify the direction of one or more aspects of an emotional response. Emotion regulation can thus serve to influence emotions, based on the *type* (i.e., which emotion one is experiencing), *intensity* (i.e., how strong the emotion is), course of *time* (i.e., when the emotion starts and how long it lasts), and *quality* (i.e., how the emotion is experienced or expressed) (Pena-Sarrionandia, 2015).

In summary, *emotion regulation* is the processes by which we influence the emotions we have, when we have them, and how we experience and express these emotions (Lewiss, 2008). Emotions are by no means always helpful (Gross, 2010) and may often lead to doing foolish things. For instance, lashing out in anger towards your manager (which you know will only worsen your situation), or purchasing a new home out of pure excitement, but which you know you cannot afford (Pena-Sarrionandia, 2015). Therefore, regulating one's emotions becomes imperative in certain situations. However, it should be explicitly noted that emotions are central to general psychological functioning and are distinctly different from clinical issues (such as mental disorders like anxiety or clinical depression).

Emotional regulation can take many forms, depending on the context. Emotional regulation can be either *intrinsic* (referring to regulating one's own emotions), or *extrinsic* (e.g., regulating someone else's emotions). Therefore, emotional regulation occurs when one activates (either implicitly or explicitly) a goal to influence the emotion-generative process (Gross & Jazaiera, 2014). Emotional regulation often involves turning down the behavioural aspect of a negative emotion, such as anger, fear, or sadness when it is not appropriate. It is important to note that positive emotions can also be regulated. For instance, looking less happy when you beat your friend in a tennis match. Also, it should be noted that emotional regulation does not need to involve only *down-regulation*. It can also involve maintaining or increasing positively-valanced emotions, for instance sharing good news with others (e.g., telling your friends and family about some positive event leading to your extreme happiness), thereby prolonging the positive effect thereof (Lewiss et al., 2008). The awareness of one's emotion, and the context in which it occurs, makes it possible to determine if the emotion should be regulated and to access knowledge about how to do so. The emotion-regulation goal determines whether emotion experience, expression, or physiology must be increased, maintained or decreased in duration and/or intensity (Pena-Sarrionandia et al., 2015). Another component of emotional regulation is coregulation. *Coregulation* is a distinct type of interpersonal emotion regulation, often termed 'social affect regulation'. In other words, coregulation is the mutual exchange of fluctuating emotional signals (including subjective experience, expressive behaviour, and autonomic physiology) between individuals, which fosters emotional and physiological equilibrium for both parties within an intimate relationship (Butler et al., 2013). For example, coregulation is when Eric's wife listens to him, giving him a hug to make him feel less anxious or stressed.

Keltner et al. (2014) propose that we should regard emotions, not in terms of the individual mind, but in terms of our relationships with others. If an interpersonal view is accepted, regulation does not focus on personal pleasantness of emotions but to balance our interpersonal concerns. Therefore, it becomes important to understand emotion regulation as a process of coordinating the various goals and strivings of an individual in a relational encounter with another individual or groups. For instance, if a person is enjoying success, but does not want to make their friend envious, one can give priority to the relationship, avoiding anything that seems like boasting.

A second framework that has examined emotion management is emotional intelligence (EI). EI provides a scientific framework for studying individual differences with regards to how individuals identify, understand, express and regulate their own and others' emotions. A critical part of EI is the individual differences in emotional regulation, where individuals scoring high on EI are assumed to regulate their emotions better, compared to those scoring low on EI.

Conclusion

To conclude, this chapter provides some broad theories as to why and how emotions originate, what emotions entail, and how long one might experience emotions. Furthermore, this chapter gives a basic understanding of the underlying theories of emotion and concepts that are related to emotion. In the chapters that follow, more nuanced ideas about very specific emotions and emotional experiences will be unpacked.

CHAPTER 2

Happiness is a Balancing Act

Linda Bosman

Time heals all wounds

The message from the telephone call shatters Mel's soul. He is gone – she will never see her friend again. Overwhelmed with grief, her tears flow from her heavy heart and roll down her face. She has often felt sadness before, in the many disappointing life events that challenged her character. Emotional by nature, she becomes intensely sad *with* others, and *for* others; her tears flow easily – as a healing ritual. From experience, she knows that, as the saying goes, time heals all wounds, and this too shall become tolerable. But this sadness, the loss of a loved one, is deeper and more intense; it occupies her body and mind. She realises that regaining balance will take more than simply struggling through a few stages. She knows that she will adapt to her new normal; her happiness will return – in sudden moments and in the simple pleasures of life, but also slowly over time, allowing her to appreciate her well-lived life once again.

Introduction

Happiness and sadness fall within the category of six basic emotions, along with fear, anger, disgust, and surprise (Compton & Hoffman, 2020). Zelenski (2020) explains a basic emotion as one of a discrete set of feeling states: They have specific causes, are brief, and have automatic consequences. Being basic emotions, happiness and sadness meet specific criteria, such as having distinct physiology in the body and brain, as well as prototypical expressions (i.e., in the face, body posture, tone of voice, and touch), experiences, and action tendencies (responses) that distinguish them from other affective states, like moods (Ortony, 2022). Basic emotions, also termed 'primary' or 'first order' emotions, are considered fundamental and universal across cultures (Ortony, 2022; Zelenski, 2020).

Non-basic emotions, such as euphoria, optimism, or tranquillity, are complex expressions and variations of basic emotions. They represent more refined emotional states, extending from or combining basic emotions. These complex emotions often arise from the interplay of various factors, including individual experiences, cognitive processes, and social influences (Compton & Hoffman, 2020).

Consider the experience of Mel, whose story exemplifies the interplay of basic and non-basic emotions. Mel's loss of a loved one triggers sadness, a basic emotion, evident in her physiological responses (tears) and prototypical expressions (sad face). Her anticipation of regaining happiness reflects optimism, a non-basic emotion, blending cognitive expectation with emotional complexity.

Situating happiness and sadness on the valence-arousal spectrum

The valence spectrum of emotions refers to the range of positive to negative experiences that individuals can feel, categorising emotions based on their pleasant or unpleasant nature (Alexander et al., 2021). This spectrum is crucial for understanding and classifying emotions according to the feelings they evoke. On the positive side of the valence spectrum, happiness – alongside emotions like joy, contentment, enthusiasm, amusement, relief, awe, and interest – comprises positively-valenced (pleasant) affective states that vary across orthogonal levels of arousal (Hartmann, 2022; Alexander et al., 2021). This orthogonality means that the experience of positive emotions, such as happiness, does not depend on arousal levels, which can range from low (e.g., relaxed or calm states) to high (e.g., excited or alert states). For instance, both calmness and happiness share a similar valence (pleasantness), but calmness is associated with lower arousal, while happiness often involves higher arousal (Alexander et al., 2021).

On the negative side of the valence spectrum, sadness – along with emotions such as fear, disgust, anger, despair, frustration, regret, anxiety, guilt, shame, envy, jealousy, resentment, and bitterness – falls into negatively-valenced (unpleasant) affective states (Sauter, 2017).

Mel, grieving her friend's loss, experiences sadness, a negatively-valenced emotion that reflects the unpleasant nature of her emotional state, highlighting the spectrum's relevance to real-life experiences.

Functions of emotions

Emotions are complex phenomena that encompass physiological reactions throughout the body, as well as alterations in subjective feelings, cognition, and behaviour (Hartmann et al., 2023). Emotions arise when different bodily and psychological systems interact (Zelenski, 2020). These are delineated through the five components of emotions: appraisals (mental assessments of circumstances, interpreting things), physiological changes in the body and brain (e.g., sweaty palms and racing hearts), expressions (evident in the face, posture, tone of voice, touch), subjective experiences (personal, lived), and action tendencies (e.g., flee, fight, freeze). Shifts in emotional states impact multiple response systems, including subjective experiences, expressive behaviour (e.g., facial expressions), and peripheral physiological responses (e.g., heart activity) (Lohani et al., 2018).

Emotions significantly influence our daily lives, guiding our responses to both positive and negative stimuli. They are integral to the intricate processes of information processing and evaluation during decision-making (Hartmann, 2022). Both positive and negative emotions fulfil significant functions (Zelenski, 2020). From an evolutionary standpoint, negative emotions, such as fear and anger, appear to hold greater importance for survival compared to positive emotions like pride and interest. This is because negative emotions are more readily interpreted as indicators of potentially life-threatening circumstances necessitating immediate action, such as the activation of the fight-or-flight response (Mortillaro & Dukes, 2018). Despite their unpleasant nature, negative emotions serve the vital role of alerting individuals to potential dangers and guiding them away from harm, thereby contributing to overall wellbeing and healthy functioning (Zelenski, 2020).

On the other hand, positive affect states (moods, emotions, traits), like happiness, are associated with success and flourishing in various walks of life (i.e. social, career, physical, psychological). Positive emotions serve to ensure the physical, intellectual, and social capacities that are required for human survival in the long run. The short-term functional role of feelings such as pleasure is to reinforce the activities that lead to one's survival, for example, food, reproduction, and societal connections (Alexander et al., 2021).

Emotions regulate behaviour and foster adaptation (Zaid et al., 2025). Sadness, for example, signals loss and elicits support. Mel's grief over her friend's death, expressed through tears as a healing ritual, reflects this function – prompting introspection and connection, aiding her gradual adjustment to a significant life change.

Expressions, sensations and detection

Emotional expressions are the behavioural component of our emotions, i.e., the way we express or communicate our internal states to others (Zelenski, 2020). We express our emotions in various ways; for example, through vocalisations (sounds), by varying pitch and tone, and also without speech, such as with sighs, giggles, and grunts. We also use gestures or changes in our posture to signal our emotions (Mortillaro & Dukes, 2018). While negative emotion expressions have more specific action tendencies (e.g., fight, freeze, or flight), this is less evident with positive emotions (Zelenski, 2020). There is an ongoing debate regarding whether expressions of emotion primarily reflect individuals' internal states (smiling because one is happy) or if the primary function of emotions is to convey social signals (smiling to indicate happiness) (Mortillaro & Dukes, 2018).

Interestingly, weight is often used as a metaphor to describe emotions on the valence spectrum: Positive emotions like happiness convey sensations of bodily lightness, while negative emotions like sadness involve feelings of bodily heaviness (Hartmann et al., 2023). Hartmann and colleagues' study reveals a consistent pattern, indicating positive emotions (e.g., happiness, love, pride) are associated with bodily lightness, while negative emotions (e.g., anger, fear, sadness, depression) evoke bodily heaviness, particularly in the chest/heart region, and are notably linked with sadness. Weight-related expressions of emotions, such as feeling light-hearted (i.e., often expressed as on cloud nine) or heavy-hearted, are cross-cultural and found in various languages. Hartmann et al. (2023) propose bodily sensation mapping (BSM) as a valuable tool aligning with an embodied view of cognition and emotion. BSM, a self-report tool, allows individuals to assess and interpret their emotions by mapping activation sensations on a body silhouette. This aids in overcoming challenges in verbally expressing or quantifying emotions, enhancing precision and efficiency.

Various emotional states have distinct physiological features, and these physiological signals can be detected through various means, for example, electroencephalography (EEG), photoplethysmography (PPG), respiration (RSP), skin conductance response (GSR), skin temperature (SKT), and electrocardiography (ECG) (Shi et al., 2017). While the discussion of these emotion detection methods is outside the scope of this chapter, the array of methods underscores the complexity of human emotion and the interdisciplinary interest in gaining a more comprehensive understanding of human emotions.

Sadness is conveyed through physical cues and felt sensations, detectable by self and others (Xie, 2024). Mel's "heavy heart" and flowing tears after losing her friend vividly express her intense sorrow. This deep, occupying sadness underscores how loss manifests, making her emotional state unmistakable.

Happiness

Humans have been captivated by the nature, sources, and promotion of happiness for centuries. From ancient Greek philosophy to contemporary wellbeing, and general positive psychology research, philosophers, theologians, and countless others have deliberated on questions like, '*What does it mean to be happy?*', '*What constitutes a good life?*' and '*What is a life well lived?*' Research on happiness and the 'good life' has surged: Dynamic and interdisciplinary studies spanning psychology, physiology, philosophy, religion, identity, politics, and economics are actively exploring happiness to unravel its mysteries, at both individual and societal levels (Lomas & VanderWeele, 2023). This section delves into perspectives on happiness, defines happiness and subjective wellbeing, and explores the consequences and pursuit of happiness.

Happiness defined

Although extensively explored and examined from various perspectives over centuries, happiness remains a complex and multifaceted construct to conceptualise and measure. As a basic emotion (Samadiani et al., 2021; Hartmann, et al 2023), happiness is an instinctive and brief emotional state experienced by people across all cultures (Zelenski, 2020). Happiness is also categorised as a positive emotion along with joy, love, pride, contentment, interest, amusement, awe, satisfaction, and gratitude (Galambos et al., 2021; Zelenski, 2020). From a biological perspective, happiness is conceptualised as a psychological state that results from the secretion of specific chemicals released by specialised brain cells (Dsouza et al., 2020). Although considered a brief emotional state, happiness is also a more long-term characteristic of people (Zelenski, 2020). For Scott (2024), happiness encompasses a spectrum of satisfying emotions that contribute to emotional and social wellbeing. These emotions, which include joy, excitement, gratitude, pride, optimism, contentment, and love, manifest in multiple forms and arise from various behaviours, life circumstances, and experiences.

A wealth of terms closely related to, or used interchangeably with happiness, is apparent in literature, including health, wellbeing, flourishing, fulfilment, contentment, satisfaction, and joy (WHO, 2021). In everyday terms, happiness refers to the state of feeling or showing pleasure or contentment (Galambos et al., 2021). Joy, frequently linked with happiness, is the delightful sensation that individuals experience when positive events occur, especially when they are unforeseen or surpass expectations (Zelenski, 2020). Joy is invigorating, and typically heightens our overall arousal and activity, which, in turn, can foster learning and the development of skills (Zelenski, 2020). While happiness can reflect a mood or state it is also often treated as a trait, or an outcome (Alexander et al., 2021).

Falk and Graeber (2020) regard happiness as a key concept and building block in contemporary societies. In this regard, happiness is often prominently positioned as a fundamental driving force, a life goal, and even a human right. Shinde (2017) clarifies happiness as a positive emotional state that is subjectively defined by each person. Happiness is, therefore, personal, and in the mind of the subject (Zelenski, 2020).

Perspectives on happiness

The roots of two major perspectives on happiness, namely hedonia and eudaimonia, can be traced to the classic Hellenic philosophy, most notably to Aristotle in the *Nicomachean Ethics* (Compton & Hoffman, 2020). In this work, Aristotle considers contenders for the good life: a life of pleasure; a life of honour; a life of wealth or health or eminence, or a life led by virtue and excellence (*areté*) (Oishi & Westgate, 2022). In the millennia since Greek philosophers deliberated on the matter, Aristotle's idea of 'the good life' has evolved into numerous refined theories of wellbeing (Oishi & Westgate, 2022). Today, research continues to explore the constituents of happiness from a view of a life that feels good (hedonic) or a life that feels right (eudemonic).

The hedonic perspective on happiness

The hedonic perspective on happiness has its roots in Ancient Greek philosophers' beliefs that pleasure is the basic components of the good life. Originating from the term *hedoné*, the philosophical term (hedonia) implies that the pursuit of wellbeing and happiness is fundamentally the pursuit of individual sensual pleasures and the avoidance of harm, pain, and suffering (Compton & Hoffman, 2020). "Eat, drink, and be merry", or the prototypical "sex, drugs, and rock 'n' roll" may very well portray the hedonic ethos of living a happy and satisfying life (Zelenski, 2020). Hedonic happiness considers what makes life pleasant or unpleasant, and is a subjective form of wellbeing, measured by cognitive evaluations of 'feeling good'. Consequently, from a hedonic perspective, a good life is a pleasant one, reflecting subjective evaluations of happiness (Guse, 2022).

Current conceptualisations of hedonic happiness focus on feelings of positive affect and life satisfaction (Oishi & Westgate, 2021). Societies have since realised the inadequacy of short-lived, self-indulgent, sensual pleasures driven by a 'me first' attitude toward life that does not lead to self-improvement and growth. Consequently, Compton and Hoffman (2020) propose a more socially responsible hedonic approach that focuses on promoting happiness for self and others in a variety of ways.

Eudemonic perspective on happiness

Contrary to a life that 'feels good' (hedonia), eudaimonia focuses on a life that 'feels right'. This perspective originates from Aristotle's philosophy on happiness and the concept of leading a good life, as articulated in *Nicomachean Ethics* (Alexander, 2021). Eudaimonia, also termed psychological wellbeing, refers to the conditions of optimal living and their effects (Alexander et al., 2021). It gauges how well individuals are 'doing', by focusing on terms related to improvement or change, such as meaning, purpose, engagement, and flow (e.g., Ryff, 2017). For the ancient Greeks, especially Aristotle, eudaimonia was linked to living a life aligned with the most desirable values and virtues, reflecting the highest good. Consequently, the eudaimonic perspective on wellbeing emphasises realising one's potential and fully developing one's skills, talents, and personality. It involves discovering and living by one's 'true nature' and 'true self'.

According to Zelenski (2020), people who behave in morally valued ways, live virtuous lives and fulfil their highest potential live eudemonic lives. This includes having a sense of inner peace, a deep appreciation of life, a sense of connection to other people, a wider perspective, and a sense that life 'feels right' (i.e., a personally fulfilling life).

Happiness as wellbeing

Defining wellbeing appears to be just as complex as defining happiness. The World Health Organization (WHO) (2021) defines wellbeing as a positive state experienced by individuals and societies. Like health, it serves as a resource for daily life and is influenced by social, economic, and environmental conditions. The WHO (2021) further explains that wellbeing includes quality of life and the ability of people and societies to contribute to the world with a sense of meaning and purpose. Emphasising wellbeing allows for tracking the equitable distribution of resources, overall thriving, and sustainability. A society's wellbeing can be measured by its resilience, capacity for action, and preparedness to overcome challenges. Not surprisingly, wellbeing is recognised as a key welfare indicator, with many countries incorporating a national happiness measurement into their economic policy objectives (Shinde, 2017).

The happiness equation

Since the term happiness is theorised differently, it is often replaced with the term "subjective well-being" (SWB), originally coined by Diener (1984)). Generally, consensus exists that SWB includes three core components (Galambos et al., 2021; Guse, 2020; Shinde, 2017 ; Zelenski, 2020):

(1) High life satisfaction (a cognitive evaluation of the quality of one's life)

(2) High positive/hedonic affect (i.e., experiencing many pleasant emotions like happiness)

(3) Low negative affect (i.e., experiencing few unpleasant emotions like sadness)

Using a simple equation, the three components of SWB are expressed as life satisfaction + high positive affect + low negative affect = subjective wellbeing (SWB) (Guse, 2020, p. 31). This equation represents a balancing act: affect balance is achieved when the key components of SWB include life evaluations and a predominance of positive over negative affect. Satisfaction in areas like marriage and work, along with specific indicators such as depression, anxiety, and anger (representing negative affect), as well as self-esteem and optimism, are additional subjective markers of wellbeing (Galambos et al., 2021). A brief overview of the three components follows.

Life satisfaction

Life satisfaction refers to one's cognitive evaluation of one's life as a whole, or as Zelenski (2020) explains, an individual's judgement that things have unfolded positively and that circumstances are favourable. Generally, life satisfaction involves a person's contentment with current, past, and future life, as well as a desire for change (Alexander et al., 2021). One is satisfied when there is little or no discrepancy between the present and what is thought to be the ideal or deserved situation. Conversely, one is dissatisfied when there is a substantial discrepancy between present conditions and the ideal standard (Zelenski, 2020).

Guse (2020) distinguishes two subdivisions of life satisfaction, namely (1) general life satisfaction and (2) domain-specific satisfaction, including satisfaction with work, relationships, leisure time, the body, and other aspects.

Positive and negative affect

Affect represents the emotional side of SWB. In addition to our measurable subjective experiences of life satisfaction, SWB encompasses affective components involving both positive and negative emotions linked to everyday experiences. Typically, SWB is characterised by high positive affect and low negative affect (Guse, 2020).

According to Zelenski (2020), on average, individuals who experience minimal unpleasant emotions (low negative affect) typically report higher levels of life satisfaction. In this regard, positive emotions (joy, love, contentment) are deemed important to our wellbeing, can promote our physiological resources, and contribute to flourishing in life (Guse, 2020).

However, the components that make up the SWB equation can diverge. For instance, consider someone immersed in constant enjoyment but dissatisfied due to a lack of accomplishments. Conversely, another person may find joy in family and career success but grapple with intense anxiety. According to Zelenski (2020), these variations carry two crucial implications. First, the happiest individuals tend to possess all three components (i.e., life satisfaction + high positive affect + low negative affect), yet focusing on just one indicator may overlook a part of the complete picture. Secondly, studying the components of SWB separately can be beneficial, as they may change differently over time, and external factors can impact one more than others. For instance, wealth exhibits a stronger association with life satisfaction than with positive emotions.

Subjective happiness measures

Happiness research was challenged by the uncertainty of how to measure it (Compton & Hoffman, 2020). In a series of scientific works, Ed Diener ('Dr Happiness') and colleagues have coined the expression "subjective well-being" (SWB), as the aspect of happiness that can be empirically measured. World-renowned happiness researchers (e.g., Diener et al., 1985) used a simple approach that allowed participants to define happiness terms for themselves. The reasoning behind the approach was that since evaluations of happiness are subjective, they should be measured through subjective reports. Several measurement instruments were devised for this endeavour, for example, Diener et al.'s (1985) Satisfaction with Life Scale (SWLS) and the Flourishing Scale (FS). When inquiring into a person's overall life satisfaction, these instruments enabled people to answer questions such as, *'Are you happy?'* or *'How happy are you?'* based on personal criteria (Zelenski, 2020). Instruments like these rested on the assumption that individuals' happiness or life satisfaction could be meaningfully translated into a numerical scale; and that if two people from vastly diverse contexts (taxi drivers, lottery winners, people living in rural areas) scored the same on the test, they had roughly the same level of happiness. Surprisingly, studies have tended to support the validity of these two assumptions.

Happiness (or SWB) is inherently personal, representing a person's own view or measurement of their wellbeing, rather than an external measurement of their wellbeing. Happiness is therefore a deeply personal and subjective aspect residing within each unique individual's mindset (Zelenski, 2020).

Societal happiness and measures

Understanding international differences in subjective wellbeing (SWB) has advanced significantly since 2005, largely due to the Gallup World Poll (GWP), which underpins the annual world happiness rankings. The GWP surveys a diverse, representative sample of individuals across nations – spanning variations in age, gender, income, and geography – to capture a comprehensive snapshot of global wellbeing (Gallup, 2024). Respondents evaluate their life satisfaction using the Cantril Ladder, a 10-point scale where 0 represents the 'worst possible life' and 10 the 'best possible life'. This self-reported measure is analysed alongside six key indicators: (1) gross domestic product (GDP) per capita, (2) social support, (3) healthy life expectancy, (4) freedom to make life choices, (5) generosity, and (6) perceptions of corruption (Helliwell et al., 2024). These indicators provide a multidimensional framework, revealing how economic, social, and governance factors interplay with personal happiness across cultures. For instance, the 2024 GWP data highlighted that Nordic countries consistently rank high, driven by strong social support and low corruption, while nations with economic instability or political oppression often score lower (Gallup, 2024).

Since its inception as a publication of the Wellbeing Research Centre at the University of Oxford in 2024, the *World Happiness Report* (WHR) has amplified this effort, responding to a growing global demand for happiness and wellbeing to be prioritised in government policy (Helliwell et al., 2024). Building on GWP data, the WHR synthesises cutting-edge happiness science to explain both personal and national variations in SWB. It goes beyond mere rankings to offer actionable insights, such as how income inequality correlates with reduced life satisfaction, or how social trust bolsters resilience during crises (Layard, 2023). The 2024 report, for example, emphasised the role of digital connectivity in enhancing social support in urbanising regions, while noting its potential to exacerbate isolation when over-relied upon (Helliwell et al., 2024). This dual focus – descriptive analytics and prescriptive advice – positions the WHR as a vital tool for evidence-based policymaking, bridging gaps between subjective experiences and objective conditions. For a deeper dive, the report's website[1] provides interactive data and detailed methodologies.

However, these measures face scrutiny for their Western bias, as highlighted by Krys et al. (2023) in their study *Happiness Maximization Is a WEIRD Way of Living*. The WEIRD framework – Western, Educated, Industrialised, Rich, and Democratic – critiques the assumption that happiness maximisation, as measured by tools like the Cantril Ladder, is a universal goal. Krys et al. argue that WEIRD societies prioritise individual happiness, often equating it with SWB, while non-WEIRD cultures may value interdependent components, like harmony, meaning, or family wellbeing over personal joy. For instance, their reanalysis of life satisfaction data across 61 countries revealed that non-WEIRD populations, such as those in collectivist societies, often idealise moderate happiness levels, with 70% of participants desiring happiness

1 https://worldhappiness.report/

above their current state but not at the "ceiling" levels typical in WEIRD cultures. This cultural variation suggests that global happiness metrics may misrepresent wellbeing in non-Western contexts, where norms against self-promotion or a focus on collective harmony can lead to underreported happiness (Krys et al., 2023).

The significance of these measures extends beyond academic interest. Governments increasingly use SWB metrics to guide resource allocation and assess societal progress, moving away from GDP-centric models that overlook emotional and social health (Stiglitz et al., 2018). Yet, the WEIRD critique underscores the need for culturally sensitive metrics. The Cantril Ladder, while reliable, may oversimplify complex emotional states, and cultural differences in reporting happiness can skew comparisons (Diener et al., 2018). Despite these limitations, the GWP and WHR offer a robust foundation for tracking societal happiness, informing policies that aim to balance economic prosperity with human flourishing, provided they evolve to account for diverse cultural ideals of wellbeing.

The universal pursuit of happiness

When posed with the question, *'What do you desire in life?'*, most people express a fundamental wish for happiness. Unsurprisingly, the desire for happiness and a happy life is universal (Oishi & Westgate, 2022). In this regard, Dsouza et al. (2020) posit that happiness is inherently sought and pursued throughout life, and is often deemed the ultimate source of pleasure.

Surprisingly, the average person experiences moderate happiness (Shinde, 2017), with happiness being a prevalent and dominant emotion for most individuals (Zelenski, 2020). Interestingly, people worldwide frequently report being in a positive mood, also known as a positive mood offset (Compton & Hoffman, 2020). Although most people experience their wellbeing as above average, researchers (e.g., Diener et al., 2009; Lyubomirsky et al., 2005) generally agree that an increase in happiness could have positive effects on various aspects of people's lives.

The consequences of happiness

Over the recent decades, a substantial body of literature has explored the intricate and interconnected factors influencing happiness on both individual and societal levels. Literature of this nature is significant given the widespread recognition of happiness as a universally valued and pursued aspect of human life. Lomas and VanderWeele (2023) emphasise that grasping the elements affecting happiness can support individuals and societies in making well-informed decisions regarding actions and policies that may enhance happiness, both at an individual and collective level.

The important function of negative emotions as survival or warning signals has already been established, but what purpose does positive emotions like happiness serve, other than that they merely feel good? What is the point of feeling happy, joyful, or ecstatic? Acknowledging that positive emotions are less critical for survival does not negate the significance of their social roles. Apart from the fact that happiness 'feels' good, evidence suggests that happiness is generally good for us, and a source of good outcomes (Potgieter & Botha, 2020). Apart from feeling pleasant, the correlates of high happiness include, among others, better health (cardiovascular, immune, and endocrine) and health behaviours, longevity, productivity at work, creativity, cooperation, higher income, delay of gratification, more and better social relationships, and service to society (volunteering, donating) (Zelenski, 2020; Lyubomirsky et al., 2005). Moreover, Mortillaro and Dukes (2018) argue that positive emotions play a role in fostering affiliation and cooperation, making them vital for adaptation.

People who feel unhappy or sad typically face a heavy psychological burden – which happiness can lift. In this regard, Hartmann et al. (2022) explain the correlation between happiness and pleasure and the release of so-called 'happy hormones' like serotonin, dopamine, oxytocin, noradrenaline, and endorphins. These hormones prepare the body for action but also alleviate pain during physical activity (e.g., endorphins and serotonin). As such, the heightened motivation and energy associated with positive states help people overcome physiological and psychological challenges, making burdens seem lighter.

Barbara Fredrickson (2001) pioneered the broaden-and-build theory of positive emotions that explains how positive affect experiences contribute to and have a long-lasting impact on our personal growth and development. In this regard, it seems as though various positive emotions serve specific functions – responding to material opportunities or social stimuli, facilitating the acquisition of new skills, and encoding novel information – necessitating distinct expressive signals for effective communication.

Generally, people who report higher levels of happiness and life satisfaction tend to succeed in diverse life domains, for example, they have happier marriages, more fulfilling social relationships, improved health, greater community involvement, enhanced coping skills, job satisfaction, and higher incomes (Ruggeri et al., 2020). In this regard, Alexander et al. (2021) regard the experience of positive emotions, feelings, and affect as essential for cultivating resilience, flourishing, vitality, happiness, and life satisfaction, ultimately contributing to overall physical and emotional wellbeing. Referring to Diener and colleagues' findings, Compton and Hoffman (2020) emphasise the significant impact of positive emotionality, ranging from higher levels of wellbeing, better romantic relationships, increased altruism and generosity, successful careers, enhanced creativity, and better health.

Dsouza et al. (2020) state that happiness, encompassing the various definitions and dimensions, can contribute to a positive perspective on life, a healthy self-concept, heightened vitality and mental wellbeing, and enhanced social and physical functioning. The aforementioned authors regard the pursuit of happiness and wellbeing as a shared human aspiration, forming the foundation for fostering global human harmony. Dsouza et al. (2020) state that happy people also often witness advancements in their social connections, professional endeavours, and overall wellness. Compton and Hoffman (2020, p. 132) conclude by stating: "The scientific consensus seems to be that being happier can help people lead more satisfying lives for themselves, the people around them, and their communities."

The downside of happiness

Dsouza et al. (2020, p. 1) argue that all humans inherently seek and pursue happiness throughout their lives, because "there is nothing else that can give more pleasure than being happy". However, the common caution for moderation – too much of a good thing can simply be bad for us – also seems to apply to happiness. In this regard, excessive positivity can have several adverse effects. Compton and Hofman (2020) caution that desiring happiness excessively can lead to loneliness, increased gullibility, and selfishness. Additionally, frequently worrying about one's happiness can lead to constant self-monitoring and create a fragile and vulnerable sense of self. Thus, the 'power of positive thinking' can have a downside for some individuals.

Essentially, being extremely happy can cause people to overlook their surroundings. When happy people make decisions, they are more likely to engage in stereotypical thinking, rely on shortcuts, and are less inclined to check for errors (Lyubomirsky et al., 2005). As such, very happy individuals may be more susceptible to the primacy effect in impression formation, quickly forming opinions based on first impressions. Additionally, being in a positive mood may increase selfish behaviour.

Similarly, Potgieter and Botha (2020) explore the concept of *dysfunctional happiness*, considering scenarios such as 'unhealthy happiness' (e.g., someone perceived as happy yet not leading a good life), or personality traits like sensation seeking that lead individuals to engage in pleasure-seeking behaviours (reckless driving, substance abuse, sexual promiscuity), often at the expense of relationships, health, and overall wellbeing.

Expressions of authentic happiness

Happiness can be detected in various ways and across the body. As such, Sauter (2017) reports a range of expressions (i.e., nonverbal, facial, vocal, and bodily cues) that communicate positive emotions. Emotions associated with happiness all have recognisable signals that are evident in the voice, face, head, body, and touch. The Duchenne smile is typically associated with several positive emotions, including happiness (Mortillaro & Dukes, 2018). Specifically, authentic smiles involve the contraction of a muscle around the eye known as the orbicularis oculi. The visible outcome is the presence of wrinkles, often referred to as 'crow's feet', at the outer edges of the eyes. While the cheek muscles can be voluntarily contracted, the eye muscles are more challenging to engage without genuine feelings of pleasure. These authentic smiles, characterised by the presence of eye wrinkles, are termed Duchenne smiles, named after the French anatomist Guillaume Duchenne, who first delineated this initially overlooked distinction in 1862. Unlike a forced or polite smile that only engages the mouth muscles, the Duchenne smile is considered a more sincere expression of happiness or joy (Mortillaro & Dukes, 2018).

The complex creation of happiness

Lomas and VanderWeele (2023) employ the term "complex creation" of happiness to emphasise that the factors and conditions fostering heightened happiness intersect and blend in intricate and sometimes unpredictable ways. As such happiness is an emergent phenomenon, not attributable to any single factor. Also supporting the complexity of happiness creation, Galambos et al. (2021) argue that the happiness levels of any individual, sample, or nation arise from distinct, interplaying factors, such as gender, socio-economic background, and migration status. Additionally, individual attributes like physical health, life events such as marriage, divorce, unemployment, and retirement, as well as community elements (e.g., corruption, social support, crime) and macro-level indicators, like economic recessions, natural disasters, and war, all play a role. Moreover, humans are not merely passively affected by their conditions, but actively shape these very conditions through their values and behaviours (Galambos et al., 2021).

Zelenski (2020) highlights both internal (e.g., personality, heritability), and external (environmental) factors influencing the creation of happiness, but – based on research evidence – regards personality traits as the strongest predictors of happiness. For Compton and Hoffman (2020), genetic make-up plays an instrumental role in people's eventual emotional lives: families offer the genetics that largely determine our base emotional responsiveness to the world. This is confirmed by Dsouza et al. (2020), stating that genetics contributes to roughly 35–50% of human happiness. For Zelenski (2020), genetics, personality, and outlook are among the best predictors of happiness, while environmental factors, such as demographic features (e.g., gender, age, education), parenting practices, or life events, have a smaller impact on long-term happiness in general.

Happiness and wellbeing are largely socio-culturally determined. While emotionality is partially genetically determined, there is considerable variation in how people express, label, and promulgate positive emotions around the world (Compton & Hoffman, 2020). To name an example, while happiness in the US may be defined as an exuberant, energetic feeling that produces outwardly expressed enthusiasm and joy, Chinese people typically view happiness in terms of quiet contentment that is a somewhat private emotion (Compton & Hoffman, 2020).

As per Dsouza et al. (2020), neurotransmitters associated with happiness include dopamine, oxytocin, serotonin, endocannabinoids, endorphins, epinephrine, norepinephrine, cortisol, and melatonin. These substances, secreted in humans, serve specific purposes in the experience of happiness. Although conclusive evidence regarding the genetics of happiness is lacking, studies indicate that 35–50% of joy may be hereditary.

Sheldon and Lyubomirsky (2021, p. 153), conclude that "happiness can be successfully pursued, but it is not 'easy'". To enhance happiness, it is crucial to choose personally meaningful activities with a focus on eudemonic pursuits rather than the direct pursuit of positive emotions. Sustained effort invested in diverse and changing approaches to these activities fosters a continuous flow of engaging, satisfying, connecting, and uplifting experiences, thereby elevating the likelihood of staying within the upper range of happiness potential.

In their pursuit of happiness, humans often chase material possessions to achieve joy, yet, as Dsouza et al. (2020) point out, it is ultimately the brain that controls when and how humans feel happy.

Hedonic adaptation (baseline happiness)

Concepts such as set point theory, the hedonic treadmill, and baseline happiness underscore the relative stability of happiness and human capacity for adaptation. Set point theory posits that genetics significantly influence long-term wellbeing, contributing roughly 35–50% to an individual's average happiness level, or "set point" (Lyubomirsky et al., 2005; Compton & Hoffman, 2020). After experiencing temporary highs (e.g., a promotion) or lows (e.g., a break-up), people tend to return to this baseline over time. Those with set points favouring positive emotionality often exhibit cheerfulness, while those inclined toward negative emotionality may lean toward pessimism or anxiety, though these tendencies can be moderated by life experiences and intentional practices (Sheldon & Lyubomirsky, 2021).

The hedonic treadmill reinforces this stability, where 'hedonic' refers to the pleasantness of experiences and 'treadmill' suggests a lack of lasting progress despite efforts to boost happiness (Zelenski, 2020). This concept describes how individuals adapt to both positive and negative events, reverting to a personal norm after an adjustment period (Scott, 2022). For example, Mel, devastated by her friend's death, feels intense sadness that disrupts her baseline; yet, she anticipates adapting over time, expecting happiness to return gradually through life's simple pleasures. Classic studies, such as Brickman et al. (1978), support this, showing lottery winners and accident victims eventually returning to pre-event happiness levels. However, adaptation is not absolute: severe, ongoing stressors like chronic illness or poverty can lower the set point durably, suggesting limits to resilience (Lucas, 2007).

This adaptability has implications for long-term wellbeing. While people are sensitive to change – celebrating a windfall or grieving a loss – they typically recalibrate emotionally, as evidenced by longitudinal data showing SWB's robustness (Diener et al., 2018). Yet, research also indicates variability: Luhmann et al. (2012) found that events like marriage yield small, sustained boosts, while widowhood can cause lasting declines, challenging the notion of complete reversion. The treadmill analogy thus captures a general truth but oversimplifies exceptions. Ultimately, internal factors – genetics, personality, and coping strategies – play a larger role in long-term happiness than transient external events, though sustained efforts (e.g., gratitude practices) can nudge the baseline upward (Sheldon & Lucas, 2014; Snyder & Lopez, 2007).

Defining sadness

The APA (2018) clarifies sadness as "an emotional state of unhappiness, ranging in intensity from mild to extreme and usually aroused by the loss of something that is highly valued (e.g., by the rupture of a relationship)." As noted earlier, sadness is considered one of the six basic emotions (Arias et al., 2020). Sadness is a common and frequently encountered human response to life events such as the loss of a loved one, facing career-related disappointment, or receiving heartbreaking news (Schimelpfening, 2023). Sadness is occasionally characterised as psychological pain, accompanied by additional feelings of loneliness, anxiety, depression, grief, and anguish (Arias et al., 2020). Sadness affects both the body and mind, with durations ranging from brief moments to several hours (Arias et al., 2020).

From the sadness-related words identified by Arias et al.'s (2020) linguistic task team, they could deduce that the feelings associated with sadness vary considerably in intensity. Sadness can range from low or dreary, to more intense feelings of distress to extreme forms such as miserable, grief, anguish. The words also refer to variations in duration, for example, from brief emotional states like displeased, to longer mood states, such as sombre or dour. The description of melancholic may coincide with clinical depression.

Arias et al. (2020) emphasise that the behaviour function and neural systems of sadness are adaptive and conserved by evolution. As such, sadness is an adaptive emotion that enables people to cope with losses, be it of resources, status, relationships, or loved ones. Loss, as described by Özel and Özkan (2020), is an integral part of life that people may experience and respond to in various and unique ways. Mourning, the deep and prolonged painful process following loss, involves a range of behavioural, cognitive, and emotional reactions, which can vary from a calm stance to a significant crisis. Mourning is a subjective process uniquely influenced by factors such as age, gender, culture, and previous mourning and coping experiences (Özel & Özkan, 2020).

Expressions of sadness

Moosavi et al. (2024) describe the eyes as "mirrors of the soul", offering nonverbal yet reliable cues about a person's emotional state and underlying traits. In essence, one can often discern another's emotions, intentions, and inner experiences simply by looking into their eyes. In the context of sadness, this emotion manifests through a range of facial expressions, many of which are shaped by what Darwin referred to as the "grief muscles" – notably the *omega melancholicum* (furrowing of the brow) and *Veraguth's folds* (drooping or shadowing at the inner corners of the eyes). These features serve as visual expressions of emotional pain, allowing sadness to be both felt and seen. These muscles contract during grief or sadness, causing the eyebrows to furrow, the corners of the mouth to turn downward, and the eyelids to droop – hallmarks of a sad expression.

Recent research (Milbank et al., 2024) expands on this, showing that sadness is not a monolithic state but comprises varied emotional facets such as melancholy, misery, bereavement, and despair, each with dissociable facial and physiological signatures. For instance, Milbank et al. (2024) found that despair involves more pronounced head tilting and eye closure, while bereavement shows greater brow raising, suggesting nuanced muscular patterns beyond Darwin's original observations.

Sadness also manifests through a slumped posture and slowed gait, and it may or may not involve crying. Physiologically, crying-related sadness typically increases heart rate and skin conductance, whereas non-crying sadness slows heart rate, reduces skin conductance, and deepens respiration (Arias et al., 2020). Milbank et al. (2024) further refine this distinction, demonstrating that melancholy elicits milder physiological arousal compared to the heightened skin conductance and heart rate responses seen in misery or despair. Neuroscientific evidence supports these variations: Nakajima et al. (2024) used multimodal imaging (functional magnetic resonance imaging (fMRI) and EEG) to reveal that sadness intensity correlates with distinct neural activity patterns – mild sadness (e.g., melancholy) activates the prefrontal cortex for reflection, while severe sadness (e.g., despair) engages the amygdala and insula, amplifying emotional distress. These facial and physiological cues are typically recognisable, facilitating emotional support from others (Arias et al., 2020).

Human beings express sadness in diverse ways (Arias et al., 2020; Folk & Dunn, 2024; Milbank et al., 2024; Nakajima et al., 2024):

› Typical facial expressions include drooping eyelids, downcast eyes, lowered lip corners, and slanting inner eyebrows (Arias et al. 2020), with Milbank et al. (2024) adding that despair may feature tightened lips and a downward head tilt.
› Specific behaviours include social withdrawal, reduced reward-seeking, slumped posture, slowed walking speed, and potential crying (Arias et al., 2020), though Folk and Dunn (2024) note that sadness can also prompt prosocial behaviours like seeking connection, depending on the context.
› Physiological changes are evident in heart rate and skin conductance, varying by sadness type – e.g., bereavement may sustain elevated arousal longer than melancholy (Milbank et al., 2024).
› Cognitive/subjective processes link to distinct physiological responses (e.g., fight, flight, freeze) (Arias et al., 2020), with Nakajima et al. (2024) suggesting that severe sadness may impair executive function due to amygdala overactivation.

While crying is most commonly associated with sadness, it often arises at emotional peaks and can also accompany intense feelings of happiness, anger, or frustration (Sharman et al., 2020). It serves multiple functions: producing biochemical changes, improving mood, and expelling toxins via tears (Sharman et al., 2020). Crying releases endogenous opioids, potentially reducing pain and aiding recovery from distress, while promoting sedation, balance, and stress coping. Sharman et al. (2020) propose that crying fosters self-soothing and emotion regulation, acting as an intrapersonal cry for help – a signal for support from others. Xie and Li (2025) build on this, showing that adaptive sadness regulation strategies (e.g., mindful crying or cognitive reappraisal) enhance long-term wellbeing more effectively than suppression, which may prolong distress. Meanwhile, Folk and Dunn (2024) highlight crying's social role, noting that it can strengthen interpersonal bonds by eliciting empathy, aligning with sadness's adaptive capacity to foster connection amid loss.

For Mel, the shattering news of her friend's death triggers intense bereavement, her tears flowing as both a healing ritual and a signal of her grief's depth. Unlike past disappointments where sadness was familiar, this loss occupies her fully, yet she trusts time and adaptive coping will restore her balance, allowing happiness to return in quiet, simple moments.

The bright side of sadness

Despite being categorised as a negative emotion both Arias (2020) and Forgas (2017) confirm the potential benefits of mild negative affective states like sadness. In its mild manifestation, sadness can provide notable advantages, fostering an adaptive, alert, and externally oriented response style (Arias et al., 2020). Compton and Hoffman (2020) argue that sadness and depression can sometimes serve beneficial purposes. Building upon Andrews and Thomson's (2009) analytical rumination hypothesis outlined in 'The Bright Side of Being Blue', they proposed that experiencing sadness allows people to introspect and examine the intricate issues underlying their emotional state. Furthermore, negative emotions like sadness can stimulate creative problem-solving strategies to navigate challenging emotions (Compton & Hoffman, 2020).

Similarly, Forgas (2017) emphasises that navigating the complexities of our social world demands intricate processing. In this regard, negative affect and moods might enhance the quality and effectiveness of cognitive processes and interpersonal behaviours, while positive affect could diminish this. People in a negative mood may exhibit lower susceptibility to judgemental errors, greater resilience against eyewitness distortions, heightened motivation, increased sensitivity to social norms, and enhanced proficiency in generating high-quality and effective communication strategies (Forgas, 2017).

Abdusattorova (2023) points to the capacity of sadness to nurture empathy and compassion for others navigating their own challenges. In this regard, a state of sadness can act as a prompt, reminding people of our shared humanity and inspiring us to offer support and understanding to those facing difficulties. Through sadness, a sense of connection and solidarity may unfold. In this context, Compton and Hoffman (2020) suggest that the capacity to feel the suffering of others or the sadness in the world may increase our empathy, social sensitivity, and sense of justice.

The beauty of sadness

Paradoxically, experiences of sadness can evoke positive emotional states particularly when perceived as aesthetically pleasing and non-threatening, for example, listening to sad music can be both an enjoyable and moving experience (Arias et al., 2020). People are naturally drawn to art forms depicting tragic narratives that elicit negative emotions. Shakespeare's *Romeo and Juliet* exemplifies this, with its needless and tragic deaths. Similarly, the melancholic themes of the blues paradoxically uplift listeners. Compton and Hoffman (2020, p. 358) describe the "power of artistic tragedy": people engage with artistic tragedy to confront the inevitability of sorrow, grief and their own mortality. Through art, people process emotions like disappointment or loss without directly experiencing them. Empathy for fictional characters fosters a sense of shared humanity, increasing compassion and altruism. Witnessing tragic narratives may inspire a resolve to prevent similar tragedies. Thus, artistic tragedy provides a safe space to engage with negative emotions, leading to benefits, such as enhanced compassion, hope, relief, empathy, and determination (Compton & Hoffman, 2020, p. 358).

Negative consequences of sadness

While mild forms of sadness can benefit people, prolonged states of severe sadness, such as depressive rumination characterised by negative perspectives on oneself, the world, and the future, are indicative of depressive disorders and lack clear evolutionary significance (Arias et al., 2020).

Rumination is characterised by repetitive dwelling on negative emotions and their causes and effects (Scott, 2022). This fixation on past problems can trap individuals in a cycle of recurring negative thoughts from which escape is difficult (APA, 2020). The more one engages in rumination, the deeper the spiral of negative feelings becomes, perpetuating the cycle (APA, 2020). In contrast to productive emotional processing, which facilitates problem-solving and progress, rumination tends to foster pessimism and negative thought patterns, hindering the adoption of active coping strategies (Scott, 2022). This propensity towards repetitive negativity exacerbates current distress and increases the risk of developing or worsening depression and anxiety (APA, 2020).

Jahanitabesh et al. (2019) regard both negative mood and ruminative thinking as unfortunate features of depression. Despite individuals' intentions to use rumination as a means of relieving distress, this approach frequently proves counterproductive. Instead of alleviating negative thoughts and emotions, rumination prolongs and amplifies them. Indeed, self-reported rumination is predictive of the emergence of depressive moods and is linked to prolonged depressive episodes.

Chronic sadness is often misdiagnosed as a depressive disorder (Horwitz & Wakefield, 2007, as cited in Arias et al., 2020). Distinguishing between sadness and depression can be challenging, as persistent sadness is one of the two defining symptoms of a major depressive episode, the other being anhedonia, which is "the inability to enjoy experiences or activities that normally would be pleasurable" (APA, 2018). According to Holmes (2023), distinguishing between normal sadness and clinical depression is crucial. Holmes (2023) regards the transitory nature of sadness as distinguishing it as different from depression. Sadness is a transient emotional response, whereas depression is a prolonged mental disorder significantly impacting daily functioning. This distinction lies in the duration and severity of the state. Sadness is time-limited, while depression persists and disrupts an individual's ability to cope with daily life.

Persistent sadness can impair wellbeing, risking depression (Zaid et al., 2025). Mel's deeper, more intense grief, consuming her body and mind, hints at such consequences following her friend's death. Yet, her belief in time's healing power suggests resilience, tempering the potential for prolonged negative effects.

Dealing with sadness and enhancing happiness

Emotions are a fundamental part of human life and play a crucial role in shaping our daily experiences and social interactions. The ability to regulate emotions in socially appropriate and constructive ways is essential for mental health, wellbeing, and effective functioning in everyday life (Zaid et al., 2025). Adaptive regulation of emotions, particularly sadness, has been shown to mitigate the effects of depression and anxiety, offering valuable insights for preventive and therapeutic interventions. Xie (2024) highlights the serious consequences of poorly managed emotions, noting that they can lead to stress-related health problems that affect both physical and psychological wellbeing. Maladaptive responses, such as venting without constructive communication, emotional suppression, escapism through substance use, or projection can escalate internal conflict, increase stress, and harm relationships. In contrast, healthier strategies such as mindfulness – observing and accepting emotions without immediate reaction – can support more thoughtful responses. Effective communication, which involves expressing emotions openly and constructively, enhances interpersonal understanding. Cognitive restructuring, or reframing irrational thoughts, can also promote emotional balance and resilience (Xie, 2024).

Alternatively, consulting mental health professionals can be instrumental in helping individuals process complex emotions, especially during periods of sadness or grief, thereby fostering personal growth and a sustained sense of wellbeing.

Dealing with sadness

The mourning process following sadness is often regarded as a series of non-linear phases and stages, with predictable characteristics that change over time (Özel & Özkan, 2020). Perhaps the most well-known strategy for dealing with sadness is the five stages of grief theory proposed by Elizabeth Kübler-Ross. Since the publication of her 1969 book, *On Death and Dying*, the five stages (denial, anger, bargaining, depression, and acceptance) have become ingrained in popular culture and widely used in bereavement treatment. In 2017, David Kessler introduced a sixth stage – meaning – in the book *On Grief and Grieving* (Daniel, 2023). Daniel (2023) challenges the validity and utility of stage theory, questioning its persistent use in bereavement counselling despite sustained academic critique exposing its limitations. He champions more contemporary, process-oriented models – such as continuing bonds, tasks of grieving, meaning-reconstruction, the six Rs of mourning, and the dual-process model – which are contextually grounded and attuned to individual differences, gaining traction as functional alternatives.

For Mel, mourning her friend's death, the predetermined stages – denial, anger, bargaining, depression, acceptance – feel misaligned with her experience. She recognises that restoring balance requires more than progressing through predefined steps. Instead, exploring modern grief models that embrace the complexity and uniqueness of her journey could offer greater support, prompting her to consider these approaches:

› The *continuing bonds* model suggests that grief is not about severing ties but maintaining an enduring connection with the deceased through memories, rituals, or symbolic interactions (Klass et al., 1996). For Mel, this might mean speaking to her friend during quiet moments or revisiting places they cherished together.

› The *tasks of grieving*, proposed by Worden (2018), frame mourning as active work: accepting the loss, processing pain, adjusting to a changed reality, and reinvesting in life. Rather than passively experiencing stages, Mel actively engages in making sense of her friend's absence.

› Similarly, *meaning-reconstruction* focuses on reshaping one's sense of identity and purpose after loss, integrating the experience into one's life narrative (Neimeyer, 2019). Mel struggles to redefine herself without her friend's presence but gradually finds meaning in continuing his legacy. The *six Rs of mourning* – recognising the loss, reacting emotionally, recollecting memories, relinquishing old attachments, readjusting, and reinvesting – provide a structured yet flexible framework for navigating grief (Rando, 1993).

› Finally, the *dual-process model* acknowledges that grieving is not a linear path, but an oscillation between loss-oriented tasks (focusing on the emotional pain) and restoration-oriented tasks (adjusting to new roles and routines) (Stroebe & Schut, 2010). Some days, Mel could find herself deeply mourning; on others, she may feel moments of normalcy and renewal.

Mel's experience illustrates how mourning is not about following a strict sequence of emotions but about navigating an evolving, deeply personal process. These contemporary models better capture grief's individuality, offering a more adaptable and compassionate approach to coping (Bonanno, 2021).

Enhancing happiness and wellbeing

From Folk and Dunn's (2024) point of view, happiness may not be the sole goal in life, but for many, it is the most significant. As such, scientific research exploring the determinants of a happy life can potentially inform this universal pursuit of happiness (Sing et al., 2023). A prominent and empirically supported framework for understanding and enhancing happiness is the PERMA model, developed by Martin Seligman, a foundational figure in positive psychology. Introduced in *Flourish* (2011), PERMA identifies five core elements of wellbeing – Positive Emotion, Engagement, Relationships, Meaning, and Accomplishment. This model integrates both hedonic (pleasure-based) and eudaimonic (purpose-based) dimensions of happiness, offering a multidimensional lens that resonates with the nuanced interplay of happiness and sadness explored in this chapter.

> *Positive Emotion* includes joy, gratitude, hope, and contentment – affective states that not only enhance life satisfaction but also build resilience. These emotions, when cultivated intentionally (e.g., through gratitude journaling or acts of kindness), act as psychological buffers against adversity (Fredrickson, 2013; Seligman, 2011).

> *Engagement*, often associated with Csikszentmihalyi's (1990) concept of "flow", refers to deep involvement in activities that match one's strengths and interests. Such immersive states produce intrinsic reward and satisfaction, contributing to a sense of vitality and fulfilment.

> *Relationships* – the presence of supportive, trusting, and meaningful social connections – are foundational to wellbeing. As both Seligman (2011) and Lomas and VanderWeele (2023) argue, emotional bonds not only enhance happiness but serve evolutionary functions by promoting cooperation, empathy, and mutual care.

> *Meaning* entails belonging to and serving something greater than the self, whether through spirituality, community, or purpose-driven work. It offers existential grounding, particularly in the face of suffering, making it a key pillar in balancing happiness with life's inevitable sadness (Steger, 2018).

> *Accomplishment* involves the pursuit and achievement of goals, which fosters self-efficacy, agency, and a sense of progress. The satisfaction derived from overcoming challenges – whether personal, academic, or professional – adds to one's overall sense of competence and wellbeing (Seligman, 2011).

To build on the PERMA framework, Donaldson et al. (2022) propose the PERMA+4 model, expanding wellbeing theory to include four additional empirically validated building blocks: Physical Health, Mindset, Environment, and Economic Security. This evolution acknowledges that wellbeing is not only psychological but also shaped by structural and material conditions.

› *Physical Health* recognises the integral link between bodily health and emotional wellbeing. Sleep, nutrition, and exercise routines not only affect mood, but support cognitive and physiological regulation of emotions, such as sadness and stress.

› *Mindset* highlights the role of beliefs, self-talk, and cognitive framing in shaping emotional experiences. Growth-oriented thinking and self-compassion enhance emotional adaptability and happiness, particularly during adversity.

› *Environment* refers to the physical, social, and cultural spaces in which individuals live and work. Safe, inclusive, and aesthetically pleasing environments contribute to psychological safety and sustained wellbeing.

› *Economic Security* acknowledges the foundational importance of meeting basic needs. Financial stability reduces chronic stress and allows individuals to focus on higher-order goals aligned with the original PERMA domains.

Together, PERMA and PERMA+4 offer a powerful, integrative framework for promoting happiness that accounts for both internal psychological processes and external life conditions. Their application in diverse sectors – from education to healthcare to community development – underscores their potential for fostering holistic flourishing. In the context of this chapter, they also illustrate how positive psychology does not deny sadness but rather contextualises it as one part of a broader emotional landscape that, when navigated adaptively, contributes to long-term wellbeing (Cabrera & Donaldson, 2024).

For Mel, devastated by her friend's death, this framework illuminates a path forward. Cultivating joy and hope (Positive Emotion), her tears flow as a ritual of healing, releasing grief to pave the way for future contentment. She anticipates re-engaging with life's simple pleasures (Engagement), finding fulfilment in 'flow' as she adapts to her new normal. Her emotional nature and past reliance on others (Relationships) suggest supportive bonds will bolster her recovery, reflecting their evolutionary role in fostering empathy. Despite her soul-shattering loss, Mel's belief in a well-lived life

(Meaning) anchors her, offering purpose as a buffer against deep sadness. Her confidence in adapting over time (Accomplishment) mirrors the agency gained through small victories, building resilience. The intense sorrow occupying her body (Physical Health) underscores the need for rest and care to regulate emotions, while her trust in time healing wounds (Mindset) reflects a growth-oriented perspective essential for navigating grief. A nurturing setting (Environment) could further support her gradual return to happiness, providing psychological safety amidst her loss. Though not explicit, her focus on emotional recovery assumes financial stability (Economic Security), reducing stress and enabling pursuit of higher wellbeing. For Mel, PERMA+4 blends immediate emotional release with long-term purpose and support, guiding her from grief to renewed appreciation of life's pleasures.

Conclusion

Embracing both happiness and sadness as integral facets of human emotions lead to a more authentic, empathetic, and enriching existence (Abdusattorova, 2023). According to Compton and Hoffman (2020, p. 180), experiencing a full life necessitates "feeling both positive and negative emotions", rather than attempting to eliminate the negative ones, as this acknowledgment of emotional diversity, or emodiversity, is linked to greater wellbeing. Furthermore, greater emotional diversity can increase resilience and counter our tendency to habituate to specific positive emotions, thereby enhancing the stability and salience of positive emotionality in our lives.

CHAPTER 3

Rotten Roots: The Physical,
Psychological and Moral Intricacies
of Disgust

Melanie Moen

A bad taste in the mouth

Eric decided to go for a long run along the beautiful riverbed that made Riverside famous. He needs time to think and reflect about his life. Something has been bothering him, but he cannot seem to pin down exactly what it is. Because of the duration of the run, he realises that he is *now late for date night with his wife*. He realises she will not be impressed if he is late – he has been away on business often of late, and he owes her a special night out. Suddenly, he trips and falls – pushing himself up, he realises he fell and landed with his hand in dog poop. His tracksuit, hand and arm are completely covered in faeces. The foul smell, and the sight of his soiled suit immediately, elicits a disgusted facial expression – a scrunched nose and curled lip immediately demonstrate his distress.

When he looks up, he sees his best friend, and their local GP, Doctor Oscar Snipe and his young teenage son enter a brothel. Disgusted by both these incidents, Eric experiences a quick flashback of when he was a teenager and a bug flew into his mouth, and he accidentally bit it in half. This whole incident with the dog poop and seeing his friend at the brothel leaves Eric with a (literal) 'bad taste' in the mouth.

Introduction

Disgust is a complicated emotion, with diverse reasons for it surfacing. Like Eric's story, there are several triggers that can elicit disgust. A wide range of actions and substances, from controversial triggers like faeces and vomit, to incest and pornography, can all elicit disgust (Tybur et al., 2009). On the one hand, disgust helps to ensure the safety of the organism by inhibiting contact with things that are toxic or dangerous. On the other hand, disgust is an emotion that is associated with creating and sustaining our social and cultural reality (Kolnai, 2004).

Darwin included disgust as one of the basic emotions as early as 1872 (Miller, 2004). Disgust is described as a universal emotion alongside surprise, sadness, happiness, fear, anger and contempt. Disgust is also described as the most visceral of the basic emotions; therefore, it appears to be one of the more natural emotions (Ryynane et al., 2013), as it is an emotion where the facial expressions and gestures are invariant across cultures (Kolnai, 2004). Disgust has a diverse set of triggers, ranging from the very concrete (for instance, bad tastes, such as Eric's memory of biting a bug in half), to extremely abstract (such as the moral transgressions such as Eric's friend visiting a brothel with his teenage son, and Eric's reaction to this) (Chapman & Anderson, 2012). Rozin and Haidt (2013) propose that disgust be divided into three domains: pathogen avoidance, sex/mating, and morality, each of which will be elaborated on next.

In this chapter, disgust will be viewed and described from a physiological and psychological perspective. An attempt will be made to define the emotion and to discuss the origins of the emotion. Disgust will also be described from the perspective of pathogen avoidance, sexual and morality. Emotions elicited by disgust, and their associated psychological challenges, will also be outlined. The concept of elevation as the polar opposite emotion to disgust will be presented, and the use of humour to deal with challenging emotions and situations will be described.

Defining disgust

The diversity of disgust complicates the definition of the emotion. Disgust is recognised as a basic and universal emotion. It is often described as a feeling of revulsion towards something that is perceived as offensive, unpleasant or dirty, such as Eric touching dog poop (Chapman & Anderson, 2012). Disgust is also described as an emotional reaction that activates the parasympathetic nervous system, generating feelings of nausea, and typically involves a characteristic facial expression. Reynolds and Askew (2019, p. 1 269) concur with this definition. They define disgust as "a type of rejection response characterised by a specific facial expression, a desire to distance oneself from the object of disgust, a physiological manifestation of mild nausea, a fear of oral incorporation of the object of disgust, and a feeling of revulsion." Therefore, one can conclude that the result of the disgust is the behavioural avoidance of the stimulus (Rottmann, 2014). Disgust is characterised by a diverse set of triggers ranging from extremely concrete (for instance, a bad taste or smells) to extremely abstract (moral transgression, e.g., incest) (Chapman & Anderson, 2012).

Strongman (2003) is of the opinion that disgust is about rejection. Disgust is associated with the rejection of something either physical or psychological. Disgust motivates people to reject anything perceived as likely to contaminate the self physically, spiritually, or threaten their status as civilised people (Horberg et al., 2009). The English word *disgust* and the French word *degout*, literally mean repugnant to taste. The Russian word *otvraschchenie* comes from a verb signifying motion. It refers to the gesture of pushing something away with the purpose of calming visceral and/or moral revulsion (Matich, 2009).

The origin of disgust

Disgust is described as one of the few uniquely human emotions, because of its cognitive complexity (Case & Stevenson, 2024; Strongman, 2003; Rottmann, 2014, p. 419). Cultural evolution suggests that it is concerned with essential humanness, as people have distinct reactions to certain physical and moral triggers (Strongman, 2003).

It is believed that the initial development of pathogen disgust takes place during early childhood. Death, due to the ingestion of pathogens, is particularly high in the early years. Therefore, some theorists place the development of disgust between the ages of three and five years' old, while others believe it only develops during middle childhood. There is also the belief that the ability to experience disgust is unnecessary in the early years, as parents fulfil this role for the young child by protecting them from pathogens (Rottmann, 2014). However, authors such as Chapman and Anderson (2012) posit that distaste responses can be seen in neonates only a few hours' old. Research conducted by Gülşen et al. (2023) noted disgust responses by certain food groups from infants between the ages of six to 11 months.

The role of disgust is dual; on the one hand, it defends the body against toxicity and disease (pathogen disgust), and on the other hand it reacts to the violation of social and moral forms of disgust (Case & Stevenson, 2024; Chapman & Anderson, 2012). On a basic level, disgust functions as a protective mechanism that helps us avoid contact with harmful substances and pathogens. For instance, the smell or sight of rotten food can trigger feelings of disgust, which in turn can prevent us from consuming contaminated food. Evolutionary theories that favour the oral origins' hypothesis of disgust, posit that humans initially had an increased risk of foodborne disease and infection due to their meat-heavy generalist diets; therefore, an oral mechanism to avoid infectious substances was deemed particularly advantageous (Case & Stevenson, 2024; Rottmann, 2014).

Researchers such as Al-Shawaf et al. (2016) believe that evolutionary psychology is too narrow in scope for a comprehensive theory on emotions. They feel that there is an unnecessary emphasis on the subset of emotions that evolved to serve a communication function. They believe that many evolved emotions have no distinct facial expression (i.e., sexual jealousy) or do not appear to serve a signalling function at all (i.e., sexual regret). However, some aspects of the emotion of disgust can be clearly explained within evolutionary psychology.

Disgust is sometimes deemed evolutionary in that it is moving from the physical world (e.g., food avoidance) to the abstract, socio-moral domain. In the case of moral disgust, the new functional role might for instance be associated with the avoidance of individuals who violate social norms (Chapman & Anderson, 2012). Social theorists disagree with the oral origin of disgust; they believe that disgust developed due to regulating social interactions (Rottmann, 2014). For instance, marrying your biological brother or sister is considered socially unacceptable and can elicit feelings of disgust (like the vignette example of the father and son who visit a brothel together). This might also be considered socially unacceptable behaviour in some cultures.

Disgust can be divided into several categories such as core disgust, animal nature disgust, interpersonal disgust, and socio-moral disgust. *Core disgust* is revulsion elicited by noxious objects, such as soft body products or offensive odours (for instance, the smell of dog poop). It is mostly characterised by unpleasant sensory experiences. *Animal nature disgust* is triggered by activities that remind people of their animal origins, such as certain sexual or eating habits. *Interpersonal disgust* is elicited by the prospect of contact with strangers, evildoers, or diseased persons. *Socio-moral disgust* is revulsion evoked by people who commit vulgar violations against others, such as child abuse or incest (Horber et al., 2009, p. 964). In general, disgust is divided in three broad categories, namely pathogen disgust, sexual disgust and moral disgust.

Pathogen disgust

The behavioural immune system (BIS) framework is an evolutionary explanation of a set of psychological functions to detect, emotionally react to, and avoid pathogen threats. These behavioural responses to pathogen threats are also observable in animals. Within the BIS, the core emotion of disgust plays a pivotal role in triggering the appropriate avoidance behaviour (Liuzza, 2020). Therefore, it is agreed that pathogen disgust guards against infectious disease by prompting avoidance (Karinen et al., 2023).

Disgust is a universal emotion, characterised by a specific facial muscle activation pattern. The facial expression of disgust seems to serve the function of expelling distasteful food and minimising air flow (Liuzza, 2020). Parasitic microorganisms pose large selection pressures on all long-lived, multicellular organisms. Pathogens' rapid reproduction at the expense of their hosts creates a coevolutionary race between host avoidance and pathogen transmission (Tybur et al., 2013). Pathogen disgust is brought forth by behaviours and objects that retain pathogenic bacteria that cause disease (e.g., rotten foods), and orchestrates the avoidance of physical contact with such stimuli (Donner et al., 2023).

Higher pathogen disgust sensitivity is associated with aggravated symptoms of anxiety disorders, such as post-traumatic stress disorder (PTSD) and obsessive-compulsive disorder (OCD), more conservative political views and more negative attitudes toward foreigners (Karinen et al., 2023).

Disgust and the senses

Disgust has a more pronounced relationship with the proximate senses of smell, taste, and touch than other basic emotions. The main carriers of disgust are the olfactory visual and tactile senses (Saluja et al., 2023). The sense of taste is related to the sense of smell. There is no single disgusting taste that could not be related to a corresponding odour. Smell and taste remain intimately bound together, with the sense of taste being absorbed by smell (Kolnai, 2004). The cortex can distinguish between 10 000 different scents. Particular scents may be variably perceived by different people. What is a pleasant odour for one person may be unpleasant for another (Sherwood, 2015). However, some disgust elicitors seem to be universal, including body odours. Body odours are relevant in regulating human interactions and, at the same time, are important disgust cues. Some humans use body odour cues to detect disease signs and regulate their social behaviours accordingly (Liuzza, 2020).

Smell and memory are closely linked. Smells are processed in the front of the brain, which sends information to the other areas of the body's central command for further processing. Odours take a direct route to the limbic system, including the amygdala and the hippocampus, the regions related to emotion and memory (Walsh, 2020). Odour memory is central to olfactory cognition. Odour-evoked memory and associations are triggered by smells, which in turn can either elicit a positive or negative memory and response (Herz, 2016).

Aural disgust is to an extent described as 'moral disgust'. Certain associations – often visual – are called forth when confronted by certain aural stimuli. For instance, if you find a certain beery voice disgusting, it might remind you of the moral disgustingness of drunkenness (Kolnai, 2004). Olfaction is deemed a key signalling system for avoiding pathogens, as it is widely acknowledged that a principal function of olfaction is to detect pathogen threats (Liuzza, 2020).

There also seems to be a clear link between fear and disgust; however, disgust distinguishes itself from fear fundamentally with regard to direction and intention. Disgust is markedly orientated outwards, whereas fear is more inwardly orientated. Disgust has a cognitive role, which seems to be lacking in fear (Kolnai, 2004). Both fear and disgust have distinct responses. Disgust has an immediate sensory rejection functioning to limit the environmental input and to avoid contamination, whereas fear has an instinctive and immediate response to a stimulus. Disgust depends on focal attention and develops slower than fear, whereas a fear response is considered automatic.

Both PTSD and OCD have traditionally been understood as anxiety disorders; however, the role of disgust has been increasingly linked to fear and anxiety. In situations where fear and anxiety are experienced, disgust is elicited as a form of rejection/revulsion response to a particular stimulus. Neuroimaging studies have identified increased activation of neural structures associated with the processing of disgust (in the context of contamination-based OCD). Disgust has been associated with a number of anxiety disorders, such as phobias, separation anxiety and health-related anxieties (Reynold & Askew, 2019).

Additionally, several cross-sectional studies have established correlations between elevated contamination fear and the trait-like vulnerabilities of disgust propensity (Badour et al., 2012). Reynolds and Askew (2019) are of opinion that disgust is associated with the etiology and/or maintenance of anxiety disorders.

Sexual disgust

Disgust is associated with decreased sexual arousal. For instance, women reported lower sexual arousal toward an erotic film after being exposed to disgusting pictures. Sexual activity can be considered disgusting in at least two ways. First, sexual activity is related the exchange of bodily fluids such as saliva, sweat, semen, and vaginal secretions, all of which increase your chances of contracting a sexually transmitted infection. Second, the body parts involved in sexual activities, such as the mouth, vagina, and anus, are also the most sensitive to intrusion and contamination (Wen et al., 2023).

As mentioned before, disgust has evolved over time to include the avoidance of two different threats, namely the contact with pathogens, and sex with individuals who are deemed low partner value. The emotion disgust has an important role to play in partner selection (Donner et al., 2023). Although the primary function of disgust is to protect individuals from ingesting harmful substances, it also has implications for intergroup relations. Disgust is an important part of BIS, which encourages individuals to avoid social situations that can possibly cause bodily contamination. Therefore, avoiding people and situations that could lead to infection is highlighted (De Barros et al., 2023).

Tybur et al. (2013) state that although sexual intercourse is necessary for reproduction, it can result in tissue damage during intercourse, the risk of pathogen transmission, and social risks namely reputational damage and direct aggression from intrasexual competitors. The prospect of having sex with genetic relatives or promiscuous individuals can lead to sexual disgust. Pathogen disgust and sexual disgust both elicit avoidant behaviours and are considered distinct disgust motives (Donner et al., 2023). When one focuses on sexual disgust, there seems to be a bidirectional relationship between disgust and mating behaviour. Disgust inhibits sexual behaviour, and sexual arousal inhibits disgust. Sexual behaviour increases your chances of pathogenic infections through the transmission of bodily fluids, but as mentioned before, sexual behaviour is also imperative to reproductive success.

A short-term mating orientation may increase one's exposure to pathogenic infections because of a propensity to engage in multiple sexual opportunities with little known information from a sexual partner. Short-term mating can inhibit disgust during a mating opportunity. This may mean that individuals oriented toward short-term mating pay lower attention to pathogen-related information. People with an uncommitted sociosexual orientation have lower levels of sexual disgust (Garza et al., 2023, p. 73). Research has found that disgust inhibits sexual arousal responses and also shows a close relation with sexual problems (Wen et al., 2023). Sexual dysfunction related to disgust can include problems with arousal, desire, orgasm, and sexual pain. A strong correlation exists between sexual disgust and sexual dysfunction in women. As mentioned before, sexual disgust has an inhibitory effect on sexual arousal and is associated with the development and maintenance of sexual pain disorder (Crosby et al., 2019). Self-related disgust has also been associated with sexual dysfunctions such as vaginismus, dyspareunia, premature ejaculation and erectile dysfunction (Phillips et al., 1998). Self-focused disgust is often associated with trauma, such as sexual trauma, which can also translate to mental disgust (Badour et al., 2014).

Moral disgust

Although disgust is usually associated with contamination agents, verbal, facial and body expressions of disgust are also observed, across cultures, in response to social behavioural violations, such as crime, paedophilia or incest (Luppino et al., 2023). Disgust amplifies the moral significance of protecting the purity of the body and soul. Disgust as a moral emotion is defined by the evaluation of purity and contamination (Horberg et al., 2009). There exists a duality in moral transgressions. Moral transgressions elicit negative emotions. The induction of negative emotions such as disgust also heightens sensitivity to moral transgressions (Chapman et al., 2009; Giubilini, 2015).

The primary function of moral disgust is to mark individuals whose behaviour suggests that they represent a threat and to avoid them. This action reduces the risk to potential exposure harm (Hutcherson & Gross, 2011). The violation of moral norms might evoke a kind of moral revulsion or disgust in victims and onlookers (Chapman et al., 2009). In the vignette at the beginning of the chapter, moral disgust was experienced by the onlooker. He considered the exposure of a teenage boy to a brothel as morally disgusting, especially with seemingly full approbation from his father. Matich (2009) is of the opinion that disgust is a sentiment that regulates transgressive experience with the purpose of enforcing social and cultural taboos.

Disgust is, therefore, about borders and challenges our senses. Disgust has an inhibitory function and therefore it motivates us to limit or avoid certain behaviours that are deemed immoral by the individual themselves or the dominant cultural group (Giubilini, 2015). As mentioned before, disgust functions as a sensory mechanism to reduce exposure to oral or olfactory threats. The two senses that are closely linked to disgust are taste and smell. For instance, a research experiment on people who were unfairly treated in a work scenario activated stronger taste sensations than those who felt they were fairly treated (Skarlicki et al., 2013).

Delight is often derived from going against 'moral good' and aesthetic beauty. The relationship between moral judgement and disgust might take one or both forms. Certain violations of moral transgressions elicit emotion. Purity violations can specifically elicit disgust. It is believed that disgust is preadapted to serve as a guardian of the sanctity of the soul and protect the purity of one's body (Kollareth et al., 2022). It is agreed that disgust migrates into the moral realm, as well as being "…prompted by filth, depravity, sexual perversion, anti-social practices and dangerously – by groups to whom such traits are attributed" (Ryynane et al., 2023, p. 20).

Many believe that disgust can be summoned as a means of social control, to ensure conformity of behaviour, and to exclude outsiders and those deemed not to fit in with the rest of the group (Ryynane et al., 2023). Disgust arises as a consequence of certain moral violations; there is evidence that disgust exerts a causal influence on moral judgements, leading people to be particularly harsh in their moral evaluations (Inbar et al., 2009). Moral disgust promotes low-cost forms of punishment, for instance gossip and physical violence (Karinen et al., 2023).

Disgust is also associated with guilt. Luppino et al. (2023) propose two types of guilt: the deontological guilt (DG; related to the transgression of an internalised moral rule), and the altruistic guilt (AG; elicited by the failure of an altruistic goal). The connection of disgust with morality seems to be particularly strong in the deontological domain. The association between deontological guilt and disgust has been emphasised on both a behavioural and a neural level (Van der Eijk & Columbus, 2023). Guilty emotions activate specific brain areas, such as the cingulate gyrus and medial frontal cortex. There are also different neuronal networks involved in different types of guilt, with the insula selectively responding to deontological guilt stimuli. Abnormal processing of specific guilt feelings might account for some psychopathological manifestation, such as OCD and depression (Basile et al., 2011).

The tendency to feel guilty for trespassing a moral norm has been positively associated with disgust sensitivity. People also often use anger and disgust interchangeably, especially in response to moral stimuli. Moral disgust is used metaphorically to express anger, for example, a man hitting a small, innocent child (Van der Eijk & Columbus, 2023). In the vignette, Eric might have felt anger towards his friend for involving his teenage son in a visit to a brothel.

Disgust and dehumanisation

Disgust has been associated with dehumanisation (Buckels et al., 2013). Giner-Sorolla and Russel (2019) propose that disgust might be uniquely associated with animalistic dehumanisation, for instance, seeing a specific group in animalistic terms. Out-group dehumanisation is deemed dangerous, as it has been associated with many wars and genocides in history. For instance, during the Rwandan genocide, television stations broadcast a call to kill the Tutsi "cockroaches", claiming they were a dirty race that should be exterminated. Nazi propaganda in *Der Strümer* depicted Jews as vermin, insects and swine. Although the causes of these atrocities are complex, a common theme is depicting the out-group to evoke disgust (Buckels et al., 2013).

However, disgust is seen as effective in persuading people to morally condemn specific individuals and groups. Historically, outgroups have been perceived as dangerous or deviant (Inbar et al., 2009). Research experiments by Giner-Sorolla and Russel (2019) found that groups perceived as being both incompetent and unfriendly fail to activate parts of the brain in the perceiver that are essential for social cognition, such as the medial prefrontal cortex. Therefore, these experiments found evidence for dehumanisation. Additionally, the two parts of the brain associated with feelings of disgust, namely the insula and amygdala, were activated in reaction to the out-groups, suggesting that disgust is related to dehumanisation.

Self-disgust

Self-disgust is an adverse self-conscious emotion that plays an important role in psychopathology and wellbeing (Aristotelidou et al., 2023). Self-disgust is a negative self-conscious emotion schema that reflects disgust towards the self (how a person perceives themself) or towards actions (how a person perceives their actions) (Ypsilanti et al., 2020). It is therefore directed at one's physical appearance, moral actions, and behaviour (Aristotelidou et al., 2023).

When disgust is not directed externally but towards oneself, it is labelled as self-disgust. Self-disgust is triggered by the violation of social and moral norms (Schöggl et al., 2014). Elevated externally, disgust proneness is associated with several mental disorders, such as phobias, anxiety, sexual dysfunctions, OCD, schizophrenia and eating disorders (Schöggl et al., 2014; Ypsilanti et al., 2020). People diagnosed with anorexia and bulimia experience disgust in relation to sexuality, certain parts of their bodies, and food (especially fattening food) (Phillips et al., 1998). Self-disgust is more commonly reported than shame and guilt among individuals diagnosed with a major depressive disorder. People prone to loneliness report more self-disgust than others (Ypsilanti et al., 2020). The negative implications of shame on the development of self-esteem have been noted. Low self-esteem is positively linked to depression and self-disgust (Phillips et al., 1998).

Disgust is a more cognitively demanding emotion and belongs to the broader category of negative self-conscious emotions, along with shame, guilt and embarrassment (refer to Chapter 4 on shame and pride) (Aristotelidou et al., 2023).

Social disgust

Social disgust is associated with disgust-related thoughts, feelings, and behaviours of individuals, and is often influenced by actual, imagined, or implied social context. Social disgust is prominent in negative human interactions, which often include prejudice and discrimination toward minority groups (Berger & Anaki, 2021).

Social disgust can be described through intergroup relations. Repulsions toward minority groups are noted when considering social disgust. For instance, healthy out-group members can be perceived the same as infected in-group members. A second aspect associated with social disgust is interpersonal disgust, which is triggered by group irrelevant contact. Here, for instance, someone might show reluctance to wear clear used clothes or sit on a warm, vacated seat. Aversion to these individuals may stem from various personal attributes, such as abnormality, misfortune, or moral taint (Berger & Anaki, 2021). Interpersonal disgust and moral disgust are often provoked by violations of social norms and orders, and are closely associated with the disgust-derived emotions shame and guilt (Kolnai, 2004). A third social disgust aspect combines intergroup and interpersonal disgust with contagion. For instance, things that have been in contact with one another can change or influence one another, even after contact has been terminated. For example, people are less likely to eat food prepared by someone who disgusts them (Berger & Anaki, 2021).

Just as the body has developed a physiological immune system, our minds have evolved a Behavioural Immune System (BIS. This psychological mechanism drives behaviours aimed at avoiding infection. Rooted in disgust, BIS prompts precautionary measures against disease threats, including withdrawal from potentially harmful situations. One manifestation of this mechanism could be the inclination to view certain out-groups with disgust. Research suggests that disgust diminishes empathy and the ability to attribute full humanity to others, thereby fostering implicit associations between out-group members and non-human entities, and facilitating the dehumanisation of norm violators. Additionally, groups perceived as lacking warmth and competence often trigger feelings of disgust, and are viewed as less capable of experiencing complex, "uniquely human" emotions and experiences (Landry et al., 2022).

Social disgust can also be understood culturally and in terms of a vertical dimension, where social disgust could be associated with God and moral perfection (above), and devils, demons and moral evil (below), and where humans are often seen as hovering in the middle of this vertical dimension. They can either rise to the godly dimension above, or sink below to the demonic and bestial dimension. Social disgust is then understood as an emotional reaction to people's behaviour of moving down to a less godlike nature. Therefore, one can deduce that humans feel revolted by moral depravity, which shows, to some extent, an overlap to pathogen disgust (Haidt, 2000).

Elevation as the opposite of social disgust

"Elevation is the emotion elicited when witnessing acts of moral beauty and is framed as the opposite of disgust" (Klebl et al., 2019, p. 158). Haidt (2000) agrees that elevation is the opposite of social disgust, and that it is triggered by witnessing acts of virtue. Elevation causes a feeling of warmth in the body and makes one feel good, whereas disgust causes nausea and makes one feel dragged down. Disgust motivates avoidance behaviour, whereas elevation prompts engagement. Elevation, therefore, promotes positive engagement and is on the upper end of the emotion (Klebl et al., 2019).

Elevation arises from witnessing acts of moral beauty and establishes a mindset whereby people want to act in a more noble, saint-like way. Elevation is also associated with reverence and the motivation to help others (Strohminger et al., 2011). Elevation is a warm, uplifting feeling that people experience when they see unexpected acts of human goodness, kindness, and compassion. It makes a person want to help others and to become a better person (Haidt, 2000).

The role of humour in dealing with negative emotions

Humour is considered a coping mechanism often used in dealing with negative emotions. It is a known fact that humour, laughing and smiling have the potential to alleviate stress and provide an opportunity to re-evaluate the situation (Lenggogeni et al., 2022). Humour is often used to assist in coping with a variety of social, emotional, and cognitive difficulties and challenges. Humour is conceptualised as a process where the appraisal of an unexpected or incongruous situation results in an amusing experience or an emotional feeling of funniness. Humour often functions as distancing one from negative stimuli, but can also assist in changing one's perspective on negative stimuli through reappraisal (Deckman & Skolnick, 2023).

Humour has been demonstrated in fostering the development and support of personal wellbeing in the face of adversity (Papousek, 2018). Humour is often associated with high-arousal positive emotions but might also be associated with high-arousal negative emotions. For instance, a scene from the movie *Pink Flamingos*, in which a character eats dog faeces elicits high-arousal emotions, and disgust in particular; but the emotion is also accompanied with feelings of amusement, especially for participants who were dispassionate observers. A benign violation hypothesis states that people find events that they construct as being wrong, but not directly involved in, as humorous. Eating faeces or touching it is a clear violation, but viewing the action from the perspective of a dispassionate observer (as the example in the vignette) helps make the violation benign (Larsen & McGraw, 2014).

The term 'coping humour' is defined as the propensity to create and appreciate humorous stimuli. It is used to cope with stressful and demanding situations. A sense of humour is also associated with lower levels of loneliness and depression. Humour also moderates the relationship between stressors and mood disturbances. Individuals who have higher coping humour are likely to interpret, experience and react to environmental stressors in a more positive manner than individuals who are low on humour (Sliter et al., 2014). A positive relationship also exists between humour and longevity. It has been postulated that humour may enhance quality of life, assist in the management of stress, and help to cope with the stressors related to ageing. For example, from a philosophical point of view, humour is not only highly valued and desired, but also considered a defining human attribute (Shammi & Stuss, 2003). Humour is one of the innate abilities that a person develops while growing up and is affected by their life experiences. Everyone has a sense of humour, but it is important to note that our ideas of humour might differ (Tanay et al., 2013).

Conclusion

In this chapter, the complex emotion disgust was viewed from both a physiological and a psychological perspective. The emotion is defined by most authors as protective measure to ensure avoidance of either a pathogen or a perceived moral transgression. Disgust is also defined as an emotional reaction that activates the parasympathetic nervous system, which generates nauseous feelings alongside pertinent facial characteristics or expressions.

The origin of disgust was outlined and also viewed from a pathogen avoidant perspective, both sexual as well as moral. It is clear from the literature that pathogen avoidance is associated with the protection of the person, while sexual disgust has a dual role. On the one hand, it protects the individual from pathogens by avoiding certain sexual behaviours, but on the other hand, it has a distinct foundation in the moral domain. In this chapter, it became clear that the origin of moral disgust is multifaceted. Moral transgressions often elicit negative emotions, while the induction of negative emotions such as disgust also heightens a sensitivity to moral transgressions.

The link between disgust and dehumanisation was also investigated. Dehumanisation is often used effectively as external moral condemnation of specific groups and individuals. When disgust is not directed externally but internally, it is labelled as self-disgust, which in turn is associated with the violation of social and moral norms. Social disgust is greatly influenced by actual, imagined, or implied social context. Sadly, social disgust is associated with negative human interactions, which often include discrimination against minority groups. Elevation, as an example of an opposite emotion to disgust, was also described in this chapter, while the use of humour (i.e., to deal with challenging emotions and situations) was outlined.

CHAPTER 4

A Kaleidoscope of Self-conscious Emotions: Shame, Guilt, Embarrassment and Pride

Yolandi-Eloïse Janse van Rensburg

A doggone shame

Nicky currently works as a data analyst in one of the biggest companies in Riverside. She has been asked to present her research to the company CEO and board of directors in the city. Finally – the big break she has been waiting for all these years has finally arrived. All the people who she admires are in the boardroom. Before her presentation starts, she feels a sense of pride in what she was able to accomplish by putting the report together in a very short amount of time.

However, during her presentation, the CEO stands up and points out a gross error in her results. Nicky realises that this mistake was due to a combination of being under severe time pressure over the past few months, but also her general lack of attention to detail. Nicky feels guilty, because she knows that she should have double-checked her work for flaws, because this error has serious implications. Nicky's sense of pride (which she held mere seconds ago) instantly turns into a feeling of embarrassment. Nicky blushes and looks down, stumbling over her words in trying to find a logical explanation for the mistake.

After the meeting, Nicky departs from the big city and goes back to her office in Riverside. She now realises that her findings have been reported incorrectly for several months, but she feels too ashamed to tell any of her colleagues. The feeling of shame festers for several weeks, making Nicky think of a horrible incident that happened in high school many years ago – making her feel stupid and dumb all over again. Despite having achieved many successes over the years, she dreads the day that her friends will remember that awful incident. These negative thoughts cause Nicky to have a lowered sense of self-worth. Too scared to make a fool of herself by talking to someone, Nicky decides to keep her pride and resign.

> "Shame cannot survive being spoken. It cannot tolerate having words wrapped around it. What it creates is secrecy, silence, and judgment. If you stay quiet, you stay in a lot of self-judgment." Brené Brown

Introduction

As seen in Nicky's case, feelings are often a result of a mix of emotions, and people rarely experience a single, pure emotion at any given time. Therefore, researchers often cluster emotions together, according to different emotional experiences, or how they originate (e.g., biological) (Ortony, 2022). One cluster of emotions is called *self-conscious* emotions, where an individual deals with (positive or negative) evaluations and judgements of the self, in relation to others, or to one's own values. More specifically, shame, guilt, and embarrassment are included in the category of negative, self-punishing, self-reflexive emotions (Niedenthal et al., 2006), whereas pride, empathy and gratitude are viewed as positive self-conscious emotions (Bastin et al., 2016). Although one might view these emotions as part of a family of emotions, which are often used interchangeably, each respective emotion is distinct and is not rooted in the same affective experience

(Tangney et al., 1996). Therefore, it is important to first consider the origin of self-conscious emotions.

The origins of self-conscious emotions

Primary self-conscious emotions (i.e., shame, guilt, embarrassment, and pride) (Lewis, 2010) are psychologically and cognitively more complex than basic emotions, and should be treated as a special class of emotions, because they require self-awareness and self-representation (Tangney et al., 1996). This cluster of emotions facilitates our social interactions and motivate us to adhere to social norms and personal standards, and are more cognitively complex (Else-Quest et al., 2012). Also, self-conscious emotions are central in motivating and regulating one's thoughts, feelings, and behaviour. And although this cluster of emotions all have an element of social control and are often experienced within a social context (Tangney, 1995), they do not always have to be experienced in a social setting (e.g., think of how Nicky experienced embarrassment in front of her audience, but felt shame for many weeks after the presentation). Certain events may generate basic emotions (e.g., happiness), but not self-conscious emotions (e.g., pride). For instance, a person may feel happy both after winning the lottery and at an athletic event. It is likely that winning the lottery will not involve self-evaluation, whereas winning a race involves social comparison and a self-evaluative process, resulting in a different emotion, pride (Strongman, 2003). Other examples of *social comparison* emotions include envy and jealousy, where one compares the self to others, to make an evaluation of the self (or hubris and pride when the evaluation of the self is positive) (Niedenthal et al., 2006).

The experience of self-conscious emotions (also referred to as moral emotions) (Tangney, 1995), may be needed for the smooth functioning of social systems (e.g., guilt may aid in why people do not act immorally or participate in criminal activities). Both shame and guilt are moral emotions that play an important role in social functioning. In fact, society has implemented various techniques to induce feelings of guilt or shame for punishing inappropriate behaviour (e.g., punishing school children for bad behaviour, or giving office colleagues the cold-shoulder when behaving inappropriately). Through acts of punishment, self-evaluative emotions are enhanced to act in more socially appropriate ways. However, sometimes one might experience self-conscious emotions (like shame) over things that are outside of one's own control (e.g., experiencing shame for having a deranged father who acts awkwardly in from of your friends).

Exactly when self-conscious emotions emerge naturally in infants is not quite clear. Some researchers believe that infants experience self-conscious emotions as early as three years of age (e.g., Tracy & Robbins, 2007a). However, evidence suggests that self-awareness (and, therefore, also self-conscious emotions) may develop even earlier, around the age of 18 months (e.g., a gaze aversion that indicates shame, or raised arms indicating pride) (Tracey & Robbins, 2004). However, basic emotions, like sadness or disgust, emerge within the first nine months of life (Campos et al., 1983). Knowing at what exact age self-conscious emotions develop is difficult, because researchers are unable to measure or assess self-conscious emotions amongst infants (Tracey & Robbins, 2004). What we do know is that embarrassment, which is less cognition dependent, emerges earlier in childhood, as compared to shame or guilt, which involves reflecting (Lewis, 2010).

As with the six basic emotions (Ekman, 1993), which have distinct facial expression, researchers have failed to find a distinct *facial expression* for any of the respective self-conscious emotions. However, physical indicators of shame include turning the face, covering the face with hands with a downward movement of the head, closing of eyes, involuntary eye movement (Walton, 2004), and blushing (when embarrassed, and which cannot be controlled). Furthermore, the upper body collapses, making the body a smaller target, as though to avoid harm. These postural changes, together with avoidance or withdrawal behaviour, may be an attempt (perhaps even symbolic) to avoid the stigma associated with moral transgression, trying to keep oneself free from condemnation (Terizzi & Shook, 2020). Pride, on the other hand, can easily be identified from an expanded posture, walking with broad shoulders while displaying an expanded upper body, and nose pointing upward into the air, enlarging one's bodily features. It is noteworthy to mention that pride cannot be recognised when observers are shown only facial features, and excluding the view of a person's body posture (Tracy & Robins, 2004).

What also sets self-conscious emotions apart from basic emotions, is that the former facilitates the attainment of complex social goals, whereas the latter facilitates survival goals. For example, fear can prompt an individual to flee from a predator, thereby increasing their chances of survival when faced with a threat, but self-conscious emotions promote the achievement of specific social goals (e.g., enhancing status and preventing social rejection) (Tracy & Robins, 2007a).

Distinguishing between shame, guilt and embarrassment

To illustrate the difference among shame, guilt, and embarrassment, we look at the case of Nicky. The whole incident starts when the CEO points out errors in Nicky's presentation. This causes social discomfort, looking bad in the face of others, and her physical reactions (blushing and stumbling over her words) make it evident that she is very *embarrassed*.

During the weeks that follow, Nicky experiences *shame*, because in her mind, she tells herself that she is not cut out for the job, and that she always messes up important details when it really matters. Through skewed self-evaluation, she starts believing that she is a bad person. The feeling of shame sabotages her confidence, and she feels like a fraudster (also known as imposter syndrome). For her, the only way to salvage herself (image) is to resign.

Initially, Nicky feels *guilty*, because she should have taken more time to check her work more meticulously. She knows that attention to detail is her own nemesis, and for this reason, she feels even more guilty for not taking the time to double-check her results. She believes she did a bad thing. This guilt is focused on her behaviour (not checking her work and rushing to complete the report). In retrospect, she thinks that she should have done things differently.

This example illustrates the primary distinction between shame (i.e., characterised by *self*-evaluation) and guilt (i.e., characterised by *behavioural*-evaluation) (Niedenthal et al., 1994). To further illustrate the differences between each of the respective emotions, it is best to discuss each emotion individually.

Shame: I am a bad person. Shame, which fits into a cluster of seven basic emotions (e.g., Tomkins, as cited in Ortony, 2021) is a negatively-valanced emotion, and is related to the way people perceive themselves (normally as bad or worthless) and how they believe others view them. Shame is defined as: "the painful emotion arising from the consciousness of something dishonouring, ridiculous, or indecorous in one's own conduct or circumstances (or in those of others whose honour or disgrace one regards as one's own), or of being in a situation which offends one's sense of modesty or decency" (Walton, 2004, p. 241).

The emotional dynamics of shame are complex and entail negative self-reflection and self-evaluation, resulting from thinking that one is unworthy of love and acceptance from others (Tangney et al., 2003). People who feel shame often attribute their wrongdoing to personal characteristics (e.g., personality or intelligence), which affects the person's core identity, because it evokes deep feelings of worthlessness, failure, and incompetence. Additionally, it is about having the desire to be a good person, but possessing equally the inadequacy to realise this desire (Bastin et al., 2016). The experience of shame often results in self-condemnation and the desire to then escape or withdraw, which leads to avoidance behaviour (Bastin et al., 2021; Terrizzi & Shook, 2020).

There are two forms of shame, namely *external shame*, which involves negative views of self as seen through the eyes of others, and *internal shame*, which involves negative views of the self as seen through one's own eyes. Although episodes of shame involve both forms, which may fuel each other, a meta-analysis by Kim et al. (2011) found that external shame (i.e., *what others think of me*) shows stronger associations with depressive symptoms, compared to internal shame (i.e., viewing oneself negatively).

However, experiencing no shame at all is also not advisable, because deficiencies in shame have been associated with an anti-social disregard for social norms and may even be linked with psychopathic behaviour (Tangney et al., 2003). Shame, like disgust, is described as a moral emotion, and might emerge from the feeling of revulsion with oneself (therefore, disgust causes shame). Terrizzi and Shook (2020) refer to the idea that shame might have evolved from a 'disease-avoidance' response, like disgust, as both disgust and shame have significant overlap, such as behavioural avoidance; both emotions involve bodily concern and encourage avoidance of social interaction. Additionally, Terrizzi and Shook (2020) found that guilt significantly correlated with moral disgust, as both these emotions concern negative behavioural evaluations (e.g., social contract violations).

Guilt: I did a bad thing. Where shame concerns the self, guilt concerns *behaviour* and is associated with a sense of remorse or regret. Guilt occurs when a person believes they have done something that violates social norms. Feeling guilty can arise from treating another person poorly, as well as from violating one's own internal moral standards (Bastin et al., 2021). Those feeling guilty often seek forgiveness for their hurtful actions, and therefore may involve specific (symbolic) reparative behaviour to restore the harm caused (Tangey, 1995).

Guilt can be a constructive emotion, which may comprise various prosocial behaviours, such as empathy, altruism, and caregiving. Also, guilt can be viewed as positive, if one learns from mistakes made, amend one's behaviour accordingly, and shows empathy towards others (Tangney, 1995). However, under certain conditions, guilt can become maladaptive. In the meta-analysis by Kim et al. (2011), they found that *legitimate guilt* (i.e., guilt that is realistic and situationally appropriate) is moderately related to depressive symptoms, whereas *maladaptive guilt* (i.e., guilt that is marked by unrealistic and inappropriate attributions of responsibility), shows stronger relations to depression.

Embarrassment: I look bad in the presence of others. Whereas shame and guilt events occur when respondents are alone, embarrassment is more likely to be experienced in social contexts (Tangney et al., 1996). Embarrassment is like shame, but differs in the sense that it is less intense. It involves presenting oneself to an audience (real or imagined), and experiencing social awkwardness, which can result in a real or perceived loss of approval from others (Lewis, 2010; Strongman, 2003). Compared to shame or guilt, embarrassment is viewed as less negative or damaging, as it causes less emotional pain. Generally, it only affects the self (and one's reputation), and does not concern others' wellbeing as in the case of experiencing guilt (Bastin et al., 2016).

Disentangling the sister-emotions – shame, guilt, and embarrassment – can be done by looking at the similarities of each emotion, respectively (Terrizzi & Shook, 2020). First, both shame and guilt have been recognised to occur when social rules are broken (Bastin, 2021). Therefore, guilt and shame may regulate moral behaviour and safeguard social norms. Second, both shame and guilt depend on cognitive, appraisal dimensions (i.e., thinking about the wellbeing of others and making amends, as with guilt, or the desire to withdraw when experiencing shame). Compared to shame and guilt, embarrassment is less dependent on reasoning, as it is experienced immediately, is experienced briefly, and is associated with bodily functions like blushing (Tracey & Robins, 2004). Of the three emotions, shame is the 'ugly' emotion, as it generates greater pain and can be a more distressing to experience, as compared to guilt or embarrassment (Bastin et al., 2016; Tangney et al., 1996). Additionally, guilt is generally perceived as more moral than shame, because making amends (associated with guilt) is more noble than hiding (associated with shame).

One distinct difference between shame and guilt is that the feeling of shame implicates the presence of other people, while guilt can arise and persist without others (i.e., also referred to as a public emotion versus a private emotion) (Michl et al., 2014). Whilst guilt and shame are both provoked in the presence of others, they may also occur when alone, in private. Adding to this, guilt versus shame situations distinguish themselves not only by the number of people present, but also by the number of people aware of the person's behaviour (Niedenthal et al., 1992). Therefore, like in the case of Nicky, it is not about how many people were in the boardroom when the CEO pointed out her error (that led to her feeling shame and embarrassment). After the meeting, when she is alone, she also feels guilty when she reflects on what she did wrong (not double-checking). Adding to this, she subsequently realises that there are even more errors in her work. To avoid the shame (of more people finding out that she was not doing a thorough job), she decides to quit her job.

Further, shame involves negative feelings about the self, whereas guilt involves negative feelings about a specific action taken (Tracey & Robins, 2004). Kim et al. (2011) highlights the critical differences between shame and guilt based on various categories: *Direction of attentional focus and focus of distress* – shame is inward, toward the self, whilst guilt is focused outward, towards relationships with others. *Phenomenology* – shame is about feeling inferior, helpless, powerless, and exposed, whereas guilt is about feeling tension, regret, and remorse. *Action tendencies* – shame is associated with wanting to avoid, hide, withdraw, escape, isolate, or having a need to disappear, whereas guilt is aimed at approaching, amending, repairing, confessing, and apologising. *Reputation* – shame is about repairing one's own reputation, whereas guilt is about repairing damaged relationships.

Additionally, research by Michl et al. (2014) aimed to demonstrate emotion-specific differences in brain activity by using functional magnetic resonance imaging (fMRI). Their results show that there are both overlap and differences in how shame and guilt are activated in the brain. More specifically, activations were found for shame in the frontal lobe, and for guilt in the amygdala and insula. A systematic review by Bastin et al. (2016) confirms that different parts of the brain do indeed play a role in the activation of self-conscious emotions. Adding to this finding, a study designed to investigate individual differences in shame and guilt in youth (aged 15–21 years) also found that shame and guilt were distinct in terms of the neural activity in regions of the brain (Bastin et al., 2021). Furthermore, the brain scans in the study showed that after making a decision about a hypothetical moral dilemma, shame and guilt are also associated with activity in brain regions involving social cognition and emotion regulation. This finding confirms that guilt and shame are indeed moral emotions that may play an important role in social functioning (Piretti et al., 2023). A recent meta-analysis on fMRIs found that shame and embarrassment are activated in areas of the brain associated with social pain and behavioural inhibition, whereas guilt engages in an area of the brain associated with social cognitive processes.

To further facilitate a better understanding of shame and guilt, two other, parallel-running, self-conscious emotions should also be discussed, namely pride and hubris. Where shame and hubris are viewed as the negatively valanced emotions, guilt and pride are positively valanced (Tracy & Robins, 2007b). Neuroimaging studies show that both pride and shame are activated in parts of the brain associated with self-referential processing and social cognitive processing.

In terms of mental health, shame and guilt play distinct roles, with shame more closely related to depressive symptoms, whereas guilt is linked to anxiety (Oh et al., 2023). Additionally, a lack of self-compassion can lead to increased shame, which may then lead to prolonged grief; however, having self-compassion is positively related to pride, which may mitigate prolonged grief (Szőcs et al., 2022).

Pride and hubris: I am proud of what I did and of who I am

Pride is often discussed as an emotion, but it is also often seen as a character strength or agential disposition (Kauppinen, 2017), which is described as a noble characteristic but also a deadly sin (Williams, & DeSteno, 2009). In fact, pride is both a positively-, but also a negatively-valanced emotion (Niedenthal et al., 2004). Whilst some academics believe that pride is one construct, comprising two facets, namely authentic pride and hubristic pride (e.g., Tracy & Robins, 2007b), others think the answer is not so clear-cut in how to explain pride (e.g., Holbrook et al., 2014). In either event, pride has been referred to as two different types. First, *authentic* or *beta pride* (Tangney, 1999) reflects a positive, emotional reaction to personal success, and feeling pleased with an accomplishment or achievement (Tangney, 1999). This type of pride reflects the affective component of genuine self-esteem and has been found to positively relate to having successful social relationships (Tracy et al., 2009). Furthermore, this pride is achievement-oriented and is often described using words such as *triumphant, achieving, confident, productive, self-worth*, and *successful*. With pride, the attribution of good behaviour is made to a specific cause, and not necessarily to the person (e.g., I worked hard to achieve this result) (Tracy & Robins, 2007c).

Second, the other (ugly) side of pride has been described as *hubristic* or *alpha pride* (Lewis, 2000; Tangney, 1999) and reflects feeling proud of the global self in an arrogant way. Hubristic pride reflects the affective component of narcissism and is positively related to aggression and antisocial behaviour (Tracy et al., 2009; Tracy & Robins, 2007b). Hubris is defined as "excessive pride or self-confidence leading to nemesis (i.e., the agent of someone's downfall)" (SA COD, 2002, p. 562). Hubristic pride is often described by using words such as *haughty, smug, arrogant, conceited, stuck-up, egotistical* and *snobbish* (Tracy & Robins, 2007c).

Self-conscious emotions and individual differences

What causes guilt- versus shame-proneness? As in the example of Nicky, one person might feel guilty when they realise that there are more erroneous results in their work. They can report the action to their supervisor, correct the mistake, and move on. Or, like Nicky, they might feel very ashamed, and unworthy, and that they cannot be trusted to do a thorough job, and as a consequence decide to resign. Finally, another person might not even shrug at the idea of making mistakes, believing that making mistakes is part of being human. To understand guilt- and shame-proneness, it is necessary to distinguish between emotion *states*, which are situation-specific experiences that lead to shame and guilt, and emotion *traits*, which are described as "stable personality dispositions representing the propensity to experience moral emotions across time and situations" (Tangney et al., 2009, p. 192).

There are two types of emotion states, which may influence whether a person experiences shame or guilt: The *anticipatory* state refers to forecasted (shame/guilt) responses, on which a person has not yet acted and is based on previous similar events or behaviour. *Consequential* state stems from feedback on actual past behaviour that evoked shame/guilt. Researchers report that individuals who are more prone to guilt/shame are susceptible to both anticipatory and consequential experiences of shame/guilt (Tangney et al., 2009). So, when shame/guilt-prone individuals encounter situations (e.g., failure or transgression), they are more likely to respond with shame or guilt. As in the case of Nicky, something happened when she was younger, and trivial incidents always take her back to that dark moment in her past.

In tracking self-conscious emotions across a lifespan (i.e., 13 to 89 years of age, using data from 2 611 individuals), Orth et al. (2010, p. 1 061) found that *shame* decreases from adolescence into middle adulthood, reaching a low point around the age of 50 years, but then increases as one gets older. Interestingly, *guilt* increases from adolescence into old age, but reaches a plateau around the age of 70 years. And finally, *authentic pride* increases from adolescence into old age, but *hubristic pride* decreases from adolescence into middle adulthood, but then increases around the age of 65 years, into old age. This study also found that women generally reported to have higher guilt and shame, as compared to men. This finding was confirmed by the results from a meta-analysis (Else-Quest et al., 2012), including 382 different studies to test gender stereotyping self-conscious emotions. The authors confirmed that women do experience more guilt, shame, and to a lesser extent embarrassment, as compared to men. But the results showed no significant differences in authentic and hubristic pride for men, as compared to women.

Shame has also been described as maladaptive because it encourages dysfunctional behaviours, such as withdrawal and avoidance behaviour and low self-esteem (Orth et al., 2006). Some studies have found that shame is a core component of narcissistic, antisocial, and borderline personality disorders (e.g., Ritter et al., 2014). Additionally, proneness to shame has been related to various antisocial and risky behaviour, such as alcohol and substance abuse, delinquent behaviour, depression, anxiety, eating-disorders, PTSD, and suicide tendencies (see Stuewig & Tangney et al., 2007). In fact, guilt and shame are very common among trauma survivors suffering from PTSD. As shame is associated to one's overall worthiness as a person (the self) the traumatic event motivates individuals to hide the source of their shame, which often ends in social isolation and withdrawal (Blum, 2008).

A study by Spice et al. (2015) on juvenile delinquents found that shame was positively related to psychopathic behaviour and characteristics, whereas guilt was significantly, negatively related. This finding makes sense, given that a critical feature of psychopathy is the lack of guilt (having remorse for doing something bad), and not necessarily the lack of shame. The reason is psychopaths often have a grandiose sense of self-worth and are high on impression management. Therefore, their source of shame might not necessarily be embedded in *I did a bad thing, therefore I am a bad person*, but rather stems from other sources of shame, like not wanting to get caught. Additionally, this study also found that shame was positively associated with numerous mental health problems. However, the relation between shame or guilt, and that of maladaptive behaviour is often tested with simple, bivariate analyses. More nuanced research is needed to understand this intricate relationship and other underlaying variables (e.g., coping mechanisms, upbringing, external triggers). Additionally, despite decades of research, there is little evidence investigating the causes of individual differences in the proneness to guilt and/or shame (Tangney et al., 2009).

A meta-analysis study (comprising $N = 64\ 698$ individuals) by Dickens and Robins (2022), found that authentic pride and hubris should be understood as the same emotion, but with two facets, as they show a significant but small relation. Furthermore, this study found that hubristic pride shows significant positive correlations with poor mental health (e.g., depression, trait anxiety, social anxiety, social phobia, loneliness, ranging between $.11 < r > .24$, $p < .01$). Whereas authentic pride, in fact, showed stronger significant negative correlations with all these respective variables (ranging between $-.39 < r > -.5$, $p < .01$). Additionally, results showed that authentic pride correlates strongly with self-esteem, status, and power (i.e., feeling confident and good about one's social status). On the other hand, those high on hubristic pride shows to have a fragile self-esteem, a low sense of prestige, and for this reason, these individuals try to act impressive and important to display confidence (which they do not possess).

Both shame and pride are referred to as *emotions of self-assessment*, because they imply a self-evaluation. A person with a high propensity for feeling shame will have a general, negative self-image (and is related to mental health issues). On the other end, a person scoring high on hubristic pride, with a grandiose assessment of the self also shows to relate to a negative self-esteem and is also significantly related to various mental health issues (depression, anxiety, loneliness, etc.). However, it is interesting to note that shame-proneness and hubristic pride shows a non-significant relationship, whilst authentic pride and shame-proneness shows to be significantly, negatively related ($r = -.24$, $p < .001$) (Dickens & Robins, 2022). This implies that neither shame, nor hubris are helpful emotions. But a realistic sense of authentic pride is healthy and may inspire oneself, or others, to persevere through difficult times.

Moving from shame to pride

As with most negatively-valanced emotions, experiencing shame for extended periods of time might lead to anxiety, depression, and a feeling of hopelessness, and induces feelings of worthlessness, inferiority, and incompetence (Tangney et al., 2011). Holding on to shame can affect one's ability to move forward; it can be incredibly difficult to cope with, and can lead to feelings of being overwhelmed and hopeless. For this reason, shame should be dealt with in an appropriate manner. The best possible action for Nicky is to take an emotional growth journey to move from shame to pride. Here are some ways to deal with shame and enhance authentic pride:

› Accept responsibility for one's mistakes by facing the consequences, without making excuses or justifying one's actions. Be kind by forgiving oneself for mistakes made. Plan how to avoid such mistakes in the future and learn from the mistakes.

› Talk about one's feelings to a close and trusted friend. By sharing one's thoughts and feelings, negative self-conscious emotions can become easier to manage. Also, by bringing the situation (of what one is ashamed) into the open, one would feel less embarrassed and might come to the realisation that the issue was trivial.

› Find healthy coping mechanisms to get rid of negative emotions, such as regular exercise, meditation, listening to good music, and humour.

› Use positive affirmations and self-talk to make a significant shift from negative to positive ideas about oneself. Self-affirmations are self-generated thoughts or experiences that lead to a positive view of the self and can enhance self-efficacy and self-confidence. Affirmations can be used to cope in situations that are perceived as threatening. Hill et al. (2020) found that pride-based self-affirmation exercises increased parents' positive self-concept. Affirmations should be written according to the following principles, with the word 'I' in them: it must describe what one wants to move towards, and not what one wants to move away from; it must be in the present tense and action orientated (e.g., *I am smart enough to secure the job interview*). Also, it must move from guilt and shame (i.e., *I have done a bad thing, therefore I am bad*) towards a notion of *I have done a bad thing; how can I move forward?*

› Move from a failure mindset to a growth mindset. Instead of focusing on what one did wrong, ask oneself, '*What can I learn from this?*'

› Having empathy and compassion is the antidote to shame. Showing empathy towards others (and oneself), and providing a genuine apology, could help repair the harm caused by immoral transgressions (Terrizzi & Shook, 2020). Also, by connecting with people, and realising that one is not alone when dealing with a struggle, will assist not only oneself, but also others, in dealing with shame. Empathy does not require that one has experienced the same situation as another person – it just shows that one is not judgemental.

Conclusion

Understanding self-conscious emotions, how they relate to certain phenomena in daily life, and how they play out in organisational settings, is important. Correctly attributed, legitimate guilt and authentic pride might be seen as positively-valanced emotions, which are related to socially acceptable behaviour and positive outcomes. However, shame and hubris are negatively valanced emotions and do not necessarily aid in functional behaviour, because they are both significantly related to mental health problems. It is quite evident that more research is needed to fully understand moral, self-conscious emotions and how they impact people's behaviour (Terrizzi & Shook, 2020). Academics that wish to further explore this field, should consider nuanced theories, confound variables, and use state-like measures (rather than trait-like assessments, which are mostly reported in the current literature), and apply advanced statistical analysis (i.e., not only bivariate correlations) to gain a deeper understanding of the antecedents of moral emotions, how they impact prosocial, or dysfunctional behaviour.

CHAPTER 5

Human Anger and Aggression:
Nature versus Nurture

Christiaan Bezuidenhout

I never get angry; why did I do it?

Eric sprints home to shower (and hopes that nobody will see him covered in dog poop). As he runs past the old clock tower in the city centre, he realises – he is not late at all. In fact, his watch was gaining time, and therefore he is actually early for his date with his wife. He has been under a lot of stress lately. After the horrible morning meeting, Eric's manager informed him that his probation period will be extended, before they make a decision on his permanent appointment with the company. Eric is eager to get home, because he had a tough day at the office. Eric opens the front door, walks up the staircase, and stops in surprise. He thought he would be home before his wife, because he never arrives home this early from work. He hears muffled noises and laughter coming from the bedroom. His heart starts to race faster as he opens the door – his wife... together with is best friend?! Betrayal from the two people he trusts most. Raging red is all he sees! One forceful swing with his golf club and Eric's wife screams "Eric, no!" His best friend is motionless on the floor.

While waiting for the ambulance to arrive, Eric is frozen. Several thoughts are rushing through his head: *I am so angry, but now I feel my aggression is dissipating... I am shivering. Could my anger of what I have witnessed make me kill my best friend in a blind rage? I have never been this angry before. I don't know what came over me. I am a kind, reasonable, balanced man. I am feeling cold, and my mouth is dry... What have I done?*

Introduction

Aggressive behaviours involve different actions where humans attempt to hurt each other, exert power over others, or stand up for themselves in ways that go beyond reasonableness. Aggressive behaviour is at the root of many social and individual tribulations. Often general human actions are hostile and confrontational with no clear motivation or intention – consider road rage in this regard (Bartol & Bartol, 2021). People often confuse anger and aggression. Aggression is the behaviour that is intended to hurt or cause harm to others or property. Anger, on the other hand, is an emotion and often occur before aggression manifests. However, anger the emotion does not always necessarily lead to aggressive actions, due to our ability to manage our emotions. Anger only becomes problematic when someone has difficulty managing it. If one is unable to manage anger, they will be prone to say or do things they often regret later. A popular belief exists (and is supported even by certain scholars) that men are frequently more outwardly aggressive compared to women, which leads to the misconception that women are less angry than males. This misconception has been disapproved by research, as it has been found that women experience anger as frequently and as intensely as men (Devlin, 2019).

Humans often choose to challenge and to act aggressively when they are confronted with antagonising situations. Humans react differently in terms of aggressive intentions. Some channel their anger inward, while others openly show their aggressive intent. There are a variety of reasons for, and ways to explain, why anger results in aggression. In this contribution are a number of theories, perspectives and factors that explain why the anger emotion can develop into aggression or result in a withdrawal from others. It is impossible to cover the wide spectrum of explanations for anger and aggression in a single chapter. The aim of the chapter is to provide enough food for thought to decide whether the anger emotion is caused by nature, or nurture, or both. The chapter will also focus on aggression, as this is often the visible outcome of anger that most affects others or their surroundings.

Defining anger, aggression and violence: The challenge

Emotions are difficult to define or explain. In this regard, Statharakos (2022, p. 21) states that "to this day, there is no scientific consensus on a definition of emotion; hence, it is a challenging concept that has been difficult for psychologists to decipher and define in an agreed-upon way." One such emotion, which is difficult to define and which is often confused with aggression, is anger. Anger occurs when someone causes resentment and animosity in a person. This often leads to antagonism toward that person, especially if one feels that they have acted with deliberate malicious intent. Importantly, anger is the emotion that all humans experience, while aggression is the action that is taken in response to the feeling of anger. Feelings of anger can be triggered by events, such as irresponsible driving by someone, or by unexpected behaviour from an animal (e.g., when a dog jumps up against your new car and scratches it). If a person becomes annoyed because of something that went wrong or because someone offended them or something bad happened to them, they will most likely experience anger. These uncomfortable feelings of irritation, rage and infuriation can be so extreme that it could cause aggressive behaviour in retaliation (The American Psychological Association, 2024). Fortunately, many people learn to manage anger, and not all angry people revert to aggression to deal with their anger. Some people channel it into positive actions like doing physical exercise or finding a solution for the problem to avert anger. Andrews and Bonta (1998, p. 123) contextualise anger as follows: "Anger is a drive that leads to drive-specific behaviours (i.e., aggression) in the presence of appropriate cues or releasers."

The concept of aggression is more challenging to define, as it has many meanings and, therefore, causes much confusion (Barnett, 1975). There are in inordinate number of words that people use when they converse about aggression, which complicates the definition even further. A few of these words include: hostility, violence, attack, assault, combativeness, encroachment, offensive, invasion, infringement, belligerence, quarrelsome, force, militant, antagonism, assertive, fierce, vigorous, domineering, feisty, strong-headed, and territorial – the list seems never-ending (Anderson & Bushman, 2002; Archer, 2009; Bartol & Bartol, 2021; Wrangham, 2018). In addition, the concepts of aggression and violence are often used synonymously. Perhaps the best way to highlight the difference is to refer to the aggression-violence continuum. All violent actions should be seen as part of the aggression spectrum. However, not all aggressive actions are deemed violent (Anderson & Huesmann, 2003). With this continuum in mind, the aim of this chapter is to simplify the discussion of aggression. Therefore, for the purposes of this contribution, aggression will be used as an all-encompassing concept to include all actions and non-actions that are manifested overtly as active acts of aggressions, or covertly as passive acts of aggression. Active and passive aggression both originate from the emotion anger.

Any action by a human aimed at another human with the intent to cause harm should be seen as aggression. Importantly, the aggressor must believe that their intended behaviour will harm the recipient – physically or emotionally. In turn, the recipient should be motivated and driven to avoid the behaviour (Anderson & Bushman, 2002; Anderson & Huesmann, 2003; Bartol & Bartol, 2021). The latter is important to deem behaviour as intentionally aggressive actions to hurt someone, because in certain situations aggressive behaviour is condoned. Consider, for example, ultimate fighting, boxing, wrestling, the National Football League or rugby, where the active participants in these scenarios know aggressive behaviour towards each other is part of the sport.

Wrangham (2017) dilutes aggression even more, as he insists that aggression as a concept is more complex, as two major types of aggression exist

– namely proactive and reactive aggression, each with its own unique, underlying drivers. In some cases, people refuse to speak to someone if they are upset, while others will use force to elicit a reaction, to hurt someone, to get something, or to retaliate physically to something that offends them. In relationships, people often do things that one could categorise as a form of aggression. Bartol and Bartol (2021) affirm in this regard that if a person refuses to speak to their partner, the action does not fit well into the definition of aggression, as it is not deemed an active attempt to harm someone (consider the aggression-violence continuum). However, in modern times, actions like these should be interpreted as an aggressive act as the *intent* is to 'punish' the partner. Remaining mute causes tension and this tension is triggered by premeditated malicious intent, which may escalate into a violent act. While the behaviour of remaining mute is passive, the indirect intent has an aggressive basis. Often this type of behaviour falls into a category of aggressive responses, known as passive-aggressive behaviour. Also, many behavioural expressions could be described as aggressive, but individuals do not necessarily intend them as such (e.g., boisterous shouting in front of the television while you are watching sport or animated screaming at a team because they are losing).

It is already clear that aggression does not entail a singular action or emotion. There are many varieties of human aggression, varying from passive non-verbal behaviour to active physical behaviour. To highlight the complexity of defining aggression, the varieties of aggression will be highlighted in Table 1.

Table 1: Varieties of human aggression

	ACTIVE		PASSIVE	
	Direct	Indirect	Direct	Indirect
PHYSICAL	Striking a person, for example, Eric hitting his best friend with a golf club. If it is an Ultimate Fighting Championship (UFC) fight between two contenders, this category of aggression is not relevant, since the violent aggression takes place with consent.	Practical joke or a booby trap, for example, hitting a male between the legs as a prank to get video footage of their reaction, without their knowledge or consent.	Obstructing a bus stop to prevent others from getting to work. Also consider a sit-in, such as during a strike for better wages.	Refusing to perform a required task, for example, refusing to complete a task when the manager is disliked.
VERBAL	Insulting a person, for example, swearing at someone and showing inappropriate hand gestures during a road rage incident or calling your partner derogatory names during an argument.	Hateful gossip, for example, spreading a rumour about somebody, at college such as telling common friends the target had several one-night stands and has a sexually transmitted disease (STD), without any evidence or sub-stantiation.	Refusing to speak, for example, a person that refuses to speak to their partner because the partner came home later than agreed from a baseball game, because the partner joined an old school friend to go to a pub after the game. The 'punishing' partner may stay mute for several days to 'chastise' the 'offending' partner and to show their dissatisfaction.	Refusing consent, vocal or written, for example, a wife who refuses to sign the divorce papers after her spouse filed for divorce, bearing in mind the spouse caught her partner in bed with her best friend.

Sources: Adapted source: Bartol, C.R., & Bartol, A.M. (2014). *Criminal behaviour: A psychosocial approach* (10th ed.). Pearson. Original source: Buss, A.H. (1971) Aggression pays. In J.L. Singer (Ed.), *The control of aggression and violence.* Academic Press. Adapted for this contribution from: Klopper, H.F. & Bezuidenhout, C. (2020). Crimes of a violent nature (Chapter 7). In C. Bezuidenhout (Ed.). *A Southern African Perspective on Fundamental Criminology* (2nd ed.). Pearson.

Although some of the categories of violence in Table 1 may overlap to some extent, it reiterates the difficulty of defining aggression. Aggression may vary from passive non-verbal behaviour to active physical behaviour, and combinations thereof (Bartol & Bartol, 2021). To complicate defining aggression even more is the fact that a distinction should be made between expressive aggression and instrumental aggression. Expressive (hostile) aggression is shown in emotionally charged situations. In most cases these situations prompt anger due to strong emotional responses that they trigger. The person who experiences the emotional discomfort aims to hurt or cause suffering to the person causing the emotional discomfort and anger. The anger should be seen as a state of arousal, which stimulates frustration or attack. It is an almost automatic and impulsive response to the other's action. The motivation is to hurt the object that caused the immediate pain, anger and hostility. Usually, crimes of this nature are extremely difficult to deter or prevent. In most cases, the heightened emotions of the situation and hostility undermine the person's ability to control their feelings and to make rational decisions (Andrews & Bonta, 1998).

Instrumental aggression is usually caused by competition or coveting something that someone else has. In the case of home invasions, instrumental aggression becomes relevant, as it usually involves criminals that focus on the acquisition of material goods with value, such as computers, smartphones, jewellery and cash. Although the initial aim is not necessarily to injure someone physically, victims will still suffer emotional and material harm (Bartol & Bartol, 2021; Brown et al., 2007, p. 197; Klopper & Bezuidenhout, 2020). However, in most cases, perpetrators will use force to attain their goal of acquiring the goods. Thus, the perpetrator places just enough pressure on victims to render them compliant. In South Africa, an anomaly exists, since many 'instrumental' robbers use extreme force and violence to get what they want. It is a matter of concern that these perpetrators often torture and kill their victims after they have satisfied their instrumental need of attaining the goods or money with concomitant force (Bruce, 2010; Geldenhuys, 2010). According to the CSVR (2009, p. 105), the use of excessive, unnecessary violence is known as gratuitous violence. The perpetrators show unnecessary violence after they have attained their instrumental goal during a robbery, such as a successful home invasion or vehicle hijacking. Perpetrators who use gratuitous violence seem to be oblivious to the impact of severely assaulting the victim(s) without any material need for it. For example, during a home invasion, they will assault the victims severely for the instrumental gain of, for instance, a few mobile phones and a small amount of cash. In this scenario, gratuitous violence is often demonstrated without weighing up the consequences of taking lives for an insignificant monetary gain.

From the above, the deduction may be made that physical violence may be impulsive, reactive, defensive, or take the form of predatory, remorseless aggression. Many factors play a role in the human's ability or motivation to experience anger and show aggression towards other humans, towards animals, or inwardly towards themselves (such as self-mutilation). In some instances, violent behaviour may be related to alcohol intoxication, drug abuse, psychosis (a mental illness), or other neuropsychiatric conditions, such as dementia (a serious loss of cognitive ability in a previously unimpaired person) (Bartol & Bartol, 2021). At this juncture, it would be helpful to consider explanations from different perspectives to provide us with a deeper account of why we show aggression.

Perspectives on anger and aggression

Over time, many opinions have emerged to explain why we have the capacity to experience anger and aggression. Important questions that these opinions or perspectives aim to answer include: Is anger and aggression learnt behaviour? Is anger and aggression innate? Are we aggressive by nature? Are human and animal aggression similar constructs? Most of the opinions and research on the topic of aggression agree that socialisation (nurture) and genetic factors (nature) play an important role in the manifestation of aggression. Rummel (2007) believes there are at least five broad perspectives that offer explanations of human aggression: (1) social learning,

(2) ethological (genetic-biological), (3) psychotherapeutic, (4) frustration-aggression, and (5) cultural.

The social learning perspective

When people become intensely frustrated or irritated due to a trigger, they react uniquely to those triggers. Some people will respond aggressively, others will withdraw, while another group will change their tactics to deal with the situation in a tactful and constructive way. In other cases, some people seem unaffected by the trigger or frustrating circumstances. A major factor for these different reactions to irritation and frustration, and the manner in which it is managed, may be past learning experiences. Human beings are very adept at learning and maintaining behaviour patterns that have worked for them in the past. The learning process begins in early childhood (Bandura, 2001; Bezuidenhout, 2024). Children develop many behaviours and skills merely by watching their parents, friends, peers and significant others in their environment. This process is widely known as modelling or observational learning (nurture).

In general, children model behaviour from three main role models:

› family members (e.g., parents, guardians, grandparents, uncles, aunts, cousins, nieces);

› members of a subculture or peer group (e.g., friends, peers at school); and

› the media (e.g., television, movies, books, magazines, video games), where the Internet and social media platforms provide abundant symbolic models, including how these models deal with frustration and aggression. Often these symbolic models are the aggressors, especially in video games. Several incidents have been reported about violent outbursts following children playing video games with violent content. In the United States (US), an 11-year-old was escorted to hospital by the police for a mental health intervention, because he became physically aggressive with his mother after losing in the *Super Smash Bros.* game. The mother indicated he had a history of violent outburst after minimal provocation in the context of video-game use (Nye, 2021).

Therefore, we can deduce that aggression is acquired through experiences, behavioural models (observational learning), and by rewards, as well as punishments. Aggression can consequently be viewed as behaviour that is learnt throughout childhood from various influences. Conditions most conducive to the learning of aggression are those in which children (1) are confronted with many opportunities to observe aggression (for instance the abusive home), (2) are reinforced for their own aggression (for example the father who commends the child for beating up another child at school), or (3) are often the object of aggression (for instance, domestic violence also channelled towards the child). The learning of aggression and how to react to annoying triggers does not only manifest in abusive households. A loving caring father who reacts with swear words and derogatory sign language while driving children to school every morning will also influence the children's way of responding to frustration when they are confronted with annoying stimuli (Bartol & Bartol, 2021). For this reason, we need to look at the four phases of social learning, namely attention, retention, reproduction and motivation. Each of these phases plays an important role in the learning processes of humans (Akers et al., 2021; Anderson & Bushman, 2002; Bandura, 1983).

Attention. Different people influence humans throughout their lifetime; however, a role model that makes a significant impression and impacts on the child is often chosen to be watched and imitated (e.g., a parent, a teacher, a coach, a peer). The child sees the role model as someone who possesses the knowledge and or skill that they crave or respect. This is how the learning experience commences. The role model must keep the child's attention and interest, or the child might shift their attention to another role model who impresses them. This will break down the eventual flow of information, as the learning process will be discontinued and learning will not take place in full. Residue of the concluding inputs could, however, still manifest in the learner from time to time.

Retention. As soon as a child resonates with a role model, they have to be able to retain and store the information that is being transferred to them. If they have certain challenges (e.g., a mental handicap), no learning, or only a limited amount will take place.

Reproduction. If a child stores information successfully, they do not necessarily know how to use it and in which context. The child needs to start imitating the influencer. Once again physical, emotional and mental ability plays a role in imitating the role model.

Motivation. Rewards and punishment play a significant role in motivating the protégé (often a child). If the influencer rewards the protégé for their newly learnt behaviour or skill, the process is usually more successful. If no reward, praise or reinforcement is forthcoming, the learning and imitation of the copied actions may fail completely. In most scenarios, rewards and reinforcement stimulate the learning process of the understudy. Regular praise and motivation from the influencer will usually allow the understudy to work harder to copy the influencer's actions and reactions and to become like the influencer. Motivation is perhaps the key element in the learning mechanisms in life. Children often try harder if they receive praise or a reinforcement, like an ice cream for good behaviour or mastering a certain action. Even an adult researcher at a university will try to improve their research outputs if they are told by management they are next in line for a promotion to a more senior level (Akers et al., 2021; Anderson & Bushman, 2002; Bandura, 1983; Bartol & Bartol, 2021; Bartol & Bartol, 2017; Huesmann, 1988).

From the aforementioned discussion, one can deduce that the mere exposure to aggressive models does not guarantee that the spectator immediately engages in similar aggressive actions at a later stage. Several key conditions may prevent observational learning from even taking place. Humans differ widely in their ability to learn from observation, and when the influencer or role model is punished for their aggressive action, the young observer may think twice before they decide to imitate the role model (Bartol & Bartol, 2021).

In addition to social learning, a human's predetermined genetic constitution — their biological, physiological and psychological programming (nature) — in some way predetermines a person's inclination to experience anger and show aggression. This complex interplay between nature and nurture eventually impacts on a human's ability to deal with and show aggression.

The biological perspective

Aggression in humans is often explained as an inborn survival function. In lieu of this, anger is often touted as the emotion that triggers the body's fight-flight-freeze response. Certain situations initiate the adrenal glands to flood the body with stress hormones, such as adrenaline, and testosterone, which in turn prepare humans for physical aggression. Over millions of years, anger has been hardwired into the brain's reward circuit. If we are confronted with something threatening, or experience unfairness, our reward system activates the amygdala in the brain to evaluate the gravity of the threat or unfairness. Whether we will react aggressively will also be determined by the aggression-enhancing influence of situational stimuli and factors (physical or emotional discomfort). The emotion is related to — but at this stage separable from — behaviour or action. Our physiological activation kicks in and the autonomic nervous system goes into overdrive; muscles tense up, teeth are clenched, and the human's neuroendocrine system (neurons, neurotransmitters and glands) is activated.

Initially, during the early stage when we are confronted with negative stimuli, mediating cognitive processes has little influence beyond the immediate appraisal that the situation is aversive, and our innate systems are activated. Some people may act immediately, as their anger is immediately turned into a violent reaction. However, many humans deliberate or evaluate the feeling of anger. They use cognitive processes to mediate and evaluate a proper course of action. They might still be angry but decide to walk away from the situation, or consider the reasons or merit for the unwanted physical or emotional triggers they experienced. The anger will likely dissipate over time and disappear altogether in the future (Bartol & Bartol, 2021;

Deffenbacher, Deffenbacher, Lynch & Richards, 2003; Devlin, 2019; Manfredi & Taglietti, 2022).

The inborn nature of aggression is especially evident in the animal kingdom, where the predator stalks their prey and protects their territory. Aggression is, therefore, seen as an instinct in both humans and animals. The study of animal behaviour, and how it relates to human behaviour, is known as ethology. In his seminal publication *On Aggression* (1966), Konrad Lorenz maintains that aggression is an inherited instinct of both humans and animals. An important function of aggression for animals and humans is to protect territory. For some animals, a certain territory in a specific natural habitat is key for their survival (consider gorillas in the rain forests of Africa). In the case of humans, they have to ensure food security, fresh water, and safe land space to enable them to settle, govern and reproduce. Many bloody and aggressive wars have been fought between humans to annex land areas to build sovereignty and territory. A recent war was sparked in 2014 when Russia annexed Crimea and began arming and abetting separatists in the Donbas region. This annexation of Crimea was the first time since World War II that a European state annexed the territory of another. It escalated in February 2022, when Russia invaded the whole of Ukraine, which sparked a bloody and aggressive war, as Ukraine believes it is independent, and that it must protect its country (territory), people, food sources and sovereignty (International Crisis Group, 2022).

The issue of territory and instinct usually comes to the fore when personal space is violated. The instinctive or genetically programmed response when someone invades a person's space is to become irritated, which predisposes them to become aggressive. Some people will immediately act aggressively and will go into attack mode. If someone jumps over a person's fence, the natural instinct will be to show an increased aggressive response toward the intruder, preventing further territory violation – invading their home. The tendency to attack space violators is referred to as 'territoriality'. In the animal kingdom, lions will fend off hyaenas with aggressive actions to protect their territory and food – similar to humans who protect their yard and home. That is why humans erect walls and install the latest warning technologies to keep intruders out. Animals do not have this luxury, and have to rely on their aggressive instincts and guile.

Lorenz (in Bartol & Bartol, 2021) believed it is an innate propensity developed through the lengthy, complex process of evolution to protect one's territory. Aggression to protect territory also serves another function. This innate aggressive behaviour among members of the same animal species (intraspecific aggression), prevents overcrowding and ensures that the best and most powerful males mate with females to guarantee their offspring. Consider how the older males in a pack are usually pushed out of the herd by the stronger young males, or when the dominant male must protect his territory against 'intruders' from the same species – intermale fighting. In the case of Bison, the bulls fight over who will have the right to mate with the females during mating season – mate-selection-related aggression. The deadlier animals are (like lions, leopards, tigers and pumas), the more intense the innate inhibitions against engaging in physical combat with members of its own species become. Deadly animals have developed weaponry through evolution (e.g., large canines, sharp long claws, medium to large body size, and remarkable strength). This innately programmed inhibition is a form of insurance for species' survival otherwise they would eventually terminate themselves if they did not manage and inhibit intraspecific physical combat. The deadlier animals opt to display their force and superiority by means of a complicated array of behaviours known collectively as ritualised aggression. They will show their fangs, roar loudly, or use their bulk to intimidate their opposition. We cannot fathom this intraspecific intricate communication system of aggression yet, but animals transmit these communication cues, after which the more powerful, dominant animal takes over while the losing animal usually bows out. The losing animal demonstrates defeat by various concession actions, like lowering their head, urinating, squealing softly, turning their back or running away. The defeated party will leave the territory of the dominant male.

Ethologists believe by understanding animal aggression, we can somehow get to grips with human aggression. Their premise is that humans are part of the animal world and undoubtedly follow many of the same basic principles.

However, they propose that humans have surpassed inhibiting aggression mechanisms and use mechanisms that are less uniquely animal-like to protect their territory. Humans have, over time, developed technologically advanced mechanisms (technological weaponry like nuclear bombs, fighter jets, rockets, radar, explosives, firearms, etc.) to protect themselves and their territories. As an alternative to developing natural weapons and ritualised aggressive options to ensure species-preservation, humans have developed the capacity to eradicate enemies and their species. Lorenz believe humans are hyper aggressive. Humans are assumed to have a conscience; a superior learning ability; and apparently, humans have outdistanced animals on the evolutionary development scale. This stands as a paradox, as humans should surely, with their 'superiority', preserve instead of destroy mother nature (deforestation, poaching to the brink of extinction, extraction of resources, etc.), maim, kill, go to war, engage in terrorism, murder their own species with impunity, reproduce irresponsibly, dump waste illegally to their own detriment, engage willingly in extractivism (e.g., deep sea mining), consume and support wider capitalistic ideals (i.e., materialism and product obsolescence and opulence) (Bartol & Bartol, 2021; Lorenz, 1966).

Nowadays, the ethological perspective has evolved into what is referred to as evolutionary psychology. Evolutionary psychology focuses on the evolution of behaviour using the principles of difference-in-degree, in terms of humans and animals. Humans are different from animals 'in degree', on a continuum, and not in kind. Evolutionary psychology and ethology agree that we have significant differences, but we are fully related. This approach corresponds to the Darwinian perspective of natural selection. It claims that human evolutionary history provides the fundamental framework for understanding human cognitions and behaviours. Evolutionary psychology does not see aggression as a pathology in humans but rather view it as something that is normal, especially for men (Bandura, 1983; Bedford et al., 2022; Berkowitz, 1973; Leach, 1973; Lorenz, 1966; Montagu, 1973; Spallone, 1998; Zillmann, 1983).

The ethological position on aggression is questioned by some behavioural scientists who believe that aggression is neither wholly instinctual nor learnt, but the outcome of an interaction between an animal's disposition, environment, and social structure (Bartol & Bartol, 2021; Rummel, 1977). The human-animal analogy to explain human aggression is still part of the mainstream discussion, but often this explanation lacks hard scientific evidence to portray humans as innately aggressive and controlled by their instincts. Some contemporary integrated theoretical explanations do adopt aspects of the biological perspectives on aggression and violence. Researchers are focusing on variables like the brain, hormones and the nervous system. It appears that aggression is mostly controlled by the amygdala in the brain. The amygdala is a small, almond-shaped group of nerve cells in the brain stem. Other areas in the brain on which researchers focus are the hypothalamus and the temporal lobe. To date, we have learnt that the amygdala is responsible for regulating our reactions and perceptions of aggression and fear. The amygdala is connected to the sympathetic nervous system, which in turn is related to the release of neurotransmitters related to stress and aggression.

To conclude the biological perspective, we need to remember that many biological variables that we often forget to consider in aggressive behaviour (like the influence of your diet or a hormonal imbalance) can too cause aggressive behaviour. It is believed that foods that contain a high sugar content, artificial colours, preservatives, and other potentially triggering ingredients can cause mood changes. Hormones like testosterone, oestrogen and progesterone are also often the topic of debate in relation to mood changes. High testosterone levels have been linked to aggressive behaviour in males, and fluctuations in oestrogen and progesterone levels during the menstrual cycle have been found to affect the mood of some women. These changes in hormone levels may trigger negative emotions, such as anger and irritability in some women. Lest we not forget – humans have mastered the ability to breed certain dog species to be aggressive (Bartol & Bartol, 2021; Coertze & Bezuidenhout, 2013; Fishbein & Pease, 1994; Tajima-Pozo et al., 2015). Therefore, aggression has a strong biological and genetic basis (i.e., nature is paramount, as compared to nurture).

The psychotherapeutic perspective

The various branches of psychotherapy represent another position to explain anger and aggression. In this perspective, anger and aggression are seen as outcomes of underlying psychological structures, processes, innate drives, and mechanisms. In short, anger and aggression are part of our psychological make-up. Anger is an emotional state we experience regularly, with different levels of intensity. Anger is part of our everyday life. Some humans struggle with chronic anger, which could inadvertently undermine meaningful relationships and psychological wellbeing, and if not managed, can cause neural damage due to the prolonged secretion of the stress hormones that accompany anger. This could lead to physical health problems, which in turn could affect sound judgement, contribute to short-term memory difficulties, and chronic anger, which can weaken the immune system. Psychologically speaking, those people who automatically react when they are angry, are angered easily and usually have a low frustration tolerance. They judge actions with subjective qualities and see triggers (which others take in their stride) as inconvenient and annoying. Anger-prone people usually grow infuriated for minor tribulations and often judge insignificant matters as unfair and unjust. The anger-prone person would interpret a situation where they are reprimanded by a line manager as unfair and this in turn will cause the motivation to react to the incident or to withdraw from the incident. Importantly, anger-prone people do not always react physically (a temper tantrum by throwing things around) or verbally (cursing the line manager or the company). In some instances, they will mope and sulk for days, and even withdraw socially. In chronic and serious cases, they can become physically ill due to the intensity of the suppressed anger (Manfredi & Taglietti, 2022; *Psychology Today*, 2024).

Aggression and anger in humans should be comprehended as a confluence of our biophysiological constitution, the inheritance of genes over our evolutionary past, and the interaction of our neurotransmitters and neurological condition with our temperament. Chemicals in our bodies like dopamine, serotonin, adrenaline, testosterone and frontal lobe brain interface seemingly play a significant role in the manifestation of aggressive behaviour. The sources of aggression lie in ourselves and cannot be linked to one dimensional explanations of animal-like instincts alone. Instinct is a mere facet of a complex psychological, neurophysiological and biological configuration of all the elements that lead to anger and aggression in humans. It is a complex array of innate and environmental cues that predispose humans to act aggressively. Globally, angry emotions that lead to aggression is perhaps the human emotion and action most exhibited daily.

Adler and Freud's perspectives on anger and aggression

During the early 1900s, Alfred Adler became the first psychotherapist to propose the existence of an innate aggressive drive. Aggression as an innate drive dominates our motor behaviour and is the organising principle of our activities and perceptions. Adler added that aggression is a confluence of other drives in humans, and a drive that we can turn inward, which could create various pathological manifestations (Adler, 1924). Adler was one of the original members of Sigmund Freud's inner circle, although they never shared a warm, personal relationship. In the early years (circa 1911), Adler was of the opinion that psychoanalysis should be much broader than the sharp focus Freud placed on infantile sexuality (libido) and human drives. He expressed his opposition to the strong sexual affection the Freudian psychoanalysis group used to explain human motivations. Adler insisted that the drive for superiority was a more basic motive than an exclusively raw sexual drive (Dennen, 2005). Freud and Adler disagreed about several issues in terms of human behaviour. When they realised that their differences were irreconcilable, Adler broke away from Freud and also resigned his presidency and membership of the Psychoanalytic Society. He and nine other former members of the Freudian circle formed their own society, namely Individual Psychology.

Adler soon reinterpreted the stance of the Freudian psychoanalysts regarding sexual drive in humans as a masculine protest (a drive to compensate for feelings of inferiority). He advanced that the drive is part of the human's upward striving for wholeness, completion or achievement.

As humans, we are driven, ultimately, to improve ourselves; to overcome our weaknesses. He saw aggression as subordinate to this drive to improve ourselves. Aggression towards others is interpreted as a pathological endeavour in pursuit of improving oneself.

Adler honed in on certain actions by people to protect themselves and their self-esteem. He believed that people create patterns of behaviour to protect their exaggerated sense of self-esteem against public disgrace. In his individual perspective of psychology, these protective actions are known as safeguarding tendencies (similar to defence mechanisms in the Freudian dogma). In both instances, in terms of safeguarding or defence mechanisms, people develop certain behaviours and symptoms as a protection against anxiety. There are important differences between these two concepts, namely that defence mechanisms operate unconsciously to protect the ego against anxiety, and it is a common trait to all humans; while safeguarding tendencies are believed to be a conscious process to shield one's fragile self-esteem from public humiliation. Importantly, safeguarding tendencies only develop when neurotic symptoms start to manifest. *Withdrawal, excuses* and *aggression* are viewed as three common safeguarding tendencies in humans (Ansbacher & Ansbacher, 1956; Meyer et al., 1993). They develop very uniquely, and are devised to maintain an elevated feeling of self-importance or to protect a style of life. This enables those with neurotic issues to hide their inflated self-image and to maintain their fictitious manner of operation.

Adler believed that *excuses* are the most common and most generally used safeguarding tendency in humans. Excuses protect the weak human's artificially inflated sense of self-worth. Excuses allow you to manipulate people into believing that you are more superior and more capable than you really are. Typical strategies include a cunning way with word-use like: *'If my father was not an alcoholic, I would have studied medicine'; 'If my wife did not have an intimate relationship with my best friend, this would not have happened'; 'If I had more opportunities, I would have been a successful businessman'; 'If only I followed my heart, I would not have married him, but now it is too late!'*

The second safeguarding technique people use is the tendency to *withdraw*, by escaping life's obstacles. People often withdraw from challenges in their life. This in turn can affect personality development. People have the ability to unconsciously escape their problems by initiating a detachment between themselves and their everyday challenges. Adler recognised four modes of withdrawal to safeguard:

› *Moving backward* (reverting to a more secure period of life to protect oneself and to prompt sympathy from others – for instance spoiled children who become parasites of the family).

› *Standing still* (people who use this strategy do not move in any direction, to avoid all responsibility and to prevent any threat of failure – for example, *'I am not applying for that job because I am overqualified'*).

› *Hesitating* (when confronted with challenges one hesitates or procrastinates in an effort to preserve an inflated sense of self-esteem – compulsive behaviours often fall into this category as it is seen as efforts to waste time (e.g., obsessive orderliness, leaving certain projects unfinished; compulsive hand washing etc.). Adler saw compulsive behaviours as intentional efforts to waste or play for time (Ansbacher & Ansbacher, 1956; Meyer et al., 1993).

› *Constructing obstacles* (aim low when confronted with a hurdle to ensure that failure can be rectified with an excuse while success of overcoming the hurdle will feed the brittle self-esteem).

Safeguarding will probably not be necessary if people give up their obsessive self-interest. Genuine acceptance of oneself and unconditional empathy and understanding of one's fellow human beings will prevent the employment of safeguarding techniques to a large extent.

The last common safeguarding tendency in humans is *aggression*. Some people use aggression to safeguard their exaggerated superiority complex. In the Adlerian dogma, people do this to protect their fragile self-esteem (Ansbacher & Ansbacher, 1956; Meyer et al., 1993). Aggression as a safeguarding technique can manifest in three ways, namely depreciation, accusation, or self-accusation.

In *depreciation* people tend to undervalue the achievements of other people and to overvalue their own achievements. The motivation is to demean another to place the critic in a favourable light (consider rumours in the unofficial communication channels at work or the critic who blames others for poor performance at work).

Accusation is the tendency to blame others for your own failures. In addition, one seeks revenge, as the revenge element provides the safeguarding of one's own fragile self-esteem. People with unbalanced unhealthy relationships and lifestyles often use an element of aggressive accusation towards others to balance out their unhealthy way of thinking and living. Unhealthy and morbid people habitually channel aggressive accusatory acts in such a way to cause the people around them – like a partner – to suffer more than *they* do.

Self-accusation is the third form of neurotic aggression. This type of aggression is demonstrated by self-torture (e.g., self-imposed distress (physical and or psychological)) and guilt. Self-imposed distress includes perversity, recklessness, masochism, depression and suicide. The hypothesis is that self-imposed distressed actions are a mechanism of hurting people who are close to you. Feelings of guilt are seen as aggressive, self-accusatory behaviour. For example, *'I should have been nicer to my ex-girlfriend while we were still dating but now it is all over and she deserves to suffer'* or *'I should not have trusted my best friend and my wife, because they were cheating and he deserved to die.'* Depreciation (devaluing others to feel better) and self-accusation (devaluing the self to inflict suffering on other people to protect one's self-esteem) are opposite strategies, although both are utilised to gain superiority in demanding emotional situations (Ansbacher & Ansbacher, 1956; Meyer et al., 1993).

As mentioned earlier, Freud's initial thoughts were dominated by self-preservation and sexual instincts (the id, ego, and superego instincts, Thanatos and Eros) (Bartol & Bartol, 2021; Marcuse, 1966). Earlier in his works, Freud did not identify aggression as a separate instinct, but rather as a component of Eros. Eros is a fundamental aspect of one's sexuality. Importantly, he saw the Eros as a tension-releasing instinct. He believed that humans were driven by two competing instincts, namely the human instinctive impulse known as Thanatos – the 'death instinct', and the 'life instinct' known as Eros. Life instinct relates to leisure, pleasure, friendships and comfort. It has an aversion to the malicious, dangerous and hostile part of life. However, in some cases, the death instinct could be channelled outwards after gaining control over the life instinct. In many cases, this is a spontaneous mental condition in humans that awakens aggression, evil, violence and destruction. Some humans channel the death instinct inwards after it gains control. Once again, this is seen as a spontaneous mental condition in some humans that leads to self-harm and even suicide. In terms of Thanatos, Marcuse (1966, p. 29) states that "the death instinct is destructiveness not for its own sake, but for the relief of tension, frustration and aggression. The descent towards death is an 'unconscious flight' from pain and want. It is an expression of the eternal struggle against suffering and repression." Hence, from the standpoint of the Freud-Marcuse thesis, in response to situations of life, Thanatos continually strives to gain dominance and control over Eros, the life instinct, thereby generating aggression and violence as a substitute for peace and harmony (Dennen, 2005; Kli, 2018; Marcuse, 1966; Olofinbiyi, 2022). As soon as Thanatos is directed inward, the libido (sex drive) confronts the death instinct and directs it outward. This is when it becomes external aggression and manifests in the human's drive for control and power. In this context, aggression is seen as a secondary instinct as the libido deflects the death instinct away from the self to preserve the human being. What is more, during the duel between them, the death instinct may combine with the Eros instinct to spawn sadism (a person who gleans pleasure from hurting or humiliating others) and masochism (a person who is gratified by their own pain). These two are some of the most malicious and worst common pathological manifestations in humans (Bartol & Bartol, 2021).

In addition to the aforementioned, Freud believed human beings are susceptible to a buildup of aggressive energies from birth. These energies must be released or drained regularly or they will reach dangerous levels – mostly linked to our sexual drives. This is known as the psychodynamic or hydraulic model. The reason for this is that it is symbolically compared to the so-called pressure-cooker pot, with a valve on top of the pot. The steam builds up, and every now and then, the valve will release steam from the pot. In humans, pressure builds up and it needs to be released. If it is not released, people will blow off steam by engaging in a tirade. This is how humans blow off their excess 'steam' (otherwise referred to as their 'aggressive energy'). Freud believed that all forms of violence are a manifestation of our aggressive energy discharge. The pressure in us builds up and reaches dangerous levels. One could release the energy by means of a catharsis – a release (Bartol & Bartol, 2021).

To Freud, then, aggression was always negative or destructive. It was antilife or pathological. Behaviour was a manifestation either of Eros, or the desire for death (Thanatos), or a combination of these. Striving for identity, self-assertion, and social interest had no role in Freud's perspective.

The psychoanalytic perspective has been influential in understanding aggressive human behaviour. Although instincts like Eros, libido, Thanatos, ego, id, superego, and catharsis are also shaped by culture, which, in turn influences individual characteristic predispositions (or personalities), as well as social behaviour, the concepts have been found useful since their inception (Bartol & Bartol, 2021; Dennen, 2005; Kli, 2018; Marcuse, 1966).

The frustration-aggression perspective

Frustration and associated anger play an important role in the manifestation of aggression. At the time of Freud's death in 1939, a group of psychologists proposed that aggression is a direct result of frustration (Dollard et al., 1939). Dollard and his colleagues proposed that humans who experience frustration will show aggressive actions. These authors believed aggression is a natural, spontaneous response to annoying circumstances. Unfortunately, researchers like Berkowitz (1962, 1969, 1973) indicated that frustration does not lead to aggression in all circumstances, and aggressive behaviours cannot always be linked to frustration. Berkowitz and colleagues indicated that people respond differently to frustration, disgust and anger. Some humans will show aggression, but others will choose to react differently to their circumstances (e.g., withdrawal).

Berkowitz revised the initial work of Dollard et al. (1939), adding that some people could show an increased probability to grow angry in frustrating circumstances. Berkowitz and his colleagues believed frustration could facilitate the show of aggressive behaviour. Also, people could react in an overt manner (physical or verbal) or covert way (wishing your bully was dead). Notably, they believe that not only anger and frustration lead to aggression. Other sensations like intense pain, or sexual arousal, which is a pleasant state, could cause aggressive behaviour (Berkowitz, 1973). Severe back pain can cause frustration and indifferent behaviour, and the person could end up scolding everyone around them. If a person has sexual intentions with someone, and they are together in a situation where the person of interest allows certain behaviours (like touching a hand or other body parts) to take place, but they then suddenly end the intimacy, the person with the intention can become annoyed with the person of interest in this supposedly pleasant situation (e.g., consider a date-rape situation). This explains the core assumption of the frustration-aggression hypothesis: if anticipated goals or expectations are thwarted, frustration is likely to result. The person must expect or predict the attainment of a goal or achievement first (a sexual encounter; a promotion at work; a recognition for hard work; making the sports team, etc.) for frustration to manifest.

Berkowitz (1973) allows for important variables, like social learning and individual differences in response to frustrating circumstances. One person will walk away from the circumstances they find frustrating, while others will respond callously. At this point, it is fair to assume we are different, and we act differently in frustrating situations. Berkowitz's revised frustration-aggression hypothesis suggests the following important process:

(1) The actual point when a person is blocked from obtaining an expected goal.

(2) This could likely cause frustration and even generate anger.

(3) The anger could predispose some, or ready them to explode and show aggressive behaviour.

Several variables play a role in whether someone engages in aggressive actions due to their frustration. Variables like social learning, cognitive development, interpretation of the situation, and their regular individual way of responding to frustration, will play a significant role in their reaction. The level of frustration and the presence of aggression-eliciting stimuli in the environment and in their culture will also play an important role in the outcomes of the behaviour (Bartol & Bartol, 2021; Berkowitz, 1989).

The cultural perspective

Similar to the social learning theory, the cultural perspective proposes that aggression is seated within a culture. Members of a specific culture learn aggression in the same way traits of their ethnic group or language are learnt. To understand aggression in a culture, one should understand the cultural context of aggression. Aggression often has a function in the preservation and progression of the culture. According to Ventura (2024), the current top 10 most peaceful countries (in descending order) are: Iceland, Denmark, Ireland, New Zealand, Austria, Singapore, Portugal, Slovenia, Japan, and Switzerland. It is possible that countries like Iceland and New Zealand are culturally more cohesive due to their geographic isolation. In short, some cultures are relatively free of collective aggression. These cultures hardly ever manifest interpersonal violence and viciousness towards other countries. Individuals always have the potential to show aggressive behaviour, but we cannot ignore the role of cultural learning, because aggressive cultures often have aggressive citizens. The premise is that external sources have an influence on learning aggressiveness collectively. The difference between the cultural approach and the social learning perspective is that social learning is mostly tested in laboratory experiments while the cultural perspective was developed by a process of naturalistic observation and an attentiveness to cultures (Rummel, 1977). In addition, the social learning perspective focuses on the individual and how the individual is influenced by a role model and the interactions between punishment, response and reinforcement (Bandura, 1973, 2001). The cultural perspective focusses less on the individual but on the totality of norms, cultural practices, meanings, and values of ethnic groups within which certain behavioural patterns develop.

Consider the so-called culture of violence in some countries. South Africa is a prime example of a culture that has embraced violence as a mechanism to cope, control, and to achieve certain goals (Pandey, 2012). The culture of violence perspective explains how cultures and societies can sanction violent acts. It basically accounts for inter-generational systems of violence and domestic violence. Violent acts like murder, rape and robbery are notoriously prevalent in South Africa and could be related to the culture of violence.

Additional perspectives on aggression

Several less-celebrated perspectives on aggression exist. These perspectives include the displaced aggression theory, the cognitive-neoassociation (CNA) model, and the excitation-transfer theory (Bartol & Bartol, 2021).

Cognitive-neoassociation model

The cognitive-neoassociation perspective is in essence a reformulation of the frustration-aggression hypothesis. It explains aggression in the following manner. An aversive event, like physical pain or psychological distress, produces a negative affect (discomfort) in most human beings. The effect of physical pain is often obvious, but the adverse effect of emotional pain is in many cases not tangible. If a supervisor scolds a person at work, or someone's partner makes a demeaning hurtful comment about them in front of friends, most people will feel angry, sad and even depressed about it during and after these incidents. Scolding, demeaning comments and malicious gossip will all invoke negative affects due to their negative desolate content and intent. This will trigger a variety of feelings, thoughts, and memories that are associated with flight (fear) and fight (anger) tendencies in animals and humans. The fight or flight response is also known as the fight-flight-freeze-or-fawn response. Walter Bradford Cannon is credited as the pioneer of this perspective. He also referred to it as hyperarousal or the acute stress response. It is seen as a physiological reaction that occurs in response to a perceived harmful event, attack, or threat to survival whenever the sympathetic nervous system prepares a human being or animal for a response to imminent danger (McCarty, 2016; Bartol & Bartol, 2021).

In most cases, a person will not consider the situation cognitively, but in an arbitrary way, as the immediate emotional pain will be too overwhelming. In some cases, someone who is the victim of a demeaning comment from a partner will, however, react immediately either by responding with a similarly hurtful comment or by turning to violence (e.g., a slap or full-blown assault). In the vignette, Eric caught his wife in bed with his best friend and he reacted with severe violence by killing him with a golf club. If someone does not react immediately (flight) and time passes, people often start to appraise the incident cognitively, which will influence their subsequent emotional reactions and experiences. The person in the situation assesses the incident cognitively and calculates a fitting course of action. As time goes by, the individual makes causal attributions about the unpleasant experience. The person in the situation thinks about the nature of their feelings and the degree of impact the incident had on them – cognitively they associate and evaluate. In some cases, people will decide it is not a 'big deal' after they cool off. In cases like Eric's, the partner can decide to file for divorce as they do not want to experience this type of humiliation again. In severe cases, unpleasant feelings and arousal can lead to the murder of a loved one (e.g., as Eric's situation shows), or to familicide, where an entire family is murdered (Bartol & Bartol, 2021; Berkowitz, 1989).

Cognitive scripts perspective

According to Huesmann (1988), social behaviour in general, and aggressive behaviour in particular, are controlled largely by cognitive scripts learnt and memorised through daily experiences. "A script suggests what events are to happen in the environment, how the person should behave in response to these events, and what the likely outcome of those behaviours would be" (Huesmann, 1988, p. 15). Cognitive scripts can be learnt by direct experience or by observing role models (Bushman & Anderson, 2001). Once learnt, the script usually determines actions and reactions. Each script is different and unique to each person, but once established, they are quite permanent like a physical feature and become resilient to change and may persist for a lifetime. For the script to become enduring, it must be repeated from time to time. In this sense, practice makes perfect, and with repetition the script will not only become encoded and maintained in memory, but it will also be more easily retrieved and utilised when the person is confronted with a problem that needs the coding of the relevant script. The person's "evaluation of the 'appropriateness' of a script plays an important role in determining which scripts are stored in memory, in determining which scripts are retrieved and utilized, and which scripts continue to be utilized" (Huesmann, 1988, p. 19). Personal standards and processes are also important in the storing and utilisation of certain scripts. Scripts that are inconsistent or violate one's internalised standards are unlikely to be stored or utilised. An individual with poorly integrated internal standards against aggression, or who is convinced that aggressive behaviour is instrumental in attaining what you need, is more likely to incorporate aggressive scripts for behaviour. Aggressive humans often use and instigate aggressive reactions from others, which in turn confirm their beliefs about the aggressiveness of human nature in a repetitive, preserving manner.

One's cognitive script to use violence will be partly determined by nature and partly by nurture. If someone grows up in an environment where their biological, socio-economic and environmental factors, as well as the community circumstances, place them at risk of showing aggressive behaviour, their cognitive script on aggression will become quite permanent and relevant in situations where they use that script to guide their behaviour. In addition, situations that trigger them to show expressive aggression will bring forward more severe violence (Anderson & Bushman, 2002; Bartol & Bartol, 2021).

Hostile attribution bias

Highly aggressive people often have a hostile attribution bias. This means they are more likely to interpret ambiguous actions as hostile and threatening than other people with less aggressive biases. They see innocent actions as deliberate actions to hurt or foil them. Dill et al. (1997, p. 275) highlight it as follows: people described as having hostile attribution bias "tend to view the world through blood-red tinted glasses." People with hostile attribution bias usually label social problems in hostile ways, choose to adopt hostile goals, and refrain from seeking additional facts in confrontational situations and desist from generating alternative solutions. They often predict few consequences for aggression and prioritise their aggressive solutions in a provoking situation (Bartol & Bartol, 2021; Eron & Slaby, 1994).

Hostile attribution bias begins to develop in childhood when a child grows up in adverse circumstances – their bias stays ingrained until adulthood. Many people who show higher tendencies toward hostile attribution biases, as well as other social cognitive deficits related to aggression, often come from backgrounds where they were confronted with a pattern of higher involvement in violent situations as children, and adversity – like abuse and maltreatment – occurred frequently (Bartol & Bartol, 2021; Klopper & Bezuidenhout, 2020).

Excitation-transfer theory

The excitation-transfer theory focuses on how humans take physiological arousal from one situation to another – often without them realising. For example, a person's supervisor talks down to them and criticises them in front of colleagues. This anger and embarrassment are bottled up inside as they cannot argue with their superior. Although they might think they are over the anger when they get home later, after the workday, some residual anger is still situated in the consciousness. Therefore, after the workday is completed, the person will go home where an insignificant incident could cause a major situation and they fly off the handle. This is the excitation-transfer mechanism in operation. The negative criticism at work indirectly caused the person to overreact at home for a less severe trigger. For example, the person who was criticised at work, walks into the front door of their home and their partner makes a patronising remark about the lawn that was not mowed over the weekend. The residue of the physiological arousal and feelings of the morning at work along with the sudden anger that is generated by the patronising remark at home, may increase the likelihood of showing aggression when they arrive home after work. Zillmann (1988) referred to this as excitation transfer. His premise is that physiological arousal, whether the source was physical or emotional, will dissipate slowly over time. It will not disappear immediately, as some residual arousal will drift in the psyche. If, for instance, one's supervisor at work makes disapproving comments about one's performance and work output in front of colleagues early in the morning, the arousal will dissipate slightly over time, but it will not disappear completely. The key premise is that one can transfer arousal from one situation to another. Importantly, it often occurs when people are unaware that they are still carrying some arousal from a previous situation to a new, unrelated one (Bartol & Bartol, 2021; Klopper & Bezuidenhout, 2020; Zillman, 1988).

Displaced aggression theory

A perspective that is easily confused with the excitation-transfer theory is the displaced aggression theory. Bushman and his co-workers propose that some people take out their physiological arousal on the wrong people, i.e., people who did not actually cause the initial arousal, but are inconveniently in the wrong place at the wrong time (Bushman et al., 2005). Accordingly, displaced aggression is likely to take place when an individual cannot aggress or react against a source of provocation like the scolding supervisor at work. However, the victim of the reprimand feels more at ease taking out their frustration and anger on an innocent family member or their partner when they get home. At this point, the theory echoes the same ideas as the excitation transfer contribution, but the key difference lies in the following process, namely rumination. The victim keeps thinking and pondering about the incident at work long after it is over.

Rumination refers to obsessive thinking about an incident, idea, situation, or choice and recurrently interferes with normal mental functioning, to self-focused attention toward one's thoughts and feelings. The importance here is that ruminative thought can harbour and maintain angry feelings on a high level without dissipating somewhat over time. In fact, the rumination can worsen the physiological storm inside the person, and it can stay at this high level of activation long after they have removed themselves from the initial provocation. Bushman et al. (2005) believe it is the ruminative thoughts that could promote later aggression against a pet, someone random, a family member, or a partner, who is perhaps mildly annoying by doing something inconsequential and undeserving of an aggressive outburst. The bottom line is that an aggressive outburst follows long after the initial trigger took place due to the continuous intruding thoughts about the trigger event. A secondary innocent target commits a minor provocative action long after the triggering event, which in turn prompts an aggressive response. This delayed displaced aggressive response is usually excessive and far more than what might be expected. To illustrate this process, take the example of Eric. Imagine, Eric's manager scolded him during an important meeting earlier in the day, in front of all his co-workers; in doing so, Eric experienced anger and shame. In his mind, Eric starts thinking that he would really like to punch his manager in his face for what he has done, but then he starts contextualising the situation. Of course, he cannot hit the manager, although he feels that he deserves it. Eric goes back to his office highly irritated and starts ruminating about what happened during the meeting. Through ruminating, he gets angrier. At the end of the day, Eric goes home, only to find his wife in bed with his best friend. Because of his anger and frustration, he swings once and gives his friend one blow to the head – unfortunately, it is just hard enough to kill him.

Most of the discussion so far has focused on a one-dimensional contribution to explain aggression. In recent years, several integrated perspectives have seen the light. Some scholars believe it is better to explain aggression from a multi-angle approach that incorporates several disciplines and perspectives. These scholars believe it is better to combine the best sections of different theories to explain aggression more holistically and eclectically.

Brown et al. (1998) posits in this regard that theory integration has become a familiar feature among scholars. Furthermore, it allows one to combine nature and nurture in explanations. Whereas concepts like the id, ego, superego, libido, Eros, Thanatos and safeguarding are difficult to measure and pinpoint, academics have employed advanced statistical analysis of their data to support their assumptions in terms of the social learning models. Also, research data and methodologies have become very advanced compared to the past. This allows academics to integrate different perspectives and to measure all correlating relevant variables to enable integration. Some of the major developments of recent decades involves attempts to integrate social, biological, physiological, psychological, emotional, criminological, personal and economic factors into one perspective to explain aggressive behaviour.

The General Aggression Model (GAM)

An example of a multi-disciplinary effort to explain aggression in general saw the light during 2011. Several perspectives and theories of explaining human aggression were combined in an effort to integrate the common features of previous efforts. Nathan DeWall and Craig Anderson (DeWall & Anderson, 2011, p. 255) state that "GAM provides the only theoretical framework of aggression and violence that explicitly incorporates biological factors, personality development, social processes, short-term and long-term processes, and decision processes." The theory attempts to include most factors that can cause aggression. It draws heavily on social-cognitive and social learning theories. Aggression and violence depend on how a person perceives and interprets the social environment, expectations about various outcomes, knowledge and beliefs about how people usually respond in certain situations and the degree to which a person believes he or she has the ability to respond effectively. Eventually, reactions might be complicated, but with time, through cultural teachings and repetitive experiences, the person's judgement and choices in different situations become automatised. Eventually a person considers situations and other people without effort based on their appearance, race, religion and other characteristics.

In addition, GAM posits that violence often occurs because of an escalation cycle. A trigger event must take place to prompt the action between two people, two groups or any type of dyad – even two countries (consider the war that was prompted by Russia and the retaliatory reaction from Ukraine). Once the trigger event occurs, the other person or group will likely retaliate. Reciprocal retaliation can occur because both parties usually deem the reaction or retaliation as unjustified. Persistence of the retaliation often occurs because the role players get caught up in a tangle as the opposing parties perceive the other party as acting with malice or evil intent and deem their own behaviour as acceptable and appropriate in the relevant situation. An important aspect of the GAM theory, which echoes the level of violent incidents between groups and individuals in violence-prone countries, is that violence and aggression can ignite in a wide range of situations and because of many triggers (Bezuidenhout, 2024; Van der Westhuizen & Bezuidenhout, 2020). To contextualise this, in this regard, DeWall and Anderson (2011, p. 26) state that "if you want to create people who are predisposed to aggression and violence, begin by depriving them of resources necessary to meet basic needs – physical, emotional, psychological, and social." Consider those countries where low levels of aggression are reported against countries that endorse violence, and where basic resources are difficult to attain (e.g., Afghanistan, Yemen, Syria, South Sudan, Congo, South Africa and Mexico) (Parker, 2023).

We can use the xenophobic attacks in South Africa as an example of where the general public is provided with multiple examples and models of aggression and violence. Aggression is a simple, direct way of solving immediate problems, conflicts and needs. These are also deemed successful tools in achieving something. If people are provided with cognitive beliefs and values that dehumanise an out-group and are exposed to events of violence against them, desensitisation will eventually occur. If the necessary cognitive scripts about an out-group exist, high levels of violence will follow (refer to the chapter on disgust to read more on dehumanisation) (Bartol & Bartol, 2017). For example, the perceptions some South Africans hold with regard to immigrants from neighbouring countries have resulted in violent xenophobic attacks. Many believe the immigrants have taken over, commit crime, take away job opportunities from locals, work for lower wages, and date local females to make the local males look superfluous (Olofinbiyi, 2022). In terms of the GAM explanation, all the relevant ingredients, like inner drives, hostile bias, adversity, expressive motivations, triggers, excuses, the Eros being overwhelmed by Thanatos, and opportunity in a culture of violence, make aggression towards foreign immigrants possible and easy.

The upside of anger and aggression

Society often holds the perception that anger and aggression are negative and increase the risk factor for exhibiting serious violent behaviour. It is true that anger could instigate an aggressive action, but we need to emphasise that anger and aggression can act as sources of strength and assertiveness in situations where it is needed. It can be utilised positively on an individual or societal level to bring change for the good. In some situations, the anger we feel can make us feel calm when the anger dissipates, and anger can empower us in fearful situations. Instead of fear and retreat, anger and aggression can motivate us to confront in a controlled and balanced way. Ellis (1976) is of the opinion that you need a bit of aggression to lead a healthy, productive life. This can be achieved with actions that promote the basic values of survival, protection, happiness, social acceptance, intimate relations and safeguarding. A certain amount of positive aggression is needed during childhood and adolescence, as it helps to build the person's autonomy and unique identity. A hint of positive aggression assists a person in cooperative and competitive activities with their peers. Humans must learn how to channel positive aggression to become balanced and self-assertive. This will eventually help humans to become independent beings who understand themselves and have the ability to master challenges from society and how they will react to these challenges. This empowers us. Anger and aggression can therefore have both negative and positive connotations.

Society socialises children to be open with their emotions, for example, when they feel down or experience anxiety, happiness, sadness, disgust; but strangely, society frowns upon those who express anger as an emotion. Due to the dissent we have placed on anger, humans usually do not uncover techniques on how to handle anger and the related aggressiveness, or how to channel it constructively. Relevant coping mechanisms often do not develop, and emotional disinterest is often the end result. However, when a person is allowed to uncover the specific triggers of anger and aggression that impact their behaviour, it will allow them to develop cognitive and emotional coping strategies to keep the relevant triggers, and will prompt to push them from a stable state to an unstable one. Once cognitive strategies of appraising the triggers have been developed, a person controls their emotions and actions more. These strategies become ingrained and will go into operation and substantially influence the subsequent emotional or physical reactions and experiences after the initial trigger. One could say that a form of automatic response is likely to develop over time and situation-relevant responses will be forthcoming when a person is confronted by provoking triggers. These developed cognitions will mediate and evaluate a proper course of action. The ability of roused people to make intellectual causal attributions about the unpleasant experience will imaginably significantly reduce aggressiveness in society. We must, therefore, endeavour to assist children from a young age, to think about the nature of their feelings and assist them to control their feelings and actions in a cognitively responsible, age-related way. Eventually, humans will be able to carefully consider the merits of a trigger or event and manage them responsibly. It is true that anger and aggression are related to our fight-flight-freeze response of the sympathetic nervous system, but it does not imply we cannot socialise humans to contextualise triggers and negative stimuli and to cognitively evaluate the merit of an aggressive response. The same energy that prepares the human to fight can be channelled positively to motivate a person, their communities and society, to oppose discrimination and unfairness by changing attitudes, and by insisting to change policy and to introduce new accommodating inclusive norms (Bartol & Bartol, 2021; Manfredi & Taglietti 2022; *Psychology Today*, 2024).

Although different perceptions exist about anger and aggression and whether they derive from nature or nurture, we must be able to socialise humans to manage their anger and related responses in a controlled and balanced way. On the one hand, scholars like Bandura contend that it is not an innate attribute of human nature to be angry and aggressive. Bandura posits that "It is important to distinguish between the proximate hormonal and neuronal regulators of aggressive behaviour and the cognitive and social influences that preside over these biological mechanisms" (Bandura, 2016, p. 17). On the other side of the continuum, Adler (Ansbacher & Ansbacher, 1956, p. 208) believed that psychology's focus on nature and nurture have made them blind to an individual's own creative contribution to their development. Adler states in this regard: "Whatever cannot be evaluated as environmental influence is evaluated as hereditary influence, while whatever cannot be referred to obscure hereditary factors, is attributed to environment" (Ansbacher & Ansbacher, 1956, p. 208). We can therefore never ignore the individual's free choice to decide how they will react to aggressive stimuli, or when and why they show aggression. With the suitable socialisation techniques and appropriate cognitive development, humans have the potential to channel anger and arousal into beneficial impacts and decrease aggressive consequences significantly. In this regard, Hebb (1955, p. 249) states that arousal "is an energizer, but not a guide, an engine but not a steering gear". It is our cognition that provides the guidance and focus to the energising effects of anger, frustration and fear. Humans have the cognitive ability to manage emotions. The ability to manage anger and the related response must be practised and rehearsed to replace aggressive responses with nonviolent or nonaggressive behaviours as solutions. It is imperative to change those cognitive scripts in favour of aggression by means of psychological treatment programmes (Bartol & Bartol, 2021). These programmes should be directed at cognitive behaviour therapy (CBT) and anger management to guide the relevant people to recognise the physiological responses that accompany their anger and aggression and identify strategies for controlling it.

Conclusion

In this chapter, several theories were considered to define anger and aggression. Nature, nurture and all the interlinking variables cannot be seen separately, as these influence and complement one another. The earlier contributions about specific drives in humans, learning processes as well as biology and psychology set the stage for the many efforts that have developed over time to explain anger and aggression.

A theorist such as Ellis (1976) is of the opinion that everyone needs a modicum of aggression to lead a healthy, productive life. This can be achieved through actions that promote the basic values of survival, protection, happiness, social acceptance, intimate relations and safeguarding. He believes that a certain amount of positive aggression is needed during childhood and adolescence as it helps to build a person's autonomy and unique identity. A hint of positive aggression assists a person in cooperative and competitive activities with their peers. Humans must learn how to channel positive aggression to become balanced and self-assertive. This will eventually help them to become independent beings who understand themselves and have the ability to master challenges from society and how they will react to these challenges.

Importantly, a person's culture often provides the nurturing ground for aggression. In this contribution, anger and aggression were explained from several angles. It was impossible to cover all the explanations in this chapter, but it is hoped that the factors that have been highlighted will leave the reader with some food for thought about the complexity of human aggression and the role of all the correlating variables. Adler believed that psychology's focus on nature and nurture has made them blind to an individual's own creative contribution to their development. We can, therefore, never ignore the individual's free choice to decide how they will react to aggressive stimuli, or when and why they show aggression.

CHAPTER 6

The Thin Line that Cuts Through Every Heart: Fear and Courage

Yolandi-Eloïse Janse van Rensburg
Palesa Luzipo
Lindiwe Masole

The bucket list

Mel has been very quiet the past week, as she is not in a good place at the moment. For this reason, Ophelia decides to call Mel for a cup of coffee. Sitting outside in the afternoon sun at the corner bakery, Ophelia says: "I think we should do something nice for a change… something adventurous! I recently read an article, titled 'The F's of fear: Fight, flight, freeze, fawn, flag, or flop'. Reading the article made me think about my personal *bucket list*. I still have so many things that I want to do before I die. I think ticking off my *bucket list* will make me feel alive again! Come on, Mel – let's be daring and go do that 10-day hike to the peak of Mount Veil that we have always been planning to do. Yes, this is exactly what we need to do… let's go hiking!"

Courage is resistance to fear, mastery of fear and not the absence of fear.
—Mark Twain

Introduction

Already in 1930, Watson (as cited in Ortony, 2022) believed that all emotions stem from three basic emotions, namely, fear, love, and rage. This idea implies that all prosocial emotions (e.g., compassion, empathy, trust, hope) may be embedded in love, whereas more intricate negative emotions (e.g., embarrassment, anxiety, trauma, sadness, and anger) are rooted in fear or rage. However, in relation to other emotions, fear (just like disgust) is a functional, primal emotion that can be a helpful response when facing immediate danger, and is needed for human survival (Izard, 1993). Although fear is essential for survival, excessive or irrational fear, for extended periods of time, can become problematic, as this may lead to avoidance behaviour, which may interfere with daily functioning.

Defining fear

Fear is a phrase very commonly used, and according to many academics (e.g., Le Doux, 2014), is one of the most extensively studied emotions. Yet, to date, there is no single agreed-upon definition of the concept in literature. In fact, there are ongoing debates about how to best define and investigate fear (Mobbs et al., 2019), whether it is a psychological construct, and what it really means to *be afraid* (Adophs, 2013).

The debate on how to define fear originates from the view that emotions, like fear, are conscious, subjective experiences that are cognitively assembled conceptions of a situation and not an innate mental state (Mobbs et al., 2019). Some researchers (e.g., Barret, 2017; Le Doux, 2017), define fear as a conscious feeling one has when one's safety is threatened, and results from the cognitive interpretation that one is in a dangerous situation. Whereas other researchers, such as Adolphs (2013, p. 79), define fear as an "intervening variable between sets of context-dependent stimuli and suites of behavioural response," and believe that fear is an innate experience that occurs across various species. While the debate on how to best define fear rages on, there is general agreement on its purpose. Fear is generally said to be an adaptive emotion, with the primary aim of mobilising the body's resources in case of danger (Steimer, 2001; Simic et al., 2021). Therefore, fear reactions are necessary to help humans (and animals) to survive in the presence of danger. Additionally, experiencing fear may also assist in predicting future threats, if one learns to associate certain neutral stimuli with danger.

Sources of fear

Fear responses can be caused by a wide range of stimuli, ranging from basic unconditioned stimuli, to complex symbolic knowledge (which may be both real and imagined) (Adolphs, 2013; Silva et al., 2016). To fully understand the process that occurs from exposure to stimuli to experiencing fear, one must first distinguish between innate fear and learnt or conditioned fear. According to Gross and Canteras (2012), *innate fear* responses are those activated by intrinsically threatening stimuli, while *learnt fear* is fear that is elicited by neutral stimuli that have been associated with innate threats. For example, seeing a snake in the wild can be expected to naturally evoke an innate fear response. Similarly, behaviours can also be elicited by exposure to a cue, associated with predator exposure, for example seeing a picture of a snake (Gross & Canteras, 2012). Fear conditioning is an example of associative learning, a process by which the brain creates memories about the relationship between two events (Simic et al., 2021). As a field of study, fear is often best researched using Pavlovian fear conditioning (Le Doux, 2014). This procedure involves repeatedly presenting a neutral stimulus (also known as a conditioned stimulus, like a tone, or light) paired with an aversive unconditioned stimulus (such as a mild electric shock). Through continuous pairing and presentation, the subject comes to learn that the conditioned stimulus is harmful and expresses a (conditioned) fear response, even when presented with the harmless conditioned stimulus alone (Panzer et al., 2007; Gunduz-Cinar, 2021).

Over a century of research on fear has led to general findings about fear according to different themes (Gullone, 2000): the structure and duration of fear, and how it is related to individual differences (e.g., age, gender, socio-economic status, and culture). To summarise the main findings of Gullone (2000): First, there is an overwhelming resemblance on how the general structure of fear looks, as there has been consistency in the results from various factor analytic studies. It seems that all fears can be classified into four broad categories: (1) interpersonal events or situations (e.g., failure, criticism, the dark); (2) death, injuries, illness, blood and surgical procedures; (3) animals, and (4) agoraphobic fears. Second, fear is short-lived and generally decreases with the increase in age or maturation (i.e., younger children report to have more fears compared to older children). Therefore, most fears subside as one grows older, apart from psychic stress related to medical conditions (which may increase with age). Third, females report to have more fears, as compared to males (which might be influenced by gender stereotyping). Fourth, children from lower social economic status (SES) report to have more fears (which, as compared to youth from middle and upper SES groups). Fifth, more research is needed in terms of cross-cultural studies on fear, as findings are inconclusive.

Epigenetic studies (e.g., Dias & Ressler, 2014; Zovkic et al., 2013) have revealed that certain fears can be inherited through the generations and might leave permanent epigenetic marks (i.e., changes in gene expression that occur without altering the underlying DNA sequence and involves modifications to the DNA) and could therefore be passed to future generations. Experimental studies on laboratory mice found that male mice, that were conditioned to associate a specific chemical scent with shocks (fear), passed down the response of the scent to the next two following generations through epigenetic changes. Therefore, although not being directly exposed, the second and third generations of mice had a heightened sensitivity to the specific chemical scent. In fact, exposure to fear-inducing situations, like war and conflict, has an epigenetic hereditary effect on the physical health of offspring (e.g., leading to decreased cortisol levels, heightened mortality risk, diabetes, and heart disease) (Raza et al., 2023).

Biological process of fear

A meta-analytic review has determined how the human brain generates emotions, in the form of a *conceptual act model* (see the open peer commentary section in Lindquist et al., 2012). To understand the brain basis of emotion, this review compares two hypotheses: (1) whether discrete emotion categories consistently and specifically correspond to distinct brain regions (i.e., referred to the *locationist approach*), versus (2) whether discrete emotion categories are constructed of more general brain networks, not related to specific to categories (i.e., the *psychological constructionist approach*). Although the findings are highly debated, Lindquist et al. (2012) found evidence to support the latter hypothesis, implying that interacting regions of the brain are involved in both emotional and non-emotional experiences across a range of emotive categories.

However, many researchers support the *locationist approach*, linking fear to the amygdala (which forms part of the limbic system), and which is generally regarded as responsible for processing emotions, especially fear, as well as the pulvinar and fronto-occipital regions (Adolphs, 2013; Tao et al., 2021). Both implicit and explicit fear processing are activated in the amygdala; however, explicit fear processing appears to elicit more activations in other parts of the brain, such as the pulvinar and the parahippocampal gyrus, suggesting that visual attention and contextual association play an important role during this process (Tao et al., 2021).

The amygdala (in particular, the central nucleus, which is often referred to as the *emotional brain*) supports the cardiovascular changes that occur during the freeze response (e.g., during 'fear learning experiments' on rats, rats freeze in response to tones previously paired with electric shocks) (Lindquist et al., 2012). There are two main pathways that lead to the amygdala – the fast pathway, which reaches the amygdala directly from the sensory nuclei of the thalamus, without prior cortical processing, and a slower pathway that activates the amygdala through the thalamus and cerebral cortex (Simic, 2016). The amygdala contributes to the fear circuits in two ways, directly by detecting the threat on an unconscious level and regulating the behavioural and physiological responses, and indirectly, through cognitive systems in the emergence of a conscious feeling of fear (Simic et al., 2021). In the face of fear, stress hormones like cortisol and adrenaline are released, and other physiological reactions occur (e.g., the heart beats faster, blood flows away from the heart, into the limbs, the mouth becomes dry). Whilst some parts of the brain and body become more active, other parts might go into "shut down mode" (e.g., the cerebral cortex that is responsible for rational thinking). Responses to fear show both within and between individual differences; therefore, responses to fear-invoking stimuli may be different for the same person, but in dissimilar situations.

Responses to fear

Fear can manifest in various ways, including *physiological* responses (such as increased heart rate, sweating, and trembling), *cognitive* responses (such as heightened alertness and anticipation of danger), and *behavioural* responses (such as avoidance or defensive actions). However, reactions may not be the same within the same individual. For instance, fear may be associated with a racing heart, feelings of uneasiness, attempts to escape, or numbness and not being able to move (Amstadter, 2008). Reactions to fear have been classified according to fighting (i.e., to regain control by displaying anger and aggression), fleeing (e.g., running away to avoid the situation or conflict avoidance), or freezing (e.g., feeling isolated or experiencing numbness) (Blanchard & Blanchard, 1989). Later, these aforementioned categories on how people might respond to fear (or trauma) have been expanded to also include (e.g., Donahue, 2020): *fawning*, which refers to abandoning one's own needs to please others; *flagging*, where one dissociates from a specific situation, and *fainting*, where one can be mentally and physically unresponsive.

The effect of prolonged fear

Fear is generally considered an adaptive emotion and crucial for survival (Hartley & Phelps, 2010; Sangha et al., 2020). However, prolonged fear response may become maladaptive and give rise to the development of psychological disorders (Hartley & Phelps, 2010; Beckers et al., 2023). For instance, persistent fear in the absence of danger has been found to lead to different anxiety disorders (e.g., panic, social, anxiety), phobias, and post-traumatic stress disorder (PTSD), where fear is experienced even in a safe context (Panzer et al., 2007; Tinoco-Gonzalez et al., 2015).

Researchers report that as many as one in three people in the world might be suffering from some anxiety disorder at some point in their lifetime (Rubin et al., 2016). Although anxiety disorders may include a diverse set of phenotypes, they all involve excessive negative affect, such as a feeling of fear and anxiety. The most significant difference between fear and anxiety disorders is that fear, is a real, external, known, and objective threat to survival, whereas the origins of anxiety are unclear, uncertain, and play a subjective role (Strongman, 2003).

Fear stimuli may result in a stress response. A stress response is a complex interplay of the nervous, endocrine, and immune systems, which prepare the body to handle the challenges presented by the stressor. If the exposure to a stressor (fear) is repetitive or prolonged, the stress response becomes maladaptive and detrimental to physiology and a heightened autonomic response may cause an increase in heart rate and blood pressure (Chu et al., 2022). Researchers have found that prolonged fear is associated with adverse mental health. Demirbas and Kutlu (2021) found that as people's fears increase, their psychological and somatic complaints increase, and their quality of life decreases. Furthermore, prolonged fear has also been associated with depression. Recent studies on fear, focused on the topical subject of COVID-19, found a significant relation between fear, COVID-19, and depression respectively (e.g., Gundogan & Arpaci, 2022; Li et al., 2022). Furthermore, perseverative thinking about the fear stimuli or ruminating, has been found to be a predisposing factor to the development of depression (Alderman et al., 2015; Sun et al., 2014). Rumination (i.e., an emotion regulation strategy that involves repetitive thoughts causing emotional distress) may maintain and exacerbate the emotion of fear by enhancing negative thinking, impairing problem solving and interfering with instrumental behaviour (Michl et al., 2013; Nolen-Hoeksema et al., 2008).

Military cohort studies also show that people who have been exposed to dangerous situations and traumatic events may suffer from an impaired immune function, contributing to the development of autoimmune diseases (Bookwalter et al., 2020). Additionally, numerous studies (e.g., see Hamai & Feletti, 2022) found a significantly strong relationship between childhood adversity, like being abused or being exposed to a dysfunctional household, and medical conditions that lead to early death.

Conquering fear

The ability to modify or control the nature of negative emotions is com--monly referred to as emotion regulation (see Chapter 1). Emotion regulation is described as actions that aim to alter either the form, frequency, duration, or situational occurrence of an event that may precede an emotional response, as well as the events that may follow an emotional response (Olatunji et al., 2017). Effective regulation of emotion is essential for both mental and physical wellbeing (Hartley & Phelps, 2010). Hartley and Phelps (2010) suggest four different types of regulatory processes:

First, *extinction* is the process of diminishing fear through learning that a previously threatening stimuli no longer signals danger. Extinction of fear occurs where, for example, a person who has a fear of heights gradually learns to climb higher on a ladder, without experiencing the emotion of fear. Second, *cognitive emotion regulation* involves using various mental strategies to modify a fear response. Positive refocusing is one example of cognitive emotion regulation, and entails directing one's thoughts to pleasant matters, whilst experiencing the emotion of fear. Third, *active coping* is used when fear is regulated through performance of behaviours that reduce exposure to a fear evoking stimulus. For example, physically changing one's fear-inducing environment for an environment where one feels safe. Fourth, *reconsolidation* is used to disrupt a fear memory through pharmacological or behavioural manipulations that block its reconsolidation. The process of reconsolidation involves recalling a fear memory and introducing behavioural manipulations or pharmacological interventions. The interventions promote the incorporation of new information, which leads to the extinction of the previous fear memory.

Additionally, *cognitive behavioural therapy* aims to alleviate distress through the development of adaptive cognitions and behaviours (Fenn & Byrne, 2013) and has been successful in helping people overcome their fears (Kaplan & Tolin, 2011).

Exposure therapy is also a form of treatment that encourages the systematic confrontation of the feared stimuli (Guo, 2021). The aim is to reduce a person's reaction to fear inducing stimuli through repetitive exposure. Systematic desensitisation is a form of exposure therapy where a person is simultaneously exposed to the fear inducing stimuli while also engaging in behaviour, such as relaxation, which generates a response that is the opposite of anxiety (Thomas et al., 2017).

Emotional Freedom Techniques (EFT), commonly referred to as *tapping therapy*, which emanates from ancient Chinese acupressure, involves the tapping of meridian points on the body while focusing on the feared object to alleviate the experience of fear (Patterson, 2016, p. 105). EFT combines the tapping of meridian points with a focus on the feared object or negative emotion to provide desensitisation to the fear. During EFT, a participant is directed to identify a concern they wish to address with the technique. While maintaining exposure to the memory, EFT clients tap with their fingertips on a series of 12 acupressure points associated with stress reduction. The tapping process is repeated until the emotional intensity is reduced to a comfortable level (Bach et al., 2019; Church et al., 2012).

Finally, *mindfulness*, according to Kabat-Zinn (2005), is defined as the awareness that arises from purposefully paying attention to the present moment in a non-judgemental way (Kabat-Zinn, 2005). As a therapeutic intervention, mindfulness therapy works by disrupting an individual's unconscious reactions associated with fear (Greeson & Brantley, 2009). During mindful meditation, the direct exposure to feared thoughts, memories or emotional states, while simultaneously and nonjudgmentally observing these thoughts, memories and emotions, and preventing a reactive emotional response, could result in the desensitisation of fear (Kummar, 2018). The benefits of the role of mindful therapy in managing fear are increasingly being investigated (Belen, 2022; Hölzel et al., 2016), and according to Analayo (2019), when combined with professional assistance, mindful meditation practices have the potential to support and facilitate the facing of difficult emotions.

Despite these recommended interventions to overcome fear, one could also decide to act courageously by facing one's fears. In fact, some people might enjoy experiencing fearful moments (like watching horror movies) or embarking on a *bucket list* journey, because they get to face their fears head-on, but in a more controlled way. Through the excitation transfer process (Zillmann as cited in Meston & Frohlich, 2003) one's body and brain become (and remain) aroused. The brain produces hormones such as dopamine, which elicits pleasure, even after the frightening experience is over (Abraham et al., 2014).

The relation between fear, courage, and the bucket list

Whereas fear is often perceived as a negative basic emotion, courage is seen as a positive virtue or character strength (Peterson & Seligman, 2004). However, courage is not synonymous with being fearless, or showing fearlessness (which might even be considered as foolish or ignorant). In fact, both courage and being fearless appear to function in opposition to fear (Rubin et al., 2016). However, studies have found that fear and courage are, in fact, not significantly related (e.g., Muris, 2009) and are therefore not, proverbially speaking, two sides of the same coin.

Adding to this, the tripartite model of fear explains the relational action of courage, according to the emotion-based changes focusing on physiological, cognitive, and behavioural changes (Rachman, 1984). For courage to be displayed, Rachman (1984) argues that, just before an action is taken, fear is at its highest and subsides immediately after the action is taken, despite the fear. Thus, in the last few minutes, just before you jump off a cliff, fall out of an aircraft, or plunge into shark-infested waters, the level of fear will be at its highest. However, as soon as a behavioural response has been committed, there is a significant reduction in the perception of fear. This school of thought emphasises the interconnectedness and independence of fear and courage. In other words, the road to courage begins with the feeling of fear, and the will to act outweighs the feeling of uncertainty (Navarini & De Monte, 2019). However, whether courage is only possible through fear, is still theoretically ambiguous and is yet to be scientifically established (Mocanu, 2019). In fact, from the ancient Greeks to present-day behavioural scientists, there is still a limited empirical understanding of courage (Pury, 2013; Rate, 2007). Research is limited as to why individuals would rise to the occasion, "defend what they believe in, or fight for the rights of others" (Pury et al., 2010, p. 232).

Adding to the notion of courage, Putman (2001) argues that both fear and confidence are two intertwined emotions that form the foundation of courage. Fear is a natural emotional response to perceived danger or uncertainty, signalling the presence of risk or threat. Thus, courage does not emerge in the absence of fear, but rather in the conscious decision to act despite it. Confidence, on the other hand, acts as the counterbalancing force that enables individuals to confront fear. Therefore, confidence stems from self-belief, prior experiences, and the perception of one's abilities to manage difficult situations. While fear highlights vulnerability, confidence reinforces the possibility of overcoming challenges. Together, these emotions create a dynamic tension, where fear acknowledges the risks involved, and confidence fuels the determination to persevere. This delicate balance between fear and confidence ultimately empowers individuals to take courageous actions in the face of adversity.

There is a clear link between fear, courage and having a bucket list. In the vignette, Ophelia decides to take up the challenge of hiking Mount Veil. She has many fears (rational or irrational beliefs about something), like being afraid of heights and hanging onto the cliffside of the mountain, fear of the unknown, and she is scared of getting lost in the mist and fog. However, her bucket list activity of hiking (i.e., presenting one's deepest desires and things that one wishes to experience before death), causes her to delve deep to expand her comfort zone and look to herself for courage. When Ophelia makes it to the top of Mount Veil, she will feel a sense of accomplishment and realise that is she is not only *alive* but living a full life, filled with a sense of personal growth and accomplishment.

Defining courage

Courage is an elusive, mysterious phenomenon (Olsthoorn, 2007), lauded as one of the cardinal virtues of positive psychology, and has recently been rediscovered as a vital characteristic, which is becoming increasingly important, even in the workplace (Koerner, 2013). Already in 350 BCE, Aristotle stated that "courage is the first of human qualities because it is the quality which guarantees the others" (Lachman, 2007, p. 131). 'Courage' comes from the Old French word *corage* (from the Latin word *cor*, meaning 'heart'), and is defined as "the ability to do something that frightens one; strength in the face of pain or grief" (SA COD, 2002, p. 265). The term 'heart' is a widespread metaphor for inner strength. However, courage without the necessary intellectual responsibility and common sense, could lead to temerity, which refers to excessive confidence and may lead to being recklessness and foolhardy (SA COD, 2002, p. 1 206). To the other extreme, a person that contemptibly lacks courage is said to be a coward. Coward originates from the old French *couard* (from the Latin *cauda*), meaning 'tail' and perhaps with reference to an animal with its tail between its legs (SA COD, 2002, p. 267).

According to Rate et al. (2007), courage is divided into explicit and implicit theoretical categories. The explicit approach measures courage based on the physiological responses to stress and fear. Research on bomb operators and bomb disposal operators established that physiological responses to fear and stress in one instance significantly reduced physiological responses to fear in similar circumstances. According to this finding, the response to fear regulates behaviour in similar situations in that the level of fear and uncertainty is reduced so that one becomes fearless for other similar situations (Cox et al., 1983). This perspective supports the idea that decreasing fear will increase courage (Barney, 2024). Farrell (2024) argues that courage is not the lack of fear, but the realisation that something greater holds more significance than the fear. Evidently, this realisation and assessment can be observed in firefighters, soldiers during war, sky divers jumping from an aircraft, and an organ donor volunteering to make personal sacrifices (to name a few).

Implicit theories, on the other hand, analyse the cognitive construction of courage. The notion proposed by Sternberg (1985) is that courage is subjective, based on how we understand it individually. Fear is equally subjective, and our responses will always differ based on the meaning we attach to situations. Woodard and Pury (2007) assert that what is courageous for one person may not be as courageous to someone else. Implicit theories are important in psychology and in the world because most judgements people make of each other are based on their implicit understanding (Sternberg, 1985). Interesting to note, there is no formal test of courage, because people evaluate each other's courage based on their own implicit theory of what courage (and perhaps fear) means to them.

The application of courage has been widely researched, resulting in the development of various definitions and theories. Shelp's work in 1984 led to the development of a conceptual foundation for the definition of courage. Shelp defined courage as the disposition to voluntarily act, perhaps fearfully, in dangerous circumstances, where relevant risks are reasonably appraised, to preserve some perceived good for oneself or others, but also recognising that the desired perceived good may not be accomplished (Shelp, 1984). Woodard (2004, p. 174) then adds to the definition, stating that it is the "ability to act for a meaningful (noble, good or practical) cause, despite experiencing the fear associated with the perceived threat exceeding the available resources." Additionally, Pury and Kowalski (2007, p. 121) includes that it is "responding to extraordinary times with behaviours that seem natural and called for in those circumstances." This view suggests that fear may not always be part of the process of a courageous reaction or behaviour. However, courage has also been defined as "the voluntary willingness to act with or without varying levels of fear, in response to a threat to achieve an important outcome or goal" (Woodard & Pury, 2007, p. 174). And finally, according to Gruber (2011, p. 274), courage is a "cognitive mental process used to enact change on a stable system for the intention of a positive outcome."

Taken together, these definitions point us to the dispositional nature of courage in regulating thinking processes, feelings and ultimately the actions we take in the face of fear. Courage is thus a systematic process that involves not only physical strength and endurance but also mental stamina that leads to behavioural changes; it has both attitudinal and behavioural components. Courage enables us to navigate through life's turbulence and reach the desired outcome and goal safely and positively. Based on the given definitions, there seems to be a golden thread: we label people's behaviour as courageous based on their exceptional response to extreme situations, acting, irrespective of experiencing fear, for the betterment of others, and acts of courage seem to involve "a desirable, important, and morally relevant goal that is intentionally pursued by the actor despite risk, threat, or other unpleasant facts" (Pury et al., 2007, p. 233).

Given the various types of courageous acts that can be observed, Navarini and De Monte (2019) note that a universal definition of courage is too complex. This complexity is further complicated by the strong argument that courage is rooted in the character strengths of bravery and persistence, and consequently some researchers use bravery and courage synonymously. There have been many controversies around the conceptualisation and application of courage, which has led to a lack of consensus over its definition (Mocanu, 2019).

Components of courage

The concept of courage is commonly accepted as a character strength in the broader field of positive psychology (Peterson & Seligman, 2004) and is considered to encompass four strengths, under the rubric of courage, which are:

Bravery. This refers to valour, or not shrinking from threat, challenge, difficulty, or pain, and acting on one's convictions, even if it would mean being unpopular; doing what needs to be done despite experiencing fear. This includes physical bravery but is not limited to it.

Perseverance. This refers to persistence or being industrious; taking pleasure in finishing what one starts, and persevering in a course of action, despite obstacles.

Honesty. Showing integrity and being authentic; speaking the truth; presenting oneself in a genuine way and acting sincerely, being without pretence, and taking responsibility for one's own feelings and actions.

Zest. Approaching life enthusiasm and energy; not doing things halfway of half-heartedly; living life as an adventure, feeling alive and activated.

Adding to this broad notion of courage as a character strength, Shelp (1984) identified four steps in understanding the components of courage and how it comes about. First, there must be a *free choice to accept* or *not to accept* the consequences of acting. The acceptance of consequences is rooted in the screening of one's available resources versus the environmental demands. In most instances, one might feel that you do not have what it takes to overcome a difficulty. However, it is the willingness to commit to the achievement of a desired goal, no matter the consequences, which fulfils this first step. Second, there must be a reasonable level of *personal threat, risk, or danger*, should an action be taken or not taken. Thus, courage involves the willingness to face danger, loss, or uncertainty. The risk could be based on threats that can be either physical (e.g., possible death), social (facing judgement from others), moral (making an ethical decision and facing the consequences alone), or emotional (becoming vulnerable and enduring possible shame). Third, risk or *uncertainty of the outcome* – there should be a level of uncertainty about the outcome, given the level of risk and potential consequences. Therefore, courage does not exist where a specific outcome is certain and secure. Fourth, acts of courage are aimed towards a *noble cause towards a worthy end* – thus doing something more than for the simple thrill of it (e.g., for justice, protection, truth). The outcome of one's courageous actions is regarded as valuable and worthwhile from the perspective of the actor and the action is done for the greater good.

Summarising these components of courage, Rate et al. (2007) proposed the components of courage to include: intentionality (the actor shows a voluntary willingness to act despite the full awareness of what is at stake), risk, a noble act, and fear. However, it appears that there is no clear synergistic link between personal risk, uncertainty, and the emotional response of fear. Simply put, uncertainty and personal risk may or may not induce the feeling of fear, depending on several factors, such as experience and confidence. Therefore, some researchers have established that though it may be expected for the emotion of fear to emerge from situations that pose personal threats and uncertainty of outcomes, acting under such conditions can constitute courage even without the element of fear (Woodard & Pury, 2007).

Finally, to illustrate these components of courage in action, let us look at courage in the example of Ophelia, planning her hike on Mount Veil. It is not obvious or guaranteed that if she decides to go on the hike, that nothing can go wrong. There are elements of *fear of the unknown* (e.g., what if the weather changes and there is mist or fog and they get lost?), the physical *threat* (e.g., what if she twists her ankle or breaks her leg when scrambling over the cliffs of the mountain?), and knowing that other hikers have gone missing while doing the hike; therefore, it is dangerous and *anything could happen*, even with all the necessary skills she has as a hiker and having the necessary safety equipment. Courage surfaces when one has thought of all the possibilities that could go wrong, but still *deliberately commits* to taking the action (e.g., Ophelia plans to face her fear of heights and go hiking, because she thinks Mel needs a good breakaway in nature).

Types of courage

According to studies (e.g., O'Byrne et al., 2000; Pury & Hensel, 2010; Pury & Kowalksi, 2007), courage can be categorised into general types: (1) *Physical (valour) courage* entails the risk of taking physical discomfort and harm that may cause bodily harm. We see this kind of courage from firefighters, rescue operators, and police officers. People in these kinds of occupations exhibit physical courage in the execution of their jobs. (2) *Moral (social) courage*, also referred to as social courage, is described as standing up for what is perceived to be morally justified. This entails actions towards the preservation of ethics, justice and serving the greater good of humanity, and standing up for what is right in the face of social disproval. There are many examples in the political and humanitarian spheres of those who have been titled as inspirational because of the courage they have exhibited in the face of adversity for the common good and benefit. (3) *Vital courage* refers to thriving in the face of a serious illness. (4) *Belief-based courage* is to stand up for one's beliefs related to religious, spiritual and political ideology. (5) *Personal or psychological courage* refers to a self-referenced measure in the context of an individual's life experience of having to face one's own destructive thoughts and habits, which can lead to risking one's psychological stability in the pursuit of the desired goal. Finally, (6) *general courage* refers to actions that would be courageous for anyone to take, being fearless and confident, implicating lowered physiological and subjective measures of fear. There may also be many other types of courage, but research supporting additional categorisation is limited.

Conclusion

What we can take from this chapter is that ruminating on thoughts that evoke (real or imagined) fear, might spiral into anxiety. One should cultivate the self-discipline to keep the mind clear of dark thoughts, because neuroscientists have shown that, once established, breaking negative thought patterns may be very difficult (see Pittman & Young, 2021). During his inauguration speech in 1933, President FD Roosevelt stated (Rosenman, 1938, p. 11): "the only thing we have to fear is fear itself—nameless, unreasoning, unjustified terror which paralyzes…". Therefore, one should have the courage to face your fears head-on.

CHAPTER 7

Tainted Roots: Trauma and its
Impact on Emotions

Tyler I. Counsil

McLean's traumatic transition

Isabelle, or as her fourth-grade class calls her, Ms Isabelle, has become concerned about McLean. Normally a happy and talkative student, Isabelle noticed that McLean has recently become quiet and withdrawn. Instead of responding with enthusiasm and delight when being called upon in class, the child now demonstrates non-verbal refusal to engage with his teacher, instead opting to shake his head 'no' with immense energy and often putting his hands up as if physically pushing back on the request. His usual cheerful demeanour has also been replaced in recent weeks with more alarming and seemingly unprompted emotions of an extreme and sometimes combative nature.

Historically, McLean was usually a student whose smile was contagious, with laughter of an infectious sort, where he would produce a deep belly giggle at the slightest sign of something humorous manifesting in the classroom environment, which frequently made Isabelle smile herself. This once-curious, everlasting happiness has instead been replaced with a furrowed brow and the occasional tear streaming down his face without explanation or causation from a classroom event of inter-student strife. When students try to engage with McLean, the typical response of robust glee has now been supplanted by a verbal, disproportionate roar, demanding that other students leave him alone. Sometimes McLean is also found missing from his seat, only to be found at the back of the class, out of sight in the coat closet, crying and tightly gripping his legs in the foetal position during normal lesson time.

Concerned about the youth and this recent change of emotions, attitude, and engagement, Isabelle seeks to learn more and discusses the recent change of emotions with the youth social worker at the school. Through that conversation, it is discovered that McLean's mother has been hospitalised over the past few weeks in relation to an event where her significant other physically harmed her to the point of serious injury. His grandmother has been taking care of him during this period. Isabelle also learns an approximate timeline of when this new adult entered the child's life, and it aligns closely with the transitional period in which the child's demeanour has shifted. She also learns that the child and his mother recently moved to Riverside specifically to be closer to the significant other. As such, both the social worker and Isabelle agree to work towards a minimal facts-finding interview with McLean to talk about his recent change in demeanour, while also notifying local authorities of this recent dynamic to assess the need for a forensic interview at a local child advocacy centre to better understand if McLean was witness to any violent events in which his mother was abused, as well as to better determine if the boy himself is also a survivor of any mental, emotional, or physical harm or neglect while trapped in this new home environment.

Introduction

The focal point of this chapter is exclusively dedicated to the phenomenon known as trauma and its impact on the emotions and wellbeing of an individual. In simple terms, trauma is a reaction to an event. That reaction – based on one's perception of the event to which they are subjected directly, witnessed in some capacity, or experienced vicariously through second-hand narratives, social media, or the news – can have disruptive, if not potentially devastating, short- and long-term effects to one's emotional repertoire, regulation, and output thereof. Furthermore, trauma can corrode critical cognitive faculties and even one's own physical health if not properly processed or mitigated from the onset of first-hand or secondary traumatic event exposure.

According to the National Council for Behavioral Health (2022, p. 1), approximately 70% of US adults having experienced one or more distressing event in their lives; trauma is an ever-present phenomenon in human life irrespective of one's position within the lifespan. The phenomenon is not exclusive to North America; a survey of the general population in 24 countries, such as Australia, Columbia, Japan, and South Africa, found similar results, with over 70% of respondents experiencing one traumatic event and 30.5% of respondents having experienced four or more traumatic events (Benjet et al., 2015, p. 2). Children, adults, and the elderly are equally susceptible to trauma, with over 1/3 of youth exposed to violence in their community, experiencing post-traumatic stress disorder (PTSD) at some point and over 8% of adults experiencing this clinical disorder at some time in their life (American Psychiatric Association, n.d.). Given the prevalence of trauma in society today, this chapter will focus on the history of the concept, including why trauma exists. It will also explore an understanding of key typologies of trauma that occur within the human population, cultural considerations to trauma, lifespan, and health impacts of the phenomenon, and how we can combat trauma's caustic effects through resiliency.

The definition of trauma

According to the American Psychological Association (n.d.), trauma is a whole-body (e.g., physical, emotional, mental) response to a shocking or devastating event, where the event may be something the individual has endured, witnessed, or learnt about through second-hand mechanisms (e.g., disclosure, investigation, news or social media). The effects of trauma may be acute (short-term) or chronic (long-term) and may vary in manifestation depending on the individual and their perspective of the situation as determined by their whole-body wellbeing, social: cultural values, resiliency or protective factors available to the individual, and the scale and severity of the event.

Seeds of woe: The history of trauma

The varied and complex phenomenon known as trauma has existed since the dawn of humankind's existence. The landscape of ancestral paintings, cave drawings, anthropological discoveries of skeletal remains demonstrating catastrophic damage from wars, sacrifices and large-scale cataclysmic natural events and historic tomes chronicling dreadful events of varying types demonstrates sufficient evidence that humanity's exposure to violent and shocking events and the impact on those survivors of such travesties is not a new phenomenon. As with most concepts, however, the ability to put a name to these events and the consequences of said moments in time has been a more recent triumph.

The first use of the word 'trauma' originates from Greece. The term was first applied around the 1690s by Greeks seeking to explain a physical wound of medical origins more concisely (*Online Etymology Dictionary*, n.d.). The notion of trauma as being correlated to more than bodily harm and being tethered to some form of psychological stress resultant from primary or secondary exposure to a challenging event did not arise until the 19th century, in fact, although there were some general allusions to the phenomenon in French philosopher René Descartes's *The Passion of the Soul*, penned in 1649. Specifically, the author outlined the complex relationship between fear, human emotional response to shocking events and impact thereof on human behaviour, indicating that he felt emotions arose in human beings because of an external force or stimulus being applied to the individual (Black & Flynn, 2020).

Some of the most historic, detailed depictions of trauma as being correlated to physical and cognitive faculties and both body and emotional dysregulation and dysfunction originate from global conflicts, most notably starting with accounts from soldiers engaged in combat during the American Civil War, World War I and World War II (Van Der Kolk, 2000, p. 7). Lasiuk and Hegadoren (2006) note that soldiers embroiled in the Civil War, for instance, suffered from 'soldier's heart' upon returning home from combat. During World War I, 'shell shock' affected many survivors of the global conflict, as well (Benedek & Ursano, 2009, Phenomenology section). As noted by *Frontline* (2015), these terms were used to help family members and caregivers of those returning from the war to better understand or come to terms with the fact that their loved ones had changed both in body and mind.

'Soldier's heart' was specifically correlated to physiological impacts on the returning soldier's body, whereby their pulse and blood pressure were notably affected after exposure to traumatic events on the battlefield. Conversely, 'shell shock' was more specifically attributed to psychological outcomes, whereby a soldier exposed to heavy ordinance explosions may have demonstrated feelings of anxiety, nervousness, fear alongside suffering from nightmares or other feelings related to these events, with these complex emotions or mentally dysregulated states being observed both during combat and outside the conflict as loud sounds or events paralleling a wartime shelling triggered the survivor's cognitive faculties and memory, bringing them back to that terrible event (History, 2017). 'Combat fatigue', now more commonly known as combat stress reaction, was a phenomenon observed in World War II, where combatants showed a decline in cognitive faculties (e.g., slowed response time, delays in critical thinking) and a depressive-like state where fatigue diminished one's ability to perform even the most basic tasks (DeLucia-Waack, Kalodner, & Riva, 2014). While these manifestations of the body's physiological and psychological responses to traumatic events were predominantly observed in the wartime populations, trauma responses were likewise being recognised in civilian populations around the same time.

In the 18th and 19th centuries, civilian life was under a period of significant advancement by way of the Industrial Revolution, but such technological and societal advances did not come without their share of strife. As reported by Obschonka (2018), shocking deaths observed on the job, health impacts of working in unsafe conditions and the stressors of employment, family caregiving focused on (in a word) economic prosperity, and environmental hazards as a result of technological advances and pollution thereof, have been shown to contribute to diminished or dysregulated cognitive faculties (e.g., reduced self-control, negative thoughts/feelings) and physical maladies (e.g., cancer, heart attack). One study examining the traumatic impacts of coal mining on US and UK populations found that there were higher manifestations of anxiety and depression, diminished conscientiousness, and significant reductions in life expectancy (Obschonka et al., 2018). Eventually, in the 1980s, researchers and scholars recognised the overall general impact of trauma on humanity irrespective of combat and social advance.

The introduction of PTSD, as noted in the 1980 American Psychiatric Association's (APA's) *Diagnostic and Statistical Manual of Mental Disorders*, Third Edition (DSM-III) was perhaps the greatest watershed moment in scientific history with respect to realising that trauma is a universal outcome for humanity (Center for Substance Abuse Treatment, 2014, Chapter 3). It is with this distinction that the world began to realise that – be it a singular, severe event, or a series of disturbing encounters – there are often consequences to one's overall health. Since that time, numerous studies have better postulated and understood trauma across generations, throughout the lifespan and expanded to explore other populations of impacted individuals – ranging from children exposed to abuse and neglect, persons reeling from the loss of a loved one, or more. Recent research previously cited (Benjet et al., 2015) and data from the World Health Organization (Kessler et al., 2017) paints a stark picture of how interwoven trauma is in the fabric of humanity.

The authors of the 2017 study (Kessler et al.) found that an overwhelming majority of the 68 894 survey participants from 24 countries examined had experienced trauma; specifically, 70.4% of the persons surveyed had experienced trauma across the lifespan and each person surveyed experienced an average of 3.2 traumas over the course of their lives. Trauma associated with interpersonal violence had the strongest correlation to PTSD onset across the survey participants. As such, trauma is ever-present in our society and can accumulate into a heavy psychological and physiological burden on humanity based on the scope, severity, number of events and personal perspectives of the trauma-laden event. To better understand trauma, and mitigate it or prevent it outright, one must examine why such an experience exists.

The roots of suffering: Exploring the existence of trauma

At the fundamental biological level, trauma is a response directly based on how human brains are wired, or more scientifically speaking, how the brain makes use of the amygdala. The amygdala is a portion of the brain designed to regulate – or control – our involuntary (autonomic) and hormone-based (endocrine) functions (Šimić et al., 2021, p. 1). As best stated by Fox et al. (2015, p. 1), "survival depends on the central extended amygdala's ability to rapidly integrate and respond to threats that vary in their immediacy, proximity, and characteristics." More specifically, the amygdala can be thought of as a 'threat detector' imbedded in the human brain, allowing it to access hormones, upregulate energy consumption, and engage in crucial functions to help an individual attempt to survive what is perceived as a potential life-threatening event (Öhman, 2005).

In plain terms, trauma is partially biological. The amygdala has developed to help humans with emotional regulation and fostering the activation of systems in our body and brain tied to decision-making and instinctual or situational awareness of environmental changes and activation of one's fight-or-freeze response. Simplifying the concept of trauma further – this phenomenon exists because our brain is hard-wired to recognise situations that can harm an individual and to elicit thoughts, feelings, and actions tied to current or even previous events, where a person may be or was historically in harm's way, as a means of protecting oneself. Since the brain stores critical incident information in this capacity, it becomes readily apparent as to how some individuals may have 'flashback' or 'triggering' events based on responses to external stimuli (National Sexual Violence Resource Center, n.d., paragraph 5). For example, McLean's recent withdrawal, heightened emotional responses, and avoidance behaviours may be indicative of his brain responding to past traumatic experiences, potentially linked to witnessing domestic violence involving his mother. His instinctual reactions – hiding, crying, and aggressively rejecting peer interaction – align with the brain's protective mechanisms when confronted with reminders of distressing events.

Those stimuli harkening back to a serious event may invoke this part of our brain to compel us to act, even when immediate danger is not present simply due to how it is designed (Frederick, 2020, paragraph 5). The greater buildup of consecutive traumatic events or the severity of even a singular traumatic event can thus trigger this portion of the brain to trigger more readily or perhaps be in a near 'always-on' scenario, which can cause the individual to enter a state of emotional dysregulation or enter a state where the constant perception of threat can permanently alter bodily functions leading to overproduction of chemicals that can lead to terminal health consequences if the stress is not mitigated in some manner (Dai et al., 2020).

Scholars have also discovered that trauma may be an inherited artefact at both the societal and social level, as well as being hereditary (Bale, 2014; Youssef, 2022). A family's history of trauma may be shared through stories and memories, creating a collective memory of trauma that is etched on the brains of the next generation. For instance, catastrophic events that impacted a family (e.g., the Holocaust) or large-scale subsets of the population (e.g., the 9/11 terrorist attacks) can create a collective memory that is shared amongst individuals across the lifespan and between generations (Hirschberger, 2018, p. 2). The collective memory is then translated into a means system, where the individual's brain imprints the collective memory or shared experience into a range of emotions experienced in a vicarious manner that can also induce trauma, which may trigger a host of protective responses at the physiological and psychological level, akin to how youth may respond with fear-laden responses when told a particularly scary story. Intergenerational trauma also appears to exist at the biological level.

In addition to family and societal events, one's own culture, too, can be a major driving factor in trauma development and response. Ford et al. (2015) found that one's sexual identity, physical make-up, immigration status, religious or spiritual beliefs, socio-economic status and more can predispose them for greater trauma exposure. Several studies support this notion that trauma can exist due to unique cultural experiences or constraints.

For example, many cultures see a disproportionate amount of abuse in child and adolescent populations, and one study of over 4 000 youth, conducted by Croft et al. (2019, p. 79), discovered that 45% of those studied had suffered from psychotic episodes where trauma negatively impacted juvenile mental health. Polanco-Roman, Danies, and Anglin (2016) studied over 700 early adults and found that racial discrimination is correlated to cognitive dissociation from this form of trauma, where the individual feels withdrawn or disconnected from themselves and the world around them. Poverty and unique community experiences, too, have an impact on trauma's existence in the living. For instance, raising children in a neighbourhood where safety concerns are present has been linked to maternal depression (Corman et al., 2016). In Haiti, a population of over 600 residents was studied and it was discovered that over 65% of those surveyed had demonstrated suicidal ideation, with a stronger correlation to ideation being tied to an increase in adverse childhood experiences (ACEs), or those experiences in one's youth that place a child at an increased risk for trauma or misfortune (Joshi et al., 2023). Thus, trauma appears to also exist as a construct of potentially one's culture: who one chooses to be, their lived experience and perceptions surrounding those events, can cause trauma to manifest.

Given that culture – how and where one is raised and the values and systems stemming from that lived experience – can cause unique trauma to exist, recent studies have also begun to examine the notion that trauma (and trauma response) is an inherited artefact in one's genetic material. In particular, the field of epigenetics explores how behaviour and environmental circumstances, such as extreme events, can change one's DNA and how that passage of heritable material can impact future offspring and their trauma reactions (Yehuda & Lehrner, 2018, p. 244). More recently, much work has been done exploring social epigenetics in particular, which examines environmental influences on genetic changes and the passage of such alterations to one's biological next of kin (Mancilla et al., 2020, p. 2). Having explored why trauma exists – as both a construct of human biology and sociocultural collective memories/information sharing – it is important to also identify the types of traumas that exist within the fabric of society.

Scars in the bark: Examining trauma typologies

Research in the field of trauma recognition has evolved extensively since the early work endeavoured to explore trauma central to industrial and combat-based experiences, and there are now numerous ways of categorising the various types of traumas that exist in society. Note that many of these typologies may and often have overlapped. For instance, a community-level trauma type, such as a civil war or social uprising, may be tied to an early childhood trauma, such as sexual assault perpetrated on a youth because of social disruption and the dissolving of protective social constructs that would normally prevent such traumatic events from befalling a child.

Bullying is a more common type of trauma that exists across the lifespan of an individual and can be both in-person or present in their online life. An estimated 35% of individuals studied in a 2014 study by Modecki et al. (p. 607) have experienced bullying, which entails deliberate actions perpetrated against somebody as being perceived as having less power than the bully, with the specific intent of inflicting some form of physical, social, psychological or emotional harm on the victim. Community violence can also be a form of traumatic experience one can endure. This form of trauma entails being subject to or witnessing some type of negative circumstance in a public area, such as being exposed to drug trade and solicitation, active shooting situations or gun violence events, or experiencing war or terrorist events (Violence Policy Center, 2017, p. 1). The most recent data from the Centers for Disease Control and Prevention (n.d.-a) indicate that injuries and violence in one's communities are the most prevalent contributors to mortality in the US for those individuals aged 1–44. Intimate partner violence (IPV) has generated a great deal of generational trauma irrespective of global location. In South Africa, for instance, 50% of women reported being a survivor of IPV, while 40% of men were reported to have perpetrated violence against a partner (George, 2023, paragraph 4). A study by Valabdass et al. (2021) found that – across 66 countries studied – nearly 14% of all homicides and almost half of all female murders were perpetrated by an intimate partner. Natural disasters – hurricanes, flash floods, tornadoes, pandemic and endemic illness, wildfires and more – may also be correlated as traumatic events that have severe health consequences to the living (Lee & Kim, 2020, p. 100).

Other types of trauma include early childhood abuse or events of neglect or situations that could be categorised as an aforementioned ACE, such as sexual or physical violence perpetrated on young children or even more nuanced events, such as a troubling experience at a healthcare provider, making a cross-country move with family, having a family member addicted to illicit or licit substances or engaging in traumatic experience with an adult at a childcare centre (Peterson, 2018). IPV has likewise been demonstrated to be a highly devastating traumatic event typology, with depression, anxiety and PTSD significantly correlated with IPV exposure (Chu et al., 2023). Medical trauma is experienced when an individual is dealing with the physical, mental, emotional and possible social consequences of being diagnosed with a chronic illness, dealing with health complications or near-death experiences, or enduring potentially painful or dramatic medical procedures (Peterson, 2018b). Finally, immigration or refugee relocation events have been studied and found to potentially induce high levels of trauma both before, during and after relocation because of the actual rearrangement event itself, due to the circumstances surrounding the transfer, or a combination thereof (Shi, Stey & Tatebe, 2021, p. 85).

Traumatic events can also be categorised based on their persistence. Acute trauma involves a severe, albeit short bout with an incident where one's fight-or-freeze response is activated, and the event is traditionally one of an extreme but often short-lived experience (Feriante, 2023). An acute trauma incident then may include a fist fight or verbal shouting match between individuals, sheltering during an intense weather event, or experiencing the death of a beloved animal, family member, or friend. By contrast, chronic trauma entails the exposure to one or multiple cumulative events over an extended period (Allarakha, 2021). Unmitigated acute traumatic events may overwhelm the individual and eventually progress into a chronic event. Examples of chronic trauma events may include enduring challenges with cancer diagnosis and treatment, dealing with a divorce, or facing extensive challenges with relocation following an armed conflict in one's country. Complex trauma occurs when a disruptive, interpersonal series of events (e.g., child abuse) are encountered, usually in youth, and may have significant and long-lasting impacts to the person's cognitive and physical development (Peterson, 2018a). Complex traumatic events include severe, repeat instances of child maltreatment, interpersonal violence, or other persistent disruptive family circumstances.

Since trauma manifests in many unique ways and can impact everyone differently, the gamut of signs or evidence of trauma impact on an individual, likewise, has the potential to greatly vary. That stated, the following list – though not comprehensive – does illustrate some of the varied symptoms and emotions tied to somebody suffering because of trauma (Center for Substance Abuse Treatment, 2014; SAMHSA, 2023):

> Irritable or short-tempered
> Crying or screaming
> Anxious or apprehensive
> Tendency towards overeating or undernourishment
> Sleeplessness or exhaustion
> Feelings of remorse, embarrassment
> Social isolation or avoidance
> Engagement in substance use or abuse
> Confusion or concentration issues
> Dissociation or numbness

› Overstimulated or understimulated

› Over-focused on traumatic events or averting

As one can discern, there are many unique classifications of trauma, and the emotional or physical symptoms can manifest across a variable spectrum of responses in each survivor. Each form of trauma is both unique in terms of its general categorisation but also distinct in terms of what event type(s) may occur and how these events are perceived and interpreted by those enduring such circumstances. To better understand how trauma impacts an individual, it is important to explore trauma and its power over the body at various timepoints in the lifespan of the average human.

A ringing history: Looking at trauma's impact on emotions across the lifespan

Much like the rings of a tree tell the story of its life, the experiences one endures at varying points across in their lifespan with respect to trauma also manifest in myriad ways. As mentioned prior, the 'mileage' of a traumatic event, or how much it impacts an individual, largely depends on the person's development and environment (Straussner & Calnan, 2014, p. 324). Numerous studies have demonstrated the impacts of trauma on one's physical and mental health, but correlation of trauma to emotional outputs – which is the focus of this tome – are less recognised and, as such, will be the focal point of this section (Centers for Disease Control and Prevention, 2021). Regardless of where one exists across the lifespan, trauma can have serious consequences on one's emotional health and reactions.

Trauma can also impair a child's ability to focus, understand, and process information, be it a simple request for information from a caregiver, recognising the social cues from a classmate or friend, successfully completing an assignment in class, or more. Specifically, trauma at an early age can impair cognitive functioning and result in diminished brain operation. A study from *Neuron* (Nemeroff, 2016) found significant alterations in both endocrine (hormone) and neurotransmitter (nervous) system pathways tied to memory, concentration, and mood regulation. As such, youth with these altered biological pathways who suffer through unprocessed trauma can display an increase in anger or feelings of hostility, especially since trauma persistence has been shown to correlate with reduced self-control in children (Straussner & Phillips, 2003). For instance, McLean's sudden shift from a joyful and engaged student to one who is withdrawn, easily distressed, and prone to aggressive outbursts suggests an impaired ability to regulate emotions and process social interactions due to the traumatic events surrounding his mother's hospitalisation. His difficulty following classroom expectations, isolating behaviours, and emotional dysregulation may stem from his brain struggling to process overwhelming stress and fear. Sadness or fear may manifest as the child encounters triggering events or recalls the trauma endured; such emotions may stem from the feelings of helplessness, despair, or anxiety they experienced and continue to experience when thinking about the event (Peterson, 2018c).

Evidence of maladapted trauma responses and emotions in children may also present in ways that adults may often confound with adolescent self-exploration or deviance associated with revolting against conventional societal expectations. Older children may also display challenges with substance abuse, engaging in risky sexual behaviour, acting on dangerous impulses (e.g., excessive speeding), or conducting self-harm activities that may often be correlated with a wide range of emotions, such as the child showcasing happiness in the moment, a sense of surprise at what they did in this spontaneous circumstance, or perhaps downstream sadness, guilt, or disgust if the event does not result in any short- or long-term gratification (Brent & Silverstein, 2013).

The emotional baggage of one's experiences as children also carries far into the future. Adults often experience heightened emotions that were also felt during triggering events or post-traumatic circumstances. In fact, adults who experienced trauma in their adolescence are 15 times more likely to develop a personality disorder and approximately three times more likely to develop a mental health issue (Newport Institute, 2023). Specifically, adults tend to display a range of emotions across the spectrum of human feelings (Veterans Affairs, n.d.). An adult may experience irritability or anger to feelings of helplessness or overwhelming sadness. Given the advanced developmental capabilities of the human brain, adults may also endeavour through emotions of overwhelming sadness or fearfulness alongside feelings of disgust towards actual or perceived responsible parties or entities correlated with the traumatic event (e.g., systems, policies or persons who 'failed' the survivor). Conversely, one may also encounter adults who feel dissociated with their feelings. While a child may dissociate and express that they are floating or in another place when enduring or recalling a traumatic event, adults tend to indicate that they may feel numb, or in a sense of shock and often express an inability to experience any emotions whatsoever (Lyons, 2020, p. 5). Adults with childhood trauma profiles also have indicated an increase in empathy-associated emotions and feelings (Greenberg et al., 2018, p. 7).

The 'bookends' of human existence – children and the elderly – are often the most disproportionately impacted from an emotional standpoint with respect to trauma (The Jewish Federations of North America, n.d.). Some emotions tied to traumatic events near the end of one's lifespan are similar to those displayed in adulthood, such as anger or irritability, profound sadness, or revulsion at a particular circumstance. Older adult populations may, however, also display emotional distancing from sharing positive feelings with caregivers or an increase in distress or helplessness given their advanced age or complications with health challenges (Moye & Rouse, 2014). Mental health conditions associated with advanced ageing or cognitive decline (e.g., dementia, Alzheimer's) may also exacerbate recall of traumatic events or delay traumatic recollection of trauma-inducing circumstances, giving the appearance to caregivers that the individual has recently suffered a shocking experience that may have, in actuality, taken place much earlier in life (Ladson, n.d., p. 47). As one might surmise, the ability to control these trauma-tethered emotions or use them in an appropriate context is a major struggle for those suffering from varying forms of trauma.

Emotional dysregulation then is a constant, irrespective of the age at which an individual encounters trauma in their life. The phenomenon occurs when an individual is unable to control the severity of their reactions to a given circumstance, be that a post-traumatic event or in correlation to a triggering event where emotions and feelings tied to the traumatic event may manifest (WebMD, 2021). Emotional dysregulation also refers to situations where the individual's emotions fail to align with conventional expectations of how one should react to a given situation (Cuncic, 2023).

As such, one might encounter a child who might react in a proliferative manner to a school fire alarm, triggering their memories of a housefire where loved ones perished, whereby they scream, cry, or shake uncontrollably during the event and have a challenging time calming down soon thereafter. An adult who struggles to cope with the punishment carried out by the justice system regarding their experience of surviving a violent sexual assault may result in the survivor laughing at similar moments discussed in the news, when one might expect a more sombre or empathetic emotional response. An elderly nursing home resident may be combative and attempt to physically strike caretakers when administering medicine based on their inability to manage their sentiments from a previous encounter with a healthcare professional that took place many years earlier.

Despite these challenges with trauma, and its impact on emotional control, there is some promising research that exists, which demonstrates that trauma and mitigating the negative emotional consequences of an extreme event of duress is possible. Encountering and being able to mitigate traumatic events earlier in life has been correlated with positive outcomes related to stress mitigation and enhanced sense of wellbeing (Shrira et al., 2012). Furthermore, evidence-based strategies and best-practice models do exist that have demonstrated improved emotional regulation in those individuals once overcome by their trauma histories (Dumornay et al., 2022, Figure 3). Thus, to overcome the detrimental effects of trauma on emotional control, it is important to review such best practices in greater detail.

Pruning the pain: Trauma mitigation through resiliency-based intervention and prevention

To combat the challenges tied to disproportionate or ill-fitting emotional yields tied to traumatic events, one must first understand the methods that exist for professional intervention in such situations. Physiological symptoms of trauma (e.g., pain or discomfort, elevated pulse or blood pressure) should be explored with the survivor's primary healthcare provider (Ahmadi et al., 2016, p. 95). Likewise, professional mental health clinicians should be a part of any survivor service strategy when trauma engages one's cognitive faculties.

All practices and methods used should be evidence-based and focused on a trauma-informed (i.e., trauma-practicing) model of care that recognises trauma as a critical part of the survivor's health history and being (SAMHSA, 2023). The goal of these practices should be to mitigate the consequences of trauma on the mental, emotional and physical wellbeing of the individual, and to replace those factors that are contributing to the maladapted response to trauma. This would be through protective factors that promote resilience and can help to mitigate future events involving triggering past event recall or to aid in enduring future challenging circumstances (Kapil, 2022). Protective factors may include helping the trauma survivor to identify and engage in healthy relationships, develop or augment new or preexisting coping skills, or connect with community organisations and services for empowerment. All interventions to be used for trauma intervention should focus on the Substance Abuse and Mental Health Services Administration's (SAMHSA's) core tenants of implementing a trauma-informed approach to care, which includes the following (Menscher & Maul, 2016).

> Patient empowerment (i.e., offered choices at any applicable intervention phase)
> Treatment choice (i.e., providing a range of treatment options)
> Collaboration (i.e., family, healthcare provider cooperative planning)
> Safety emphasis (i.e., treatment location and events focused on patient wellbeing)
> Trustworthiness (i.e., setting clear expectations, transparency in all steps)

There are several evidence-based methods that exist when specifically attempting to address emotional dysregulation related to trauma. Eye movement desensitisation and reprocessing therapy (EMDR) entails requiring the survivor to "to briefly focus on the trauma memory while simultaneously experiencing bilateral stimulation (typically eye movements), which is associated with a reduction in the vividness and emotion associated with the trauma memories" (American Psychological Association, 2017, p. 1). Exposure therapy has been historically used in a safe space to allow the survivor to 'confront' their apprehensions and emotions tied to a traumatising event or circumstances thereof (American Psychological Association, 2017a). Trauma-focused cognitive behavioural therapy (TF-CBT) has also shown promise in reducing emotional dysregulation in youth by empowering the child and applicable caregivers with skills to combat negative thoughts and feelings while exposing them to increasing triggers or reminders of a traumatic event so that they begin to rely on those resiliency competencies learnt in a graduated fashion (Cohen & Mannarino, 2015; Kliethermes & Wamser-Nanney, 2017). Each example posited herein has significant research demonstrating positive impacts on trauma mitigation and emotional regulation (Sin et al., 2017, p. 4).

While intervention methods have grown extensively in more recent times, no intervention can sufficiently replace trauma prevention. A trauma-prevention focused response for all individuals across the lifespan involves multiple levels of social-ecological engagement (e.g., individual, relationship, community, and societal level) and focusing on augmenting protective factors at each level while combatting the quantity and variety of trauma-inducing factors present (Centers for Disease Control and Prevention, n.d.-b). At the individual level, prevention may take the form of providing the person with coping skills and self-care strategies to deal with stressful events (American Psychological Association, 2023). Relationship level prevention could entail the ability to confide feelings and thoughts about a troublesome event with a friend or loved one, while community level resiliency might involve equitable, affordable access to wrap-around services for individuals struggling to cope with a traumatic encounter. Societal level prevention will endeavour a much bolder strategy – to work to curb trauma-based perspectives and values – which may be a seemingly insurmountable challenge but is feasible with the right vision and planning for such an endeavour. One need to look no further than to publications such as *Unto the Third Generation* (Vieth, 2005) for a glimpse into how society can change for the better and erase trauma-laden experiences for future generations.

Conclusion

The concept of trauma has existed since the dawn of humankind. Largely a protective mechanism engrained at the biological level, trauma is tied to emotions and feelings from a given event to safeguard persons from repeated, harmful encounters. Many types of traumas exist, and each event has the potential to impact one's health from a physical and mental perspective either in a temporary capacity or over an enduring period. Trauma is often tied to extreme and unexpected displays of emotions, including but not limited to fear, anger, sadness, and revulsion, through a process known as emotional dysregulation; moreover, inappropriate exhibits of emotions – such as happiness or disbelief – may develop at seemingly abnormal moments because of the trauma survivor's inability to control their feelings. Several evidence-based therapies exist to intervene when one's emotional gamut runs uninhibited based on trauma response, but prevention is the ultimate antidote for trauma and its toxic impact on one's emotional state.

CHAPTER 8

Passion: The Known Unknown

Sifiso Shabangu

Oh... you will just know, you know?

Tim remembers his high school graduation, and the words of Principal Bell in his final speech as though it were yesterday: "So, when you leave high school, and begin the journey of 'adulting' – as young people refer to adult responsibilities – find your passion! Chase your passion! Hold onto it because you will be lost without it."

As Tim sat in the audience listening, he leaned over to his mother and asked: "Mom, what is passion, and what if I have many of them, like, I don't know, many things that I am passionate about?" Tim's mother whispered back: "Oh Timmy, passion is that thing that will pull you towards it and demand your attention. It will push you away from other things. You will just know when you found your passion." Tim replied: "But what if there are many things that do the pulling and the pushing?" Upon which his mom smiled and responded:

"Well, in that case, figure out what is pulling most of the time and that's the one." To this day, Tim is thankful for Principal Bell and his mother's advice. It really guided him through all the years and helped him to make the right decisions in life (and to avoid making terrible mistakes, like almost marrying the wrong woman)!

Introduction

Passion, whether it is chasing it, finding it, or demonstrating it, is often invoked as though it is universally agreed and expected that each person should have it. Passion is one of the most known unknown emotions as it appears to have multiple identities. For Principal Bell and Tim's mother, passion was a singular external entity that should have been discovered. In religious spaces, faith is viewed as "the highest passion in a person" (Westphal, 2011, p. 88), and scholars have proposed passion is rooted in biology and one's socio-cultural environment (Mullen, 1991; Tsai, 2021). Passion is said to lead to excellence, and it is an instrument for developing a meaningful existence (Vallerand, 2008). For Tim, passion was a thing he needed to find in the world, without anyone guiding him, or having a proverbial manual as to the '*how*' and a definition for the '*what*' his passions would be.

Inversely, passion has also been associated with negative emotional outcomes, rigidity in pursuits, and poverty of a balanced existence (Vallerand, 2012). This is suggestive of passion being a contributor to positive and negative outcomes, a scenario that was not pointed out to Tim – at least not the undesirable passion-related consequences. Indeed, passion is known to bring out the best or the worst in individuals – "the dualism inherent in passion" (Vallerand, 2012, p. 3). This dualism has been highlighted by Ripand et al. (2012, p. 574), who indicated that "passion appears to energize and direct both peaceful and extremist ideologically inspired movements." Though passion can result in maladaptive outcomes, the biological and social functions of passion are essential for continued existence and adaptation (Szymańska, 2023).

Passion is inherent in our everyday lives and has been found to play a role in sport (Vallerand et al., 2008), romantic/passionate love (Hatfield & Rapson, 2006; Hatfield & Sprecher, 1986), music (Bonneville-Roussy et al., 2011), education (Carbonneau et al., 2008), career (O'Keefe et al., 2022), creativity (Grohman et al., 2017), physiological responses (Vallerand et al., 2022), dramatic arts (Vallerand et al., 2007), and developing meaningful existence (Vallerand, 2008).

Passion: Origins and definitions

The mind, body and our social environments are known to shape our emotional experiences. Darwin believed even the most primitive of societies, as they were viewed, were innately embedded with emotions – emotions are universal and human (Konstan, 2005). Recently, researchers have indicated that positive and negative emotions can result from the different types of passion we engage in our lives (Zhang et al., 2014). However, this was not always the case. During the Middle Ages, passion was understood as a self-activation of the body, and one was then at the mercy of these delicate activations (Luhmann, 1986). In the earliest writings on the emotional aspects of passion, Plato (429–347 BCE) and Spinoza (1632–1677) viewed passion as a psychological state with the individual as the victim, defenceless due to their passions, and therefore behaving unintentionally, without reason, but not unaccountably (Luhmann, 1986). According to this 16th century conceptualisation of passion, the thoughts arising from passions were unacceptable, as the individual was afflicted with suffering (Latin word 'passio', meaning suffering) (Vallerand et al., 2003). In this period, the 'restless' emotions were viewed as passions (Averill & Sundararajan, 2020), the implication being that passion did not serve any discernible function. Later, an evolved, passion-positive concept of passion was brought forward by Descartes who proposed that there was reason underlying passion, and it was connected to one's physiology and could be subject of scientific study (Radcliffe, 2015). This view was echoed by Hegel (1770–1831), who stated that passion was a necessary ingredient for optimum achievement (Radcliffe, 2015; Vallerand, 2012). Further still, in his theory of emotion of 1884, William

James, viewed passion as a scientifically valid pursuit (Charland, 2019). Passion, if controlled, can therefore be an asset for positive adaptation.

Psychologists have lagged in passion research, but the phenomenon has begun scholastic uptake in the last two decades. Prior to the last two decades, research on passion focused on the motivational elements of passion. For instance, Frijda et al. (1991) defined passion as high-priority goals with emotionally significant consequences. To achieve these emotionally important outcomes, individuals will invest time and effort. Passion has also been explored in the context of love/romantic relationships. Baumeister and Bratslavsky (1999, p. 52) defined passion as "involving strong feeling of attraction for the other person". These strong feelings are characterised by physiological arousal and a desire to be united with the other person in a variety of ways, such as conversational engagement – a sentiment echoed by Hatfield and Walster (1985). For Sternberg (1986, p. 119), passion refers to the "drives that lead to romance, physical attraction, sexual consummation, and related phenomena in loving relationships." From these definitions, we can surmise that passion was understood to involve intense motivation and a magnification of emotions towards individuals or objects. Indeed, passions "help organize and orient emotions, from which they are distinct" (Charland, 2011, p. 84). However, as is the nature of scholarship, others viewed passion itself as an emotion and therefore susceptible to the nature of emotions and their presentation (Aron & Aron, 2014; Berscheid, 2006). Further, passion can be triggered by many other emotions such as pleasure and pain, and this stimulation can be adaptive or maladaptive (Hatfield & Rapson, 1987).

In the last two decades, Vallerand and colleagues have brought forward a focus on passion towards an activity. They understand passion as "a strong inclination toward an activity that people like, that they find important, and in which they invest time and energy" (Vallerand et al., 2003, p. 757). They further propose passion as a dichotomy with the Dualistic Model of Passion (DMP) with *harmonious passion* (HP) and *obsessive passion* (OP). HP proposes that the individual's engagement with the activity is controlled, voluntary, there are no contingencies attached to it, and the activity does not impair functioning in other areas of life (Vallerand, 2008). OP results in maladaptive existence as the passionate activity controls the individual, there is almost a compulsion to engage with the activity often due to contingencies attached to it, such as social acceptance or self-worth (Bélanger et al., 2019), resulting in impairment in other areas of functioning. The DMP proposes that for individuals to develop, they must explore their environment via activities and in turn, those activities contribute to a meaningful and passion-fuelled existence (Vallerand, 2012). Through sustained engagement, trial and error, some activities will fall off, while others will be maintained, particularly enjoyable interests enabling the satisfaction of the needs for competence, autonomy, and relatedness (Vallerand et al., 2003); to the point of excellence and the person becoming the activity – that is, the passion activity becomes engrained in their identity.

For example, after graduation, Tim decided that he had a strong inclination for music and started playing multiple musical instruments. Over the years, he realised that he mostly enjoyed playing the piano, and hence stopped playing all other instruments. He focused on becoming one of the best pianists in Riverside. In fact, Tim became so passionate about playing the piano, that he saw it as being part of his core identity. Over the years, he seemed he really struck a good work-life-family balance, as he successfully pursued a career playing the piano for a living, and he made time for friends, as well as his wife and family (who also shared his passion for playing music). Thus, Tim had achieved *harmonious passion*. Contrarily, in *obsessive passion*, if Tim only made playing the piano his passionate activity to please others (e.g., to please his mom or for his community) – this relates to attached contingency, and social acceptance. In such an instance, Tim would be less likely to be in control of his engagement with playing the piano, and his other areas of functioning might have suffered. Obsessive passion eventually results in the Latin meaning 'passio', or suffering. However, obsessive passion is not addiction; granted there is a similarity in phenomenology, such as the inability to resist the behaviour, but with obsessive passion, increased involvement in the valued activity results in enjoyment, but with addiction, enjoyment is low (Ratelle et al., 2013; Reynaud et al., 2010). The difference between passion and addiction are explained later in this chapter. Therefore, passion is a major source of fuel for sustaining activity engagement to the point of excellence and internalising that activity into one's identity (Vallerand et al., 2007).

Scholars have since proposed that passion is related to our minds, bodies, and social environments, as a necessary ingredient of life that motivates behaviour. Passion is not a hurdle to be overcome, but rather a tool of logic and precise purpose (Buss, 2000; St-Louis et al., 2021). Passion has been studied in relation to the context of romantic relationships or passionate love via brain scans and physiological observation – which we will explore next. Currently, the dominating school of thought is that passion is a strong inclination towards an activity deemed important and afforded time and energy. Passion can have positive outcomes where autonomy is present (harmonious passion) and negative outcomes where autonomy is absent (obsessive passion).

Passion and physiology

In this section, we will explore the known relationship between passion, the brain, and our physiological responses. The experience of passion has been investigated in the functioning of our brains, as well as our physiological responses. The development of data-gathering tools such as functional magnetic resonance imaging (fMRI), has shed significant light on brain function regarding our emotional word. Emotions are rooted in our biology (Mullen, 1991; Sebastian & Ahmed, 2018) and therefore our minds perceive and interpret these emotions, while our physiology can determine how intensely we feel these emotions (Hatfield & Rapson, 1987). Passion is essential for brain health. The development of strong interests and passions encourages learning and acquisition of new skills and information, which helps keep the neural network functional by, for example, reducing brain atrophy over time (Sigmundsson et al., 2022). Passion is also related to the dopamine system, which plays a role in rewards, attention, and goal orientation (Tarlaci, 2012). Thus, because Tim has a passion for the piano, Tim's brain system rewards practice and sustains his attention and intended goal of being a pianist. Therefore, Tim, the pianist, sustains healthy neural pathways by continued practice, learning new musical note combinations, and enjoys working collaboratively with other musicians who share his passion.

The triggering of dopamine is further associated with specific mate selection and highly concentrated motivation towards their wellbeing (Fisher, 2006; Reynaud et al., 2010). According to Cacioppo et al. (2012), if one is experiencing highly passionate love, presentation of an image of their loved one stimulates activity in the reward, pleasure, and cognitive pathways. Specifically, these include activity in the hippocampus, caudate head, putamen, insular cortex, anterior cingulate cortex cerebellum and ventral tegmental area (Cacioppo, Grafton & Bianchi-Demicheli, 2012; Fisher et al., 2006). However, others have found that passionate love has a "specific neural network that surpasses a dopaminergic-motivation system" (Ortigue et al., 2007, p. 1 218). These brain areas are located in other parts of the brain outside the subcortical region – where the network of passionate love is found (Cacioppo et al., 2012) – but also in brain regions known to also mediate other functions, such as social cognition, body image, abstract concepts, self-representation, and metaphors (Bianchi-Demicheli et al., 2006; Fisher et al., 2006). Activity in this system supports the understanding of passionate love as positive and motivating emotional experience where the beloved craves emotional union beyond sexual contact with their lover (Bianchi-Demicheli et al., 2006; Fisher, 2006).

Our physiology can sometimes function as the windowpane through which we can observe or infer what is taking place cognitively. For example, the insular cortex generates restlessness when in passionate love, which can manifest in our physiology via heightened palpitations, elevated blood pressure, and perspiring (Tarlaci, 2012). Further, the *ventral tegmental area* (VTA) and *substantiva nigra* are responsible for over 90% dopamine produced, they are involved in all reward stimuli, such as creativity, arousal, and ecstasy (Fisher et al., 2006; Tarlaci, 2012). If the arousal and ecstatic feelings are not reciprocated, or a lover ends the romantic love, the individual's health can be compromised as they experience insomnia, lethargy, anxiety, loss of appetite, depression, and, in extreme cases, suicidality and heart attacks (Fisher et al., 2016).

Passion and love

In this section, we will explore love and its role in passion, specifically romantic/passionate love. The nature of love has been the subject of debate for centuries in literature, music, politics, family relations, romance and virtually every other sphere of existence. Love has resulted in the birth of generations; it has resulted in murder, suicide, marriage, billion-dollar entertainment industries, eloping, Valentine's Day, and people being named Love, Thando, Lerato – all meaning or relating to love. Owing to the vastness of love's expression and presentation, a uniform understanding of its nature has been a challenge to develop. Love and passion have been reported to have definitional and theoretical intersections (Mouton & Montijo, 2017), and they have been utilised interchangeably in literature on the subject (Hatfield & Rapson, 1987). To define love, we often find ourselves giving examples of what we will call love-in-action scenarios (what academics call operationalisations), such as random hugs or check-ups, which, one could argue, is the behavioural component of love. So, what is love?

Love has been defined as a disease, a madness that chains its victims and requires no explanation or justification, "love [is] its own justification" (Luhmann, 1986, p. 44). Others define love as a product of processes with an intention, that is, love is defined as thoughts, emotions and actions motivated by a desire for establishing or maintaining closeness with a particular person (Aron & Aron, 2014). It appears love engages the person holistically to achieve a desired relationship, some have dared say that love passion is an addiction plausibly deserving of being rendered a disorder (Reynaud et al., 2010).

Additional, in defining love, there have been scholastic attempts to group love (Fehr & Russell, 1991), to locate it in the brain (Sternberg & Sternberg, 2018) and to measure love (Masuda, 2003; Sternberg, 1997). In these undertakings, love's components, styles, and theories have been posited. For example,

Hendrick and Hendrick (1986) highlight Lee's six love *styles*: Eros (passionate love), Ludus (game-playing love), Storge (friendship love), Pragma (logical love), Mania (possessive, dependent love), and Agape (altruistic love). They viewed these love styles comprehensively, as "love styles that formed a closed circle" (p. 393). Sternberg (1986) proposed different *kinds* of love, such as companionate love, passionate love, infatuated love, liking and so forth. Sternberg argued, in the triangular theory of love, that the kind of love experienced would influence the intensity of passion within it. The triangular theory of love proposes that the type and intensity of love one experiences is dependent on the status of the intimacy (closeness, connectedness), passion (the fuel for the romance, physical and sexual attraction), and decision/commitment (decisions in short term, *'I love the person'*, and in the long term, *'I am committing to the love experienced'*) (Sternberg, 1986).

In this section, the focus is on romantic/passionate love. This is because romantic/passionate love is often marked and differentiated from other forms of love by the presence of passion (Davis & Todd, 1982). Romantic relationships are relationships that generally include sexual intimacy, dating, thought and chemical processes, with goal-direction (Aron et al., 2006; Bianchi-Demicheli et al., 2006). Additionally, the intimacy and passion are often pervasive (Kansky, 2018). Romantic love is also a universal phenomenon across societies and often begins when one appraises another as exceptional and special, and this passion is towards one individual at a time (Berscheid, 2006; Fisher et al., 2006; Tarlaci, 2012). Hatfield and Rapson (1987) define passionate love (being in love) as "a state of intense longing for union with another", resulting in fulfilment (p. 260). If the desire is unreciprocated, emptiness and despair are the outcome. Recently, Ratelle and colleagues (2013) have defined romantic love in line with the DMP, that is, passion is "a strong inclination toward a romantic partner that one loves, in a relationship that is deemed important, and into which significant time and energy is invested" (p. 108). This also implies that harmonious passion and obsessive passion are outcomes within romantic love, and these will be discussed in the following paragraphs.

It has been proposed that one must submit to passion when entering a close relationship of love (Luhmann, 1986). Passion and intimacy are identified as powerful and prominent features of love and "passion involves exceptionally strong positive feelings toward the partner" (Baumeister & Bratslavsky, 1999, p. 51). A passion of love is driven by the desire for closeness and the enrichment of the other's wellbeing, just like the emotion of love is stimulated by the achievement of that closeness (Frijda et al., 1991). Passion and love are presented as having a very strong association, and this was echoed in earlier works by Sternberg (1986), who stated that passion is what could initially propel the individual towards the relationship, which is then sustained by intimacy. This sustenance from intimacy was further reiterated by Baumeister and Bratslavsky (1999), who stated that passion in romantic love is influenced by intimacy, and stable intimacy sees low passion, and an increase in intimacy results in increased passion. This is all suggestive of passion as deteriorating over time, and this was reported among married couples (Sims & Meana, 2010). However, others have argued that passion does not necessarily wane with time, because this is dependent on the type of passion developed. According to Ratelle and colleagues (2013), with harmonious passion, the pursuit of the continued romantic engagement is voluntary and not conflicting with life's other spheres, and if the passion is obsessive, romantic engagement is rigid, and negatively impairs not only the romantic love, but other life domains, such as employment performance.

Passion and love appear to intersect at strong and intense desire towards the other, but passion can influence relationship initiation. Passion has been referred to as the fuel for love. This often culminates in romantic love and a sense of fulfilment when there is reciprocation. Passionate love makes the individual want to positively complement the other's life and invest time and effort. Harmonious passion is healthy for romantic love although this does not mean it is void of conflicts. Obsessive passion, on the other hand, is maladaptive, lacks autonomy and can be potentially emotionally exhausting, which can lead to relationship termination or abuse. The role of obsessive passion in addiction will be briefly expounded on in the next sections.

Passion and addiction

In this section we discuss addiction and passion, specifically obsessive passion, and how they differ and feed into each other. Obsessive passion, marked by rigidity and maladaptive outcomes, has been identified as a conduit to addiction while harmonious passion is not (Le, 2023; Szabo et al., 2022). The obsessively passionate individual creates relationship dependency or uses the passionate relationship to escape life's problems (Vallerand et al., 2008), which makes it difficult for them to stop engaging in the relationship or activity (Newland & Aicher, 2023). This is so, even when negative outcomes of the continued engagement in an activity or relationship are evident. The obsessively passionate individuals are very defensive of these outcomes (Rip et al., 2012). This could be considered an indicator of a shift from obsessive passion to addiction because one of the hallmarks of addictions is a deception of self and others. The spiralling from normal passion towards an addictive sphere may not be easily noticeable (Reynaud et al., 2010), because the addiction-related behaviours resemble and are perceived as normal desires (Summers, 2015). This is sooner evident as addiction demands to be attended, whereas passion, if harmonious, is fulfilling. Obsessive passion resembles behaviour observed in addiction.

Addiction to a substance is characterised by compulsive engagement with a substance, loss of control in limiting use, and negative emotional experience if access to the substance is disallowed (Koob, 2011). Addiction has profoundly maladaptive outcomes, such as job loss, criminal engagement, and strained family relations (Lüscher et al., 2020). Regarding maladaptive outcomes, these have been observed in, for example, brands and consumerism, where obsessive passion moderates the love emotion for the brand *towards* addiction to the brand (Le, 2023). This is evident in thoughts, compulsions, financial spending, and the desire to consume more of the brand, even when it is economically unsound. Further, the relationship between exercise addiction and obsessive passion has been demonstrated by the presence of addiction markers, such as poverty of involvement in other life domains, withdrawal if barred, compulsion to exercise, and loss of control (Schreiber &

Hausenblas, 2015). Addiction nurtures a withdrawal from supportive others, channelling all emotional, economic, and social resources towards itself.

In addition to marketing and exercise, the positive relationship between obsessive passion and addiction is also found in video games and gambling (Holding et al., 2021), anorexia nervosa (Szmukler, 2013), and (as mentioned before) in romantic/passionate love (Reynaud et al., 2010). Regarding gambling, if obsessive passion for it develops, problematic outcomes, such as anxiety, poor mood and diminished concentration on daily tasks are highly likely (Ratelle et al., 2004; Whelan et al., 2021). In anorexia nervosa, the rigidity and persistence characteristic of obsessive passion is the pursuit of thinness (Lim et al., 2007). This rigid and persistent avoidance of weight gain and pursuit of thinness is the fuel that sustains anorexia nervosa as a passion over time (Charland et al., 2013).

Scholars have touted the idea of love, specifically romantic/passionate love, being an addiction and potentially deserving of a diagnosis (Reynaud et al., 2010). Love addiction is a process addiction, beginning with pleasurable emotions and obsessive thoughts, punctuated by cycles of elation and cravings for union with the partner, and followed by diminished adaptive functioning that is persistent (Sussman, 2010). In the context of passionate love that has become addiction-led, "love addiction may also exhibit consequential [substance] dependence-like features" (Sussman, 2010, p. 33), and the addict partner can experience withdrawal-like symptoms in the partner's absence (Simson, 1982). The 'addict partner' has a compulsive need for the other, spends significant and increasing time on the relationship (cognitively or physically), and engages in persistent but unsuccessful attempts to control their maladaptive behaviour, even in the face of negative outcomes (Fisher et al., 2016; Newland & Aicher, 2023; Reynaud et al., 2010).

Love addiction makes resistance to 'cravings' for the partner futile, and one is "led away from [themselves] as a victim or prisoner of [their] compulsions" (Simson, 1982, p. 253). Love addiction is an all-consuming, self-focused endeavour that demands consistent and persistent gratification (Newland & Aicher, 2023; Simson, 1982), while passionate love, as pointed our earlier, desires intimacy and the enhancement of the partner's interests and comfort (Frijda et al., 1991). Although addiction is a process, its eventual primary focus is experiencing the pleasurable outcome even if it negatively impacts all else. Love addiction is often characterised by deception, while passion is process driven, authentic, maintains healthy engagements with other aspects of life, and can be stopped voluntarily without adverse effects.

Further, the neurological basis for the love-is-addiction argument is that passionate love and drug or behavioural addiction demonstrate neural activity within the brain reward systems (Fisher et al., 2016). The reward system includes brain areas, such as the *ventral tegmental area* (VTA), *caudate*, and *accumbens*, associated with craving, heightened attention and addiction (Ortigue et al., 2007; Tarlaci, 2012). Earlier, Bianchi-Demicheli et al. (2006) demonstrated that beyond the subcortical reward activity, the emotion and motivation centres gave love focus and influenced cognitive processing. This, potentially, implies emotional motivation for addictive behaviour towards a romantic partner beyond the behaviour-reward interaction. It has been highlighted that both obsessive passion and addiction have maladaptive outcomes, and these might include abuse and criminal acts. These are explored next.

Passion, abusive relationships, and crime

In this section, we will discuss how passion, specifically obsessive passion, plays a role in abuse within the context of romantic relationships. Further, we explore the linkage of passion, abuse, and criminal activity.

Romantic relationships encompass romantic love. Romantic love, as discussed above, is also natural, often positive but can also be powerfully negative and addictive (Fisher et al., 2016). The lover 'craves' the partner who often excitedly intrudes in their thoughts (Reynaud et al., 2010), and takes up to 85% of their conscious state, which can develop into a compulsive and excessive yearning for closeness (Fisher et al., 2016). The negative, threatening and darker side of passion can manifest in abuse within romantic relationships (Buss, 2000), such as intimate partner violence

(Pocock et al., 2020), particularly when the passion is obsessive (Bélanger et al., 2021). Passion is utilised as a manipulative tool in romantic relationships where physical violence is present (Pocock et al., 2020). Further, this facilitates coercion, and control is often dressed up as misguided passion (Keeling & Fisher, 2012). Excessive passion is a known leading contributor to psychopathology (Charland, 2015) – which can be marked by paranoia and delusional thinking.

The obsessively passionate partner's self-worth and self-esteem are contingent on the relationship. The individual becomes emotionally dependent on the relationship and "adversity heightens their passion" (Fisher, 2006, p. 88). This places an emotional toll on the partner. The partner must consistently satisfy the contingencies placed on them, which is a strenuous undertaking. The persistence of the obsessively passionate partner impairs healthy functioning in other domains, such as social, occupational, and within the very partner-relational domain. This creates an autocratic relational environment where the ego needs of the partner supersede every other emotion, need, and concern. Romantic passion has been identified as "a catalyst that induces fear of abandonment" if the contingencies placed on the relationship are appraised by the obsessively passionate as under threat (Bélanger et al., 2021, p. 1160). An escalation develops in the form of verbal and physical abuse to establish dominance, control, and, above all, to continue emotionally and psychologically benefitting from the, for example, self-worth and self-esteem contingencies attached to the relationship.

This stifling passionate love is marked by abusive acts, such as aggression and violence, which inadvertently leads to acts of criminality against the partner, such as stalking and in extreme cases murder (Bélanger et al., 2021; Buss, 2000). Concurringly, Buss (2000) reminds us that passion is an emotional fire marked by calmness and doting dedication, which can move towards brutal eruptions resulting in the harshest suffering of those in its wake. Stalking, also referred to as obsessive following, or obsessive relational intrusion, is a crime involving acts of repeated and unsolicited attention or contact, instilling fear and raising safety concerns for the victim (Bélanger et al., 2021; Meloy, 1996, 1998), and in 1% of US cases, it results in murder (Rai et al., 2020). There are two predominant types of stalkers: the one rejected by an ex-lover with whom sexually intimacy was shared, and the other who is pursuing a stranger or acquaintance with whom no previous intimate relationship exists (Fisher et al., 2016). Many stalkers are men, and most victims are women (Meloy & Fisher, 2005). Further, stalking has been presented as an evolutionary adaption to retain/acquire a mate, guard and fend off competitors, and poach the mates of others (Duntley & Buss, 2012).

Obsessive passion can lead to an abdication of the romantic relationship, which can give rise to a stalker. Stalking has been likened to addiction (Meloy & Fisher, 2005). Neurologically, brain systems associated with obsessive thinking, attention and energy appear to be rewarded in stalking behaviour (Meloy & Fisher, 2005). A rejected lover can engage in extremely inappropriate and dangerous efforts to regain lost love (Fisher, 2006) such as coercion, constraint, and violence towards the stalked (Meloy & Fisher, 2005). The most common and most violent cases of stalking are amongst former intimate partners (Bélanger et al., 2021), and these include homicide outcomes. Rejected lovers, globally, are known to be depressed, commit suicide and sometimes homicide (Fisher, 2006; Fisher et al., 2016).

Obsessive passion can lead to murder, "humans kill because we love" (Broussard, 2012, p. 181) and "the stronger a love is, the more violent the emotions it arouses" (Reynaud et al., 2010, p. 262). Historically, the crime of passion or heat of passion, has been legally accepted as mitigation in the event a partner murdered the other if caught in the act of infidelity (Broussard, 2012; Goldstein, 2002). This argument often resulted in the downgrade from murder to manslaughter charge, as the murderous reaction was deemed provoked and reasonable due to blinding passion, defined as intense anger and rage that is uncontrollable, which any other reasonable person could have committed (Mousourakis, 2007). Passion legally validated murder because "passion prompts violent action, but reason counsels control" (Mullen, 1991, p. 596). Crimes such as stalking and crimes of passion/ heat of passion, have all leaned on passion as a mitigating factor, much like Plato (429–347 BCE), who viewed passion as an overwhelming force towards the individual. However, this view of passion has been opposed by both law and psychology scholars (Dressler, 1982; Fontaine, 2009; Steinberg, 2005), even indicating that "psychology can only inform the law, but cannot force changes in law" (Sherman & Hoffmann, 2007, p. 449).

Passion and lust

Lust, known as one of the seven deadly sins or capital vices according to Christian beliefs, is often associated with behaviours considered immoral. Traditionally, lust referred to a natural proclivity towards sexual activity, but lust acquired negative associations due to the early Christian Church's "excessively anti-carnal attitudes" (Stafford, 1977, p. 295). Lust is characterised by the cravings and motivations for sexual gratification, a biological necessity (Fisher, 2015; Yu, 2013). According to Gordon and McKinney (2014), lust is the extreme end of the love-lust spectrum within the context of passionate love, the sex-without-love pole. In general, lust is thought to be void of all the positive emotions associated with sexual intimacy. However, neuroscience indicates that the love-lust dyad works in tandem, and the strongest passionate relationships boast the presence of both emotional states (Cacioppo & Cacioppo, 2013).

Lust, from an evolutionary perspective, aides the initiation of the mating process and in so doing ensures the continuation of the human species (Fisher et al., 2002; Ridley et al., 2006). Further, lust can occur within the context of passionate love, and outside of this romantic context (Cacioppo & Cacioppo, 2013; Fisher, 2015). Lust is part of the emotion-motivation brain network evolved for mate selection and attachment (Fisher et al., 2002; Ridley et al., 2006). The core function of lust is mating, unlike passion, which includes the function of developing a meaningful life. However, passion has a role in the initiation of a relationship beyond lust (Sternberg, 1986).

Contrary to the continuation of humanity via reproduction, lust can also motivate aggression which can in extreme cases end in a loss of life. Humans have an intrinsic disposition towards lust for violence and this is associated with criminal acts such as sexual murder (Elbert et al., 2017). Sexual murder, specifically lust murder – also known as erotophonophilia – is the sexual gratification from the act of killing (Chopin & Beauregard, 2021). This lust-related murder is often motivated by sexually deviant behaviours which promote violent actions. For example, in piquerism, whereby sexual gratification is gained from piercing the person's skin with sharp objects, the need to satisfy this paraphiliac craving becomes the very motive for the murder (Arrigo & Purcell, 2001). Like the negative outcomes of obsessive passion, lust might have undesirable fatal consequences in its quest to be gratified.

Absence of passion, pleasure, and expression

Apathy – Lack of passion

Passion, if absent, could lead to the individual in a state of apathy. 'Apathy' is a derivative term from the Greek 'pathos' meaning passion, and 'apathés' describes "lack of passion" or "free of passion" (Ishizaki & Mimura, 2011; Starkstein & Leentjens, 2008). Apathy is defined as a lack of motivation and diminished emotions (Van Reekum et al., 2005; Voorend et al., 2024). To clarify, the "lack of motivation is not attributable to a diminished level of consciousness, an intellectual deficit, or emotional distress" (Mann, 1990, p. 22). However, Stuss and colleagues (2000) argue that 'lack of motivation' is too simplistic and propose that apathy is an absence of reactivity to stimuli, which is evident in the individual's lack of initiative. The presence of an apathetic state is characterised by diminished motivation with cognitive, behavioural, and affective symptoms (Lanctôt et al., 2017; Levy et al., 1998). These symptoms can include "less motivation, fewer goal-directed behaviours, fewer emotions, and less social engagement" (Voorend et al., 2024, p. 163).

Apathy is reportedly caused by malfunction of the frontal subcortical systems (Van Reekum et al., 2005), such as damage to the basal ganglia (Stuss et al., 2000). Apathy has a high prevalence in individuals with neurodegenerative diseases, such as Alzheimer's (Nobis & Husain, 2018) and contributes to cognitive decline and a progression to dementia (Lanctôt et al., 2017). Furthermore, apathy is implicated in decreased functionality and treatment response, which results in poor treatment outcomes (Van Reekum et al., 2005). Passion, however, is associated with activation of the subcortical region of the brain, which is responsible for motivation and reward (Cacioppo, Grafton & Bianchi-Demicheli, 2012). The apathetic individual can then present with diminished goal-oriented and emotionally connected behaviour (Ishizaki & Mimura, 2011), profoundly impairing their quality of life (Le Heron et al., 2019).

Anhedonia – Lack of pleasure

Passion provides meaning to people's lives by providing pleasure through harmonious engagement with activities (Vallerand, 2008). Persons unable to experience pleasure, are therefore likely to experience an existence with diminished meaning, that is, lacking passion. Anhedonia, the lowered ability to experience pleasure or normally pleasurable experiences (Chapman et al., 1976; Rizvi et al., 2016), is one of the two core symptoms (the other being a persistently depressed mood) of clinical depression, which can sometimes results in hopelessness and suicide (De Fruyt et al., 2020; Winer et al., 2014). Anhedonia has been observed within the context of passionate love when one is separated from their love (Reynaud et al., 2010). Beyond the lack of pleasure, the anhedonic state is implicated in impaired desire, creativity, motivation, social engagement, ecstasy, and pleasure anticipation – the passions of human existence (Barkus, 2021; Heinze & Heinze, 1999).

Alexithymia – Lack of expression

Darwin proclaimed emotions as innately human and universal, and they function to enhance adaptive functioning (Hogeveen & Grafman, 2021; Konstan, 2005). However, to serve their adaptive purpose, one must be able to identify and describe emotions, have continued imaginative activity such as dreams, differentiate between emotional and physical sensations, and demonstrate flexibility in their cognitive style, as opposed to one fixed to an external orientation (Hogeveen & Grafman, 2021; Zackheim, 2007). Failure to achieve this is known as alexithymia, a constant psychological trait whose name is derived from the Greek, meaning 'absence of words for emotions' (Martínez-Sánchez et al., 2003; Zackheim, 2007). These cognitive and emotional deficits impair empathy and interpersonal relationships (Kauhanen et al., 1993) and this potentially encourages social withdrawal, isolation, conflict within passionate love (Wells et al., 2016), and disconnection from passion activities. Alexithymia is common with patients with anxiety and depression (Honkalampi et al., 2000; Leweke et al., 2011). Generally, alexithymia is associated with poor wellbeing, including diminished meaning in life (Timoney et al., 2013), which is aided and developed by the presence of passion (Vallerand, 2008).

Emotion regulation to enhance passion

Situations, both external and internal, trigger our emotions and demand our attention and appraisal (Jamieson et al., 2018; Smith et al., 2012). Emotions influence more than our subjective experiences but also our behaviours and physiological responses, such as posture and physical withdrawal or confrontation (Mauss et al., 2007). Generally, emotions are helpful in guiding us regarding a course of action, like joy to bolster social connection, and fear to avert danger (Gross & Jazaieri, 2014). However, emotions can be harmful due to duration, intensity, frequency, and a mismatch to the situation (Gross, 2015). Hence the need to regulate our emotions for positive health outcomes.

Humans are not passive in the emission of emotions, but we participate explicitly or implicitly in the process (Gross & Jazaieri, 2014; Mauss et al., 2007). Emotion regulation entails using specific strategies to manage and influence emotion-generative processes (St-Louis et al., 2021). Specifically, emotion regulation influences which emotions we feel, when we feel them, and how we express and experience these emotions. (Gross, 2015). Strategies for emotion regulation include: *situation selection*, which is a forward-looking strategy that encompasses being selective about situations that can lead to undesirable or desirable emotions; *situation modification*, which refers to direct action to alter a situation to moderate its emotional impact (Gross, 2015), and *cognitive change/reappraisal*, which refers to modifying one's appraisal of a situation, internally or externally (Gross & Jazaieri, 2014), "to diminish the perception of adversity early in the emotion process and consequently to greatly diminish its negative emotional impact on ill-being" (St-Louis et al., 2021, p. 1 794). Harmonious passion is positively associated with cognitive reappraisal, which is in turn linked with wellbeing (St-Louis et al., 2021).

Conclusion

Historically, passion is known to be part of humanity, but the nature and function of passion has been debatable. Advancement in scholarly tools has provided varied perspectives from which passion can be viewed, including attempts to locate it in the brain's systems. This chapter presented the adaptive or maladaptive role of passion in different aspects of our lives. To avoid an apathetic and anhedonic state, it becomes imperative to emotionally regulate ourselves.

CHAPTER 9

Looking at You to See Me:
Exploring Empathy and
Compassion

Elsa Etokabeka
Melanie Moen

To care for you, I must care for me

After high school, Ophelia decided to become a clinical psychologist so that she could help others. Currently, she works with trauma patients at the Riverside hospital. She describes herself as empathetic and compassionate. Her husband and children often comment on her inclination to help the 'underdog' and take in stray animals. She also volunteers at a local shelter some weekends, and she runs a disability support group. Recently she has been complaining of headaches, feeling fatigued, and having nightmares, waking up in the middle of the night, distressed and sweating. She loves her job as a therapist and cannot imagine doing anything else. One morning, during a session with a patient who was recounting her trauma of being raped, Ophelia starts sweating and begins to mimic the patient's facial expressions. Ophelia also starts imagining herself being raped, experiencing physical pain in several body parts. The psychological and physiological reactions to the trauma of her patient become overwhelming to her. Her patient notices Ophelia's distress and becomes agitated and scared. When Ophelia jumps up and runs out of the room screaming, the patient starts crying. A few days later, Ophelia is diagnosed with *post-traumatic stress disorder* (PTSD), *empathetic distress*, and *compassion fatigue*. The head of the hospital, and also her friend, Dr Oscar Snipe, decides she must be booked off for three months, and her patients are referred to other therapists. Dr Snipe calls her in and recommends that she takes a long vacation.

Introduction

Confusion about empathy and compassion permeates literature. Compassion is thought to be closely related to qualities such as sympathy and empathy. *Empathy* is the ability to sense, feel and understand another's emotions, while *compassion* is defined as an emotional response to another's pain or suffering with an authentic desire to help. Hence, empathy is a cognitive and affective understanding of someone else's experience, while compassion is an affective response to pain and suffering (McCullough et al., 2022).

Empathy enables us to resonate with others' positive and negative feelings (Singer & Klimecki, 2014). In other words, the emotion encapsulates a person's ability to comprehend feelings of others (Aslan & Akyol, 2020). This includes evaluating experiences and events, and the outlook of others, which enables the means to share common emotions (Simon & Nader-Grosbois, 2021). The feelings evoked include compassion and sympathy, which is the reason empathy is often interchanged with both words. Compassion is an emotion that centres on the feeling of showing care, whereas sympathy involves the ability to understand the problem. When both compassion and sympathy are combined, they enable empathy (Spinrad & Gal, 2018). Interestingly, a person can understand a problem without caring; however, they cannot care without first understanding the problem. Therefore, when people empathise, they combine both these strengths.

Humans have strong social inclinations, such as engaging in conversations or attending events (Young, 2008). To facilitate effective communication, people often employ language skills to articulate information to others. Additionally, people also use their social abilities, such as empathy and perspective-taking, to infer the emotions and mental states of others (Van Leeuwen et al., 2018). The cognitive aptitude for making inferences about the beliefs, intentions, and thoughts of others is referred to as *mentalising*. This capability enables a person to comprehend that other people have their own opinions and ideas, which may differ from one's own. Conversely, the ability to share the feelings of others is known as *empathy* (Singer & Kilmecki, 2014). Empathy is defined as the ability to understand (i.e., cognitive empathy) and vicariously share (i.e., affective empathy) the emotional states of others, which is considered critical for prosocial behaviour (Depow et al., 2021).

Empathy is therefore a multilayered framework that incorporates the cognitive, affective, and behavioural operations (Ornaghi et al., 2020). The term embodies self-recognising thoughts, which assists one in placing oneself in someone else's shoes, as in the case of Ophelia (Spinrad & Gal, 2018). As a result, cognitive processes that occurred on the inside produced an outward feeling. Empathy comprises three parts, which include an occurrence, feeling, and differentiating perspectives. With occurrence, the idea encapsulates an event. This event presents a situation where the person would have to evaluate what has taken place (Aslan & Akyol, 2020). In evaluating and experiencing the event, emotions transpire based on knowledge that has been provided. The emotions that emerge often include concern, distress, or unease, which then enable the person to help or show compassion towards the other. In other words, the feeling occurs because it is first experienced by another person and does not originate within (or is created by) the self (Ornaghi et al., 2020).

Compassion is a feeling *for* and not feeling *with* the other. It embodies another person's suffering, accompanied by the motivation to help (Singer & Klimecki, 2014). According to Strauss et al. (2014), compassion consists of five elements: recognising suffering, understanding the universality of human suffering, feeling for the person suffering, tolerating uncomfortable feelings, and motivation to act/acting to alleviate suffering.

Differentiating between empathy and compassion

Empathy is defined as the ability to sense, feel, and understands another person's emotions; compassion is an emotional response to someone else's pain and suffering, with an authentic desire to help (Patel et al., 2019, p. 2). Empathy refers to one's general capacity to resonate with others' emotional states irrespective of their valence – positive or negative (Singer & Klimecki, 2014). In this case, empathy is taken to be an affective and cognitive grasp of another person's experience; whereas compassion is an affective response to pain and suffering (McCullough et al., 2022).

Empathy relates to the ability to cognitively understand or to emotionally feel what another person is experiencing or, more simply, to care for another person. Research shows that empathy among adults already starts in infancy (Zuckerman & Tronick, 2020). Therefore, children learn empathy and caring from their parents, teachers, and religion. Although parents and others talk to their children about values, children learn best when they see them in action, such as adults modelling empathic caring.

Although empathy is viewed as a single being, its existence contains different attributes. The three attributes include cognitive, affective, and behavioural empathy (Ornaghi et al., 2020). Cognitive empathy includes understanding how another person feels; this would require speaking or experiencing the matter to understand the event that has transpired. Affective empathy centres on feeling what the other people feel. Emotions become apparent and are then internalised; this enables understanding and feeling to both take place. Lastly, behavioural empathy mostly centres on actions of help towards others. These actions include showing care and concern, as well as supporting fellow peers (Hodgkins, 2022). Together, the cognitive, affective, and behavioural frameworks determine how a person responds to a situation; this is why the three attributes relate to empathy.

As previously mentioned, compassion is described as a feeling of concern for someone else's suffering, which is accompanied by the motivation to help. It is, therefore, regarded as a prosocial motivation (Singer & Kilmecki, 2014). Strauss et al. (2014, p. 16) describe compassion as "being moved by another's suffering and wanting to help", while Crawford et al. (2014, p. 3 591) define compassion as "involving and awareness of or sensitivity to the pain and suffering of others that results in taking verbal, nonverbal or physical action to remove, reduce or alleviate the impact of such affliction." The authors further state that compassion encompasses an openness of attention, awareness of suffering, motivation, and action. A compassionate mentality is highlighted, which includes attributes such as kindness, gentleness, concern, tolerance, and affection to name but a few.

While the attributes of compassion centre on the motivation to care, a capacity for sympathy and an ability to tolerate unpleasant emotions, compassion is also the capacity for empathic understanding, non-judgement and -condemnation (Gilbert, 2019). Compassion is characterised by distress tolerance and other-orientated concern for people. It is an openness to other's distress without suppressing or making the situation about oneself. This is why the word 'empathy' is typically described as conscientiousness or the ability to tolerate distress. There is a genuine concern for the victimised person and a focus on helping in a constructive way (Steinvik et al., 2013).

The origin and development of empathy and compassion

Although empathy and compassion have existed for centuries, the scientific study is relatively young. The term 'empathy' has its origins in the Greek word 'empatheia' (passion), which is composed of 'en' (in) and 'pathos' (feeling). The word compassion is derived from the Latin 'com' (with/together) and 'pati' (to suffer). It was later introduced into the English language through the French word 'compassion' (Singer & Kilmecki, 2014).

Empathy can be developed in various ways; this mostly occurs through cognitive development, as well as social experiences (Simon & Nader-Grosbois, 2021). Under cognitive development, Hoffman (2000) outlined five stages that lead towards the development of empathy; these include *newborn reactive cry*, where a baby cries as a result of hearing another baby cry); the *egocentric empathic distress* stage entails reacting to the other person's pain; the *quasi-egocentric empathic distress* stage recognises when someone feels pain and tries to alleviate it by means of action; under the *veridical empathic distress* stage, there is the ability to grasp the perspective of others and try to help, and lastly, the *empathic distress beyond the situation* stage includes understanding that people can feel emotions in various circumstances and not only in the present moment. Each stage represents different abilities to express emotions. These emotions can be noted in the ability to differentiate oneself, trying to understand or show concern, as well as engaging in actions that would help others (Hoffman, 2012). Hence, cognitive development is achieved through social interaction combined with life experiences. The result is what theorists consider to be maturity – a progress of understanding children attain over a period of time (Wagers & Kiel, 2019).

If we consider Piaget's development theory, empathy cannot develop without decentralisation first taking place. The term 'decentralisation' incorporates the ability to grasp the viewpoint of others instead of only focusing on one's own ideas – this state equates to outgrowing the ego stage (Ornaghi et al., 2020). One of the ways decentralisations may occur is through parents delegating social responsibilities to children, for example, participating in household chores, or by owning a pet and learning how to take care of it. Both these methods have been noted to develop care and concern in a person. It is believed that affection shown towards a chore or pet is also transferable to people (Poresky, 1990).

Piaget outlines four stages of children's cognitive development (Piaget, 1956). His theory explains how children cognitively mature by means of reasoning and analysing different situations. Since empathy involves the ability to understand, as well as share, the emotions of others, Piaget's cognitive development is a framework that explains how a child learns to understand the emotions of others (Piaget, 1978). The second stage in the cognitive development, which is most relevant to empathy, is called the *preoperational stage*. This stage clarifies the operation of a child's mind and how they begin to comprehend things (Levine & Munsch, 2016). During this stage, a child practises the use of language and memory, and how they think about things starts to evolve. During this phase, imagination develops, given that children often engage in make believe and start to comprehend the idea of time (notions about the past or future). The preoperational stage develops from the age of two and lasts until seven years (Marwaha et al., 2017). The more challenging aspect of the preoperational stage is the ability to understand cause-and-effect relationships. This is because children's intellect is rather illogical and very self-centred. In this phase, children are very egocentric (Piaget, 1978), where they view the world according to their own beliefs and perspectives. Their understanding is governed by their own outlook, therefore hindering the ability to understand perspectives other than their own (Gaspar & Esteves, 2022). The phase is greatly characterised by thinking of oneself and objectifying others; empathy is only shown towards children their own age. Empathy matures from the age of nine, when a child outgrows the preoperational stage and moves on to the next stage, called the *concrete operational stage* (Gaspar & Esteves, 2022).

Authors Singer and Klimecki (2014) investigated the neuroscientific perspectives of empathy. Functional Magnetic Resonance Imaging (fMRI) has demonstrated that engaging with someone else's emotions involves the activation of neural networks also implicated in experiencing those emotions firsthand. One particularly noteworthy approach to examining these *shared neuronal networks*, related to empathic encounters, is within the realm of pain (Lu et al., 2021). In paradigms exploring *empathy for pain*, participants undergoing scanning are generally subjected to painful stimuli on their own body parts, or exposed to images and/or cues signalling that another individual is presently enduring pain (Jauniaux et al., 2019). By comparing the brain activations triggered by firsthand experiences of pain with those exclusively prompted by observing another person in pain, researchers have consistently discovered evidence supporting the presence of shared neuronal networks (Khatibi et al., 2023; Kragel & LaBar, 2016). For instance, meta-analyses on studies related to empathy for pain have consistently identified the activation of a portion of the anterior insula and a specific segment of the anterior cingulate cortex. These activations were consistent both during the personal experience of pain and when empathetically sharing in the suffering of others (Jauniaux et al., 2019).

Significantly, the intensity of these empathy-related activations is influenced by how participants report experiencing negative emotions, while empathising with others (Khatibi et al., 2023). This was the case when Ophelia started sweating and mimicking facial expressions after hearing her patient's experience of being raped. Ophelia too started experiencing physical pain in several parts of her body. Although empathy has been extensively explored in the context of pain, similar paradigms have been applied to investigate empathy based on touch, disgust, taste, and social rewards. Depending on the specific emotion under examination, shared networks were observed in the somatosensory cortex for vicarious neutral touch, the medial orbitofrontal cortex for vicarious pleasant touch, the ventral striatum for shared social rewards, and parts of the anterior insula during empathetic responses to taste and disgust (refer to the chapter on disgust).

McCullough et al. (2022, p. 47), believe that "sympathy regulated by the virtues of tenderness and steadiness becomes compassion. Compassion is the affective capacity to engage in the experience of another and consequently to be moved (sympathy updated) to affective (tenderness updated) and self-disciplined (steadiness updated) engagement in another's experience and then to respond effectively to it." It needs to be practised on a regular basis to sustain its ability. Compassion is therefore the regular exercise of the affective capacity of a person to engage with another human being; this is to ultimately relieve distress and suffering. Its moral virtue generates and disciplines behaviour in a person.

From an evolutionary perspective, compassion can be traced back to Darwin's work. He stated that those communities that included the greatest number of sympathetic members would flourish and have the most offspring (Strauss et al., 2014). Compassion sometimes stems from the initial emphasis of self-preservation (safeguarding one's offspring); however, it extends concern and care of others (outside one's immediate family.) In primates, compassion may have developed as a favourable trait for mate selection and fostering cooperative bonds with individuals beyond kinship ties (Strauss et al., 2014). What distinguishes compassion from basic non-human caring is that human compassion requires a particular set of cognitive competencies. These competencies include a range of complex reasoning abilities enable mentalising, self-awareness and symbolic thinking. Hence, human empathy and compassion operates on a conscious awareness level (Gilbert, 2019).

Types of empathy and compassion

Empathy can further facilitate empathic distress, empathic anger, or compassion, which in turn results in different interpersonal behaviours. Excessive sharing of another's distress is described as *empathetic distress* (Steinvik et al., 2013). Empathetic distress refers to a strong aversive and self-orientated response to the suffering of others, accompanied by the desire to withdraw from a situation to protect oneself from excessive negative feelings (Kristeller & Johnson, 2005). Empathetic distress is also described as a phenomenon characterised by an amplified vicarious emotional reaction to a person's emotional turmoil. This entails the individual becoming so deeply immersed in the person's distress that they adopt and feel it as if it were their own. Research has indicated that females show more empathetic distress compared to males. This can be explained by the evolutionary history where females were mostly responsible for caretaking and supportive roles to ensure the survival of their offspring (Smith, 2015). In the vignette in the beginning of this chapter, Ophelia became extremely distressed when her patient started relaying her traumatic experience of being raped. Ophelia had an amplified vicarious reaction to her patient's distress, resulting in her escaping the traumatic experience to protect herself. Sadly, Ophelia should have realised long before this traumatic session that she needed self-care and support to buffer against her emotional turmoil.

Empathic anger is related to empathy when witnessing the unfair and or intentional harmful treatment of others. In other words, empathy may take the form of anger on the person who has been victimised. Empathetic anger is not only concerned with helping someone, but can also be associated with the desire to punish the person who is responsible for the distress of the victim (Steinvik et al., 2013). Additionally, *empathetic concern* is organised around the wellbeing of others and can include feelings of concern, sympathy, tenderness, compassion, softheartedness to name a few (Lin & Janice, 2020).

According to Cavanagh (1995), there are different types of compassion; these include authentic compassion, conditional compassion, gentle and tough compassion, easy and difficult compassion, and pseudo-compassion. *Authentic compassion* means that as much as humanly possible, one person sees, hears, and feels with the heart of the other person. *Conditional compassion* is negotiated: "I will be compassionate with you, if...", in other words, there is a condition associated with compassion. *Gentle compassion* is what most people have in mind when they think of compassion. For instance, giving the love and support to a family member who lost a loved one, while *tough compassion* relates to, for instance, a wife who places her alcoholic husband under an ultimatum to seek help for his addiction. *Easy compassion* is, for instance, showing compassion towards a woman who has lost her baby, or in the case of Ophelia, who showed compassion towards her patient who was raped. The situation evokes a natural reaction to compassion, while *difficult compassion* is, for instance, having empathy for a child molester who has cancer, although everyone needs compassion at some point in their life. *Pseudo-compassion* relates to false compassion that lacks one or more critical elements (affective or behavioural) of true compassion. For instance, a man who shows compassion for his neighbour who lost his job but does not reach out to assist him (Cavanagh, 1995).

Another type of compassion is *compassionate love*. Underwood (cited in Fehr et al., 2014, p. 576) defines *compassionate love* as "attitudes and actions related to giving of self for the good of the other." Underwood's view on compassionate love also includes actions that promote the flourishing of the other and not just reducing distress. Compassionate love includes a deeper introspection by setting aside your own agenda for the sake of the good of another person (Kristeller & Johnson, 2005). Berscheid (in Fehr,

2014, p. 576), defines compassionate love as "concern for another's welfare and taking actions to promote it, regardless of whether those actions are perceived to result in future benefits to the self." Similarly, Kim et al. (2022) describe compassionate love as a type of other-focused love defined as an affective, cognitive, and behavioural attitude toward others out of concern or care for them. It is believed that compassionate love is a more enduring type of attitude, as compared to empathy or other related constructs (e.g., forgiveness and compassionate love are similar in that they both involve one's desire to do good).

Compassionate care is "a deep feeling of connectedness with the experience of human suffering that requires personal knowing of the suffering of others and a virtuous response that seeks to address the suffering and needs of a person through relational understanding and action" (Coffey et al., 2019, p. 2341). Compassionate care is also described in terms of the relationship that exists between vulnerable human beings that must be nurtured (Coffey et al., 2019). Compassionate care requires understanding others' values, establishing relationships with them, and responding to others in meaningful ways (Pehlivan & Güner, 2020).

Measuring empathy and compassion

With the ability to show empathetic characteristics, one then wonders what tests can be conducted to determine actions and feelings that pertain towards the emotion? In essence, how can empathy be identified or measured? Fortunately, literature highlights different ways that this can be done. Since empathy involves concerning emotions, one would need to analyse feelings that centre on care, worry or distress. Fury, anger, sadness, and fear are the emotions often associated with sensing empathy (Simon & Nader-Grosbois, 2021), often because it enables the understanding and experiences of events. Hence, researchers develop tests that includes the means to identify these feelings. Apart from tests assessing empathy as an emotion, we also find performance-based measures such as the Young Children's Empathy Measure (YCEM) (Poresky, 1990), and the Kids' Empathic Development Scale (KEDS). The apparatuses evaluate actions and behaviour that are associated with empathetic characteristics, to particularly show the ability to understand, as well as share the same feelings as another (Poresky, 1990).

Compassion is mostly measured as compassionate care in health and spiritual settings, which is assessed by using the Compassionate Care Assessment Tool (CCAT) (Burnell & Agan, 2013). This tool measures both the constructs of compassion and care, which comprise 28 sub-facets. Additionally, the Spiritual Needs Questionnaire (Galek et al., 2005) is used to assess seven different constructs, of which compassion is one. Finally, the Caring Behaviors Inventory (CBI-24) (Wolf et al., 1994) is often used in medical settings to assess compassion-related behaviour, for instance showing concern and meeting patient needs (Burnell & Agan, 2013).

The advantages of empathy and compassion

There are various benefits that result from having empathy. For example, cognitive, social, and emotional development transpires. With regards to cognitive development, this can be seen in the ability to analyse different perspectives. Empathy helps us to understand different experiences of people. To be empathetic, one needs to pay attention to, as well as analyse a problem. The recipient thereafter needs to consider possible solutions and develops problem solving skills. Problem solving in return promotes mental flexibility. The final example of cognitive development includes asking questions and conversating. Engaging as well as sharing information allows the ability to consider the knowledge of others (Aslan & Akyol, 2020).

In terms of emotional development, some of the evident examples include the ability to express emotions, acknowledge the emotions they feel, handle one's emotions constructively, engage about what you feel, understand some of the reasons and effects of emotions, as well as regulate certain distresses cause by empathy. These skills help people to understand emotions, as well as communicate them effectively (Spinrad & Gal, 2018). Lastly, social development is enhanced when a person manages to uphold their behaviour in socially appropriate ways. This includes being open to others' perspectives (cooperate), respect social conventions or rules, understand the emotions of others, communicate more effectively with others and resolve inter-personal problems actively and in a positive manner.

The importance of compassion is recognised in many divisions of society. There are several religious traditions that place compassion at the centre of the belief system. In Buddhism for instance, loving-kindness and compassion meditations are important practices to counter negative interpersonal attitudes (Zhou et al., 2023). Several professional bodies, such as education, healthcare and the justice system, also emphasise the importance of compassion and incorporate these principles in their guidelines and ethos (Strauss et al., 2014). Gilbert (2019) is of the opinion that compassion is an identity by which many strive to live, in other words, a desire to become a compassionate person. The lifestyle is linked to mindful living, where a person strives to be helpful and not harm others.

Self-compassion is an important self-regulatory strategy to cope with personal pain, failure, inadequacies, and uncomfortable feelings. In the case study at the beginning of the chapter, Ophelia was booked off due to compassion fatigue. One could argue that she did not have good self-regulatory strategies in place to assist her in dealing with emotionally taxing situations. It is believed that people who are compassionate toward themselves can mitigate the harmful effects of self-critical thinking when they are depressed. Multiple sessions of self-compassion interventions have positive outcomes in most health domains, with the strongest effects observed on global physical health, functional immunity, sleep, and danger avoidance (Phillips & Hine, 2021).

Support and nurturing from significant others at an early age can also enhance self-compassion (Zhang et al., 2023). Self-compassion has been associated with a negative predictor to anger and violence. Self-compassion also has a stronger negative predictor of personal distress and shame, and a stronger positive predictor to social functioning in sex offenders. There is also a strong link between self-compassion and positive social connectedness (Morley, 2015).

Hindrances to empathy and compassion

Struggling to empathise has been linked to various disorders, which include psychopathy, and anti-social personality disorder. The disorders mark little emotional responses, as well as poor behavioural skills. Hence, empathy enables emotional understanding and behavioural control to be able to effectively care and engage with others (Schonert-Reichl et al., 2011). In understanding the benefits of having empathy, the literature also elaborates on individuals with little to no empathetic skills. One of the first problems of not having empathy, involves unfavourable social behaviour, like saying hurtful things or only satisfying one's own needs. When people behave with little/no empathy, this can lead to arguments and aggression due to provocations or creating unpleasant environments (Camassa, 2024; Larson et al., 2024). In fact, children and adults with low empathic abilities can display anti-social behaviour (Miller & Eisenberg, 1988). The inability to understand emotions and other's experiences limits the means to talk, as well as share ideas. This could ultimately lead to a person withdrawing from society, because they struggle to engage with others. Another problem concerns communication, such as the inability to provide a suitable response after hearing a distressful event (Simon & Nader-Grosbois, 2021). Responses indicate whether the matter has been understood, therefore, inappropriate answers eliminate chances of helping others in distress. The ego prevents the ability to consider someone else's thoughts (Wagers & Kiel, 2019).

The development of empathy can be affected by various negative experiences. Especially the case where negative experiences are long, intense, and frequent. An example of a negative experience is adversity, given that it has been found to cause developmental delays, like the inability to manage and express one's emotion. The unfortunate problem with adversity is that it tends to create a negative outlook of life. Adversity also incites negative emotions for example, anger, aggression, conflict, and seclusion (Simon & Nader-Grosbois, 2021). Wagers and Kiel (2019) noted that these negative emotions further lead to internal and external problems hindering empathy from effectively developing. Internal problems can be understood as cognitive conditions that embody negative feelings, which include feeling anxious, depressed, and desiring isolation. External problems encompass negative behaviour towards others; these include aggression, irritability, or defiance noted in a person. Negative emotions hinder the ability to engage with positive emotions and without this ability, it becomes challenging to develop positive emotional skill (Wagers & Kiel, 2019). Both problems prevent the means to show care, concern, or consideration of others, which embodies empathy and compassion.

There is a growing concern in our society that compassion is a dying virtue, gradually being smothered by narcissism, competition, prejudice, and revenge (Berardi et al., 2020; Gilbert, 2021). Psychologists and philosophers agree that compassion is at the heart of the behaviour that keeps individuals, families, institutions, and societies alive through caring, altruism, justice, morality, and love (Sugianto, 2020). There are, however, certain *fears*, *blocks* and *resistance* that can hinder compassion from developing. Certain *fears* might relate to becoming more empathetically compassionate; one might fear becoming overwhelmed by distress and feeling personally undeserving. *Blocks* can relate to wanting to but not knowing how to show compassion in certain contexts. For instance, working at a hospital where one has limited time to spend with a patient, one might not know how to confront hospital management who prescribes these time limitations that hinder relationship building and compassion. *Resistance* is when individuals are neither frightened nor blocked, but simply do not want to be compassionate. For instance, when they do not want to help immigrants because immigrants are too costly to the country (Gilbert, 2019).

Compassion has also been associated to prosocial lying. Prosocial lies are false statements made with the intention of misleading and benefitting someone else. Prosocial lies are intended to benefit the other and have minimal or substantial consequences. Altruistic white lies are also associated with compassion and are lies that benefits the listener at the expense of the liar (Fang et al., 2020). Although prosocial lies can sometimes be deemed altruistic and compassionate, they might have some negative consequences for both the liar and the party who is lied to.

The importance of enhancing empathy

Empathy is important and should be explored for various reasons. The first reason is that many children still face social development concerns that include the inability to recognise or manage their emotions. Understanding the nature of empathy grants the opportunity to study children's socio-emotional strengths, as well as their weaknesses (Simon & Nader-Grosbois, 2021). One of the biggest socio-emotional conflicts faced in schools today is the issue of bullying. Since empathy incorporates the ability to understand the perspective of others, bullying could be combatted by means of creating an environment where the children involved are able to share their thoughts, feelings, and experiences on the matter (Spinrad & Gal, 2018). Learning from these different angles could strengthen the existing body of literature.

Having empathy and compassion cultivates the means to harness social and emotional skills. The opportunity to help others combat externalising behaviour since it teaches caring and considering others, understanding their needs, as well as cultivating patience. Helping others teaches us to comprehend positive and negative outlooks people experience (Poresky, 1990).

Social interaction has been one of the greatest ways children learn. This is because children obtain the means to observe and practise their experiences. The most emphasised form of teaching empathy is done through parental interactions (Schonert-Reichl & Oberle, 2011). Parents are the people closest to the child, therefore, they are the primary group that would teach children how to engage with others. If parental interaction with the child excludes attitudes and behaviour of empathy, the child becomes accustomed to never expressing it (Spinrad & Gal, 2018). Parental warmth is believed to enhance empathy. This is because the same attitude and actions shown at home will most likely be practised outside, fostering the ability to become nurturing. Parental interaction raises the awareness of our emotions; specifically, to help identify and comprehend our experiences (Ornaghi et al., 2020).

Outside parental interaction, empathy can also be developed through reinforcement. Reinforcement can be understood as actions that strengthen a particular behaviour or attitude. Empathic reinforcement in this case transpires in two different ways – through physical reward and non-physical (intangible) reward. Physical reward comprises receiving gifts for helpful behaviour and forming friendships, while intangible rewards relate to showing approval by means of action rather than offering gifts; these actions would include praising or encouraging prosocial behaviours. It is worth noting that the purpose of instilling reinforcement is to mostly show the benefits and goodness that come from helping others (Spinrad & Gal, 2018). We get to expose the feeling and knowledge that comes with helping others; this would be to inspire and promote prosocial behaviour with others.

Apart from a person's parental upbringing, there are different ways empathy can be developed. Some of these forms can be seen through activities that help understand the perspective of others. According to Aslan and Akyol (2020), understanding other peoples' point of view plays an important role in developing empathic behaviour and prosocial skills. Furthermore, it helps people engage effectively and settles inter-personal challenges in more positive ways (Battistich, 2003).

Enhancing compassion

There are several ways to enhance compassion, both on a personal and interpersonal level, but also through therapeutic interventions. These interventions include self-compassion, compassionate communication, compassion focused therapy (CFT), and meditative practice, which will be briefly explained next.

Self-compassion is an important concept in enhancing self-love and limiting negative emotions. Self-compassion is described as the non-judgemental acceptance of one's own suffering, while also directing kindness towards oneself. Self-compassion has been found to modify negative emotions and elicit more positive emotions. Self-compassion involves three dimensions namely self-kindness (to treat oneself instead of self-criticism or judgement); common humanity (acknowledging that suffering is a common human experience), and mindfulness (accepting suffering while holding it in balanced awareness versus over-identification with suffering) (Inwood & Ferrari, 2018).

Compassionate communication is often used in educational settings, but also as part of social justice and human possibility. Compassionate communication is founded on language and communication skills that strengthen our ability to remain human, even in trying situations. Compassionate communication trains us to observe carefully, and to be able to specify behaviours and conditions that are affecting us (Hao, 2011).

Compassion focused therapy (CFT) is an integrated form of psychotherapy developed for working with people who have high levels of shame. CFT has been developed as a therapeutic approach to support people who have endured shame because of their early life experiences. Compassion fatigue, as in the case of Ophelia, is often diagnosed in clinicians who work with trauma patients. Techniques suggested by clinicians who work with trauma and emotionally taxing cases include "information-processing techniques: gaining distance by imagining that a patient's trauma narrative was just a movie; splitting one's focus so that one was partly an 'objective observer'; taking time out by pushing trauma images aside, thinking about other things, and then regrouping; and reminding oneself of past successes. Breathing and relaxing techniques are also used, while many clinicians also find consulting with colleagues helpful" (Taylor et al., 2017).

Meditative practice has been known to cultivate experiences of compassion and loving kindness. A two-stage model is proposed. The first stage involves an awareness of habitual reactions and disengagement from the usual preoccupation with self-reinforcing, self-defeating, or self-indulgent behaviours and reactions. Seeing that compassion requires engagement with others, the second step involves the development of compassion through meditation, which involves focused engagement with others through empathy and love. There is a belief that as the self transcends, the mind is open to the possibility to full engagement with others. Once the preoccupation with the self diminishes, the openness to others increases (Kristeller & Johnson, 2005). Marshall et al. (2015) concur that self-compassion moderates the influence of self-esteem on mental health. Low self-esteem has little effect on mental health when self-compassion is high. People should be taught that every person is imperfect and feels inadequate sometimes, therefore it is important to treat oneself with kindness, patience, and forgiveness.

Conclusion

There is still a need to balance the extent to which we should be empathetic and compassionate towards others. If we overstep our own boundaries of empathy and compassion, we might end up in a spiral of self-destruction, similar to what Ophelia experienced.

However, it has been established that empathy and compassion have more positive outcomes than negative. There are several benefits to practising empathy and compassion as the development of these emotions include cognitive and social development to name but a few (Riess, 2017). Both emotional experiences are focused on the wellbeing of the self, as well as others. Both empathy and compassion are also important emotions in understanding ourselves and others. These are emotions that should be developed and practiced ensuring a society that is sensitive towards the needs and experiences of our fellow human beings.

CHAPTER 10

Trust: Taking Risks Until Scepticism
is Trounced

Judite Ferreira-Prévost

Sketching the circle of trust

After a long holiday, Ophelia was back at it again – she really missed working with people in the community. Ophelia looked at each person sitting in the circle before her. Each had allowed a different story to be sketched on their face, but all had come tonight for the same reason – to be vulnerable but also to redeem their confidence. After the necessary introductions, Ophelia asked each person to express their understanding of the concept of trust, using as many senses as they wished. A paraphernalia of pictures, stationery, paints, instruments, moulding clay and even spices were laid bare for their use.

Pono took immediately to the moulding clay, shaping and twisting it into a pikorua as his mother had shown him – intertwined and reminding him of the strong bonds he had with his family and friends.

Shinrai picked up an old, rusty key and thought back to the woman who had held the one to his heart. As he stared at Pono's clay creation, it prompted him to think of how she had used more sign language near the end when she could not talk, slowly forming two fists and rotating them towards each other before eventually collapsing one on top of the other – I trust.

Thembeka was drawn to the easel and started adding paint to the curved trunk and flapping ears of the animal she associated with loyalty and steadfastness. She could smell the dust on its rough skin and hear its trumpeting as she formed the brushstrokes.

Tom remained seated in his chair. He had attended these kinds of groups before, and it had not made a difference. It was not something his family or culture were used to, and he did not see the point of engaging. He wondered if trying to think about it differently would make a difference.

Fidel had gone through some rough storms lately, and paused in front of the photo of the lighthouse. He could almost hear the waves crashing against the rocks, rupturing into minute and defenceless droplets. He smelled the salt air and tasted it against his face. At least there was that one light of beacon that kept him from going astray.

Introduction

Trust is generally accepted to be the most important building block or adhesive for effective and healthy social interactions. It can act as a strong pillar in relationships and strengthen connections with friends, foes, and systems and is therefore a vital ingredient in our social survival. Just as it can give strength, trust is also ironically fragile and prone to break easily (Ma et al., 2018). It is therefore important to understand as much as possible about trust as it can influence every interaction we experience in life.

As this chapter about trust forms part of a greater volume of work on human experiences and emotions, we could understand the presumption that trust can only be linked to affect and feeling. However, from all the emotions you read about in this book, trust may possibly surprise you the most and display a myriad of elements and dimensions.

It is not easy to define something as complex as trust. However, in our attempt, we rope in various perspectives and theories regarding the origin or development of trust, to recent empirical findings, including the possibility of trusting a non-human (Riedl, 2021). The biological, psychoanalytical and psychosocial approaches (Klein, 1935; Erikson, 1963; Winnicott, 1965; Bowlby, 1969) will be given preference in the attempt to understand the origins of trust.

We will also briefly explore distrust and discover how, although associated with negative valences of emotions, it can be used positively (Kujala et al., 2016) to better manage our decisions and relationships. Finally, we will discover possible ways to manage trust in emotion, belief, decision and behaviour. As you explore this concept further, be conscious of the words and images that resonate most with you in this chapter.

Definition of trust

As the vignette at the beginning of the chapter suggests, trust evokes different images for different people. A variety of definitions and perspectives have been provided over the years with words such as expectation, vulnerability, risk-taking, belief, and integrity being cited.

Although three decades old, a definition for trust still often quoted in literature is that of Mayer et al.'s (1995). Trust is described as a willingness to be vulnerable to the actions of another person, while also expecting those actions to align with what one deems important and ethical, irrespective of whether there is control or not. Therefore, rather than an emotion, this definition implies an approach, behaviour or decision that is consciously chosen, where one is aware of the risks but also expects and presumes the goodwill of those involved. This is a more optimistic manner of viewing trust and is again reflected in the work of Filkowski, Anderson and Haas (2016, p. 326), who describe trust as a "positively-valenced interpersonal attitude".

Kee and Knox (1970) developed one of the first conceptualisations of trust more than half a century ago. They focused on an individual's previous experience and disposition, as well as the context (situational factors) that influences us, eventually trusting another person's motives and ability (or not). Motives and abilities, as well benevolence and integrity, were also noted by Mayer et al. (1995), who emphasised the trustworthiness of the person being trusted, and how these aspects could influence the dynamics of a trust relationship.

Ingenhoff and Sommer (2010) asserted that trust is multi-faceted and dynamic. It comprises different aspects, such as thought, feeling, norm, motivation and behaviour, and can change and evolve over time and space, depending on the role-players and contexts. The facets or dimensions of trust – the cognitive, affective, social and behavioural aspects – are now elucidated, whereafter the role-players in a trust relationship – the trustor and trustee, as well as the actual context in which the role-players interact – will be explored.

Dimensions of trust

Some scholars (Christie, 2012; Kujala et al., 2016; Lockey, 2017; Lauharatanahirun & Aimone, 2021; Saleem et al., 2020) acknowledge the cognitive, affective and behavioural dimensions of trust, whether it is played out inter-personally, between people in a relationship or organisation, or intra-personally, within oneself (Kryazh & Grankina-Sazonova, 2018). At times, trust can be viewed even as impersonal, when it refers to trust of an abstract conception, such as the future or the world or a large organisation, such as the government.

Cognitive trust or cognitive aspects of trust refer mainly to thoughts, belief, knowledge and information processing, including what we think of another's capabilities. In the vignette at the start of this chapter, Tom, although reluctant to participate in the group, begins to value the importance of how his thoughts, and specifically how his thinking is different to the ways his family and culture, and how this could ultimately lead him to trust and engage more. Affective trust or affective components of trust link to emotions, moods, values and interests, and is particularly important when the information we have at our disposal is lacking. How we feel (e.g., our mood) and how we feel about others (e.g., their welfare) may have long-lasting effects on the decision to trust or not. There is also inevitably a social dimension as trust is predominantly interpersonal and involves some form of social risk (Lauharatanahirun & Aimone, 2021). Within this interpersonal relationship, Zhang (2021) proposes two dimensions related to trust, namely one that is other-focused, dependent on the trustee, and one that is self-focused, dependent on our traits and inclination to trust or not.

There are therefore numerous variables and dimensions to consider when trying to define, understand or influence trust. Apart from the biological, cognitive, emotional and social aspects of the person trusting, the environment and one's learned experiences all vie for attention in how trust develops. All these factors need to be considered not only as they pertain to the trustor, but also to the trustee – the person or entity being trusted (or not). We now focus our attention on these role-players.

The trustor

Jones and Shah (2016) refer to the trustor as the individual rendering trust judgments. It is the person (or entity in the case of a group or organisation) who experiences the feelings, thoughts, expectations and ultimate behaviour associated with trusting, or not trusting. The trustee, by implication, is the one being trusted.

Theories and models of trust that have been proposed and adapted over the last few decades have gradually acknowledged the influence of the trustor (and not only the trustee) on the trust relationship. Previous experience and dispositional factors, such as motivational orientation, personality and attitudes (Kee & Knox, 1970), as well as perception of risk (Mayer et al., 1995), expectations and the willingness to be vulnerable (Lockey, 2017), along with mood, emotional intelligence and sense of control (Christie, 2012) are all acknowledged as being significant to the dynamics of a trust relationship.

Research from various studies has noted that trust behaviour is impacted by our personal beliefs, attitudes towards taking risk, and our tendency towards altruism (Chetty et al., 2020), as well as what we consider and expect (according to our cultural background) to be appropriate and the norm for the particular context (Matthiesen et al., 2022). Chuah et al. (2016) noted in their study that people who are similar in religiosity and affiliations, tend to trust each other more and have trust reciprocated, particularly within their own groups. Those who are outside these groups may also tend to believe that religious others in general are probably more trustworthy.

There appears to be a strong link between trust and overall wellbeing. In Young and McGrath (2021), health and longevity correlated positively with trust, as did character traits, such as kindness, self-inhibition, curiosity and cooperation. Trust was furthermore found to facilitate the relationship between emotional intelligence and psychological wellbeing and resilience (Kryazh & Grankina-Sazonova, 2018). If we as trustors are aware of and understand our own emotions, as well as those of others, and if we can manage and adapt to these emotions appropriately, then our willingness to trust others will result in us being more self-confident, resilient, purposeful and socially content.

The dyadic model of trust in relationships introduced by Simpson and Vieth (2021, p. 19) reminds us that neither "the level nor the trajectory of trust in relationships can be fully understood without considering the dispositions and actions of both relationship partners." Now that we have looked at the one relationship partner of the trustor, we move on to explore the other, namely the trustee.

The trustee

The ambivalence, benevolence and integrity (ABI) model of Mayer et al. (1995) focuses on the trustworthiness of the person being trusted, namely the trustee, with particular attention on the ability, benevolence and integrity of the trustee. This is also echoed in Matthiesen et al. (2022), who highlight the importance of the trustee's competence, as well as moral calibre in the trusting relationship. In order to be trusted, the trustee should be capable of doing and being what they profess and should actualise this in goodwill.

In their study of various literature, Simpson and Vieth (2021) differentiated trustees according to the contexts of their relationships. The following are some examples and findings:

> **Trustee as a stranger:** the more willing we are to share of ourselves and be open to experiences, the more trusting we could be of those seemingly different to us. Having common social issues, however, facilitates this process.

> **Trustee as a work colleague:** this context is usually an involuntary one with the result that one could be forced to trust someone for the sake of cohesion and to get a project completed. Again, this process is facilitated if we are perceptive enough to how others view us as being either trustworthy or untrustworthy. Saleem et al. (2020) also found that servant leadership – leading by example and holding high standards of morality – will most likely motivate employees to trust their leader and be task-orientated.

> **Trustee as a family member or friend:** it is assumed that trust is generally high in this context, although trust is made easier if the family member or friend displays self-control and behaves appropriately. Ma et al. (2018) also found that children's interpersonal trust in someone will improve if the other person apologises for a wrongdoing.

> **Trustee as a romantic partner:** it bodes generally well when both partners in a romantic relationship trust each other, rather than only the one. Partners tend to trust each other more and are even more open to forgiving the other person's past wrongdoings if they believe there is commitment to remain in and promote the relationship. When partners trust each other more, they also tend to adapt better to changing roles, such as if they take on the role of parenthood. In the case of one of our story characters, Shinrai, there seems to have been a change in the ability of his partner to communicate as she had done before, resorting to sign language. The trust and bond between them, however, appears to have remained strong, through the adaptation to change.

Many variables can affect the assumptions and findings mentioned above and nothing is fool-proof or even always fair. The reputation of the trustee for one, and by implication the trustor's previous knowledge, can significantly affect and even bias judgement about trustworthiness (Bellucci & Park, 2020; Brudner et al., 2021). The bias could extend to preventing the trustor from revising their opinion of the trustee, even when the situation deems it necessary and beneficial to do so.

Lee et al. (2022) draw attention not only to the trustor and trustee as individuals in the trust relationship, but also to their combined and interactive experiences together. Just as certain chemicals remain inert if left alone but are reactive when put together, each interpersonal exchange brings forth its unique reactions and outcomes.

Apart from the trustor and trustee, the context within which the individuals in a relationship exist and interact, in terms of space and time, is also significant. These contextual dimensions of space and time are briefly outlined below.

The space and time

The dimensions of space and time affect and are affected by the trustor and trustee and are crucial in understanding trust holistically. Trust appears differently in different contexts of relationships. The degree of control, power dynamics, and role expectations vary significantly, depending on whether the relationship is with a stranger, romantic partner, work colleague, family or friend. As an example, we presume that you would have a greater sense of control with a close friend or family than with your colleague, boss or even a stranger. An even greater sense of control is proposed in a relationship with a professional, such as a counsellor, where we possibly impel ourselves to confidently trust the other person in therapeutic trust or a type of 'self-fulfilling prophecy' (Pace, 2020, p. 3). Such professionals might be perceived in troubling times as the lighthouse or beacon of trust, just as described in the earlier story through Fidel's character.

Interestingly, and contrary to what has just been mentioned, Matthiesen et al. (2022, p. 669) implied that we might not have as much control over trust as we think. They took a stance, based on the work of the philosopher Knud E. Løgstrup, that trust is "a spontaneous and sovereign expression of life" and that, not only do we have little control over trust, but can also not force ourselves to experience it, nor expect or impose it on others.

Over space, various contexts lend themselves to experiencing trust to a greater or lesser degree. We would naturally feel more confident and be perceived possibly as more trustworthy in a space that is familiar to us and in which we can prove to others that we have the necessary capabilities and understanding. Similarly, we would possibly tend to trust those who emit this confidence in 'their space'. As an example, it would make sense to trust your doctor's advice in a hospital but not necessarily their opinion on plumbing problems you are facing at home!

Over time and developmentally, we perceive trust differently throughout our lifetime and experiences. Typically, a baby will trust its primary caregiver and gradually become warier of strangers. Trust and mistrust form part of the psychosocial 'crisis' that Erik Erikson (1963) suggested infants must experience in the first of eight stages. Early childhood, as well as later-life social experiences, affect how we trust throughout life. As children mature and become more aware of others around them, the 'who', 'what' and 'how' to trust become more complicated, as more variables are considered in the decision-making.

Now that we have a better understanding of what trust is and what it looks like in different contexts, we explore from where it possibly arises.

Origin of trust

Trust has been studied largely in the disciplines of philosophy, psychology and sociology. Recently the study of trust has also added significant value in the fields of business and management (organisational trust). According to Lockey (2017), there is historically and predominantly cognitive and behavioural approaches to trust in the literature, with a focus on reasoning, decision-making and the ultimate outcomes of these processes. Other theories have, however, also recognised the relational, affective and moral dimensions of trust, as well as neurological and genetic factors that have proven to play important roles in this regard. We explore the origins of trust through neurological and genetic lenses, as well as through psychosocial theories of development.

Neurological and genetic factors

Our tendency to trust and our choices on who is deemed trustworthy, appears to be closely linked to neural activity in certain regions of the brain. Studies have shown that activity is noted particularly in the ventromedial prefrontal cortex, anterior insula and amygdala (Haas et al., 2015; Filkowski et al., 2016), as well as the temporoparietal junction, posterior cingulate cortex and frontoparietal regions (Bellucci & Dreher, 2021). These areas are often associated with, amongst other functions, emotional regulation, sensory information processing, decision-making, memory and behaviour.

In the forebrain, the hypothalamus synthesises oxytocin – unique because it not only is a hormone, but also acts as a neurotransmitter, chemically stimulating our neurons in the brain to communicate better with each other. Oxytocin is informally known as the 'feel-good' hormone, because it is associated with pleasant emotions and found to lessen social anxiety by decreasing the amygdala's reactivity to fear (Baumgartner et al., 2008). Oxytocin plays an integral part in mother-child bonding (attachment theory), regulation of stress responses (Takayanagi & Onaka, 2021), social behaviour, and inevitably emotions that influence social decision-making (Engelmann & Fehr, 2017).

Zak (2017) and Diaz-Dorronsoro (2020) confirm the importance of oxytocin in the work environment, asserting that actions such as hugging or acts that make one feel good, enable people to be more generous, confident and cooperative and to develop a feeling of trust. Krueger et al. (2012) are also of the belief that oxytocin enhances trust, and that trust behaviour is inherited, reliably correlating it with a genetic variation in the oxytocin gene.

Reimann et al. (2017) endorse the importance of genetics and found in their study that trust behaviour is significantly affected by heritability and furthermore reinforced by our unique experiences throughout life. They also purport (i.e., referring to 2008 research by Cesarini et al.) that because certain genes help regulate oxytocin, it follows that trust is influenced by genetic factors.

Although neurological and biological factors are key to understanding the origins of trust, our psychosocial development is paramount, as trust can never be fully comprehended outside a social setting. Trust needs people to be realised in the psychosocial space of relationship.

Psychosocial stages of development

Erikson's theory of psychosocial development (1963) proposes that humans develop through eight stages from birth to death, and that specific challenges or 'crises' need to be mastered at each of these stages, so that one can progress psychosocially to the next level.

The first stage covers the first 18 months of life and involves overcoming the tension or crisis of *trust versus mistrust*. It proposes that if an infant has its basic needs met and regularly experiences security and love, it should develop the quality of hope and become more willing to trust others and itself. Should the opposite be experienced, where the child is neglected or inconsistently fed, bathed, clothed and cared for, the seed of mistrust and insecurity could likely be planted.

Being the first stage of life, this period therefore forms the foundation of trust (or distrust) for future relationships that we will have in life. Furthermore, it is likely that this foundation, affecting all types of relationships and associations, would also most likely have a significant impact on the formation of our personality (which includes the view of ourselves) and our view of the world around us.

The first psychosocial stage is comparable to the object relations and attachment theories explained in the following section. It also underscores the importance of a safe environment and secure primary relationship in early childhood education for the development of trust in future relationships.

Theories and models of trust

Object relations and attachment theories

Object relations theory – often associated with the works of Melanie Klein (1932) and Donald Winnicott (1965), amongst others – emphasises our earliest childhood experiences and particularly our relationship with our mother or significant other. The 'object' refers to the internalised image we have of our significant other, or even of a part of them. Initially, this image is experienced as a part of ourselves, in a similar way that a baby views its mother's breast as part of itself. A 'good' object, such as parenting that is attuned to the needs of the child, enables ego development and empowers the infant to differentiate itself gradually from its mother, bridge the gap between inner and outer realities, and express itself freely. Such an association with a stable object will lead to confidence and wellbeing and a higher probability of trusting others. When the relationship with the object is characterised by inconsistency, neglect and absence, the child may become fearful, anxious and distrustful of others. Ultimately, maturity is evident when one can accept and adapt to the ambivalences and complexities of life and relationships in a coherent way of living (Mueller, 2023).

Like object relations theory, attachment theory, often associated with Bowlby (1969), promotes the importance of young children's bonds with their primary caregiver to effect emotional development and healthy social interactions later in life. Rather than mental images, it advocates for real and physical attachments with at least one primary caregiver (often the mother) and proposes that a high level of trust with those who are closest to us growing up, can help us manage stressful situations better and bond easier with adults who are responsive and consistent. Simpson (2007) further notes that those reported to be securely attached or with a high self-esteem, also appear to trust more in their relationships. Such bonds remind us of the pikorua that Pono was forming out of clay in the story at the beginning of the chapter.

A model that links closely to attachment theory is the Circle of Security, created by Cooper, Hoffmann and Powell (2017). The circle refers to a psychological space in which children feel safe to explore, make mistakes, learn, love and be loved. The model represents the significant other or caregiver as two strong and open hands: one hand acts as a secure base sending out and encouraging the child to explore and take risks while still assuring it will watch over and revel in the child's experiences; while the other hand acts as a safe haven, inviting the child back for protection, comfort and validation. Such a space creates a sense of belonging and enables those within it to trust, but also be more trusting.

Social learning theory

The final approach offered as a possible explanation for the foundation of trust highlights relationships with people and situations, rather than an introspective approach. Albert Bandura's social learning theory purports that learning occurs when we interact directly with the environment, especially through what we observe and experience. We use the feedback we receive from others' behaviour and responses to determine whether what they say also matches what they do – in essence, whether we can trust them.

From the beginning, humans have had to discern trust in others, as well as display trusting behaviour in themselves, to survive and ultimately evolve. Christie (2012, p. 40) adds that the "[i]nterplay between one's values, attitudes, moods and emotions... enables trust to develop over time" and that it is important to be aware of how others are feeling in order to know if we can trust them.

Simpson and Vieth (2021) assert that trust in ourselves and in others is not so much an issue of genetics, as many other human traits and abilities seem to be, but that it ultimately stems from and is developed through interpersonal and cultural processes. As we interact with our environments and gather information from others, we start forming impressions about who is trustworthy or not. Similarly, Van Lange (2015) shares what he believes to be "basic lessons on trust". These include the conviction that culture outweighs genetics in its influence on trust, and that social interactions with people as well as networks and media form the very foundation of trust. Although we might tend to underestimate the trustworthiness of others, we are in a learning process, admittedly shaped by our earlier experiences and knowledge, but changing and adapting to what we experience interpersonally.

Bellucci and Park (2020, p. 85) caution that social learning can become "a learning impairment" when the impressions and ultimate beliefs we form about others regarding their trustworthiness, become habits that are difficult to change. These habits are learning patterns that should be monitored not only personally, but also through research. Since these patterns can now be viewed through neuroimaging of the brain, future research in social learning theory would do well to make use of neurocomputational findings in this regard (Bellucci & Park, 2020).

The theories and models of development and learning described up to now allow us to appreciate trust more as a process rather than merely a collection of separate components. As a way to integrate what we have explored up until now and assimilate it into a more structured form, a representation of trust as a process is proposed to help us have a better understanding of trust.

A proposed representation of trust as process

The following points are noted as preparation for the representation but also as a summary of what we have shared until now:

› Trust includes cognitive, emotive, behavioural and normative elements or dimensions.

› Trust involves a willingness to risk (otherwise it is merely hope) and be vulnerable.

› Trust generally has a positive expectation and assumption in the ability, goodwill (benevolence) and morality (integrity) of the other.

› Previous experience and prior knowledge affect our disposition and decision to trust.

› Early childhood experiences and our sense of attachment to a primary caregiver can form the foundation of how we trust the world, others and ourselves.

› Our beliefs, knowledge, personality, mood, culture, emotional intelligence and sense of control, amongst other things, influence whom and how we trust.

› Our development stage, genetics, and the way our brain has been 'wired', affect how we think, feel and act.

› Context is key. The time and space in which the interpersonal interaction takes place can determine the trajectory of the trust behaviour.

› What we observe, read, hear and know about others' experiences and opinions in the media can affect our perception of trust and how we react.

› Our socio-economic status and sense of security in our environment affect the prioritising of values and lead us to trust more or less depending on the threats that are present.

Being reminded of the afore-mentioned, Figure 1 is presented to better understand trust and its multidimensionality. As the representation displays, the process of trust is continuously influenced by the contexts of space and time. Various factors associated with both the trustor and trustee – such as previous experience, values, attachment and capabilities to name a few – jointly create a perception of trustworthiness and risk that is integral to any relationship. At this stage, we as individuals experiencing this process, would make a cognitive decision to trust and act, or not trust and act. The decision to not decide is also a possibility, although not included in the figure. The outcome of our decision and action would subsequently inform the perception of trustworthiness and risk as time moves on and situations change. In this way, trust as a process continues to change and adapt to varying contexts in which we find ourselves.

Contexts of space and time

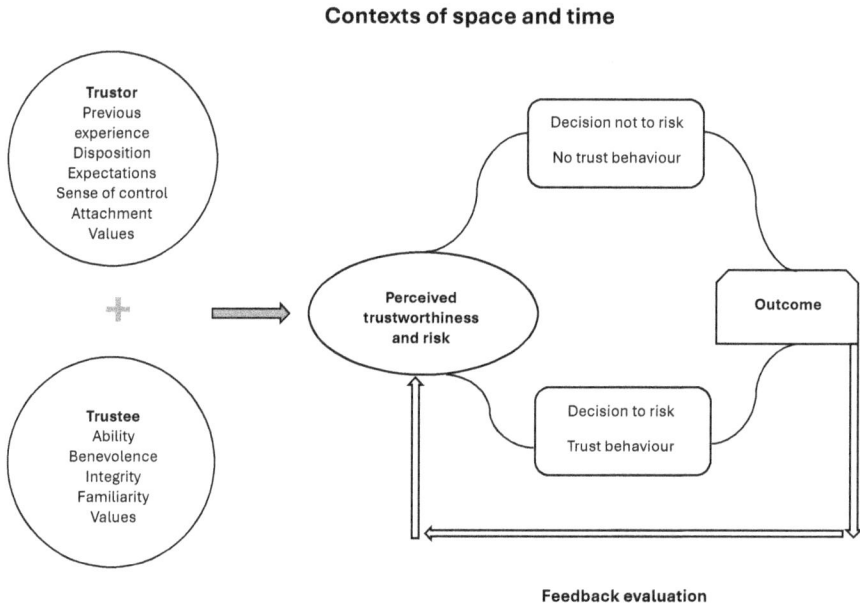

Figure 1 Model of the trust process

With a better understanding of trust, we delve briefly into some interesting findings about trust and how it can impact important facets of our daily life.

Empirical findings in trust

The values we hold as communities can often be associated with where we come from and the era in which we live. The World Value Survey (Haerpfer et al., 2022) assesses how values influence the social, political and economic development of countries and societies. In the latest findings (2017–2022), it was noted that societies associated with a strong sense of individual agency and existential security, tend to follow what is known as secular-rational and self-expression values rather than traditional and survival values. These latter sets of values emphasise commitment to religion, respect for authority and security, amongst others, but also correlate mostly with a sense of distrust in strangers. It is hence possible that trust, in contrast, would correlate more with those societies that value self-expression, self-determination and openness to difference.

Considering life circumstances and socio-economic status, Van Lange (2015) noted that societies with a more equal income distribution appear to display a more generalised willingness to trust, compared to societies where there is unequal distribution. Simpson and Vieth (2021) found that those living in lower socio-economic environments, tended to be more distrustful as they often had to weather more hazards and continuously make decisions on which resources to prioritise. When there are fewer options from which to choose, trust could therefore take on a very different character and experience for us.

Interactions between parents and teachers, or between parents and therapists, could also be considered a space in which there are fewer options available. The parent-professional relationship at times is one not sought for, but Matthiesen et al. (2022) found that there was a definite need and almost demand for trust to be present there. In such relationships each role-player could display an "exaggerated effort" (p. 682) in the relationship to prove to the other that they were trustworthy. Pace (2020) also confirmed that in therapeutic trust, such as between a patient and counsellor, each party strives to motivate the other to trust them more.

Finally, as a possible curveball to our definition and understanding of trust, Riedl (2021) considered the era in which we live and highlighted the era of digitalisation experienced in the last few decades. Technology has seemed to trade in real time for virtual time and face-to-face human communication so that we have the chance to interact with a trustee that is not necessarily human. Our understanding of trust would therefore have to accommodate or distinguish social relationships between human beings and those including non-humans.

There will always be times when we feel we have a good grasp on our understanding of trust, but then other times when we need some tips on how to reach this point again. When trust has been impaired, there are ways to repair the process or relationship, and empower ourselves to be more resilient to life's challenges. The section that follows explores how we can enhance trust in various ways, including and concluding with how we could also decrease our distrust.

> *It is a vice to trust all, and equally a vice to trust none*
> *— Seneca, Letters to Lucilius*

Increasing and preserving trust

A good place to start when exploring how best to manage trust would be to go through this chapter and note the correlations between trust and studied variables, for example, increasing oxytocin could make us more trusting; possessing greater agency (self-determination) and having more prior knowledge would probably assist us to make better trust decisions, and displaying traits of benevolence and integrity would likely make us appear more trustworthy. In its simplest form, however, we learn from Ma et al. (2018) and their study with children, that trust is reciprocal – namely, that one trusts more if one wants others to trust more. Reciprocity generates familiarity so that we feel more confident in making good decisions.

Briefly revisiting the strong link between oxytocin and trust, we mention some management behaviours identified by Zak (2017), which have been found to stimulate oxytocin, hence creating feelings of trust: acknowledging excellence, empowering others with more control over what they do, keeping people informed, showing vulnerability, and caring for people holistically.

High levels of trust have been correlated with higher emotional intelligence, i.e., being able to manage our own emotions and accurately perceive those of others (Christie, 2012). Although some people are naturally good at this, we can also learn to be more emotionally intelligent and it would therefore be prudent for organisations challenged with trust issues, to invest in 'EQ' training for its staff.

Gustafsson et al. (2021, p. 1 419) propose what they call 'trust preservation practices' (i.e., ways to keep the trust once it is there). Although set in the context of organisational trust, it is applicable for any interpersonal interaction:

› Cognitive bridging – understanding and agreeing together what should be done to make things better for the future, in a way that still connects us to what we had in the past.
› Emotional embodying – expressing how we feel and valuing the expressions of others so that everyone feels valued and emotionally safe.
› Inclusive enacting – similar to emotional embodying, everyone involved has their voice heard, but not only regarding how they feel, but particularly what they think, joining in decision-making and having a greater sense of control in the situation.

Engaging in activities that we enjoy and are good at, or educating ourselves to be good at something, can boost our confidence and self-esteem and give us a sense of more control over ourselves and our situations. A generally positive attitude and mood goes a long way to feeling happy and enhancing trust (Farolfi et al., 2021).

Repairing trust

Apart from building and even preserving trust (Gustafsson et al., 2021), there come times when we need to repair trust. Offering an apology, and by implication forgiving, are important actions in this regard. In a similar vein, Guo et al. (2017) proposes three approaches to repairing trust, namely verbal responses, compensation, and a concerted effort to avoid future and repeated harm. This would entail, where possible, talking respectively with the other person, offering some sort of repayment or action that would ameliorate the tension in the relationships, and mechanisms (such as contracts even) to prove to the other that their safety and wellbeing are of priority to us.

Building resilience

Confidence and resilience can be regarded as two dimensions of faith (Pace, 2017). Although faith is not the same as trust, there is much to learn from this. Confidence empowers us to take risks as it gives us a sense of control. When trials arise and distrust develops, resilience helps us persist in a sensible manner.

Resilience is essentially our psychological strength to adapt to challenges and persevere with a positive mindset. Tabibnia and Radecki (2018) propose behavioural and cognitive strategies to help us build resilience. Some of these, as well as other ideas, are listed below for you to peruse and practise:

› Stress reduction by controlling stressors and (where appropriate) facing our fears
› Improving physical health through diet, exercise, sleep and a healthy lifestyle
› Connecting socially with others
› Being grateful and perhaps journaling this on a regular basis
› Identifying, voicing and appropriately expressing our emotions
› Mindfulness training where we use all our senses to focus and meditate on the present moment over and over again, rather than looking at the past or future
› Positive affirmations and holding a growth mindset – focusing on what is possible and what already are strengths, rather than on what is challenging and seemingly lacking

Decreasing distrust

Our digital era has seen the increase in misinformation and disinformation. Debunking false information, discerning what is a reliable source (trusting), and verifying it with other reliable sources are all paramount to getting to the truth.

We can decrease distrust often by increasing trust. Particularly when feeling unsure and suspicious, a positive sense of control creates the perception of success and boosts feelings of trust (Christie, 2012).

Again, learning from studies with children, if there has been a fallout, an apology can decrease perceptions of distrust that are already present and developing (Ma et al., 2018). A general display of goodwill and integrity, along with showing that we have the capabilities to do what we say we will do, will increase others' perceptions of trustworthiness in us.

Paradoxically, Lupoli et al. (2020) also found that people who are perceived to be compassionate can be distrusted by others, because they appear to place more value on kindness than integrity or justice. Again, the context plays an important role in all these interactions, with the best course of action always being the one that is most transparent. As Bernard M. Baruch was noted to say, "Be who you are and say what you feel, because those who mind don't matter, and those who matter don't mind."

Although decreasing distrust may enhance trust, distrust in of itself is not necessarily something to be avoided but can be indeed beneficial to our decision-making and our daily living, as Tennessee Williams reminds us.

> We have to distrust each other. It's our only defense against betrayal.
> — Tennessee Williams

Distrust

There are various perspectives on distrust. We can view distrust as a complete absence of trust, or as the lower end on a continuum of trust, such as in Filkowski et al.'s (2016, p. 326) definition of distrust as a "negatively-valenced interpersonal attitude". The image of a continuum or gradual move from trust to distrust can be viewed developmentally. Vanderbilt et al. (2011)

found in their study that children under the age of four years tended to be very trusting. Between the ages of four and five years, children appeared to understand that others could think and feel differently to them, but in behaviour, still trusted. Only from the age of five years, were children able to transcend the understanding into action and discern who they could trust and not, acknowledging that others could show an emotion or action that was not sincere.

We could also interpret trust and distrust to be completely two different constructs, functioning separately from each other. Lockey (2017) noted that studies involving neuroimaging showed how trust and distrust stimulated different areas in the brain and appeared to suggest that trust developed slower than distrust. In addition, the study of Reimann et al. (2017) found that although genetics appeared to be closely related to trust, this was not the case with distrust, with the latter being more influenced by socialisation. The differences in their 'origins' therefore seemed to prove that they were indeed two separate concepts.

Lockey (2017) purports that trust and distrust are distinct but related. Kujala et al. (2016) likened the affective (emotion-based) and cognitive (thought-based) components of both trust and distrust with each other when studying organisational trust. He found that trust and distrust can co-exist in various possibilities of a relationship. Examples noted were when cognitive trust and affective distrust were observed together, resulting in cynicism in relationships. Another was when affective trust and affective distrust together resulted in hypervigilance in the relationship. It, therefore, appears that, however one views distrust – as separate or part of trust – there are benefits associated with it.

Excessive distrust in for instance organisations can lead to poor performance and an anxiety-provoking work environment. However, it is also possible to have 'too much' trust, as when we find ourselves gullible and believing fake news. High levels of trust can also unite people to such an extent that we find the phenomenon of groupthink when we refuse to consider new ideas and even new members. Distrust can provoke uncertainty and scepticism, but also a willingness to problem-solve honestly, make changes and be aware of those who have different values or subcultures to us (Kujala et al., 2016).

Lumineau (2015, p. 15) speaks of the "dark side of trust and the bright side of distrust" and confirms the benefits of distrust such as monitoring weaknesses and pitfalls. In a digital era, where fake news, misinformation and disinformation are rife (McIntyre & Rauch, 2021), distrust is necessary to confirm validity and reliability of sources. With this vigilance in mind, let us now finally explore how to make the most of trust and distrust in our interactions with others.

Conclusion

Our ability to trust others and ourselves is key to our survival. We do not live alone and in our interactions with the people and contexts around us, trust is fundamental to experiencing successful, stable and happy relationships.

Trust is a complex, interactive and ever-changing construct. It is part of our emotions, thoughts and actions, and is influenced by myriad variables, from within us and without. Throughout life, we will trust and distrust continuously, being influenced by space, time, our own moods and motives and our perceptions of the trustworthiness of others. We will sometimes be the one being trusted and at other times be willing to become vulnerable and trust another.

Kryazh and Grankina-Sazonova (2018, p. 328) regard trust as "an important inner resource that will help the personality to function optimally in an imperfect world: trust to the world, trust to other people and trust to myself."

Just as Ophelia, at the start of this chapter, encouraged the people in her circle to risk becoming vulnerable to each other and themselves, to better understand their own relationship with trust, we hope that the reader has come to a deeper understanding of this multifaceted concept.

CHAPTER 11

Awe: Vastly Beyond Surprise

Mathieu Gagnon

Nicky and the awe-inspiring mountain

Nicky has been dealing with a great deal of work-related stress lately. She recently decided to move away from Riverside to a new town and start a new job. She is currently facing changes in her work organisation, leading to regular conflict with colleagues. Sensing that she needs a break, her close friends, Ophelia and Mel invite her for a hike along a wooded nature trail. "It would do you good. You have never taken the time to enjoy the region's sights. All you do is work!" argued Mel. After a light lunch, they drive up to the trail and start the hike. For two hours, Nicky seems to pay little attention to the sights and sounds nature provides her and is fully absorbed by her work concerns. She keeps ruminating about them, as though stuck in a loop. However, Ophelia has a trick up her sleeve: she knows this trail well, having hiked it many times before; she expects Nicky's mood to be transformed by the end of it. As expected at the end of trail, the forest suddenly opens and, in the distance, an enormous mountain appears. It is of such formidable vastness that Nicky is speechless. Faced with the grandeur of its towering peaks reaching for the sky, all notions of her daily problems and concerns seem to melt away. Time slows down for Nicky. She has goosebumps and feels dwarfed by the immense beauty in front of her. After admiring the mountain for several minutes, they start their walk back down the trail. Nicky feels much more peaceful and calmer than before. She speaks about her work issues in a different tone: "You know, I think I've been looking at this work situation the wrong way. I forgot about my core values, and I didn't really take the time to get to know my colleagues better. Maybe if we work together around a common goal, we can make the best of this difficult situation. After all, we're all in the same boat." "That's the Nicky I know," responds Mel, pleased with the outcome of her plan. Weeks later, Nicky remembers that mountainside experience as one that helped her navigate this difficult phase in her professional life and finds deeper meaning in her life and career.

Introduction

We think Nicky's mountainside experience is best described in terms of awe. However, you may ask why it could not simply be described as surprise. After all, Nicky did not expect to see the mountain, and surprise is very much related to unexpectedness (Reisenzein et al., 2017), in addition to being considered by many as a basic emotion (Kowalska & Wróbel, 2017). However, we believe that while Nicky may have been surprised upon discovering the mountain, this concept does not go far enough in describing her experience and its subsequent impact on her. Indeed, her story is about more than suddenly realising something unexpected – or different from her expectations – has happened. It is a story about transcending her momentary self and feeling small in the face of grandeur. Surprise may be a part of it, but it is not all of it. In fact, some dictionaries define awe as "a feeling of great respect, usually mixed with fear or surprise" (Cambridge, n.d.). Moreover, contrary to surprise, awe offers an opportunity for profound transformation, a deeper sense of connection, and a meaningful life, which is why it has long been explored in writings from religion, sociology, and philosophy (Keltner, 2023; Keltner & Haidt, 2003). For these reasons, we believe it is important to understand, value and cultivate awe in your daily life.

The nature of awe

Psychologists often group different emotions into categories, classes, or families. For instance, you may have heard of basic emotions (Tracy & Randles, 2011), self-conscious emotions (Robins & Schriber, 2009) or moral emotions (Greenbaum et al., 2020). This may lead one to ask the following question: "What kind of emotion is awe?"

Awe as self-transcendent emotion

Although authors vary in this respect, we agree with those who categorise awe as part of the family of self-transcendent emotions (Chirico & Yaden, 2018; Shiota et al., 2014; Yaden et al., 2016). These are emotions that make one focus less on one's present needs and desires, increase the sense that one is part of something larger beyond oneself, and promote a sense of connection, cooperation and group cohesion (Stellar et al., 2017). Examples of other emotions from this family include compassion, gratitude, inspiration and admiration (Abatista & Cova, 2023).

Nicky's mountainside experience clearly illustrates how awe can take us beyond our daily personal goals and struggles and allow us to transcend the boundary between ourselves and the rest of the world (Yaden et al., 2017). When the mountain appears to her, her work-related concerns suddenly melt away, and she becomes fully absorbed in the present moment. Moreover, she comes out of this experience with a new outlook, an increased sense of connection with her colleagues, and a desire to find mutually beneficial solutions.

The many shades of awe

Nicky's story may lead you to infer that awe is by default a positive experience. Indeed, many emotions from the self-transcendent family are thought of as inherently positive (e.g., love, admiration, etc.) (Stellar et al., 2017). However, awe is complex and can take different forms depending on the situation. It can indeed be a pleasing aesthetic experience as Nicky is awestruck by the immensity and the beauty of the mountain (Keltner & Haidt, 2003; Konečni, 2005). That said, it can also manifest as a mixture of pleasantness and unpleasantness. For instance, she could have felt enthralled by the mountain but also partly overwhelmed by the intensity of the moment. This is perhaps best illustrated by Keltner and Haidt (2003), who describe awe as existing "in the upper reaches of pleasure and on the boundary of fear" (p. 297). Pushing this logic further, awe can also be a fully threatening experience. To illustrate this point, imagine that Nicky, Ophelia, and Mel suddenly witnessed part of the mountain collapsing, triggering a gigantic landslide heading their way, filling the air with a deep rumble, and causing the very ground they stand on to shake. Their reaction would be one of threat-based awe accompanied by feelings of dread, fear, or terror (Chaudhury et al., 2022).

In a sense, this ambiguous nature is imbedded in the term 'awe' itself. Even though native English language speakers generally use this word to denote a positive experience (Shiota et al., 2007; Stellar et al., 2017), it originates from older English and Norse words expressing terror or dread (Keltner & Haidt). In fact, modern dictionaries often describe awe using terms such as "dread, veneration, and wonder" (Merriam-Webster, n.d.).

Although awe cannot be fully categorised as a purely positive or pleasant experience, the remainder of this chapter will deal exclusively with non-threatening (i.e., positive) awe. This is because we know much more about it than its threat-based counterpart, and it is associated with a host of benefits for a person's life.

The object of awe

One might understand awe as a self-transcendent emotion that can take on different forms. However, one might wonder what exactly causes us to feel awe in the first place. In other words, what exactly is awe about? Why did Nicky experience this emotion at the sight of the mountain?

A response to vastness

To answer this question, we need to introduce two related psychological concepts: "appraisal of vastness" and "need for accommodation" (Chirico & Yaden, 2018; Keltner & Haidt, 2003). The first refers to the fact that some stimuli or experiences are appraised as being vast, "much larger than the self, or the self's ordinary level of experience or frame of reference" (Keltner & Haidt, 2003, p. 303). When the mountain appeared to Nicky, she automatically appraised it as being vast (i.e., ever extending in the distance). The second refers to the sense that our current understanding of the world is too limited to make sense of a new experience and needs to be changed (i.e., accommodated) (Schaffer et al., 2023). When Nicky saw the mountain, its vastness defied her everyday normal understanding of the world, and she could not make sense of it.

Vastness beyond the physical dimension

Nicky's experience clearly shows that the concept of vastness is central to awe. However, it would be wrong to assume that awe can only be experienced in response to physically vast sceneries or objects like mountains, waterfalls, canyons, etc. Although such geological formations do represent powerful elicitors of awe, humans can also tap into vastness in a more metaphorical or abstract way (Keltner, 2023; Keltner & Haidt, 2003). To illustrate this point, let us imagine that while Nicky was on her hike, her brother Jonathan was miles away in the maternity ward of his local hospital, experiencing his own moment of awe: the birth of his first child. How could this situation lead to an appraisal of vastness from Jonathan? From a strictly physical perspective, he was not in the presence of a vast object or scenery extending into the distance. However, he was in the presence of an event that was to change him forever and reorganise his everyday understanding of life. In other words, the vastness was not in terms of physical size but rather in terms of importance, meaning, and depth of human experience. Upon holding his newly born son, he was overcome with the realisation that he was now part of a long chain of fathers and sons stretching back to the beginning of humanity. He also realised the unending love his father had felt for him (as he now felt for his own son), and his wife's incredible power to create, nurture, and birth new life into the world. This was not an ordinary event that could be understood with his everyday expectations and notions. Hence the experience of awe.

The idea that vastness can be appraised from a more abstract perspective is in part what allows for different thematic versions or 'flavours' of awe (Keltner & Haidt, 2003). One of these relates to beauty: you could feel awe for an aesthetically pleasing piece of music or work of art. Think of the many millions of visitors who travel to the Louvre Museum to see Leonardo Da Vinci's *Mona Lisa* every year. Another relates to ability: you can feel awe and admiration at witnessing someone's "exceptional ability, talent, and skill" (Keltner & Haidt, 2023, p. 305), such as during an athletic competition or while reading about the contributions of a great historical scientist. One also relates to virtue: you can feel awe upon witnessing an individual's strength of character, resilience, or generosity. Think about people like Mahatma Ghandi or Nelson Mandela, and their impact on society. Notice that none of the examples imply vastness in terms of physical size. Instead, their magnitude is to be understood in terms of importance, meaningfulness, profundity, beauty, ability, or character.

As a final illustration, consider the fact that you may be awestruck by small sensory details like "a drop of pond water that contains an elaborate world of its own" (Shiota et al., 2017, p. 363). For instance, on their way up the trail, Nicky, Ophelia, and Mel may have crossed another hiker who was marvelling at a leaf picked up from the ground. Examining it closely through the sunlight, he could have been in awe of the vastly complex and beautiful organisation of its many laminae and veins. This idea is particularly well captured by the first four lines of William Blake's poem 'Auguries of Innocence':

> *To see a World in a Grain of Sand*
> *And a Heaven in a Wild Flower*

Hold Infinity in the palm of your hand

And Eternity in an hour.

—Blake, 1997

The different components of awe

Now that one understands the conditions under which awe emerges (i.e., an appraisal of vastness and a need for accommodation), let us explore its different components in terms of brain and body physiology, subjective impression, and expressive behaviour. Like all emotions, awe leads to specific changes at each of these levels and understanding them may help you recognise this emotion in yourself and others.

Awe and the brain

In terms of the brain, research suggests that awe reduces the activity of the default mode network, which is usually associated with our ability to mind wander and think about ourselves (Van Elk et al., 2019). It may also involve changes in brainwave patterns – specifically theta and beta wavelengths – contributing to increased attention (Reinerman-Jones et al., 2013). Taken together, these effects explain why Nicky's daily concerns seemed to evaporate as she witnessed the mountain, and why she felt fully immersed in the present moment.

Awe and the body

In terms of body-physiology, awe is thought to trigger both the parasympathetic (i.e., relaxation) and sympathetic (i.e., arousal) branches of the nervous system in a repetitive back-and-forth manner (Takano & Nomura, 2023). This makes sense, given the previously described ambiguous nature of this emotion. It can also induce piloerection (Quesnel & Riecke, 2018; Schurtz et al., 2012) as well as a "behavioural freezing" response (Joye & Dewitte, 2016). This explains why Nicky appears silent and frozen in time upon witnessing the mountain – as opposed to jumping up and down for joy. It also explains why her breathing is deep and why she feels goosebumps all over her body.

Awe and the mind

Turning to subjective experience, awe alters our senses of time, space, and self (Piff et al., 2015; Rudd et al., 2012, Yaden et al., 2017). Specifically, our attention broadens, and we become absorbed in the present moment (Sung & Yih, 2015). This effect can also make us feel like we have more time available to us (Rudd et al., 2012). Moreover, we feel our self-becoming smaller (Piff et al., 2015), and experience a deeper sense of connection (Chen & Mongrain, 2021). This can be in relation to concrete elements like our social network or community, but it can also be abstract like humanity, nature, or the world in general (Bai et al., 2017; Shiota et al., 2007; Van Cappellen & Saroglou, 2012). This fits with the observation that Nicky felt tiny in relation to the mountain and came away with a deeper sense of connection with her colleagues at work.

Awe and behaviour

Finally, in terms of expressive behaviour, awe can be recognised by a more pronounced breathing pattern and the way we extend our head forward, open our mouth and drop the jaw (Shiota et al., 2003). Mel and Ophelia may have also noticed how Nicky's eyebrows raised, and her eyes widened (Campos et al., 2013) as she let out vocal sounds like "whoa" or "wow" (Cordaro et al., 2016). Sometimes, awe may cause us to smile but at other times it may lead to a more ambivalent facial expression (Chirico et al., 2017).

Awe versus wonder, happiness, and flow

We began this chapter by explaining that surprise was different from awe and that this matters to understand Nicky's story. Indeed, while both have an element of unexpectedness, surprise is not inherently about vastness. Stated otherwise, it does not imply that we are faced with something of immense size, meaning, beauty, power, or influence, like awe does. On her way back down the trail, many things may surprise Nicky. For instance, she may be surprised upon learning that her brother Jonathan's baby was just born, even though they were not due for another three weeks. But unless she perceives this "earlier than expected" birth as profoundly meaningful in a way that leads her to transcend her momentary self and feel small in the face of such grandeur, she is unlikely to experience awe.

Still, you may ask, why could Nicky not simply be described as experiencing wonder instead of awe? While it is quite likely that Nicky will feel wonder as part of her experience, research suggests that people mean subtly different things by 'awe' and 'wonder'. Indeed, awe seems to be about observing a stimulus, while wonder is about trying to understand or explain it (Darbor et al., 2016). In other words, there is a reflective component to wonder as one attempts to make sense of one's experience (Gallagher et al., 2014). Therefore, Nicky's experience may start with awe as she is initially absorbed in observing the mountain, and gradually morph into wonder. On the way down the trail – and perhaps for many following days – she may be filled with questions about the nature of the mountain, the vast geological forces that shaped it, how it impacts the ecology around it, what stories it has inspired in the local people, etc. This wonder may lead her to become curious and seek out answers to her questions. This relationship between awe, wonder and curiosity, is partly why some authors think of awe as an epistemic emotion (i.e., one related to knowledge and understanding) (Noordewier & Gocłowska, 2023).

What about flow? Why could Nicky not simply be described as *in a state of flow* upon seeing the mountain? How is that different from awe? Once again, flow and awe have many similarities: both involve a certain level of absorption and a reduction in ego concern (Kim et al., 2023). That said, there are also important differences. Fundamentally, awe is about vastness and involves a type of "zooming out," while flow is about challenge and skill level and involves a type of "zooming in" on a task (Csikszentmihalyi, 1991; Kim et al., 2023; Shiota et al., 2007). In other words, Nicky could have been in flow during her ascent up the trail if she considered it a particularly challenging hike and perceived that she had the necessary skills to live up to the challenge.

Lastly, what about joy or happiness? Could Nicky not simply be described as deeply happy upon seeing the mountain? The difference is clear. At its root, happiness or joy has little to do with vastness and everything to do with "motive consistency": we feel happy or joyful when we perceive moving towards or attaining a valued goal or motive (Ellsworth & Smith, 1988a; Scherer, 2001). For instance, Mel may have experienced happiness upon seeing Nicky's reaction to the mountain because she had succeeded in her valued goal of changing her friend's mood.

The origins and functions of awe

We have now described what awe is, how it manifests, and how it differs from other related emotions such as wonder, surprise, or happiness. But what about its reason for being? Why does awe exist in the first place? Does it have any functions? In other words, how and why did awe become part of the human emotional repertoire? To explore this question, we will use an evolutionary and functionalist perspective (Fischer & Manstead, 2008; Keltner et al., 2006; Nesse, 1990). According to such an approach, emotions are the product of evolution, as they initially provided an adaptive response to a variety of challenges routinely faced by our early human ancestors. This begs the question: which common adaptive problems did awe help to solve during our evolution?

Social cohesion and habitat selection

One problem faced by all our ancestors is that of social cohesion (Keltner & Haidt, 2003). Indeed, group living is difficult to coordinate and can easily break apart to the detriment of all group members (Sober & Wilson, 1998). Keltner and Haidt (2003) have suggested that awe allowed our ancestors to overcome this problem by motivating them to revere, gather around, and submit to a leader with vast power and social influence. It also helped by increasing feelings of interconnectedness and motivating prosocial behaviours.

Another likely – though very different – survival problem was that of habitat selection (Northrup et al., 2021). Specifically, our ancestors needed ways to identify potential environments that provided safety and shelter from dangers. Chirico and Yaden (2018) have proposed that awe may have functioned as a signal that one was in the presence of such an environment. For them, hunter gatherers who felt a strong awe reaction at the sight of a vista that afforded a vantage point and shelter were more likely to select such an environment to settle down, thereby increasing their chances of survival.

The fact that awe can be experienced in relation to individuals who hold vast influence and power (e.g., great leaders) as well as by large natural vistas (e.g., Nicky's mountain experience) seems to support both proposals. At first sight, you may think this is contradictory, but it is possible that awe first evolved to solve one type of problem and was later recruited to solve another. For instance, Keltner and Haidt (2003) argued that although we first evolved to appraise vastness in terms of social power and influence, this ability gradually generalised to other stimuli beyond the social domain (like mountains or canyons). In other words, Nicky might be responding to the mountain's vastness by way of a psychological mechanism that first evolved to respond to vastness in terms of the power and social influence of great leaders. However, it is also conceivable that awe first evolved for habitat selection and only gradually morphed into a response to great social influence. This would fit more neatly with the observation that natural sceneries are more likely to trigger awe than powerful leaders (Yaden et al., 2018) and that awe-inspiring physical environments positively impact ratings of leaders' charisma (McGuire et al., 2024).

Learning and adaptation to complex environments

In addition to group cohesion and habitat selection, early humans were routinely confronted with a complex environment that was rich in information, difficult to predict, and often offered an ambiguous mix of potential advantages and dangers (Richesin & Baldwin, 2023). Awe may have evolved as it helped our human ancestors navigate this complex landscape in different ways. It could have done so by motivating them to explore and make meaningful sense of it via constant learning and reorganising in their thinking and beliefs (Ihm et al., 2019; Valdesolo et al., 2017). Because it promotes systematic observation instead of impulsive approach, it may have been a better response to this complexity than fear (which could have led to loss of opportunity) or curiosity (which could have led to harm or death) (Richesin & Baldwin, 2023). Moreover, awe may have also helped them respond to such challenges more creatively, and promoted higher cognitive functions such as planning, prediction making, and testing (Griskevicius et al., 2010; Lucht & Van Schie, 2024). Lastly, by increasing the sense of connectedness, it could have led them to share the product of their exploration with others in a cumulative and collaborative effort (Ihm et al., 2019; Richesin & Baldwin, 2023).

Mate selection and attraction

Another challenge of all early humans was that of attracting or selecting potential mates (Geary et al., 2004). Indeed, bonding with the wrong individual could have important negative outcomes in terms of survival and reproduction. Therefore, it is conceivable that awe-proneness may have been seen as favourable trait in a potential partner. For instance, in some communities, it could suggest that the individual had some form of privileged and "private access to the supernatural" (Konečni, 2005, p. 31). In addition, because of awe's effect in terms of prosociality (Piff et al., 2015), awe-prone individuals may have been viewed as better potential childrearing partners. Lastly, given that peak experiences like awe tend to promote psychological wellbeing, Lucht and Van Schie (2023) have proposed that awe proneness could act as a cue that someone would be a more psychologically healthy mate.

Awe during childhood and beyond

As is the case for all emotions, human infants do not arrive in the world with a fully formed adult-like ability to experience awe. Instead, it is likely the case that children must gradually develop this ability as they interact with the physical and social world around them (Barrett, 2017). What do we know about this process? And why do some people grow to be more, or less awe-inspired than others?

The emergence of awe during childhood

We often look back at our childhood as a time of great awe. However, one may be surprised to learn that the research on awe in children is surprisingly small. Of the few studies on this topic, one suggests awe can be experienced by children between the age of four to five years (Colantonio & Bonawitz, 2018), while others have observed it in children between eight and 10 years' old (Stamkou et al., 2023; Van Limpt et al., 2020). That said, we have little information as to the steps that children go through as they gradually develop the ability to experience awe. From a theoretical perspective, Prade (2022) proposes that to experience awe, children must first possess self-awareness and self-reflection, abilities which emerge around 18 to 24 months of life. For their part, O'bi and Yang (2024) have observed that four- to nine-year-olds were able to distinguish awe-inspiring visual stimuli (e.g., an image of a waterfall) from other kinds of images (e.g., a kitchen) and that such stimuli increased their motivation to explore and understand. However, they also found that they did not always lead to a change in sense of connection, which suggests that not all components of awe emerge simultaneously. Perhaps those that require more abstract thinking – like sense of connection – are particularly slower to develop as part of children's awe response. Much remains to be done to understand when and how awe develops as part of children's emotional repertoire, what roles parents, peers, teachers and media play in this process and how children think about and understand their own awe experiences and those of others.

Individual differences in awe proneness

In addition to the way awe develops during childhood, we have yet to understand why some individuals grow to be more awe-prone than others. From a biological perspective, Anderson (2016) suggests a possible genetic component to awe proneness. Specifically, it may relate to the length of alleles for a specific gene (DRD4) involved in the production of dopamine receptors. In addition, there may also be a constellation of personality and character traits that make you more likely to experience awe. For instance, awe proneness has been found to be positively correlated with *openness to experience* (Shiota et al., 2006; Silvia et al., 2015), and *trait absorption* (Van Elk et al., 2016). It is also negatively correlated to *need for cognitive closure* (Shiota et al., 2017). Stated otherwise, awe-prone people may also be the ones who are more open to novelty and change, comfortable with ambiguity, and able to attend fully to the world around them. They may also possess certain character strengths including appreciation of beauty, gratefulness, creativity, and love of learning (Güsewell & Ruch, 2012). That said, we do not know if and to what extent such personality and character factors contribute to awe proneness. Nor do we know the measure to which repeated experiences of awe impact the aforementioned factors.

Why awe matters

At this point, one may be wondering: So what, and why should one care? Indeed, understanding what awe is and how it functions is interesting, but why does it merit an entire chapter of its own? Like all emotions, awe impacts our mental and social functioning, as well as our behaviour. In this section, we will present different ways in which awe can be helpful to people. First, we will address awe's relationship with mental health and wellbeing. Then we will explore how awe impacts conduct – specifically prosocial behaviour. And finally, we will delve into awe's influence on decisions and choices as consumers.

Mental health and wellbeing

According to the GBD 2019 Mental Disorders Collaborators (2022, p. 137), "mental disorders are among the top 10 leading causes of burden worldwide, with no evidence of global reduction in the burden since 1990." Although the causes of such disorders are complex, awe may play a supportive role in mental health maintenance. One of the ways it might help, is by impacting immune functions. Indeed, awe-prone individuals may have lower levels of proinflammatory cytokines, specifically IL-6 (Stellar et al., 2015). Although such cytokines play an important role in immune system function, their overabundance may also play a role in anxiety and depressive disorders (O'Donovan et al., 2010; Ting et al., 2020). Awe may also support your health by increasing vagal tone (Monroy & Keltner, 2023), which is associated with faster recovery from stress (Souza et al., 2007). Moreover, some awe experiences may even lead to increased production of oxytocin (Thomson & Siegel, 2017), the dysfunction of which is involved in mood and anxiety disorders (Cochran et al., 2013).

In addition, awe may promote mental health by helping us shift our focus away from ourselves (Campos et al., 2013; Monroy & Keltner, 2023; Shiota et al., 2007; Stellar et al., 2018). Notice that this is in contrast to many psychological disorders (e.g., depression, anxiety, substance abuse, eating disorders), which involve an overactive self-focused attention (Mor & Winquist, 2002; Spurr & Stopa, 2002). Also, because humans are such social creatures, the increased sense of connection derived from awe is probably an important contributor to psychological wellbeing (Monroy & Keltner, 2023). Indeed, the association between social connection and mental health is well known (Wickramaratne et al., 2022), and some researchers remark that "prescribing social interactions and encouraging friendships has the potential to have a healing effect on patients" (Martino et al., 2017, p. 467).

In sum, awe is good for your mental health. It has a positive influence on mood and leads to lower levels of negative emotions, and higher life satisfaction (Anderson et al., 2018; Bai et al., 2021; Chirico et al., 2018; Monroy, & Keltner, 2018; Rankin et al., 2019; Sun et al., 2023; Zhao et al., 2019). Evidence also suggests it plays a role in resilience, feelings of self-worth, and self-compassion (Braswell et al., 2023; Thompson, 2023; Zhang et al., 2023; Yuan et al., 2025). Finally, awe may also contribute to a higher sense of meaning or purpose, which also has important consequences on mental health (Monroy & Keltner, 2023; Park, 2010).

Prosocial and moral behaviour

The early 21st century has brought with it several global crises, relating to finance, terrorism, warfare, global health, food insecurity, climate change, etc. (Wernli et al., 2023). Solving these emergencies requires global coordinated action as we put away our differences and focus on our common identity and goals. Although this process needs to play out at a societal level, awe can help by getting you to focus on the welfare and interests of others rather than your own (Piff et al., 2015). Indeed, awe is well known for its influence on prosocial behaviour (Acevedo & Tost, 2023; Bai et al., 2017; Li et al., 2019; Meng & Wang, 2022; Piff et al., 2015; Prade & Saroglou, 2016; Rudd et al., 2012; Stellar et al., 2017; Stellar et al., 2018; Van Kleef & Lelieveld, 2022).

In short, "awe shifts us from a competitive dog-eat-dog mindset to perceive that we are part of networks of more interdependent, collaborating individuals" (Keltner, 2023, p. 37). This even appears to apply to online behaviour (Goldy et al., 2022; Lin et al., 2021) and appreciation of multicultural diversity (Zhang et al., 2023). Moreover, awe also seems to be beneficial on the moral front. For instance, Song et al. (2023) found awe to be associated to a greater tendency to regard other beings (human or not) as worthy of moral concern and treatment, while Lv et al. (2023) and Luo et al. (2022) have found awe to weaken the stigmatisation and dehumanisation of people with AIDS and those suffering from obesity. In addition, Jiao and Luo (2024) showed that awe-prone individuals were less willing to engage in corrupt behaviour (e.g., giving and accepting bribes). Given increasing awareness that prosociality is to be regarded as a public health priority (Kubzansky et al., 2023), we believe we have a responsibility to promote awe as a powerful tool to make one a better social actor and a force for good.

Decision-making and consumption

Materialism and consumerism are growing issues with many deleterious effects on a global scale in terms of biodiversity and climate (Hoekstra & Wiedmann, 2014; Isbell et al., 2023), and on individual and societal scales, in terms of reduced wellbeing (Dittmar et al., 2014; Moldes & Ku, 2020). Interestingly, a growing body of research suggests that awe can help you become a more ethical, socially responsible, and pro-environmental consumer. Many authors have suggested that awe can promote eco-friendly consumption choices (Kaplan et al., 2023; Wang et al., 2019; Xu et al., 2023; Yin & Lee, 2023). Moreover, awe has been linked to a reduction in both compulsive consumption and importance attributed to money (Hu et al.,

2018; Jiang et al., 2018), a preference for experiences rather than material goods (Rudd et al., 2012), a less negative reaction to losing possessions (Koh et al., 2019), and a greater intention to engage in a sharing economy (Wang et al., 2022). The importance of awe for such issues is perhaps best illustrated in the following quote from Mary Migdley:

> There are more important things than humanity, things that awe and stupefy us with their longevity, their imperturbability, and their indifference to us. They have vast, nonhuman greatness and value, value that we do wrong to threaten. Faced with such values, the appropriate human virtues are self-restraint, hesitation, a respect for the mystery of the world, and a willingness to leave it at that (Migdley, 1994).

Cultivating awe in your daily life

By now, why awe matters and why it should be experienced more in daily life should be clear. This probably leads one to wonder where to start. This final section aims to explore this question. Our goal is not to provide a prescriptive list of awe-inducing strategies because not everything works for everybody. Each person is best equipped to know what triggers their awe. However, in this chapter we offer some suggestions in the hope that a person might adapt them in their own way.

Nature

As we have learnt from the beginning of this chapter, awe is the result of an appraisal of vastness – whether physical or metaphorical/conceptual – and an ensuing need for accommodation (Keltner & Haidt, 2003). As the opening vignette on Nicky's experience suggests, one rich source of awe is nature, specifically large natural sceneries and vistas like mountains, canyons, or waterfalls (Shiota et al., 2007). If a person lives in the vicinity of such wonders, they should get out there and experience awe. That said, not everyone has direct access to such natural sites, nor the time or financial means to visit them. So how can one live a more awe-rich life without such a privilege?

Thankfully, one can experience awe through indirect exposure to nature by way of images or videos, simulated virtual reality (VR), or even reflecting on past experiences in memory (Schaffer et al., 2023). One can therefore use image search engines, for example Google Images, video sharing websites like YouTube, or VR apps to view awe-inspiring sceneries and deliberately experience this emotion. The intensity of one's awe experience may be somewhat dampened when using these indirect strategies, but research suggests it is enough to promote the different benefits mentioned in the previous section. In fact, most of the studies referred to in this document have used some indirect way (often video clips) to evoke awe in their study-participants. In addition, remember that vastness can also be found in the rich details of natural objects all around us (Shiota et al., 2017). So, pay attention to the complex shapes, colour patterns and many features of the natural world around you. Each person will be amazed by how much there is, that they have not noticed before.

Human-made structures

One may also look for awe beyond nature. Indeed, many human-made structures (e.g., historical, cultural or religious sites, beautiful architecture, tall skyscrapers) may be awe-eliciting (Joye & Dewitte, 2016; Negami & Ellard, 2023). Here again, if these are not easily accessible in one's local environment, they can be accessed indirectly through images, videos, VR or recall from memory. Also, one must remember that vastness does not always relate to physical size and we must look for awe in terms of the significance, beauty or meaning of different human-made works of art, cultural or historical artefacts, or sacred objects.

Events

Aside from objects – natural or human-made – we may also look for awe in events. Some of these may be private or involve a limited number of individuals, like the birth of a child (Dahan, 2023). Others may be more social, such as celebrations, concerts, art festivals, worshipping ceremonies, cultural practices, etc. (Forstmann et al., 2020; Khan et al., 2016; Van Cappellen & Rimé, 2014; Wlodarczyk et al., 2021). Once again we can do this either by experiencing these events, recalling them from memory, or learning about them through reading, podcasts, documentaries and movies.

Beauty and exceptionality

One may also look for awe in music (Konečni, 2008; Yaden et al., 2019) and in the actions of individuals with exceptional talent (Shiota et al., 2014) as well as those of great character, resilience, or generosity (Keltner & Haidt, 2003). Biographies and documentaries can be a wonderful portal into such awe experiences.

Conclusion

Knowing that awe is important, how or where to find it, and how to enhance it, we hope that everyone makes time for more *awe*some experiences, because these moments make life worth living.

CHAPTER 12

The Superpower of Hope

Melissa Greenberg
Palesa Luzipo
Lobna Chérif
Yolandi-Eloïse Janse van Rensburg

A spark of hope

Mel returned home from her walk in the mountains with a wonderful feeling of awe. Unfortunately, when she walked into the room, Sam was sitting on his bed, quiet, looking sunken, almost lifeless. Mel gently embraced Sam, knowing it was about the bullying he was facing at school. "I don't want to go to school tomorrow," Sam mouthed softly. They sat and talked for a while. Mel had already spoken to the teachers, and, in turn, the teachers had repeatedly reprimanded the students and also addressed their parents. There had been a few signs of improvement, but then there were days like this. Nevertheless, Mel knew the only thing she and Sam could control was themselves. So, she calmly reviewed some strategies with Sam again. The following day, Mel dropped Sam off at school, saying: "Now, remember our gameplan when Billy hassles you again." Sam smiled with a sparkle in his eyes, as he walked away. Mel grinned when she realised Sam was wearing his favourite Superman t-shirt. As she drove off, she looked back in the rearview mirror and saw something that she had not seen in Sam before... hope.

Introduction

Although a vast amount of research shows that in-the-moment *mindfulness* is beneficial for wellbeing and flourishing, new research shows that future-orientated *hope* is especially important during difficult times. In a recent study, Scott et al, (2024) found that when individuals are "stuck in a rut", being hopeful is associated with being happy, whereas being mindful, is not. More specifically, hope comprises three main aspects, namely *desire* (i.e., wanting something in the future), *belief* (expectations that a hoped-for future is possible), and a positive *feeling* (e.g., Milona & Stockdale, 2018). So, when Sam is going through dire times (like being picked on by the school bully), he breaks the feeling of despair by envisioning his future self as 'super' and strong; he starts believing that the school bully will stop harassing him, and even possibly start liking him, and this feeling of hope makes him feel happy. Adding to his newfound feeling of hope, wearing his favourite t-shirt also makes him feel confident (also referred to as a tactic of *enclothed cognition*; Adam & Galinsky, 2012). Thus, cultivating hope, and having a forward-thinking mindset is especially important during negative or uncertain times (TenHouten, 2023).

Hope is defined as "an optimistic state of mind" grounded in "the possibility or expectation of positive outcomes regarding specific goals, events, and social circumstances", as well as "one's general sense of self" (TenHouten, 2023, p. 77). However, hope differs from *blind optimism*. Whereas optimism is characterised by a general expectation that things will turn out well, hope includes not only positive expectation but also the perceived capacity – or at least a plan – for pursuing a better and desired future.

According to Seligman's theory of learnt optimism, optimists are more likely to attribute negative events to external, variable, and specific causes (Seligman et al., 1979). Similarly, hopeful individuals tend to explain adverse events in ways that are external, specific, and temporary. Yet they go a step further, by emphasising their own agency and capacity for action. While optimism and hope are often conflated, Lazarus (1999) delineates key distinctions: optimism primarily concerns positive expectations about future outcomes, while hope entails an engagement with uncertainty and risk. It is especially salient in contexts of adversity, where maintaining hope requires cognitive flexibility and emotional resilience. Hopefulness also involves a metacognitive awareness (i.e., thinking about one's thinking), particularly in staying focused on goal attainment and navigating out of difficult situations (Scott et al., 2024). Thus, hope is not merely a feeling but a cognitive strategy, one that presupposes intentionality and planning (Gwinn & Hellman, 2018). Rather than succumbing to 'what if' scenarios, self-blame, or perceived insurmountable obstacles, the hopeful thinker draws upon an optimistic, action-oriented mindset. This orientation provides both motivation and strength, particularly in times of adversity.

Origins of hope

Over more than 30 years, academic literature has become abundant with research, well-established theories, and definitions of hope. More specifically, the theoretical understanding of hope has generated more than 26 theories, and numerous definitions of hope (Colla et al., 2023; Lopez et al., 2003). This steadfast focus on hope highlights how essential it is because the world needs hope, today more than ever. According to Graham (2024), research shows that where there is a downward spiral in hope, there is an incline in the number of deaths of despair (e.g., deaths due to suicide, drug and alcohol overdoses). More people, especially teenagers, are reporting feelings of persistent sadness (Graham, 2024).

Erickson's research in 1964 (as cited in Eliott, 2005) focuses on epigenetic development, which endorses the idea that hope, observed amongst children, is an outcome of healthy relations and interactions with their primary caregiver. Bowlby's attachment theory (see Bowlby & Holmes, 2012), highlights the importance of infant attachment patterns, which play a significant role in a child's personality development. Further, hope is highly correlated with an early development of secure attachment, prosocial behaviour, and character development (Demirtaş, 2019; Hastings et al., 2007; Schornick et al., 2023). Sadly, when children cannot develop a healthy relationship with their guardians, they become confused, having to deal with self-doubt, fear, and mistrust; they eventually develop poor interpersonal relationships, and may even suffer from depression (Snyder, 2002). Therefore, the process of hopeful thinking, versus despair, already starts in early childhood. In fact, studies investigating pre-adolescents, middle school, and university students show that early, secure attachment predicts greater hope (Demirtaş, 2019). However, even if one did not learn lessons of hope as a child, all is not lost. Research shows that hope can be cultivated through specific interventions (Magyar-Moe & Lopez, 2015), which are discussed in more detail at the end of this chapter.

Understanding hope both as a cognitive process and as an emotion

Researchers agree that hope is a multifaceted human attribute, mostly discussed in the domain of positive psychology, a field rich with insights into positive states and innate resources that are conducive to human flourishing (Bruininks, 2012). Trailblazers such as Martin Seligman in championing positive psychology (Seligman et al., 2005), as well as Rick Snyder and Shane Lazarus in formulating hope theory (1991), have underscored hope's pivotal role in navigating our daily lives (Colla et al., 2023). Snyder et al. (1991, p. 570) define hope as "the perceived capability to derive pathways to desired goals and motivate oneself via agency thinking to use those pathways." Hope, in this model, is conceptualised as a positive motivational state that emerges from a cognitive process involving three key components: goals, pathways, and agency (Snyder et al., 1991). First, *goals* refer to clearly defined, meaningful aims that provide individuals with direction and purpose. Second, *pathways* thinking (sometimes referred to as *Waypower*) involves the perceived capacity to generate multiple routes or strategies to achieve those goals, particularly in the face of obstacles. This component reflects one's ability to cognitively map out alternative courses of action when challenges arise. Snyder and colleagues emphasised that high-hope individuals are better able to recognise barriers and creatively identify viable paths to their desired outcomes. Finally, *agency* thinking (or *Willpower*) denotes the motivational energy and determination to pursue those pathways. It is the belief in one's ability to initiate and sustain goal-directed efforts over time.

Additionally, an extension of Snyder's hope theory, as proposed by Colla et al. (2023), includes a contextual motivational component (*Whypower*), adding that one can best understand hope when unpacking what motivates and gives individuals energy to achieve their goals on an intrapersonal level. In this way, hope also stems from a sense of connectedness, representing an individual's ability to tap into resources from their social system, within the context of relationships (*Wepower*). These authors add to the notion of hope, suggesting it can best be understood as "an energy system" where there is a "dynamic interplay between the parts" (Colla et al., 2023, p. 10).

Importantly, hope in this theory is not restricted to specific situations but is seen as a generalised mindset characterised by both motivation and cognitive flexibility (Snyder et al., 2002). Building on this, Pleeging (2022) conceptualises hope as a combination of agency and resourcefulness – highlighting that the hopeful individual not only possesses the will to act but also perceives access to the means necessary to achieve their goals.

Hope, from the cognitive perspective, is viewed as the mental determination to do whatever it takes to achieve one's goals, the ability to identify ways to pursue them, and has been defined as the "processes of reflection, examination, and assessment" (Walker, 2006, p. 552). Greenway and Smith (2016) expand on this notion, asserting that hope acts as a motivation to stimulate action. This internal state propels individuals into action, as it is often centred on a positive outlook, holding on to the idea of a better outcome (goal setting), while taking action (following through), and persevering (coping and adapting).

The corollary is also true: the general belief that our goals are attainable exudes positive emotions, while the belief that the attainment of our goals may not be possible elicits negative emotions (Feldman & Snyder, 2005;

Feldman & Jazaieri, 2024). Positive emotions are described as "fleeting and subtle pleasant states" (Fredrickson et al., 2008), while negative emotions are the antithesis, defined as an "unpleasant or unhappy emotion, which is evoked in individuals to express a negative effect towards an event or person" (Lazarus,1999). Significantly, positive or negative emotions not only flow from goal-pursuit success or failure but cause them. Just as positive emotions (e.g., pride and happiness) facilitate achieving goals, negative emotions (e.g., fear and sadness) can similarly prevent goals from being achieved. So, individuals who are able to generate realistic ways to reach their goals are more likely to feel optimistic and energetic, whereas individuals who cannot attain (or find ways to reach) their goals may begin to feel pessimistic and frustrated. And hence, the *emotion perspective* of hope emerges. Although emotions and goal achievement are not synonymous, they are causally linked: emotions will arise because of the outcomes of the goal achieved. Therefore, if Sam remains hopeful, he can imagine a future contrary to his current circumstances, giving him the motivation to actively work towards this envisioned future. Hope is therefore the emotion that provides feedback for the past, leading to motivation for future goals and behaviour (Snyder, 2002; Schornick, 2023). Further, hope results in a change of behaviour, also referred to as *subjective affect*. Like the experience of other emotions – which can range on a continuum from low to high (like experiencing sadness or fear and all the many emotions in between) – hope triggers activation to mobilise action (Lazarus, 1999; Feldman & Jazaieri, 2024).

Adding to the idea of cognition as the cornerstone of hope, setting goals and achieving them evokes emotion. Snyder's hope theory proposed that our thought-processes or cognitions lead to emotions. This is affirmed by Lazarus (1999, p. 663), stating that "hope is a response to goal outcomes and as such it should be treated as an emotion." Hope draws out emotions of positivity, desire, enthusiasm, anticipation, and an expectation of good things yet to come (Lazarus, 1999; Snyder et al., 2002).

Recent research involving seven studies demonstrated that exposure to hope-inducing stimuli – such as images of sleeping infants or plants thriving in unlikely environments – elicits a distinct positive emotional response, thereby supporting the classification of hope as an emotion (Edwards, 2024). Within scholarly literature, however, divergent perspectives persist regarding whether hope should be primarily conceptualised as a cognitive or emotional phenomenon (Peh et al., 2017; Lazarus, 1999; TenHouten, 2023). This duality has led to varied definitions and theoretical classifications of hope across disciplines.

According to Van Zomeren et al. (2019), hope is also viewed as a coping strategy during experiences of adversity with two functions, problem-solving and managing one's emotional state. Hope's problem-solving function serves to bring about a solution to the perceived stressor by crafting the goal, while hope's emotional-managing function regulates how the stressor is appraised. This is corroborated by the analysis of Lazarus (1999), which emphasises that when a challenge is appraised as *due to resistance to change* or *a change in expectations*, hope's coping function dominates; whereas, when a challenge is appraised as *within one's reach* and *control*, hope's problem-solving function dominates.

In summary, and aligning with Snyder's framework, we propose that hope originates as a cognitive process involving goal-directed thinking – specifically, the generation of pathways and agency – but acknowledge that emotional processes are integral to sustaining motivation and engaging in problem-solving. Thus, we have highlighted conceptualising hope as both a cognitive and emotional phenomenon, wherein the interplay between thought and feeling is essential to its motivational power and adaptive function.

Hope to foster positive outcomes

In positive psychology, hope is recognised as a character strength that supports an optimistic outlook and is strongly linked to wellbeing and life satisfaction (Peterson & Seligman, 2004; Park et al., 2005). Individuals high in hope tend to excel in personal endeavours and exhibit sustained commitment toward achieving their goals (Moss-Pech et al., 2020). Goal attainment, in turn, contributes positively to collective wellbeing and societal flourishing (Thomas et al., 2023).

Chérif et al. (2022) found that hope is strongly associated with the experiential dimensions of serenity, including inner peace, trust, acceptance, and harmony in life. This dynamic interplay between hope and inner peace fosters a balanced, resilient mindset and supports a holistic approach to wellbeing (Lu et al., 2021). High-hope individuals report elevated levels of positivity, inspiration, energy, confidence, self-worth, and a sense of being positively challenged by goal pursuit (Snyder, 2002; Snyder et al., 2002). Moreover, hope and hopeful thinking have been shown to predict flourishing, psychological wellbeing, and life satisfaction, and are positively associated with healthy intimate relationships and meaningful contributions to family, community, society, and the common good (Schornick, 2023).

Over decades, theorists and practitioners alike have recognised the pivotal role of hope in promoting positive, performance-related outcomes across diverse life domains. This explains why research has found a significant relationship between possessing hope and performance, both in the academic domain and on the sport field. More specifically, hopeful thinking is associated with higher grades at school and at university level (see Colla, 2023 for a review), and college athletes who have high hope perform significantly better in track and field than those with low hope (Snyder et al., 2002). The contrary is also true – low hope can predict lower success in both academic and athletic performance (Snyder, 2002). Rather than allowing low-hope children to struggle, become more discouraged, and eventually drop out, educators and psychologists can help turn things around. Studies have successfully used hopeful thinking interventions at all elementary, high school, and university levels (and during college orientation) to improve academic performance, self-esteem, and wellbeing (Snyder et al., 2002). Hope is also a significant component of educational leadership, allowing teachers to be empowered and to empower their students (Walker, 2006).

According to Walker (2006, p. 552), when people are hopeful and feel supported, their confidence and wellbeing – which includes feelings of "trust, optimism, assurance, happiness, and strength of belief" – increase. Li et al. (2022) are of the opinion that hope is positively correlated with optimism and motivation to pursue goals or overcome challenges. When your motivation pushes you to work harder and your hopeful thinking helps you work smarter, your abilities improve, leading to more and more confidence in your abilities to achieve those goals. Being supported provides the necessary encouragement, resources, and assistance. Together, these three elements create a powerful combination that can contribute to resilience, growth, and achievement. It may be important to note that self-efficacy differs from hope. Whereas self-efficacy is specific to a particular situation and relates to the belief in oneself to solve a problem, hope is grounded in action, reflects the intention or will to take on or continue a goal, and endures over different situations (Trzmielewska et al., 2022, p. 23; Schornick, 2023; Abramson, 2024).

Hope to prevent negative outcomes

Researchers have found that cultivating hope can help as a buffer against the stress and trauma of adversity. Viewing hope through the cognitive construct lens emphasises the role of hope in shaping thoughts, beliefs, and behaviours. In this regard, hope drives motivation, resilience, and wellbeing, which may significantly reduce depression, anxiety, and illness (Moss-Pech et al, 2020; Schornick et al., 2023; Long et al., 2020). In fact, longitudinal research has found that people with more hope throughout their lives have fewer chronic health problems; are less likely to be depressed or anxious; have stronger social support, and tend to live longer (Long et al., 2020). Additionally, hope has helped patients successfully deal with a broad range of chronic ailments, such as physical disabilities, burns, spinal cord injuries, rheumatoid arthritis, fibromyalgia, chronic fatigue, blindness, and pain (Abramson, 2024; Carter et al., 2023; Hirsch & Sirois, 2016, Jackson et al., 1998; Pasyar et al., 2023; Saadatmehr et al., 2024; Steffen et al., 2020; Xu et al., 2017; Zuchetto et al., 2020). Some studies have also observed that hope contributes to active coping strategies that predict better adjustment, for instance in cancer patients (Peh et al., 2017). Moreover, hope has been shown to help people of all ages overcome fear, build strategies to deal with addictions (Saboor et al., 2019), trauma, and post-traumatic stress disorder (PTSD) (Long, 2022).

Interestingly, hope has also been shown to be beneficial on a societal level by targeting audience members through television advertisements who are in despair: viewers have been engaged using goal setting (*get help when you feel sad*), through pathways (*call this hotline*), and agency (*you are not alone*) (Snyder et al., 2002c, p. 265). Similarly, laying the foundation of hope in legal frameworks can empower people to make good decisions, preventing crises and accidents (Snyder et al., 2002). Furthermore, hope has also positively contributed to enhanced resilience and effective coping among survivors of domestic violence (Munoz et al., 2017; Li et al., 2022). Finally, hope is central in reducing depression and hopelessness in children and youth (Kwok et al., 2016; Berry et al., 2021), as well as in the elderly (Irving et al, 2004; Zhu et al., 2017). And like in the case of Sam, strategies of cultivating hope can also assist adolescent victims of bullying (Totan et al., 2017).

Despair and hopelessness

Unlike fleeting moments of sadness, despair is a profound and pervasive state characterised by overwhelming hopelessness, powerlessness, disillusionment, and a loss of faith in the future. It constitutes a deep emotional void in which optimism withers and a sense of futility prevails (Lazarus, 1999).

From a cognitive perspective, despair distorts perception, leading to pervasive negative thinking patterns, where optimism becomes a remote and inaccessible construct. Emotionally, despair engulfs individuals in profound sadness, grief, and emptiness. These emotional states are often accompanied by withdrawal, lethargy, and an absence of motivation, which in turn hinder personal growth and meaningful engagement with life (Beck, 1967).

The origins of despair are multifactorial, encompassing biological, psychological, and socio-cultural dimensions. According to Graham (2024, p. 2), despair reflects "a condition in which people do not care whether they live or die and therefore lack a narrative for their own future." Avoidant behaviours and emotional withdrawal may exacerbate distress, as individuals fail to address the underlying issues contributing to their suffering (Scott, 2024; Graham, 2024).

Moreover, in states of sustained despair, individuals may become more susceptible to misinformation, conspiracy theories, and even radicalisation (Graham, 2024). This vulnerability is particularly pronounced among disenfranchised or hopeless individuals, including some youth, who may turn to radical protest movements as a means of asserting agency or reclaiming a sense of purpose (Shafieioun, 2023).

A practical guide to foster hope

Researchers have found that interventions relying on hope, for both individuals and groups, can be used for physical and psychological conditions to find new meaning in life (e.g., Azimian et al., 2021; Snyder, 2002). Feldman et al. (2021) have successfully cultivated hope amongst cancer patients through regular workshops on hope. As an incubator of hope, positive psychology interventions also offer various evidence-based strategies to foster and sustain hope, especially when people are experiencing hopeless times, despair, and death. Once again, evidence suggests that hope can be learnt and strengthened through strategies which enhance goal-setting, pathways-thinking, agency and motivation (e.g., Feldman et al., 2021; Magyar-Moe & Lopez, 2015), as detailed next.

Goal-setting (Whypower). A person must know what drives them – what they would like to achieve in life, and their own purpose and destiny. Ensure short-, medium-, and long-term goals that are intrinsically meaningful by adding to their life's purpose. *Intrinsically meaningful goals* are things that one does not necessarily have to do, but want to do, to make life more meaningful. Find the *golden thread*, evident in one's self-selected life's purpose, which links short-, medium-, and long-term goals and leads to personal satisfaction (Bronk et al., 2009).

Pathways-thinking (Waypower). Individuals with high levels of hope can generate multiple pathways to achieve their goals. To find all the many ways one can achieve one's goals, a person must sit with a pen and paper and brainstorm on different ideas. One can also get more ideas and input from trusted friends and family members (Feldman et al., 2021).

Agency and motivation (Willpower). Gratitude, a core concept in positive psychology, is about the appreciation for what one receives, whether tangible or intangible. Gratitude can be understood as a two-step process: recognising that one has received a positive outcome and acknowledging that there is an external source for this positive outcome (Emmons & McCullough, 2003). Gratitude is a multidimensional construct that can be interpersonal (toward benefactors), transpersonal (toward deities or the universe), or existential (toward life itself) (Emmons & Stern, 2013). Research has shown that individuals who regularly practise gratitude report higher levels of positive emotions, greater life satisfaction, and lower levels of depression and anxiety (Wood et al., 2010). Gratitude is also linked to better physical health, including improved sleep quality and stronger immune systems (Emmons & McCullough, 2003; Wood et al., 2010). Additionally, gratitude enhances social relationships by fostering feelings of connectedness and prosocial behaviour (Algoe et al., 2008). Evidence-based gratitude interventions that enhance hope, include *gratitude journaling*, which involves regularly writing down things for which one is grateful. This practice helps individuals focus on the positive aspects of their lives and develop a habit of recognising and appreciating these aspects. Research by Emmons and McCullough (2003) found that individuals who kept gratitude journals reported higher levels of wellbeing, optimism, and physical health. Participants in this aforementioned study were asked to write about things for which they were grateful on a daily or weekly basis, which led to significant improvement in participants' psychological and physical health. Similarly, research by Seligman et al. (2005) and subsequent studies suggest that the simple practice of *reflecting on three positive events* each day increases the frequency and intensity of positive emotions (such as joy, gratitude, and contentment). Also, by focusing on positive experiences, individuals can counteract the effects of negative emotions such as sadness, anxiety, and despair. This shift in focus helps to reduce rumination and negative thinking patterns, which are often associated with depression and anxiety (Sin & Lyubomirsky, 2009).

Mindfulness. Mindfulness, defined as a state of active, open attention to the present moment (Kabat-Zinn, 1994), has gained substantial attention in positive psychology for its potential to enhance psychological wellbeing. Mindfulness-based interventions have been shown to significantly reduce stress, enhance emotional regulation, and promote overall psychological wellbeing across diverse populations (Goldberg et al., 2022; Niemiec & Lissing, 2016; Khoury et al., 2015). In the context of hope theory, mindfulness helps individuals clarify their goals, values, and aspirations. Several mindfulness-based interventions have been developed to enhance psychological wellbeing, and their application in fostering hope is supported by empirical evidence. For instance, evidence-based mindfulness interventions may include *loving-kindness meditation* rooted in Buddhist traditions, encouraging individuals to cultivate compassion for themselves and others. This practice has been shown to significantly reduce symptoms of anxiety and depression (Fredrickson et al., 2008).

Mindfulness-Based Cognitive Therapy (MBCT). MBCT integrates mindfulness practices with cognitive-behavioural techniques to prevent the recurrence of depression. By teaching individuals to observe their thoughts and feelings without becoming entangled in them, MBCT can reduce negative rumination and increase psychological flexibility. This approach helps individuals maintain a hopeful outlook by reducing negative thinking patterns and enhancing coping abilities (Kabat-Zinn, 2003).

Interpersonal connections (Wepower). One must examine their environment for people and resources that remind one that they are cared for and loved. Having close connections with friends, family, and colleagues who care can enhance one's sense of hope (Martino et al., 2017).

A final thought

Even in the midst of utter despair, when the possibility of changing paths is unrealistic and all hope is lost, hopeful thinking still matters. For example, if Sam were to find out that the school is no longer willing to work on improving things with his classmates, and has suggested he change schools, hopeful thinking is still a necessary and important coping mechanism. Even when people face tragedy and imminent death, according to Wrigley (2019), hopeful thinking or 'hope talk' can be beneficial, resulting in a 'good death', moving from a 'hope for me' towards a 'hope for us' based upon communal bonds of solidarity. These shared ties are evident in Adlerian theory, which approaches psychotherapy holistically and optimistically, with all three attributes of faith, hope, and love as necessary conditions (Mosak & Bluvshtein, 2019). Furthermore, Adlerian therapists are instructed to maintain hope from the outset and have faith in their patients to be agents of change.

The interconnectedness between faith, hope, and love is described best by the late Harold Mosak, co-founder of the Alfred Adler Institute (now Adler University), when explaining what he, as a therapist, needs to provide to his dying patient: "He may need hope. And when there is not much hope, he may need faith. And when faith cannot handle all that comes, he will need my love" (Mosak & Bluvshtein, 2019).

Conclusion

Hope may help people cope, recuperate, find purpose, and learn to lead better lives, despite illness, trauma, addiction, tragedy, and loss. Even when all hope is lost, hopeful thinking may play a vital role. Hope can even be infectious, springing from social commerce and hopeful-thinking communities, simultaneously uplifting ourselves and those around us. Ultimately, hope and hopeful thinking continue to be areas ripe for further exploration. Even in the bleakest of moments and darkest of times, hope is the beacon that guides us forward. In the words of Magyar-Moe and Lopez (2015, p. 500): "Hope is a human strength that fuels our pursuit of the good life. The more we understand about hope, the closer we get to a good life for all." So, do not waste another moment, we must don our capes – or a Superman t-shirt – and go find our *Superpower of Hope!*

CHAPTER 13

Emotional Intelligence Research
Over Four Decades: Implications
for Researchers and Practitioners in
Basic Emotions

Gina Görgens-Ekermans

Intricate emotions on the playground

One of the third-grade boys, Sidney, was shivering from the cold, on the playground. Today, it was Ms Isabelle overseeing the playground, and she asked Sidney if he owned a warm jersey and decent shoes. Sidney answered: "No, Ms Isabelle, my mum cannot afford to buy me new clothes." After school, Isabelle decided to purchase a new jersey and shoes, and gifted them to Sidney the next morning. However, a few days later, two older boys noticed the new items. Loudly, and making sure that others heard his accusation, Billy repeatedly shouted: "Thief, thief! Where did you steal that from?" – while pointing to Sidney in his new jersey and shoes. As Sidney denied the accusation, by shouting angrily at them, the boys started to violently berate him, with the altercation turning physical. Swiftly, the headmaster and Isabelle arrived on the scene to break up the confrontation. In this process, one of the accusers shouted at the headmaster: "You suck eggs!" "You suck eggs!" the headmaster replied angrily.

In the aftermath of this, Isabelle pondered on how a gift could cause such pain and negative emotions. The headmaster pondered how he could lose his temper with a pupil. The teacher of the class in which the troublemakers were, was stunned at their behaviour, pondering her ability to teach them about appropriate behaviour. In unpacking this situation, sophisticated reasoning is clearly needed. More importantly, what information about emotions and feelings can help resolve this situation? What can be done about the headmaster's guilt? Why were Billy and the other accusers so angry? How can Isabelle reframe her regret about the gift? What resilience is needed by Sidney to absorb this incident and not let it define his character in terms of the shame he experienced? How could empathy be grown in an environment where the majority is deprived of financial, and often emotional, support? Reasoning that takes emotions into account, in part, is what emotional intelligence (EI) is about.

Introduction

Since its inception as an academic construct in 1990, through seminal publications in prominent journals focused on cognitive intelligence (Mayer & Salovey, 1990; Mayer, Caruso & Salovey, 1999) and emotion (Mayer, Salovey, Caruso & Sitarenios, 2001), EI has continued to appeal to a wide audience of scholars and practitioners. The utility of EI has been demonstrated in many areas of psychological science, as evidenced through recent meta-analyses in educational (e.g., MacCann et al., 2020; Quílez-Robres, Usán, Lozano-Blasco & Salavera, 2023) and organisational domains (e.g., Doğru, 2022; Marinova, Anand & Park, 2025; Pirsoul, Parmentier, Sovet & Nils, 2023), as well as theoretical developments in neuroscience (Smith et al., 2018). Notably, a large body of research underscores the psychological health benefits of EI, measured from different perspectives. For example, meta-analytic evidence suggests a notable association between EI and subjective wellbeing (e.g., positive and negative affect and general life satisfaction) in both adolescents (Llamas-Díaz et al., 2022) and adults (Sánchez-Álvarez et al. 2016). Further underscoring the impact of EI on psychological adjustment over the lifespan, the results of various meta-analyses have solidified its significant effect on psychological health, e.g., mental and physical health (Martins et al., 2010; Schutte et al., 2007), and optimism (Glassie & Schutte, 2024), with evidence of a clear link to reduced incidents of depression in clinical samples (Downey et al., 2008), as well as suicidal behaviour (Domínguez-García & Fernández-Berrocal, 2018).

In addition to cognition, perception and motivation, emotions are generally regarded as one of the most basic and central functions of the human psyche. Broadly, EI is generally defined as the competence to identify and express emotions, understand emotions, assimilate emotions in thought, as well as reflectively regulate both positive and negative emotions in the self and others (Matthews, Zeidner & Roberts, 2002; Salovey & Mayer, 1990), while promoting emotional and intellectual growth (Mayer & Salovey, 1997). Indeed, preceding the identification of EI as a unique, scientifically viable construct, various influential psychologists have alluded to the notion that alternative types of intelligence may account for general life success, wellbeing and a range of other positive outcomes. For example, the work of Thorndike (1920), Weschler (1943), and Gardner (1983) all contained the notion of considering a more holistic perspective on human intellectual capabilities. In essence, they argued for the broadening of the comprehension of intelligence beyond cognitive domains, by adding emotional and affective components. References to 'social intelligence', defined as the demonstration of wisdom in interpersonal relationships by Thorndike (1920), was later evident in the work of Weschler (1943). He not only acknowledged the need and potential benefit of including non-intellective factors in traditional conceptualisations of cognitive intelligence, but also included items to this effect in his intelligence test batteries (i.e., measuring emotional components). Several decades later, Gardner (1983) solidified this notion into a theory, with this publication, *Frames of Mind: The Theory of Multiple Intelligences*, which clearly acknowledged interpersonal and intrapersonal sub-dimensions as part of traditional conceptualisations of intelligence. This chapter will endeavour to provide a brief review of EI research over the last four decades, in an attempt to highlight implications for researchers and practitioners, predominantly working in the domain of emotions.

The foundational role of emotions in emotional intelligence

Although there is some debate about the exact nature of how emotions are organised in the human brain (see Shackman & Wagner, 2019), most scholars would agree that basic emotions – fear, anger, disgust, happiness, sadness, and surprise – exist, and are associated with distinct feelings and expressions. Emotions hold the potential to alter thinking in numerous ways (Mayer & Salovey, 1997). Generally, anxiety or fear disrupt cognition (Tarasiuk, Ciorciari & Stough, 2009), while signalling that an imminent powerful or uncontrollable threat exists. Typically, anger could reflect feelings of injustice, while happiness indicates harmonious relations with others. Positive and negative emotions, however, influence the cognitive system, prioritising attention to what is important (Salovey et al., 2002). Moreover, human emotion is "profoundly social" (Shackman & Wagner, 2019, p. 7). For example, universals in emotional expression exist, and individuals should be able to recognise them. Thus, emotional reasoning encompasses issues of relationships, as clearly illustrated in the opening vignette of this chapter. Consider, for example, the question of what would be the most appropriate emotional response to the shouting at the accusers, in the vignette, by the headmaster? How should she interpret her displayed reaction (shouting with intense anger) to counter feelings of dread and guilt? The answers to such questions would likely depend on a complex net of historic and present-day social cues and learnt emotional behaviours – and often, no correct answer exist. If the headmaster, for example, had a history of being exposed to shouting in a secure and safe, relational context (e.g., married parents that shouted often, but then resolved their conflict) it is likely that her response would be different, than if her parents yelled constantly at each other, and eventually got divorced. That is, the former could be interpreted as 'shouting releases frustration and is an appropriate emotional reaction to release irritation', whereas the latter would most likely represent the idea of 'shouting equals hatred'. Further complicating this, would be the social role that the headmaster fulfils, and the display rules (i.e., known organisationally mandated roles about appropriate emotional behaviour) that would govern good emotional behaviour, in such an instance (in front of colleagues and pupils). Mayer and Salovey (1997, p. 9) further illustrate this idea with the following example: "...an insulted person might feel anger, or if the person was insecure and non-assertive, might feel shame, humiliation – or repressed anger. Recognizing these reactions requires some form of intelligence", alluding to the construct of EI. Here, EI encapsulates the ability to almost automatically understand and efficiently manage emotions (both in oneself and of others).

Exactly *how* EI relates to emotions in a broader sense, is an area of investigation that is constantly evolving and revealing new insights. Research (e.g., Megías-Robles et al., 2019) has shown, for example, that individuals higher on EI are generally more adept at not using suppression or rumination, which are regarded as problematic emotion regulation strategies. Moreover, such individuals are also more skilled in distinguishing emotional from non-emotional information in a cognitive processing task (Gutiérrez-Cobo, Cabello & Fernández-Berrocal, 2017), as well as effectively using emotional information in decision-making via cognitive control (Checa & Fernández-Berrocal, 2019). The effect of EI on social functioning is quite pervasive. Higher levels of EI have been shown to not only influence general satisfaction with social relationships (Lopes et al., 2003), likely reflected in larger, and more fulfilling social support networks (Ciarrochi et al., 2001), but also influence perceptions of sense of belongingness (i.e., rejection or inclusion) (Moeller et al., 2020), which predicted depression, anxiety and stress in a group of college students.

Moreover, EI has been extensively studied in terms of its relationship with emotional regulation, most notably, that of emotional labour. Emotional labour, also referred to as 'emotion work' (Hochschild, 1983) is generally described as the management of emotions and feelings to meet organisationally prescribed display rules for effective social interactions (Agnew et al., 2006). Research on Emotional labour and EI, specifically illustrates the intricacies of how EI is embedded in the social context and resultant interactions stemming from reciprocal emotional exchanges. Consider, for example, that emotional labour is, amongst other strategies, enacted through two emotional regulation techniques, namely surface acting and deep acting (Holman et al., 2002). According to Chu et al. (2012), surface acting describes the suppression of experienced emotions, as well as the feigning of unfelt emotions. Deep acting describes the portrayal of required feelings (i.e., display rules) through the *adjustment* of internal emotions to truly encounter the felt or authentic feeling (Hoffmann, 2016). Returning to the vignette, the teacher of the class in which the accusers were, would display surface acting in the class situation by deliberately repressing her frustration and disappointment with these students, or ignoring her anger related to the situation. Meta-analytic research evidence (Hülsheger & Schewe, 2011) has shown that, in the long term, surface acting is detrimental to psychological health, partly due to the likely emotional dissonance it creates, which results in feelings of a subsequent loss of the authentic self (Hoffman, 2016), due to perceiving the emotional experience (e.g., expressing frustration) as a threat to their identity (e.g., wanting to be a supportive teacher) (Jansz & Timmers, 2002). Furthermore, the negative emotion (i.e., anger) is not undone by this regulation strategy (Messerli et al., 2016). In fact, it is well-known through the work of Frederickson (2001) and colleagues that positive emotions are needed to undo the aftereffects of negative emotions. This is known as the "undoing hypothesis" (Frederickson & Levenson, 1998), further underscoring the important effect of experiencing positive emotions. Conversely, if this teacher, however, would work through her own shame and regret at their behaviours, and adjust her emotional reaction, to voice an appropriate measure of disappointment to them, it will most likely resolve her internal conflict about her (potential peripheral) contribution to this situation. Consequently, she will likely experience some positive emotions (e.g., hope, resilience) in the process, which may trigger an upward spiral of emotional wellbeing, as predicted by the broaden-and-build theory of positive emotions (Frederickson, 2001). More specifically, the mechanism underlying the gain spiral is explained as,

...suspected reciprocal relations among positive emotions, broadened thinking, and positive meaning suggest that over time the effects of positive emotions should accumulate and compound. The broadened attention and cognition triggered by earlier experiences of positive emotion should facilitate coping with adversity, and this improved coping should predict future experiences of positive emotion. As this cycle continues, people build their psychological resilience and enhance their emotional well-being (Frederickson, 2001, p.9).

However, this self-regulation process presupposes a certain level of emotional self-awareness (perception of emotion), as well as the reflective regulation of emotions, to facilitate positive long-term health outcomes – underscoring the importance of EI in this process.

Conceptualisation and measurement of emotional intelligence

EI is a relatively 'young' psychological construct, compared to cognitive intelligence, which is supported by almost 115 years of research. Hence, research on EI clearly carries a distinctive trait of maturing paradigms (Kuhn, 1962) – the emergence and differentiation of specific theories. The centre of the debate, regarding the conceptualisation and measurement of EI, has been focused on the conceptual distinction/categorisation of different models and measures. Two main approaches have been used: ability EI and trait EI (Petrides & Furnham, 2000), with the 'trait' approach being previously referred to as 'mixed models'. More recently, Boyatzis et al. (2017) proposed that the 'mixed models' approach should further be split into 'trait EI' and 'behavioural' EI.

The ability approach to EI. EI is often regarded as an ability, measured through maximum performance tests, e.g., the Mayer Salovey Emotional Intelligence Test (Mayer et al., 2002). Here test items measure emotional abilities that tap into the individual's ability to process and recognise, and regulate emotionally laden information, where the scoring of 'correct' answers is often dependent on expert or consensus[2] criteria. The assessment of EI as a mental ability relies on the assumption that answers to stimuli, i.e., test items, developed to assess various facets of feelings, can be scored as correct or incorrect (Mayer & Salovey, 1997). An example item, illustrating this, is as follows: "Joan felt stressed, and became a bit anxious when she thought about all the work she needed to do. When her manager brought her an additional project, she felt (a) overwhelmed, (b) depressed, (c) ashamed, (d) self-conscious, or (e) jittery (select the best answer)." The correct answer to this question is 'overwhelmed'.[3] If expert scoring is used, the 'correct' answer would have been dictated by the individuals who were identified as 'experts' at the time of developing the instrument, to develop the scoring key (who – inadvertently – were male and Caucasian, reflecting the demographic make-up of the developers of the test). However, Ekermans (2009) provided a compelling argument for why expert scoring may perpetuate measurement bias by pinpointing inconsistencies in research results between cultural groups, based on which type of scoring method is used. Broadly interpreted, measurement bias refers to a range of factors that introduce disturbances in cross-group (e.g., cultural) assessment, which influences that comparability of scores over different groups (Ekermans, 2009). For example, on the 'Emotion identification-perception' branch item, noted above, the 'correct' answer may well be open to interpretation, implying that it may not be possible to contrast scores from individuals of different groups (e.g., males versus females, or African versus Caucasian respondents) on this branch, in terms of total scores. For example, Roberts, Zeidner and Matthews (2001) noted that, on the Multi-Factor Emotional Intelligence Scale (MEIS) (Mayer et al., 1999), a precursor to the well-known MSCEIT ability instrument, different scoring methods yielded contradictory

---

2 With expert scoring, experts in the field of emotions determine with their 'best judgement' on emotional meanings presented in the test items (i.e., emotional content). The test taker then receives credit for ratings on test items that correspond with expert judgements. Consensus scoring implies that the test taker receives credit for endorsing the response that the group endorses (i.e., pooling the answers of everyone in the sample), as the consensus group response is used as the 'correct' answer.

3 www.psychometricinstitute.com.au

findings. That is, "when consensus-based scores were used, white and ethnic minority group participants were not reliably discriminable. However, when expert scoring criteria [was] used, white participants scored significantly higher than their ethnic minority counterparts" (Roberts et al., 2001, p. 219). In addition, there is evidence of the cascading nature of EI skills/traits/competencies (Joseph & Newman, 2010; Görgens-Ekermans & Roux, 2021), originally proposed by Mayer and Salovey (1997), with the suggestion that EI abilities are organised hierarchically from basic (i.e., perception, appraisal and expression of emotion), to more psychologically integrated processes (reflective regulation of emotions). To this end, the idea that 'right responses' exist, is even further challenged. For example, what would be the 'right response' for Sidney being mocked and insulted by his peers, which would likely require the reflective regulation of emotions (the higher order branch of the MSCEIT)? Most likely, the best or 'right' response will depend on various factors. For example, the situation within which this scenario occurred will play a role. Perhaps he has been previously mocked by them, or he knows they are part of a larger, potentially dangerous gang in the school? The physical threat he experiences will also play into his emotional response, which is likely in this case, to be timid, and non-confrontational. Sidney's experience with being insulted and cultural norms about how to respond in such situations may also dictate the 'right' answer for this situation. For example, he may be inclined to maintain group harmony, which is more indicative of a collectivist cultural orientation. Conversely, his position in the status hierarchy (e.g., he is popular) may favour him to exerting himself, which would be more indicative of an individualistic orientation, as his self-identity is strong enough to override cultural norms in this case. For example, Ekermans (2009) has highlighted how individualistic cultures value emotions signalling assertiveness, independence and authenticity, whilst the emotional norm in largely collectivistic cultures may endorse emotions signalling interdependence and harmonious relationships (e.g., compassion and empathy). Hence, the scoring of ability-based EI models has been the subject of much scrutiny (see e.g., Matthews et al., 2002). However, the theoretical contribution of the Mayer and Salovey EI model has been very significant, as it provided the basis for the development of numerous self-report instruments, with associated EI theories, based on the four-branch, Mayer and Salovey model.

Hence, a brief discussion of the four-branch Mayer and Salovey model (1997) follows. The lowest branch, branch one, involves the ability to *perceive, appraise and express emotions accurately*. This implies that an individual can identify emotions and emotional content in themselves, but also in other individuals (through language, appearance), as well as in inanimate objects. It further implies that the individual can express needs related to experienced emotions, as well as discriminate between characteristic of expressions of emotional displays (e.g., accurate/honest versus inaccurate/ dishonest). The second branch, *emotional facilitation of thinking*, implies that emotions help prioritise thinking by aiding judgement and memory. Emotional states are, for example, within this branch, deemed to encourage problem solving approaches (e.g., happiness can facilitate creativity). Branch three, *understanding and analysing emotions*, describe the ability to employ emotional knowledge in terms of emotions in the social context. For example, this branch taps into the ability to interpret meanings that emotions convey about relationships, blends of emotions (e.g., fear and surprise), as well as transitions between emotions (e.g., from anger to satisfaction). Lastly, branch four is focused on the *reflective regulation of emotions* to promote emotional and intellectual growth. This branch taps into abilities related to being open to both negative and positive feelings, to reflectively engage or detach from an emotion given the cognitive appraisal of the emotion, being able to reflectively monitor emotions in oneself and in relation to others, as well as the ability to manage emotions in oneself and others (enhancing positive emotions and diminishing negative emotions). As indicated previously, branch one encompasses the simplest EI ability (perceiving and expressing emotions) with branch four representing the most psychologically integrated emotional processes (the conscious, reflective regulation of emotion). Each branch, also, within itself, contains four abilities that represent early and later developmental milestones. Generally, the abilities become more integrated in a well-functioning adult. That is, an emotionally mature adult can more easily and reflectively regulate based on their own identified emotions, as well as emotional cues from the environment.

The trait approach to EI. In addition to the ability approach, the trait approach measures EI as a constellation of personality dispositions. Here test takers self-report on behavioural tendencies and abilities, rather than utilising a test that objectively assesses their EI abilities (see Schutte et al., 1998). That is, the measures tap into typical behaviours of emotion-relevant situations (e.g., "*I know why my emotions change*" and "*I ruminate on things that make me angry*"). Examples include the Bar-On Emotional Quotient Inventory (EQ-i; Bar-On, 1997), the Trait Emotional Intelligence Questionnaire (TEIQue; Petrides & Furnham, 2001), the Genos Emotional Intelligence Inventory (Genos EI) (Gignac, 2008), the Self-report Emotional Intelligence Test (SREIT) (Schutte et al., 1998), as well as the Situational Tests of Emotional Management and Understanding (MacCann & Roberts, 2008). The latter three tests were based on the Mayer and Salovey (1990) model, while the former two represent 'expanded models' (Ashkanasy & Daus, 2005, p. 443), with components not included in the Mayer and Salovey EI theory. In addition to the 'ability' and 'trait' models distinction, for which Petrides and Furnham (2000) are generally credited, the term 'mixed models' has also been used frequently (Ashkanasy & Daus, 2005). EI models in this category include a mixture of personality and behavioural (e.g., social skills and competencies) items. An example of such a measure is the Emotional and Social Competence Inventory (ECSI) (Boyatzis, 2009), which includes sub-dimensions of self-awareness, self-management, social awareness and relationship management. A full review of all the most prominent instruments and measures utilising the trait EI approach, is beyond the scope of this chapter (for a recent review, see O'Connor et al., 2019). However, there is sufficient evidence that most of these theories and subsequent measurement instruments share sufficient conceptual overlap, which can be interpreted to describe the core facets of EI. Notably, much of these resemble the four branches identified by Mayer and Salovey (1990, 1997). These include facets relating to "(1) perceiving emotions (in self and others), (2) regulating emotions in self, (3) regulation emotions in others, and (4) strategically utilising emotions" (O'Connor et al., 2019, p. 3).

For example, the TEIQue (Petrides & Furnham, 2001) measures four factors and 15 facets of EI. The (1) 'emotionality' subscale represents perceiving emotion; (2) the 'self-control' subscale measures self-regulation of emotions; (3) regulating emotions in others is measured with the 'sociability' subscale, while (4) a 'wellbeing' subscale measures the extent to which an individual can strategically utilise emotions in everyday situations. The sampling domain of trait EI, measured with the TEIQue, was based on a content analysis of early EI constructs and related constructs, which included alexithymia, empathy, emotional expression and affective communication (Petrides, 2009). Individuals high on 'emotionality' are described as being in touch with their own, and other individual's feelings. Such individuals can perceive and express emotions and use these qualities to build and sustain close relationships. 'Self-control' describes a healthy degree of control over impulses and being able to regulate external pressures and stress. Responses are, therefore, neither repressed, or overly expressive. 'Sociability' describes the extent to which an individual is proficient in social interaction, which then naturally translates into social networks and good negotiation skills (or not). Lastly, 'wellbeing' describes a generalised sense of wellbeing, which is reflected in self-reported scores on items measuring facets, such as feeling positive, happy and fulfilled. Low scorers, generally, have low self-regard and present with a general discontent/disappointment about their life (Petrides, 2009).

Another prominent trait of the EI measure, the Genos EI inventory, contains seven dimensions, which measure an individual's typical application of emotionally relevant skills or abilities (Gignac, 2008). The original instrument (i.e., the Swinburne University Emotional Intelligence Test (SUEIT)) was originally developed through a large factor-analytic study on prominent measures of EI (at the time), which included the MSCEIT (Mayer, Salovey & Caruso, 2000a); the Bar-On EQ-i (Bar-On, 1997); the TAS-20 (Bagby, Paker & Taylor, 1994a); the EI scale by Schutte et al. (1998), and the Trait Meta-Mood Scale (TMMS) (Salovey, Mayer, Goldman, Turvey & Palfai, 1995). Mirroring personality research on the Big Five, this approach to uncovering a 'taxonomy' for EI resulted in dimensional communality, with five sub-dimensions being identified (Palmer, Gignac, Ekermans & Stough, 2008). These included, (1) emotional self-awareness and expression, (2) emotional self-awareness of others, (3) emotional reasoning, (4) emotional self-management, and (5) emotional control. In the revised instrument (renamed to the Genos EI inventory) emotional self-awareness and expression were split into separate dimensions, while emotional self-management was distinguished from emotional management of others (Gignac, 2017).

The broader Bar-On EQ-i model (1997, 2004, p. 14) defines EI as an "array of noncognitive capabilities, competencies, and skills that influence one's ability to succeed in coping with environmental demands and pressures." The instrument measures 15 malleable components that combine into five composite subscale scores. These include (1) intrapersonal EI (including aspects, such as self-regard, emotional self-awareness, assertiveness), (2) interpersonal EI (empathy, social responsibility, interpersonal relationship), (3) adaptability (flexibility, problem solving), (4) stress management (stress tolerance, impulse control), and (5) general mood (happiness and optimism). In addition to clarifying the different theoretical orientations to EI (and their associated measurement implications), the question about the malleability of EI regularly arises as an important issue pertaining to the construct. Hence, the next section reflects on this issue.

Can emotional intelligence be developed and are there benefits to such training interventions?

The proliferation of studies indicating the significant effect of EI on psychological wellbeing (e.g., Hong & Lee, 2016; Sarrionandia et al., 2018), success in the workplace (e.g., Joseph & Newman, 2010; Joseph, Jin, Newman & O'Boyle, 2015; Harms & Credé, 2010; Miao et al., 2017) and in the academic environment (e.g., MacCann et al., 2020; Rauf & Iqbal, 2024), has spurred an abundance of studies on EI interventions. Such studies typically address the questions of (1) whether EI scores can indeed be increased through training, and (2) if such increased EI skills/competencies hold beneficial outcomes (e.g., better psychological wellbeing, organisational commitment). A few examples of outcomes that have been linked to increased EI through training include emotional self-efficacy (Dacre Pool & Qualter, 2012), academic self-efficacy (Görgens-Ekermans, Delport & Du Preez, 2015), as well as psychological and physical wellbeing, social relationships, and employability (Nelis et al., 2011).

Even though some have argued against the idea of EI being an 'intelligence' (Roberts, Zeidner & Matthews, 2001), a perhaps more pressing question about the plasticity of EI and efforts to increase it, centre on the idea of emotional competence, loosely translated to EI in terms of emotional recognition and management, itself. Saarni (2000), in the *Handbook on Emotional Intelligence* (Bar-On & Parker, 2000) argued that emotional competence predominantly describes a *transaction*, not necessarily only a characteristic of the person. This view encapsulates the idea that emotional competence should be accounted for as a complex net of factors, which include, for example, (1) the individual's efficacy motivation for engaging in an emotion-eliciting encounter, (2) contextual demands and affordances available to the individual, and (3) the values and beliefs the individual brings into the emotional experience. To this end, Schutte, Malouff and Thorsteinsson (2013, p. 63) have argued that EI training might mainly impact emotional self-efficacy, "…and that an increase in emotional-competence confidence leads over time to practice-related changes in emotional intelligence ability and trait emotional intelligence." In this sense, Saarni (2000) captures the essence of what emotional competence affords the individual: the ability to function emotionally effectively, relative to the individual's goals. That is, the real test of emotional competence, loosely translated to EI in terms of emotional recognition and management, often lies in an awareness only available *after* an encounter. For example, Sidney may, with the benefit of hindsight be able to reflect on the effectiveness of his emotional reaction (i.e., shouting angrily, becoming physically violent), in the light of this goal (defending himself). Importantly, his belief in his emotional resilience would undoubtably influence his reaction to the emotionally laden interpersonal challenge (the encounter). If his belief is fragile (because the context or emotional challenge is unfamiliar – he is not used to conflict and outright confrontations) or poorly developed (due to absent parental modelling of healthy emotional regulation), then this encounter is likely to result in ineffectual outcomes. It is through this lens that the efficacy of EI training interventions should ultimately be viewed and measured. For example, Lane argued that,

> ...optimal social adaptation requires the ability to appreciate the differentiated feelings of the self and others and integrate this information into a plan of action that permits attainment of personal goals in a manner that also fits with the social context (2000, p. 185).

Yet, most of the current research on EI interventions perhaps fail to account for the complexity of such contextual variables. With this in mind, the efficacy of current EI intervention research is reviewed. Thereafter, some practical recommendations for interventions, set within the unifying framework of social and emotional learning (SEL, Graczyk et al., 2000) are presented.

One of the earliest theoretical reviews on EI interventions was conducted by Schutte et al. (2013). As a first indication of the type of effect size that could be expected for EI interventions, they selected four rigorous studies (i.e., randomised control trails with at least 50% retention of participants, $N = 435$) and calculated a meta-analytic moderate overall effect size of $g = .46$, indicating the impact of training of EI. They noted that this compared to other meta-analysis effects sizes reported for other positive psychology interventions, such as mindfulness training. More recently, Hodzic et al. (2018) analysed 28 samples over 24 studies ($N = 1\,986$) that utilised interventions to increase EI. The results of this study yielded a similar result to Schutte et al. (2013), with a moderate effect size of $g = .51$, being indicated for the impact of EI training. Notably, this study also found that trainings that are based on ability-based EI models, showed significantly higher effects. Hence, it would seem reasonable to conclude the EI interventions do increase EI levels, at least to a moderate extent, in answer to question one posed above.

On addressing the issue of whether such increased EI skills/competencies hold beneficial outcomes (Question 2), a clear body of research evidence exist. Many studies in the organisational domain, specifically focused on job satisfaction (e.g., Turner & Lloyd-Walker, 2008), teamwork and conflict management (e.g., Clarke, 2010), organisational climate (Pérez-Escoda et al., 2012), employability (Nelis et al., 2011), and workplace incivility (Kirk, Schutte & Hine, 2011) have documented significant positive changes linked to an EI intervention. Further evidence in other domains include intervention studies in the education environment. Here, perhaps the most comprehensive meta-analysis on SEL intervention studies was conducted by Durlak et al. (2011), with weak (emotional distress, $d = .24$; increased academic performance, $d = .27$) to moderate (social emotional skills, $d = .57$) effect sizes being reported. Notably, a recent systematic review (Kotsou et al., 2018, p. 9) of 46 intervention studies on adult samples (nine on ability-based measures, and 37 on trait-based measures) concluded that, overall, "…groups receiving EI interventions improved compared to control groups." This review, however, further highlighted that the most promising results lie within the realm of improving EI for psychological health, which concurs with the view of Matthews et al. (2002) – that much of the EI literature is essentially aimed at stress reduction. However, much more research evidence on the sustainability of such changes is needed. For example, Kotsou et al. (2018) noted that only about one-third of the studies included in their review, evaluated the potential sustained long-term outcomes of the training programmes. In addition, recent evidence for the effectiveness of specifically, experiential-based EI interventions (i.e., active training, which incorporates practical activities and targeted feedback), should be noted as another area of potential fruitful investigation to increase the efficacy of EI interventions (Mattingly & Kraiger, 2019; Năstasă et al., 2023).

Key features and practical considerations for EI training interventions

Given the promise of EI interventions in increasing social and emotional competencies, Matthews et al. (2002) presented a list[4] of desirable features that such programmes should ideally contain. As a first recommendation,

---

4 For an in-depth discussion on these features, please see Matthews et al. (2002, pp. 460–464).

such programmes should have a strong conceptual framework and focused, measurable goals. Accordingly, Hodzic et al. (2018) have argued that the intensity of improvement in EI is likely strongly dependent on the theoretical grounding of the intervention. The importance of realistic expectations and well-defined goals have also been highlighted by Cherniss (2000).[5] To this end, emotional self-efficacy (Bandura, 1997) is a crucial ingredient for successful social and emotional learning in adults, as expectations are likely to become self-fulfilling prophecies.

> Training programmes will be more effective if they include activities designed to help learners develop positive expectations for the training, in other words, to realize that it is possible (although not necessarily quick and easy) to improve whatever competencies they are interested in improving (Cherniss, 2000, p. 446).

Secondly, effective programmes will be comprehensive, contain multiple components, and have a systematic orientation. To this end, the *Dimensional Model of Emotional Intelligence* (see Schutte & Malouff, 2014) could be a good starting point. For example, multiple facets of emotional competence, social problem solving, and social and emotional understanding, should ideally be covered. Together with this, interventions should have a multi-level orientation. For example, in the educational environment, peers, parents and community members should be involved. In an organisational environment, this principle will translate to the involvement of line management and team members. Social and emotional change needs to occur in a safe and supportive setting (Cherniss, 2000) and is optimal with live modelling (e.g., taped role-plays).

Thirdly, an emphasis on key skills (e.g., self-awareness of feelings, emotional regulation, impulse control and empathy), as well as opportunities to practice and reinforce these skills (through role playing, modelling, play), are key elements of successful interventions, as evidenced by recent meta-analytic

---

5 Cherniss (2000) also compiled a list of best practice guidelines, which could be helpful in the design of EI development interventions.

research on experiential EI interventions (e.g., Mattingly & Kraiger, 2019). According to Salovey, Bedell, Detweiler and Mayer (2008), the cultivation of successful emotional interactions involves not only increasing the awareness of emotional competencies, but also internalising these strategies, thinking about how they could be applied, and then practising the application of these skills in everyday life. Absolutely key to this process is environmental feedback on an individual's performance of these skills. The challenge with emotional learning is that there are often strong response habits that must be altered. According to Cherniss (2000), social and emotional learning involves change that affects the core of personal identity, "...we are what we *feel* much more than what we *think*" (p. 445), therefore repeated modelling, practice and corrective feedback is needed to alter deeply embedded neural pathways in the emotional centres of the brain.

Conclusion

So how would Sidney's encounter be solved with emotional intelligence? A multi-layered approach could be used to address the emotional content that played out for every individual in the example. First, the headmaster and staff could start by modelling appropriate emotional behaviours. For example, the headmaster could have a session with all the boys and 'own' her negative emotional comment, but also explain that perceived injustice is a known trigger for heightened anger responses on her part. This gives context and creates understanding to her emotional behaviour. It also models emotional self-recognition and awareness. This could then facilitate an open discussion to directly deal with the emotional content that played out from the offender's side. Isabelle could request that the boys who started the fight write letters of apology, specifically under the guidance of a school counsellor/ trusted teacher. This should encourage reflection and self-awareness about empathy and emotional control, and potentially help them gain insight into their own triggers for bullying behaviour (feeling inferior, hopeless, because they may also be poor). Moreover, Sidney could be encouraged to reflect on his experience with a trusted adult. For example, how could he utilise this experience to build emotional resilience, and in an adaptive way resolve the shame he felt? The headmaster could devote a staff and student morning to EI training, and perhaps even encourage parents to join in this session. Teachers could have regular peer support sessions to discuss examples of patterned behaviours that could be addressed with social and emotional skills training in the school environment. Staff could make time for team talks to create a safe emotional support system for each other. These are just a few examples of how the situation could potentially be solved in an emotionally intelligent manner to reach the goal of healthy, well-functioning individuals, and organisations/schools within which they operate.

REFERENCES

A

Abatista, A. G., & Cova, F. (2023). Are self-transcendent emotions one big family? An empirical taxonomy of positive self-transcendent emotion labels. *Affective Science, 4*, 731–743. https://doi.org/10.1007/s42761-023-00194-1

Abdusattorova, B. (2023). Revealing emotions of joy and sadness. *International Scientific Online Conference: Intellectual Education Technological Solutions and Innovative Digital Tools, 2*(20). https://interonconf.org/index.php/neth/article/view/7230/6241

Abe, J. A., & Izard, C. E. (1999). The developmental functions of emotions: An analysis in terms of differential emotions theory. *Cognition and Emotion, 13*(5), 523–549. https://doi.org/10.1080/026999399379177

Abraham, A. D., Neve, K. A., & Lattal, K. M. (2014). Dopamine and extinction: A convergence of theory with fear and reward circuitry. *Neurobiology of Learning and Memory, 108*, 65–77. https://doi.org/10.1016/j.nlm.2013.11.007 researchgate.netneurotree.org

Abramson, A. (2024). Hope as the antidote. *Monitor on Psychology, 55*(1). https://www.apa.org/monitor/2024/01/trends-hope-greater-meaning-life

Acevedo, E. C., & Tost, J. (2023). Self-transcendent experience and prosociality: Connecting dispositional awe, compassion, and the moral foundations. *Personality and Individual Differences, 214*, Article 112347. https://doi.org/10.1016/j.paid.2023.112347

Adam, H., & Galinsky, A. D. (2012). Enclothed cognition. *Journal of Experimental Social Psychology, 48*(4), 918–925. https://doi.org/10.1016/j.jesp.2012.02.008 researchgate.netscirp.org

Adler, A. (1924). *The practice and theory of individual psychology.* Harcourt Brace.

Adler, A. (1930). Individual psychology. In C. Murchison (Ed.), *Psychologists of 1930* (pp. 395–405). Clark University Press.

Adolphs, R. (2013). The biology of fear. *Current Biology, 23*(2), R79–R93. https://doi.org/10.1016/j.cub.2012.11.055

Agnew, J., de Castro, A. B., Curbow, B., Fitzgerald, S. T., & Haythornthwaite, J. A. (2006). Measuring emotional labor among young workers: Refinement of the Emotions at Work Scale. *Workplace Health and Safety, 54*(5), 201–209. https://doi.org/10.1177/216507990605400503

Ahmadi, A., Bazargan-Hejazi, S., Heidari Zadie, Z., Euasobhon, P., Ketumarn, P., Karbasfrushan, A., AminiSaman, J., & Mohammadi, R. (2016). Pain management in trauma: A review study. *Journal of Injury and Violence Research, 8*(2), 89–98. https://doi.org/10.5249/jivr.v8i2.707

Akers, R. L., Sellers, C. S., & Jennings, W. G. (2021). *Criminological theories: Introduction, evaluation, and application* (8th ed.). Oxford University Press.

Alderman, B., Olson, R. L., Bates, M. E., Selby, E., Buckman, J. F., Brush, C. J., Panza, E. A., Kranzler, A., Eddie, D., & Shors, T. J. (2015). Rumination in major depressive disorder is associated with impaired neural activation during conflict monitoring. *Frontiers in Human Neuroscience, 9*, 269. https://doi.org/10.3389/fnhum.2015.00269

Alexander, R., Aragón, O. R., Bookwala, J., Cherbuin, N., Gatt, J. M., Kahrilas, I. J., Kästner, N., Lawrence, A., Lowe, L., Morrison, R. G., Mueller, S. C., Nusslock, R., Papadelis, C., Polnaszek, K. L., Richter, S. H., Silton, R. L., & Styliadis, C. (2021). The neuroscience of positive emotions and affect: Implications for cultivating happiness and wellbeing. *Neuroscience & Biobehavioural Reviews, 121*, 220–249. https://doi.org/10.1016/j.neubiorev.2020.12.002

Algoe, S. B., Haidt, J., & Gable, S. L. (2008). Beyond reciprocity: Gratitude and relationships in everyday life. *Emotion, 8*(3), 425–429. https://doi.org/10.1037/1528-3542.8.3.425

Allarakha, S., MD. (2021, February 8). What are the 3 types of trauma? *MedicineNet.* https://www.medicinenet.com/what_are_the_3_types_of_trauma/article.htm

AlShawaf, L., Conroy-Beam, D., Asao, K., & Buss, D. M. (2016). Human emotions: An evolutionary psychological perspective. *Emotion Review, 8*(2), 173–186. https://doi.org/10.1177/1754073914565518

American Psychiatric Association. (n.d.). What is post-traumatic stress disorder (PTSD)? *American Psychiatric Association.* https://www.psychiatry.org/patients-families/ptsd/what-is-ptsd

American Psychological Association. (n.d.). Trauma. *American Psychological Association.* https://www.apa.org/topics/trauma

American Psychological Association. (2017, May 25). Eye Movement Desensitization and Reprocessing (EMDR) therapy. *American Psychological Association.* https://www.apa.org/ptsd-guideline/treatments/eye-movement-reprocessing

American Psychological Association. (2017a, July 31). What is exposure therapy? *American Psychological Association.* https://www.apa.org/ptsd-guideline/patients-and-families/exposure-therapy

American Psychological Association. (2018a). Hedonic level. In *Dictionary of Psychology.* https://dictionary.apa.org/hedonic-level

American Psychological Association. (2018b). Hedonism. In *Dictionary of Psychology.* https://dictionary.apa.org/hedonism

American Psychological Association. (2018c). Flourishing. In *Dictionary of Psychology.* https://dictionary.apa.org/flourishing

American Psychological Association. (2018d). Anhedonia. In *Dictionary of Psychology*. https://dictionary.apa.org/anhedonia

American Psychological Association. (2018a). *Dictionary of Psychology: Hedonic wellbeing*. https://dictionary.apa.org/hedonic-wellbeing

American Psychological Association. (2018b). *Dictionary of Psychology: Eudaimonic wellbeing*. https://dictionary.apa.org/eudaimonicwellbeing

American Psychological Association. (2018c). *Dictionary of Psychology: Sadness*. https://dictionary.apa.org/sadness

American Psychological Association. (2020). Rumination: A cycle of negative thinking. *American Psychological Association*. https://www.psychiatry.org/news-room/apa-blogs/rumination-a-cycle-of-negative-thinking

American Psychological Association. (2023, October 17). How to cope with traumatic stress. *American Psychological Association*. https://www.apa.org/topics/trauma/stress

American Psychological Association. (2024). Anger. *American Psychological Association*. https://www.apa.org/topics/anger#:~:text=Anger%20is%20an%20emotion%20characterized,has%20deliberately%20done%20you%20wrong

Amstadter, A. (2008). Emotion regulation and anxiety disorders. *Journal of Anxiety Disorders, 22*(2), 211–221. https://doi.org/10.1016/j.janxdis.2007.02.004

Analayo, B. (2019). The insight knowledge of fear and adverse effects of mindfulness practices. *Mindfulness, 10*, 2172–2185. https://doi.org/10.1007/s12671-019-01198-4

Anderson, C. A., & Bushman, B. J. (2002). Human aggression. *Annual Review of Psychology, 53*(1), 27–51. https://doi.org/10.1146/annurev.psych.53.100901.135231

Anderson, C. A., & Huesmann, L. R. (2003). Human aggression: A socialcognitive view. In M. A. Hogg & J. Cooper (Eds), *The Sage handbook of social psychology* (pp. 296–323). Sage Publications.

Anderson, C. L. (2016). *The relationship between the D4 dopamine receptor gene (DRD4) and the emotion of awe* (Publication No. 10130107) [Doctoral dissertation, University of California]. *ProQuest Dissertations & Theses Global*. https://www.proquest.com/docview/2136365861

Anderson, C. A., Monroy, M., & Keltner, D. (2018). Awe in nature heals: Evidence from military veterans, at-risk youth, and college students. *Emotion, 18*(8), 1195–1202. https://doi.org/10.1037/emo0000442

Andrews, D. A., & Bonta, J. (1998). *The psychology of criminal conduct* (2nd rev. ed.). Anderson Publishing Company.

Ansbacher, H. L., & Ansbacher, R. R. (Eds). (1956). *The individual psychology of Alfred Adler: A systematic presentation in selections from his writings*. Basic Books.

Arias, J. A., Williams, C., Raghvani, R., Aghajani, M., Baez, S., Belzung, C., Booij, L., Busatto, G., Chiarella, J., Fu, C. H., Ibanez, A., Liddell, B. J., Lowe, L., Penninx, B. W. J. H., Rosa, P., & Kemp, A. H. (2020). The neuroscience of sadness: A multidisciplinary synthesis and collaborative review. *Neuroscience & Biobehavioural Reviews, 111*, 199–228. https://doi.org/10.1016/j.neubiorev.2020.01.006

Aristotelidou, V., Overton, P. G., & Vivas, A. B. (2023). Frontal lobe-related cognition in the context of self-disgust. *PLOS ONE, 18*(8), e0289948. https://doi.org/10.1371/journal.pone.0289948

Aron, A., & Aron, E. N. (2014). Love and sexuality. In K. McKinney & S. Sprecher (Eds), *Sexuality in close relationships* (pp. 25–48). Psychology Press.

Aron, A., Fisher, H. E., & Strong, G. (2006). Romantic love. In A. L. Vangelisti & D. Perlman (Eds), *The Cambridge handbook of personal relationships* (pp. 595–614). Cambridge University Press. https://doi.org/10.1017/CBO9780511606632.033

Arrigo, B. A., & Purcell, C. E. (2001). Explaining paraphilias and lust murder: Toward an integrated model. *International Journal of Offender Therapy and Comparative Criminology, 45*(1), 6–31. https://doi.org/10.1177/0306624X01451002

Ashkanasy, N. M., & Daus, C. S. (2005). Rumors of the death of emotional intelligence in organizational behaviour are vastly exaggerated. *Journal of Organizational Behaviour, 26*(4), 441–452. https://doi.org/10.1002/job.320

Aslan, D., & Akyol, A. K. (2020). Impact of an empathy training program on children's perspective taking abilities. *Psychological Reports, 123*(6), 2394–2409.

Averill, J. R., & Sundararajan, L. (2020). Passion and qing: Intellectual histories of emotion, West and East. In K. Pawlik & G. d'Ydewalle (Eds), *Psychological Concepts* (pp. 101–139). Psychology Press.

Azimian, M., Arian, M., Shojaei, S. F., Doostian, Y., Ebrahimi Barmi, B., & Khanjani, M. S. (2021). The effectiveness of group hope therapy training on the quality of life and meaning of life in patients with multiple sclerosis and their family caregivers. *Iranian Journal of Psychiatry, 16*(3), 260–270. https://doi.org/10.18502/ijps.v16i3.6251

B

Bach, D., Groesbeck, G., Stapleton, P., Sims, R., Blickheuser, K., & Church, D. (2019). Clinical EFT (Emotional Freedom Techniques) improves multiple physiological markers of health. *Journal of Evidence-Based Integrative Medicine, 24*, Article 2515690X18823691, 1–12. https://doi.org/10.1177/2515690X18823691

Badour, C. L., Bown, S., Adams, T. G., Bunaciu, L., & Feldner, M. T. (2012). Specificity of fear and disgust experienced during traumatic interpersonal victimization in predicting post-traumatic stress and contamination-based obsessive–compulsive symptoms. *Journal of Anxiety Disorders*, 26(5), 590–598. https://doi.org/10.1016/j.janxdis.2012.03.001

Badour, C. L., Ojserkis, R., McKay, D., & Feldner, M. T. (2014). Disgust as a unique affective predictor of mental contamination following sexual trauma. *Journal of Anxiety Disorders*, 28(7), 704–711. https://doi.org/10.1016/j.janxdis.2014.07.007

Bagby, R. M., Taylor, G. J., & Parker, J. D. A. (1994). The Twenty-Item Toronto Alexithymia Scale: Part II, convergent, discriminant, and concurrent validity. *Journal of Psychosomatic Research*, 38(1), 33–40. https://doi.org/10.1016/0022-3999(94)90006-X

Bai, Y., Maruskin, L. A., Chen, S., Gordon, A. M., Stellar, J. E., McNeil, G. D., Peng, K., & Keltner, D. (2017). Awe, the diminished self, and collective engagement: Universals and cultural variations in the small self. *Journal of Personality and Social Psychology*, 113(2), 185–209. https://doi.org/10.1037/pspa0000087

Bai, Y., Ocampo, J., Jin, G., Chen, S., Benet-Martinez, V., Monroy, M., Anderson, C., & Keltner, D. (2021). Awe, daily stress, and elevated life satisfaction. *Journal of Personality and Social Psychology*, 120(4), 837–860. https://doi.org/10.1037/pspa0000267

Bale, T. L. (2014). Lifetime stress experience: Transgenerational epigenetics and germ cell programming. *Dialogues in Clinical Neuroscience*, 16(3), 297–305. https://doi.org/10.31887/DCNS.2014.16.3/TBale

Bandura, A. (2001). Social cognitive theory: An agentic perspective. *Annual Review of Psychology*, 52, 1–26. https://doi.org/10.1146/annurev.psych.52.1.1

Bandura, A., & Walters, R. H. (1977). *Social learning theory* (Vol. 1). Prentice Hall.

Barkus, E. (2021). The effects of anhedonia in social context. *Current Behavioral Neuroscience Reports, 8*(2–3), 77–89. https://doi.org/10.1007/s40473-021-00232X

Barnett, S. A. (1975). *The rat: A study in behaviour* (Rev. ed.). University of Chicago Press.

Barney, R. (2024). *Gopal Sreenivasan, emotion and virtue: Five questions about courage. Criminal Law and Philosophy, 18*(1), 253–263. https://doi.org/10.1007/s1157202309672w

Barrett, L. F. (2012). Emotions are real. *Emotion, 12*(3), 413–429. https://doi.org/10.1037/a0027555

Barrett, L. F. (2017). The theory of constructed emotion: An active inference account of interoception and categorization. *Social Cognitive and Affective Neuroscience, 12*(1), 1–27. https://doi.org/10.1093/scan/nsw154

Bartol, C. R., & Bartol, A. M. (2014). *Criminal behaviour: A psychosocial approach* (10th ed.). Pearson.

Bartol, C. R., & Bartol, A. M. (2017). *Criminal behaviour: A psychosocial approach* (11th ed.). Prentice Hall.

Bartol, C. R., & Bartol, A. M. (2021). *Criminal behaviour: A psychological approach* (2nd customized ed., KRM 310 [B] Psychocriminology). University of Pretoria Custom Edition.

Basile, B., Mancini, F., Macaluso, E., Caltagirone, C., Frackowiak, R. S., & Bozzali, M. (2011). Deontological and altruistic guilt: Evidence for distinct neurobiological substrates. *Human Brain Mapping, 32*(2), 229–239. https://doi.org/10.1002/hbm.21009

Bastin, C., Harrison, B. J., Davey, C. G., Moll, J., & Whittle, S. (2016). Feelings of shame, embarrassment and guilt and their neural correlates: A systematic review. *Neuroscience & Biobehavioral Reviews, 71*, 455–471. https://doi.org/10.1016/j.neubiorev.2016.09.019

Bastin, C., Rakesh, D., Harrison, B. J., Davey, C. G., Allen, N. B., Müller, S., & Whittle, S. (2021). Feelings of shame and guilt are associated with distinct neural activation in youth. *Biological Psychology, 159*, Article 108025. https://doi.org/10.1016/j.biopsycho.2021.108025

Battistich, V. (2003). Effects of a school-based program to enhance prosocial development on children's peer relations and social adjustment. *Journal of Research in Character Education, 1*, 1–17.

Baumeister, R. F., & Bratslavsky, E. (1999). Passion, intimacy, and time: Passionate love as a function of change in intimacy. *Personality and Social Psychology Review, 3*(1), 49–67. https://doi.org/10.1207/S15327957PSPR0301_3

Baumgartner, T., Heinrichs, M., Vonlanthen, A., Fischbacher, U., & Fehr, E. (2008). Oxytocin shapes the neural circuitry of trust and trust adaptation in humans. *Neuron, 58*(4), 639–650. https://doi.org/10.1016/j.neuron.2008.04.009

Becker, D. V., Kenrick, D. T., Neuberg, S. L., Blackwell, K. C., & Smith, D. M. (2007). The confounded nature of angry men and happy women. *Journal of Personality and Social Psychology, 92*(2), 179–190. https://doi.org/10.1037/0022-3514.92.2.179

Beckers, T., Hermans, D., Lange, I., Luyten, L., Scheveneels, S., & Vervliet, B. (2023). Understanding clinical fear and anxiety through the lens of human fear conditioning. *Nature Reviews Psychology, 2*, 233–245. https://doi.org/10.1038/s44159-023-00156-1

Bedford, L., Mann, M., Foth, M., & Walters, R. (2022). A post-capitalocentric critique of digital technology and environmental harm: New directions at the intersection of digital and green criminology. *International Journal for Crime, Justice and Social Democracy, 11*(1), 167–181. https://doi.org/10.5204/ijcjsd.2191

Bélanger, J. J., Collier, K. E., Nisa, C. F., & Schumpe, B. M. (2021). Crimes of passion: When romantic obsession leads to abusive relationships. *Journal of Personality, 89*(6), 1159–1175. https://doi.org/10.1111/jopy.12642

Bélanger, J. J., Schumpe, B. M., & Nisa, C. F. (2019). How passionate individuals regulate their activity with other life domains: A goal-systemic perspective. *Journal of Personality, 87*(6), 1136–1150. https://doi.org/10.1111/jopy.12463

Belen, H. (2022). Fear of COVID19 and mental health: The role of mindfulness during times of crisis. *International Journal of Mental Health and Addiction, 20*(1), 607–618. https://doi.org/10.1007/s11469-020-00470-2

Bellucci, G., & Dreher, J. (2021). Trust and learning: Neurocomputational signatures of learning to trust. In F. Krueger (Ed.), *The Neurobiology of Trust* (pp. 185–218). Cambridge University Press. https://doi.org/10.1017/9781108770880.011

Bellucci, G., & Park, S. Q. (2020). Honesty biases trustworthiness impressions. *Journal of Experimental Psychology: General, 149*(8), 1567–1586. https://doi.org/10.1037/xge0000730

Benedek, D. M., & Ursano, R. J. (2009). Posttraumatic stress disorder: From phenomenology to clinical practice. *Focus, 7*(2), 160–175. https://doi.org/10.1176/foc.7.2.foc160

Benjet, C., Bromet, E. J., Karam, E. G., Kessler, R. C., McLaughlin, K. A., Ruscio, A. M., Shahly, V., Stein, D. J., Petukhova, M., Hill, E., Alonso, J., Atwoli, L., Bunting, B., Bruffærts, R., Caldas-DeAlmeida, J. M., De Girolamo, G., Florescu, S., Gureje, O., Huang, Y., ... Koenen, K. C. (2015). The epidemiology of traumatic event exposure worldwide: Results from the World Mental Health Survey Consortium. *Psychological Medicine, 46*(2), 327–343. https://doi.org/10.1017/S0033291715001981

Berardi, M. K., White, A. M., Winters, D., Thorn, K., Brennan, M., & Dolan, P. (2020). Rebuilding communities with empathy. *Local Development & Society, 1*(1), 57–67. https://doi.org/10.1080/26883597.2020.1794761

Berger, U., & Anaki, D. (2021). "And my soul shall abhor you": Implicit processing of social disgust. *Personality and Individual Differences, 168,* Article 110360. https://doi.org/10.1016/j.paid.2020.110360

Berkowitz, L. (1962). *Aggression: A social-psychological analysis.* McGrawHill.

Berkowitz, L. (1969). The frustration-aggression hypothesis revisited. In L. Berkowitz (Ed.), *Roots of aggression* (pp. 1–137). Atherton Press.

Berkowitz, L. (1973). Words and symbols as stimuli to aggressive responses. In J. F. Knutson (Ed.), *The control of aggression* (pp. 113–143). Aldine.

Berkowitz, L. (1989). Frustration-aggression hypothesis: Examination and reformulation. *Psychological Bulletin, 106*(1), 59–73.

Berry, C., Hodgekins, J., Michelson, D., Chapman, L., Chelidoni, O., Crowter, L., Sacadura, C., & Fowler, D. (2021). A systematic review and lived-experience panel analysis of hopefulness in youth depression treatment. *Adolescent Research Review, 7*(2), 235–266. https://doi.org/10.1007/s40894-021-00167-0

Berscheid, E. (2006). Searching for the meaning of "love." In R. J. Sternberg & K. Weis (Eds), *The new psychology of love* (pp. 171–183). Yale University Press. https://doi.org/10.12987/9780300159318-009

Bezuidenhout, C. (2024). Traditional theoretical explanations for youth misbehaviour. In C. Bezuidenhout (Ed.), *Child and youth misbehaviour in South Africa: A holistic approach* (5th ed.). Van Schaik.

Bianchi-Demicheli, F., Grafton, S. T., & Ortigue, S. (2006). The power of love on the human brain. *Social Neuroscience, 1*(2), 90–103. https://doi.org/10.1080/17470910600976547

Black, L. L., & Flynn, S. V. (2020). *Crisis, trauma, and disaster: A clinician's guide* (1st ed.). SAGE Publications. https://doi.org/10.4135/9781483397498

Blake, W. (1997). *The complete poetry and prose of William Blake* (D. V. Erdman, Ed.). Anchor Books.

Blanchard, R. J., & Blanchard, D. C. (1989). Antipredator defensive behaviours in a visible burrow system. *Journal of Comparative Psychology, 103*(1), 70–82.

Blum, A. (2008). Shame and guilt, misconceptions and controversies: A critical review of the literature. *Traumatology, 14*(3), 91–102.

Bonneville-Roussy, A., Lavigne, G. L., & Vallerand, R. J. (2011). When passion leads to excellence: The case of musicians. *Psychology of Music, 39*(1), 123–138. https://doi.org/10.1177/0305735609352441

Bookwalter, D. B., Roenfeldt, K. A., LeardMann, C. A., Kong, S. Y., Riddle, M. S., & Rull, R. P. (2020). Posttraumatic stress disorder and risk of selected autoimmune diseases among US military personnel. *BMC Psychiatry, 20*, Article 1–8. https://doi.org/10.1186/s12888-020-02605-4

Bowlby, J. (1969). *Attachment and loss: Vol. 1. Attachment.* Basic Books.

Bowlby, J., & Holmes, J. (2012). *A secure base.* Routledge.

Boyatzis, R. E. (2009). Competencies as a behavioural approach to emotional intelligence. *Journal of Management Development, 28*(9), 749–770. https://doi.org/10.1108/02621710910987647

Boyatzis R., Rochford K., & Cavanagh K. V. (2017). Emotional intelligence competencies in engineer's effectiveness and engagement. *Career Development International, 22*, 70–86. 10.1108/CDI-08-2016-0136

Braniecka, A., Trzebińska, E., Dowgiert, A., & Wytykowska, A. (2014). Mixed emotions and coping: The benefits of secondary emotions. *PLOS ONE, 9*(8), Article e103940. https://doi.org/10.1371/journal.pone.0103940

Braswell, J. M., & Prichard, E. C. (2023). Awe correlates with resilience to COVID19 stressors independent of religiosity. *Psychological Reports*. Advance online publication. https://doi.org/10.1177/00332941231165240

Brehm, J. W., & Miron, A. M. (2006). Can simultaneous experience of opposing emotions really occur? *Motivation and Emotion, 30*(1), 13–30. https://doi.org/10.1007/s11031-006-9007-z

Brent, D. A., & Silverstein, M. (2013). Shedding light on the long shadow of childhood adversity. *JAMA, 309*(17), 1777. https://doi.org/10.1001/jama.2013.4220

Bronk, K. C., Hill, P. L., Lapsley, D. K., Talib, T. L., & Finch, H. (2009). Purpose, hope, and life satisfaction in three age groups. *The Journal of Positive Psychology, 4*(6), 500–510. https://doi.org/10.1080/17439760903271439

Broussard, D. B. (2012). Principles for passion killing: An evolutionary solution to manslaughter mitigation. *Emory Law Journal, 62*(1), 179–215. Available at Emory Scholarly Commons

Brown, S. E., Esbensen, F.-A., & Geis, G. (1998). *Criminology: Explaining crime and its context* (3rd ed.). Anderson Publishers.

Brown, S. E., Esbensen, F.-A., & Geis, G. (2007). *Criminology: Explaining crime and its context* (6th ed.). Anderson Publishers.

Bruce, D. (2010, December). Anger, hatred, or just heartlessness? Defining gratuitous violence. *SA Crime Quarterly, (34)*. Institute for Security Studies.

Brudner, E., Karousatos, A., Fareri, D., & Delgado, M. (2021). Trust and reputation: How knowledge about others shapes our decisions. In F. Krueger (Ed.), *The Neurobiology of Trust* (pp. 155–184). Cambridge University Press. https://doi.org/10.1017/9781108770880.010

Bruininks, P. (2012). The unique psychology of hope. In J. Begbie & T. Hart (Eds), *Patterns of Promise: Art, Imagination, and Christian Hope*. Ashgate Publishing.

Buckels, E. E., & Trapnell, P. D. (2013). Disgust facilitates outgroup dehumanization. *Group Processes & Intergroup Relations, 16*(6), 771–780. https://doi.org/10.1177/1368430212471738

Burnell, L., & Agan, D. L. (2013). Compassionate Care: Can it be defined and measured? The development of the Compassionate Care Assessment Tool. *International Journal of Caring Sciences, 6*(2), 180–187.

Bushman, B. J., Bonacci, A. M., Pederson, W. C., Vasquez, E. A., & Miller, N. (2005). Chewing on it can chew you up: Effects of rumination on triggered displaced aggression. *Journal of Personality and Social Psychology, 88*, 969–983.

Buss, D. M. (2000). *The dangerous passion.* Free Press.

Butler, E. A., & Randall, A. K. (2013). Emotional coregulation in close relationships. *Emotion Review, 5*(2), 202–210. https://doi.org/10.1177/1754073912451630

C

Cabrera, V., & Donaldson, S. I. (2024). PERMA to PERMA + 4 building blocks of well-being: A systematic review of the empirical literature. *The Journal of Positive Psychology, 19*(3), 510–529. https://doi.org/10.1080/17439760.2023.2208099

Cacioppo, J. T., & Gardner, W. L. (1999). Emotion. *Annual Review of Psychology, 50*, 191–214. https://doi.org/10.1146/annurev.psych.50.1.191

Cacioppo, S., Bianchi-Demicheli, F., Hatfield, E., & Rapson, R. L. (2012). Social neuroscience of love. *Clinical Neuropsychiatry, 9*(1), 3–13.

Cacioppo, S., & Cacioppo, J. T. (2013). Lust for Life. *Scientific American Mind, 24*(5), 56–63. https://doi.org/10.1038/scientificamericanmind1113-56

Cacioppo, S., Grafton, S. T., & Bianchi-Demicheli, F. (2012). The speed of passionate love, as a subliminal prime: A high-density electrical neuroimaging study. *NeuroQuantology, 10*(4), 715–724. https://doi. org/10.14704/nq.2012.10.4.509

Camassa, M. (2024). Lack of empathy and dehumanisation. In M. Camassa, *On the Power and Limits of Empathy*. Palgrave Macmillan. https://doi. org/10.1007/978-3-031-37522-4_15

Campos, B., Shiota, M. N., Keltner, D., Gonzaga, G. C., & Goetz, J. L. (2013). What is shared, what is different? Core relational themes and expressive displays of eight positive emotions. *Cognition & Emotion, 27*(1), 37–52. https://doi.org/10.1080/02699931.2012.683852

Campos, J. J., Emde, R. N., Sorce, J. F., & Svejda, M. (1983). Emotional signaling: The differential effects of maternal expressions on infant behavior. *Developmental Psychology, 19*(2), 195–206.

Carbonneau, N., Vallerand, R. J., Fernet, C., & Guay, F. (2008). The role of passion for teaching in intrapersonal and interpersonal outcomes. *Journal of Educational Psychology, 100*(4), 977–987. https://doi.org/10.1037/ a0012545

Carter, B., Jordan, A., Forgeron, P., Qualter, P., & Saron, H. (2023). A shared love: Reciprocity and hopefulness in romantic relationships of young adults with chronic pain. *Frontiers in Pain Research, 14*(4), Article 1179516. https://doi.org/10.3389/fpain.2023.1179516

Case, T. I., & Stevenson, R. J. (2024). Evaluating the presence of disgust in animals. *Animals, 14*(2), 264. https://doi.org/10.3390/ani14020264

Cavanagh, M. E. (1995). Rediscovering compassion. *Journal of Religion and Health, 34*(4), 317–328. https://doi.org/10.1007/BF02248741

Center for Substance Abuse Treatment. (2014). Understanding the impact of trauma. In *Trauma-informed care in behavioral health services* (Treatment Improvement Protocol No. 57). Substance Abuse and Mental Health Services Administration. https://www.ncbi.nlm.nih.gov/books/ NBK207191/

Centers for Disease Control and Prevention. (n.d.-a). Injuries and violence are leading causes of death. https://www.cdc.gov/injury/wisqars/ animated-leading-causes.html

Centers for Disease Control and Prevention. (n.d.-b). The social-ecological model: A framework for prevention. https://www.cdc.gov/ violenceprevention/about/social-ecologicalmodel.html

Centers for Disease Control and Prevention. (2021, August 23). Preventing adverse childhood experiences. https://www.cdc.gov/vitalsigns/aces/ index.html

Centre for the Study of Violence and Reconciliation (CSVR). (2009). *Why does South Africa have such high rates of violent crime?* Supplement to the final report of the study on the violent nature of crime in South Africa. Submitted to the Minister of Safety and Security, Justice, Crime Prevention and Security (JCPS) cluster. https://www.csvr.org.za/docs/ study/7.unique_about_SA_crime.pdf

Chapman, H. A., & Anderson, A. K. (2012). Understanding disgust. *Annals of the New York Academy of Sciences, 1251*, 62–76.

Chapman, H. A., Kim, D. A., Susskind, J. M., & Anderson, A. K. (2009). In bad taste: Evidence for the oral origins of moral disgust. *Science, 323*(5918), 1222–1226. https://doi.org/10.1126/science.1165565

Chapman, L. J., Chapman, J. P., & Raulin, M. L. (1976). Scales for physical and social anhedonia. *Journal of Abnormal Psychology, 85*(4), 374–382. https:// doi.org/10.1037/0021-843X.85.4.374

Charland, L. C. (2011). Moral undertow and the passions: Two challenges for contemporary emotion regulation. *Emotion Review, 3*(1), 83–91. https:// doi.org/10.1177/1754073910380967

Charland, L. C. (2015). Passion and decision-making capacity in anorexia nervosa. *AJOB Neuroscience, 6*(4), 66–68. https://doi.org/10.1080/21507740 .2015.1105879

Charland, L. C. (2019). William James on passion and emotion: Influence of Théodule Ribot. *Emotion Review, 11*(3), 234–246. https://doi.org/10.1177/1754073918821438

Charland, L. C., Hope, T., Stewart, A., & Tan, J. (2013). Anorexia nervosa as a passion. *Philosophy, Psychiatry, & Psychology, 20*(4), 353–365. https://doi.org/10.1353/ppp.2013.0049

Chaudhury, S. H., Garg, N., & Jiang, Z. (2022). The curious case of threatawe: A theoretical and empirical reconceptualization. *Emotion, 22*(7), 1653–1669. https://doi.org/10.1037/emo0000984

Checa, P., & Fernández-Berrocal, P. (2019). Cognitive control and emotional intelligence: Effect of the emotional content of the task. *Frontiers in Psychology, 10*, Article 195. https://doi.org/10.3389/fpsyg.2019.00195

Chen, S. K., & Mongrain, M. (2021). Awe and the interconnected self. *The Journal of Positive Psychology, 16*(6), 770–778. https://doi.org/10.1080/17439760.2020.1818808

Chérif, L., Niemiec, R., & Wood, V. (2022). Character strengths and inner peace. *International Journal of Wellbeing, 12*(3), 16–34. https://doi.org/10.5502/ijw.v12i3.2195

Chetty, R., Hofmeyr, A., Kincaid, H., & Monroe, B. (2020). The Trust Game Does Not (Only) Measure Trust: The RiskTrust Confound Revisited. *Journal of Behavioural and Experimental Economics, 90*, Article 101520. https://doi.org/10.1016/j.socec.2020.101520

Chirico, A., Cipresso, P., Yaden, D. B., Biassoni, F., Riva, G., & Gaggioli, A. (2017). Effectiveness of immersive videos in inducing awe: An experimental study. *Scientific Reports, 7*, Article 1218. https://doi.org/10.1038/s41598-017-01242-0

Chirico, A., Ferrise, F., Cordella, L., & Gaggioli, A. (2018). Designing awe in virtual reality: An experimental study. *Frontiers in Psychology, 8*, Article 2351. https://doi.org/10.3389/fpsyg.2017.02351

Chirico, A., & Yaden, D. B. (2018). Awe: A self-transcendent and sometimes transformative emotion. In H. C. Lench (Ed.), *The function of emotions: When and why emotions help us* (pp. 221–233). Springer International Publishing. https://doi.org/10.1007/978-3-319-77619-4_11

Chopin, J., & Beauregard, E. (2021). Body dismemberment in sexual homicide cases: Lust murder or rational decision? *Psychology, Crime & Law, 27*(9), 869–889. https://doi.org/10.1080/1068316X.2020.1863403

Christie, A. M. H. (2012). An examination of the role of emotions in trust and control [Unpublished doctoral dissertation]. Griffith University. http://hdl.handle.net/10072/366921

Chu, B., Marwaha, K., Sanvictores, T., & Ayers, D. (2022). Physiology, stress reaction. In *StatPearls*. Retrieved from https://www.ncbi.nlm.nih.gov/books/NBK541120/

Chu, K. H., Baker, M. A., & Kurrmann, S. K. (2012). When we are onstage, we smile: The effects of emotional labor on employee work outcomes. *International Journal of Hospitality Management, 31*(3), 906–915. https://doi.org/10.1016/j.ijhm.2011.10.009

Chu, Y., Wang, H., Chou, F., Hsu, Y., & Liao, K. (2023). Outcomes of traumainformed care on the psychological health of women experiencing intimate partner violence: A systematic review and metaanalysis. *Journal of Psychiatric and Mental Health Nursing*. https://doi.org/10.1111/jpm.12976

Chuah, S., Gächter, S., Hoffmann, R., & Tan, J. H. W. (2016). Religion, discrimination and trust across three cultures. *European Economic Review, 90*, 280–301. https://doi.org/10.1016/j.euroecorev.2016.03.008

Chung, V., Mennella, R., Pacherie, E., & Grezes, J. (2024). Social bonding through shared experiences: The role of emotional intensity. *Royal Society Open Science, 11*(10), Article 240048.

Church, D., Yount, G., & Brooks, A. J. (2012). The effect of Emotional
    Freedom Techniques on stress biochemistry: A randomized controlled
    trial. *The Journal of Nervous and Mental Disease, 200*(10), 891–896. http://
    dx.doi.org/10.1097/NMD.0b013e31826b9fc1

Ciarrochi, J., Chan, A. Y., & Bajgar, J. (2001). Measuring emotional
    intelligence in adolescents. *Personality and Individual Differences, 31*(7),
    1105–1119. https://doi.org/10.1016/S0191-8869(00)00207-5

Clarke, N. (2010). The impact of a training program designed to target
    the emotional intelligence abilities of project managers. *International
    Journal of Project Management, 28*(5), 461–468. https://doi.org/10.1016/j.
    ijproman.2009.08.004

Cochran, D. M., Fallon, D., Hill, M., & Frazier, J. A. (2013). The role of
    oxytocin in psychiatric disorders: A review of biological and therapeutic
    research findings. *Harvard Review of Psychiatry, 21*(5), 219–247. https://doi.
    org/10.1097/HRP.0b013e3182a75b7d

Coertze, S., & Bezuidenhout, C. (2013). The perceptions of youths in early
    adolescence concerning the role obesity plays in bullying. *Child Abuse
    Research in South Africa, 14*(1), 67–81.

Coffey, A., Saab, M. M., Landers, M., Cornally, N., Hegarty, J., Drennan,
    J., Lunn, C., & Savage, E. (2019). The impact of compassionate care
    education on nurses: A mixed-method systematic review. *Journal of
    Advanced Nursing, 75*(11), 2340–2351. https://doi.org/10.1111/jan.14088

Cohen, J. A., & Mannarino, A. P. (2015). Trauma-focused cognitive behaviour
    therapy for traumatized children and families. *Child and Adolescent
    Psychiatric Clinics of North America, 24*(3), 557–570. https://doi.org/10.1016/j.
    chc.2015.02.005

Colantonio, J., & Bonawitz, E. (2018, May 16). Awesome play: Awe increases
    preschoolers' exploration and discovery. *Open Science Framework.* https://
    doi.org/10.31219/osf.io/pjhrq

Colla, R., Williams, P., & Oades, L. G. (2023). "A new hope" for positive psychology: A dynamic systems reconceptualization of Hope Theory. *Frontiers in Psychology, 14*, 1292756. https://doi.org/10.3389/fpsyg.2022.809053

Compton, W. C., & Hoffman, E. (2020). *Positive psychology: The science of happiness and flourishing* (3rd ed.). SAGE.

Consedine, N. S., & Magai, C. (2006). Emotional development in adulthood: A developmental functionalist review and critique. In C. Hoare (Ed.), *Handbook of adult development and learning* (pp. 209–244). Oxford University Press.

Cooper, G., Hoffman, K., & Powell, B. (2017). Circle of security in childcare: Putting attachment theory into practice in preschool classrooms. *Zero to Three, 37*(3), 27–34. Retrieved from https://www.semanticscholar.org/paper/ircleofSecurityinChildCare%3APuttingTheoryinCooper Hoffman/91a30d23e51f40c8e44677cca8ad9bb05cb19cb0

Cordaro, D. T., Keltner, D., Tshering, S., Wangchuk, D., & Flynn, L. M. (2016). The voice conveys emotion in ten globalized cultures and one remote village in Bhutan. *Emotion, 16*(1), 117–128. https://doi.org/10.1037/emo0000100

Corman, H., Curtis, M. A., Noonan, K., & Reichman, N. E. (2016). Maternal depression as a risk factor for children's inadequate housing conditions. *Social Science & Medicine, 149*, 76–83. https://doi.org/10.1016/j.socscimed.2015.11.054

Cox, D., Hallam, R., O'Connor, K., & Rachman, S. (1983). An experimental analysis of fearlessness and courage. *British Journal of Psychology, 74*(1), 107–117.

Crawford, P., Brown, B., Kvangarsnes, M., & Gilbert, P. (2014). The design of compassionate care. *Journal of Clinical Nursing, 23*(23–24), 3589–3599. https://doi.org/10.1111/jocn.12632

Croft, J., Heron, J., Teufel, C., Cannon, M., Wolke, D., Thompson, A., Houtepen, L. C., & Zammit, S. (2019). Association of trauma type, age of exposure, and frequency in childhood and adolescence with psychotic experiences in early adulthood. *JAMA Psychiatry, 76*(1), 79–86. https://doi.org/10.1001/jamapsychiatry.2018.3155

Crosby, C. L., Buss, D. M., & Meston, C. M. (2019). Sexual disgust: Evolutionary perspectives and relationship to female sexual function. *Current Sexual Health Reports, 11,* 300–306. https://doi.org/10.1007/s11930-019-00220-4

Csikszentmihalyi, M. (1991). *Flow: The psychology of optimal experience: Steps toward enhancing the quality of life.* HarperCollins.

Cuncic, A. (2023, May 3). How to deal with dysregulation. *Verywell Mind.* https://www.verywellmind.com/what-is-dysregulation-5073868

D

Dacre Pool, L., & Qualter, P. (2012). Improving emotional intelligence and emotional self-efficacy through a teaching intervention for university students. *Learning and Individual Differences, 22*(3), 306–312. https://doi.org/10.1016/j.lindif.2012.01.010

Dahan, O. (2023). Birthing as an experience of awe: Birthing consciousness and its long-term positive effects. *Journal of Theoretical and Philosophical Psychology, 43*(1), 16–30. https://doi.org/10.1037/teo0000214

Dai, S., Mo, Y., Wang, Y., Xiang, B., Liao, Q., Zhou, M., Li, X., Li, Y., Wang, X., Li, G., Guo, C., & Zeng, Z. (2020). Chronic stress promotes cancer development. *Sec. Molecular and Cellular Oncology, 10.* https://doi.org/10.3389/fonc.2020.01492

Daniel, T. (2023). The stubborn persistence of grief stage theory. *OMEGA - Journal of Death and Dying, 0*(0). https://doi.org/10.1177/00302228221149801

Darbor, K. E., Lench, H. C., Davis, W. E., & Hicks, J. A. (2016). Experiencing versus contemplating: Language use during descriptions of awe and wonder. *Cognition & Emotion, 30*(6), 1188–1196. https://doi.org/10.1080/02 699931.2015.1042836

Darwin, C. (1998). *The expression of emotions in man and animals.* John Murray.

Davis, K.E. and Todd, M.J. (1982) Friendship and Love Relationships. In: Davis, K.E. and Mitchell, T.O. (Eds), *Advances in Descriptive Psychology,* Vol. 2, 79–122, J.A.I. Press, Greenwich.

De Barros, A. C., Sadika, B., Croteau, T. A., Morrison, M. A., & Morrison, T. G. (2023). Associations between subcategories of disgust sensitivity and homonegativity: Examining intergroup contact as a moderator. *Psychology & Sexuality, 14*(3), 453–473.

Deckman, K. A., & Skolnick, A. J. (2023). Targeting humor to cope with an unpleasant emotion: Disgust. *Current Psychology, 42*(19), 16356–16367. https://doi.org/10.1007/s12144-020-00798-x

Deffenbacher, J. L., Deffenbacher, D. M., Lynch, R. S., & Richards, T. L. (2003). Anger, aggression, and risky behaviour: A comparison of high and low anger drivers. *Behaviour Research and Therapy, 41,* 701–718.

De Fruyt, J., Sabbe, B., & Demyttenaere, K. (2020). Anhedonia in depressive disorder: A narrative review. *Psychopathology, 53*(5–6), 274–281. https://doi.org/10.1159/000508773

DeLucia-Waack, J. L., Kalodner, C. R., & Riva, M. T. (2014). *Handbook of group counseling & psychotherapy* (2nd ed.). SAGE Publications. https://doi.org/10.4135/9781544308555

Demirbas, N., & Kutlu, R. (2021). Effects of COVID-19 fear on society's quality of life. *International Journal of Mental Health and Addiction, 20,* 2813–2822. https://doi.org/10.1007/s11469-021-00550

Deng, Y., Chang, L., Yang, M., Huo, M., & Zhou, R. (2016). Gender differences in emotional response: Inconsistency between experience and expressivity. *PLOS ONE*, 11(6), e0158666. https://doi.org/10.1371/journal.pone.0158666

Dennen, J. M. G. V. D. (2005). Theories of Aggression: Psychoanalytic theories of aggression. *Default journal*. https://core.ac.uk/download/pdf/148195022.pdf

Depow, G. J., Francis, Z., & Inzlicht, M. (2021). The experience of empathy in everyday life. *Psychological Science*, 32(8), 1198–1213. https://doi.org/10.1177/0956797621995202

Devlin, H. (2019, May 12). Science of anger: How gender, age and personality shape this emotion. *The Guardian*. https://www.theguardian.com/lifeandstyle/2019/may/12/science-of-anger-gender-age-personality

DeWall, C. N., & Anderson, C. A. (2011). The general aggression model. In P. R. Shaver & M. Mikulincer (Eds), *Human aggression and violence: Causes, manifestations, and consequences* (pp. 15–33). American Psychological Association.

Dias, B. G., & Ressler, K. J. (2014). Parental olfactory experience influences behaviour and neural structure in subsequent generations. *Nature Neuroscience*, 17(1), 89–96. https://doi.org/10.1038/nn.3594

Dickens, L. R., & Robins, R. W. (2022). Pride: A metaanalytic project. *Emotion*, 22(5), 1071–1087.

Diener, E. (1984). Subjective well-being. *Psychological Bulletin*, 95(3), 542–575.

Diener, E., Emmons, R. A., Larsen, R. J., & Griffin, S. (1985). The Satisfaction With Life Scale. *Journal of Personality Assessment*, 49(1), 71–75.

Diener, E., Wirtz, D., Tov, W., Kim-Prieto, C., Choi, D., Oishi, S., & Biswas-Diener, R. (2009). New measures of wellbeing: Flourishing and positive and negative feelings. *Social Indicators Research*, 39, 247–266.

Diener, E., Diener, C., Choi, H., & Oishi, S. (2018). Revisiting "Most People Are Happy" – And discovering when they are not. *Perspectives on Psychological Science, 13*(2), 166–170. https://doi.org/10.1177/1745691618765111

Dill, K. E., Anderson, C. A., Anderson, K. B., & Deuser, W. E. (1997). Effects of aggressive personality on social expectations and social perceptions. *Journal of Research in Personality, 31,* 272–292.

Dittmar, H., Bond, R., Hurst, M., & Kasser, T. (2014). The relationship between materialism and personal wellbeing: A meta-analysis. *Journal of Personality and Social Psychology, 107*(5), 879–896. https://doi.org/10.1037/a0037409

Doan, T., Ong, D. C., & Wu, Y. (2025). Emotion understanding as third-person appraisals: Integrating appraisal theories with developmental theories of emotion. *Psychological Review, 132*(1), 130–153. https://doi.org/10.1037/rev0000507

Doğru, Ç. (2022). A meta-analysis of the relationships between emotional intelligence and employee outcomes. *Frontiers in Psychology, 13,* Article 611348. https://doi.org/10.3389/fpsyg.2022.611348

Domínguez-García, E., & Fernández-Berrocal, P. (2018). The association between emotional intelligence and suicidal behaviour: A systematic review. *Frontiers in Psychology, 9,* Article 2380. https://doi.org/10.3389/fpsyg.2018.02380

Donahue, J. J. (2020). Fight-flight-freeze system. In *Encyclopedia of Personality and Individual Differences* (pp. 1590–1595). Springer.

Donaldson, S. I., Van Zyl, L. E., & Donaldson, S. I. (2022). PERMA+4: A framework for work-related well-being, performance, and positive organizational psychology 2.0. *Frontiers in Psychology, 12,* Article 817244. https://doi.org/10.3389/fpsyg.2021.817244

Donner, M., ChagasBastos, F. H., Jeremiah, R., & Laham, S. (2023). Pathogens or promiscuity? Testing two accounts of the relation between disgust sensitivity and binding moral values. *Emotion, 23.* Advance online publication. https://eurekamag.com/research/090/496/090496678.php

Downey, L. A., Johnston, P. J., Hansen, K., Schembri, R., Stough, C., Tuckwell, V., & Schweitzer, I. (2008). The relationship between emotional intelligence and depression in a clinical sample. *European Journal of Psychiatry, 22*(2), 93–98. https://doi.org/10.4321/S0213-61632008000200005

Dressler, J. (1982). Rethinking heat of passion: A defense in search of a rationale. *Journal of Criminal Law & Criminology, 73*(2), 421–470. https://doi.org/10.2307/1143104

Dsouza, J. M., Chakraborty, A., & Veigas, J. (2020). Biological connection to the feeling of happiness. *Journal of Clinical & Diagnostic Research, 14*(10), VE01–VE05. https://doi.org/10.7860/JCDR/2020/45423.14092

Dumornay, N. M., Finegold, K. E., Chablani, A., Elkins, L., Krouch, S., Baldwin, M., Youn, S. J., Marques, L., Ressler, K. J., & Moreland-Capuia, A. (2022). Improved emotion regulation following a trauma-informed CBT-based intervention associates with reduced risk for recidivism in justice-involved emerging adults. *Frontiers in Psychiatry, 13,* Article 951429. https://doi.org/10.3389/fpsyt.2022.951429

Duntley, J. D., & Buss, D. M. (2012). The evolution of stalking. *Sex Roles, 66*(5–6), 311–327. https://doi.org/10.1007/s11199-010-9832-0

Durlak, J. A., Weissberg, R. P., Dymnicki, A. B., Taylor, R. D., & Schellinger, K. B. (2011). The impact of enhancing students' social and emotional learning: A meta-analysis of school-based universal interventions. *Child Development, 82*(1), 405–432. https://doi.org/10.1111/j.1467-8624.2010.01564.x

E

Edwards, M. E., Cook, K., & King, L. A. (2024). A new hope induction. *Emotion, 24*(8), 1937–1949. https://doi.org/10.1037/emo0001396

Ekermans, G. (2009). Emotional intelligence across cultures: Theoretical and methodological considerations. In C. Stough, D. H. Saklofske, & J. A. D. Parker (Eds), *Assessing Emotional Intelligence: Theory, Research, and Applications* (pp. 259–290). Springer Science + Business Media.

Ekman, P. (1992). Are there basic emotions? *Psychological Review, 99*(3), 550–553. https://doi.org/10.1037/0033-295X.99.3.550

Ekman, P. (1993). Facial expression and emotion. *American Psychologist, 48*(4), 384–392. https://doi.org/10.1037/0003-066X.48.4.384

Elbert, T., Moran, J. K., & Schauer, M. (2017). Lust for violence: Appetitive aggression as a fundamental part of human nature. *eNeuroforum, 23*(2), 77–84. https://doi.org/10.1515/nf-2016-A056

Eliott, J. A. (2005). What have we done with hope? A brief history. In J. A. Eliott (Ed.), *Interdisciplinary Perspectives on Hope* (pp. 3–45). Nova Science Publishers.

Ellis, A. (1976). Healthy and unhealthy aggression. *Humanitas, 12*(2), 239–254. https://scholar.google.com/scholar_lookup?journal=Humanitas&title=Healthy+and+unhealthy+aggression&author=A+Ellis&volume=12&publication_year=1976&pages=239-254

Ellsworth, P. C., & Smith, C. A. (1988). From appraisal to emotion: Differences among unpleasant feelings. *Motivation and Emotion, 12*(3), 271–302. https://doi.org/10.1007/BF00993115

Ellsworth, P. C., & Smith, C. A. (1988a). Shades of joy: Patterns of appraisal differentiating pleasant emotions. *Cognition and Emotion, 2*(4), 301–331. https://doi.org/10.1080/02699938808412702

Else-Quest, N. M., Higgins, A., Allison, C., & Morton, L. C. (2012). Gender differences in self-conscious emotional experience: A meta-analysis. *Psychological Bulletin, 138*(5), 947–981. https://doi.org/10.1037/a0027930

Emmons, R. A., & McCullough, M. E. (2003). Counting blessings versus burdens: An experimental investigation of gratitude and subjective wellbeing in daily life. *Journal of Personality and Social Psychology, 84*(2), 377–389. https://doi.org/10.1037/0022-3514.84.2.377

Emmons, R. A., & Stern, R. (2013). Gratitude as a psychotherapeutic intervention. *Journal of Clinical Psychology, 69*(8), 846–855. https://doi.org/10.1002/jclp.22020

Engelmann, J. B., & Fehr, E. (2017). The neurobiology of trust and social decision-making: The important role of emotions. In P. A. M. Van Lange, B. Rockenbach, & T. Yamagishi (Eds), *Trust in Social Dilemmas* (pp. 33–56). Oxford University Press.

Erikson, E. (1963). *Childhood and society*. W. W. Norton & Company.

Eron, L. D., & Slaby, R. G. (1994). Introduction. In L. D. Eron, J. H. Gentry, & P. Schlegel (Eds), *Reason to hope: A psychological perspective on violence and youth* (pp. xiii–xv). American Psychological Association. https://doi.org/10.1037/10161-000

F

Falk, A., & Graeber, T. (2020). Delayed negative effects of prosocial spending on happiness. *Proceedings of the National Academy of Sciences, 117*(12), 6463–6468. https://doi.org/10.1073/pnas.1914324117

Fang, X., Chen, L., Wang, J., Zhang, Q., & Mo, L. (2020). Do all types of compassion increase prosocial lying? *Psychology Research and Behavior Management, 13*, 437–451. https://doi.org/10.2147/PRBM.S238246

Farolfi, F., Chang, L.-A., & Engelmann, J. B. (2021). Trust and emotion: The effects of incidental and integral affect. In F. Krueger (Ed.), *The*

Neurobiology of Trust (pp. 124–154). Cambridge University Press. https://doi.org/10.1017/9781108770880.009

Fehr, B., Harasymchuk, C., & Sprecher, S. (2014). Compassionate love in romantic relationships: A review and some new findings. *Journal of Social and Personal Relationships, 31*(5), 575–600. https://doi.org/10.1177/0265407514533768

Fehr, B., & Russell, J. A. (1991). The concept of love viewed from a prototype perspective. *Journal of Personality and Social Psychology, 60*(3), 425–438. https://doi.org/10.1037/0022-3514.60.3.425

Feldman, D. B., & Jazaieri, H. (2024). Feeling hopeful: Development and validation of the trait emotion hope scale. *Frontiers in Psychology, 15*, Article 1322807. https://doi.org/10.3389/fpsyg.2024.1322807

Feldman, D. B., O'Rourke, M. A., Corn, D., Subbiah, I. M., Manasseh, M., Hudson, M. F., Agarwal, R., Bakitas, M., Fraser, V. L., Fowler, L. A., & Corn, B. W. (2021). Hope-enhancement workshops in the SWOG Cancer Research Network: Feasibility of an online intervention. *Journal of Clinical Oncology, 39*(28, Suppl.), 210. https://doi.org/10.1200/JCO.2020.39.28_suppl.210

Feldman, D. B., & Snyder, C. R. (2005). Hope and the meaningful life: Theoretical and empirical associations between goal-directed thinking and life meaning. *Journal of Social and Clinical Psychology, 24*(3), 401–421. https://doi.org/10.1521/jscp.24.3.401.65616

Fenn, M. K., & Byrne, M. (2013). The key principles of cognitive behavioural therapy. *InnovAiT, 6*(9), 579–585. https://doi.org/10.1177/1755738012471029

Feriante, J. (2023, August 2). Acute and chronic mental health trauma. *StatPearls.* NCBI Bookshelf. https://www.ncbi.nlm.nih.gov/books/NBK594231/

Filkowski, M. M., Anderson, I. W., & Haas, B. W. (2016). Trying to trust: Brain activity during interpersonal social attitude change. *Cognitive, Affective &*

Behavioral Neuroscience, 16, 325–338. https://doi.org/10.3758/s13415-015-0393-0

Fischer, A. H., & Manstead, A. S. R. (2008). Social functions of emotion. In M. Lewis, J. M. Haviland-Jones, & L. F. Barrett (Eds), *Handbook of Emotions* (3rd ed., pp. 456–468). The Guilford Press.

Fishbein, D., & Pease, S. E. (1994). Diet, nutrition, and aggression. *Journal of Offender Rehabilitation, 21*(3–4), 117–144. https://doi.org/10.1300/J076v21n03_08

Fisher, H. (2006). The drive to love: The neural mechanism for mate selection. In R. J. Sternberg & K. Sternberg (Eds), *The New Psychology of Love* (pp. 87–115). Yale University Press.

Folk, D., & Dunn, E. (2024). How can people become happier? A systematic review of preregistered experiments. *Annual Review of Psychology, 75*, 467–493. https://doi.org/10.1146/annurev-psych-022423-030818

Fontaine, R. G. (2009). Adequate (non) provocation and heat of passion as excuse not justification. *University of Michigan Journal of Law Reform, 43*(1), 27–77. https://doi.org/10.36646/mjlr.43.1.adequate

Ford, J. D., Grasso, D. J., Elhai, J. D., & Courtois, C. A. (2015). Social, cultural, and other diversity issues in the traumatic stress field. In *Elsevier eBooks* (pp. 503–546). https://doi.org/10.1016/B978-0-12-801288-8.00011-X

Forgas, J. P. (2017). Can sadness be good for you? *Australian Psychologist, 52*(1), 3–13. https://doi.org/10.1111/ap.12232

Forstmann, M., Yudkin, D. A., Prosser, A. M., Heller, S. M., & Crockett, M. J. (2020). Transformative experience and social connectedness mediate the mood-enhancing effects of psychedelic use in naturalistic settings. *Proceedings of the National Academy of Sciences, 117*(5), 2338–2346. https://doi.org/10.1073/pnas.1918477117

Fox, A. S., Oler, J. A., Tromp, D., Fudge, J. L., & Kalin, N. H. (2015). Extending the amygdala in theories of threat processing. *Trends in Neurosciences, 38*(5), 319–329. https://doi.org/10.1016/j.tins.2015.03.002

Frederick, R. (2020, August 3). Why your brain is on the lookout for danger. *Center for Courageous Living.* https://www.cfcliving.com/brain-threat-detector/

Fredrickson, B. L. (2001). The role of positive emotions in positive psychology: The broaden-and-build theory of positive emotions. *American Psychologist, 56*(3), 218–226. https://doi.org/10.1037/0003-066X.56.3.218

Fredrickson, B. L., Cohn, M. A., Coffey, K. A., Pek, J., & Finkel, S. M. (2008). Open hearts build lives: Positive emotions, induced through loving-kindness meditation, build consequential personal resources. *Journal of Personality and Social Psychology, 95*(5), 1045–1062. https://doi.org/10.1037/a0013262

Frijda, N. H. (1993). The place of appraisal in emotion. *Cognition and Emotion, 7*(3–4), 357–387. https://doi.org/10.1080/02699939308409191

Frijda, N. H., Mesquita, B., Sonnemans, J., & Goozen, S. H. M. (1991). The duration of affective phenomena or emotions, sentiments and passions. In K. T. Strongman (Ed.), *International review of studies on emotion: Vol. 1* (pp. 187–225). Wiley.

Frontline. (2015, November 18). Experts – "Soldier's heart" and "shell shock:" Past names for PTSD. In *The soldier's heart.* PBS. https://www.pbs.org/wgbh/pages/frontline/shows/heart/themes/shellshock.html

G

Galambos, N. L., Krahn, H. J., Johnson, M. D., & Lachman, M. E. (2021). *The Ushape of happiness across the life course: Expanding the discussion.*

Perspectives on Psychological Science, 15(4), 898–912. https://doi. org/10.1177/1745691620902428

Galek, K., Flannelly, K., Vane, A., & Galek, R. (2005). *Assessing a patient's spiritual needs: A comprehensive instrument*. Holistic Nursing Practice, 19(2), 62–69. https://doi.org/10.1097/00004650-200503000-00006

Gallup. (2024). *Gallup World Poll: Global research methodology and data.* Gallup. https://www.gallup.com/analytics/318875/global-research.aspx

Gallagher, S., ReinermanJones, L., Sollins, B., & Janz, B. (2014). *Using a simulated environment to investigate experiences reported during space travel*. Theoretical Issues in Ergonomics Science, 15(4), 376–394. https://doi.org/1 0.1080/1463922X.2013.869370

Gardner, H. (1983). *Frames of mind: The theory of multiple intelligences*. Basic Books.

Garza, R., Pazhoohi, F., AlShawaf, L., & Byrd-Craven, J. (2023). *An eye-tracking study examining the role of mating strategies, perceived vulnerability to disease, and disgust in attention to pathogenic cues*. Adaptive Human Behavior and Physiology, 9(1), 72–87. https://doi.org/10.1007/s40750-022-00209-5

Gaspar, A., & Esteves, F. (2022). *Empathy development from adolescence to adulthood and its consistency across targets*. Frontiers in Psychology, 13, Article 936053. https://doi.org/10.3389/fpsyg.2022.936053

GBD 2019 Mental Disorders Collaborators. (2022). *Global, regional, and national burden of 12 mental disorders in 204 countries and territories, 1990–2019: A systematic analysis for the Global Burden of Disease Study 2019*. The Lancet Psychiatry, 9(2), 137–150. https://doi.org/10.1016/S2215-0366(21)00395-3

Geary, D. C., Vigil, J., & Byrd-Craven, J. (2004). *Evolution of human mate choice*. The Journal of Sex Research, 41(1), 27–42. https://www.jstor.org/stable/3813401

Geldenhuys, K. (2010). *SA farms = War zones? (Part 1)*. Servamus Communitybased Safety and Security Magazine, *103*(4), 8–13.

George, L. (2023, July 26). *Gender-based violence against women in South Africa.* Ballard Brief. https://ballardbrief.byu.edu/issue-briefs/gender-based-violence-against-women-in-south-africa

Gignac, G. E. (2017). *Genos Emotional Intelligence Inventory technical manual (2nd ed.).* Genos Pty Ltd.

Gignac, G. E. (2010). Seven-Factor Model of Emotional Intelligence as Measured by Genos EI: A confirmatory factor analytic investigation based on self- and rater-report data. *European Journal of Psychological Assessment: Official Organ of the European Association of Psychological Assessment, 26*(4), 309–316. https://doi.org/10.1027/1015-5759/a000041

Gilbert, P. (2019). *Explorations into the nature and function of compassion.* Current Opinion in Psychology, *28*, 108–114. https://doi.org/10.1016/j.copsyc.2018.12.005

Gilbert, P. (2021). *Creating a compassionate world: Addressing the conflicts between sharing and caring versus controlling and holding evolved strategies.* Frontiers in Psychology, *11*, Article: 582090. https://doi.org/10.3389/fpsyg.2020.582090

GinerSorolla, R., & Russell, P. S. (2019). *Not just disgust: Fear and anger also relate to intergroup dehumanization.* Collabra: Psychology, *5*(1), Article 56. https://doi.org/10.1525/collabra.230

Giubilini, A. (2015). *What in the world is moral disgust?* Australasian Journal of Philosophy, *94*(2), 227–242. https://doi.org/10.1080/00048402.2015.1070887

Glassie, S. L., & Schutte, N. S. (2024). *The relationship between emotional intelligence and optimism: A meta-analysis.* International Journal of Psychology, *59*(3), 353–367. https://doi.org/10.1002/ijop.13108

Goldberg, S. B., Riordan, K. M., Sun, S., & Davidson, R. J. (2022). *The empirical status of mindfulness-based interventions: A systematic review of 44 meta-analyses of randomized controlled trials.* Perspectives on Psychological Science, 17(1), 108–130. https://doi.org/10.1177/1745691620968771

Goldstein, M. A. (2002). *The biological roots of heat-of-passion crimes and honor killings.* Politics and the Life Sciences, 21(2), 28–37. https://doi.org/10.2990/1471-5457(2002)21[28:TBRHOC]2.0.CO;2

Goldy, S. P., Jones, N. M., & Piff, P. K. (2022). *The social effects of an awesome solar eclipse.* Psychological Science, 33(9), 1452–1462. https://doi.org/10.1177/09567976221085501

Görgens-Ekermans, G., Delport, M., & Du Preez, R. (2015). *Developing emotional intelligence as a key psychological resource reservoir for sustained student success.* SA Journal of Industrial Psychology, 41, Article 1251. https://doi.org/10.4102/sajip.v41i1.1251

Görgens-Ekermans, G., & Roux, C. (2021). Revisiting the Emotional Intelligence and Transformational Leadership Debate: (How) Does Emotional Intelligence Matter to Effective Leadership? *SA Journal of Human Resource Management,* 19, a1279. https://doi.org/10.4102/sajhrm.v19i0.1279

Graczyk, P. A., Weissberg, R. P., Payton, J. W., Elias, M. J., Greenberg, M. T., & Zins, J. E. (2000). Criteria for evaluating the quality of school-based social and emotional learning programs. In R. Bar-On & J. D. A. Parker (Eds), *The handbook of emotional intelligence* (pp. 391–432). JosseyBass.

Graham, C. (2024). *Hope and despair: Implications for life outcomes and policy.* Behavioral Science & Policy, 9(2). https://doi.org/10.1177/23794607231222529

Greenbaum, R., Bonner, J., Gray, T., & Mawritz, M. (2020). *Moral emotions: A review and research agenda for management scholarship.* Journal of Organizational Behavior, 41(2), 95–114. https://doi.org/10.1002/job.2367

Greenberg, D. M., BaronCohen, S., Rosenberg, N. E., Fonagy, P., & Rentfrow, P. J. (2018). *Elevated empathy in adults following childhood trauma*. PLOS ONE, 13(10), e0203886. https://doi.org/10.1371/journal.pone.0203886

Greenway, F. L., & Smith, S. R. (2016). Current research and future hope. In G. M. Steelman & E. C. Westman (Eds), *Obesity: Evaluation and treatment essentials* (p. 139). CRC Press. https://doi.org/10.1201/b19716

Greeson, J., & Brantley, J. (2009). Mindfulness and anxiety disorders: Developing a wise relationship with the inner experience of fear. *Complementary Health Practice Review*, 14(1), 10–18. https://doi.org/10.1007/978-0-387-09593-6_11

Griskevicius, V., Shiota, M. N., & Nowlis, S. M. (2010). The many shades of rose-colored glasses: An evolutionary approach to the influence of different positive emotions. *Journal of Consumer Research*, 37(2), 238–250. https://doi.org/10.1086/651442

Grohman, M. G., Ivcevic, Z., Silvia, P., & Kaufman, S. B. (2017). *The role of passion and persistence in creativity*. Psychology of Aesthetics, Creativity, and the Arts, 11(4), 376. https://doi.org/10.1037/aca0000121

Gross, J. J. (2010). *Emotion regulation: Past, present, future*. Cognition & Emotion, 13(5), 551–573. https://doi.org/10.1080/026999399379186

Gross, J. J. (2015). *Emotion regulation: Current status and future prospects*. Psychological Inquiry, 26(1), 1–26. https://doi.org/10.1080/1047840X.2014.940781

Gross, J. J., & Jazaieri, H. (2014). *Emotion, emotion regulation, and psychopathology: An affective science perspective*. Clinical Psychological Science, 2(4), 387–401. https://doi.org/10.1177/2167702614536164

Gross, C. T., & Canteras, N. S. (2012). *The many paths to fear*. Nature Reviews Neuroscience, 13(9), 651–658. https://doi.org/10.1038/nrn3301

Gross, J. J., & Jazaieri, H. (2014). Emotion, emotion regulation, and psychopathology: An affective science perspective. *Clinical Psychological Science, 2*(4), 387–401. https://doi.org/10.1177/2167702614536164

Gruber, C. (2011). *The psychology of courage: Modern research on an ancient virtue.* Integrative Psychological and Behavioural Science, 45, 272–279.

Gullone, E. (2000). The development of normal fear: A century of research. *Clinical Psychology Review, 20*(4), 429–451. https://doi.org/10.1016/S0272-7358(99)00034-3

Gülşen, M., Aydın, B., Gürer, G., & Yalçın, S. S. (2023). AI-assisted emotion analysis during complementary feeding in infants aged 6–11 months. *Computers in Biology and Medicine, 166,* Article 107482. https://doi.org/10.1016/j.compbiomed.2023.107482

Gundogan, S., & Arpaci, I. (2022). Depression as a mediator between fear of COVID19 and death anxiety. *Current Psychology: A Journal for Diverse Perspectives on Diverse Psychological Issues, 43,* 12990–12997. Advance online publication. https://doi.org/10.1007/s12144-022-03120-z

GunduzCinar, O. (2021). The endocannabinoid system in the amygdala and modulation of fear. *Progress in Neuropsychopharmacology and Biological Psychiatry, 105,* 1–11. https://doi.org/10.1016/j.pnpbp.2020.110116

Guo, R. (2021). Exposure therapy for phobia treatment. *Advances in Economics, Business and Management Research, 203,* 1563–1566.

Guo, S.-L., Lumineau, F., & Lewicki, R. J. (2017). Revisiting the foundations of organizational distrust. *Foundations and Trends in Management, 1*(1), 1–88.

Guse, T. (2020). Feeling good: The hedonic perspective on wellbeing. In M. P. Wissing, J. C. Potgieter, T. Guse, I. P. Khumalo, & L. Nel (Eds), *Towards flourishing: Embracing wellbeing in diverse contexts* (2nd ed., pp. 29–56). Van Schaik.

Güsewell, A., & Ruch, W. (2012). Are only Emotional Strengths Emotional? Character strengths and disposition to positive emotions. *Applied Psychology: Health and WellBeing, 4*(2), 218–239. https://doi.org/10.1111/j.1758-0854.2012.01070.x

Gustafsson, S., Gillespie, N., Searle, R., Hope Hailey, V., & Dietz, G. (2021). Preserving organizational trust during disruption. *Organization Studies, 42*(9), 1409–1433. https://doi.org/10.1177/0170840620912705

GutiérrezCobo, M. J., Cabello, R., & Fernández-Berrocal, P. (2017). The three models of emotional intelligence and performance in a hot and cool go/nogo task in undergraduate students. *Frontiers in Behavioural Neuroscience, 11*, Article 33. https://doi.org/10.3389/fnbeh.2017.00033

Gwinn, C., & Hellman, C. (2018). *Hope rising: How the science of hope can change your life*. Morgan James Publishing.

H

Haas, B. W., Ishak, A., Anderson, I. W., & Filkowski, M. M. (2015). The tendency to trust is reflected in human brain structure. *NeuroImage, 107*, 175–181. https://doi.org/10.1016/j.neuroimage.2014.11.060

Haerpfer, C., Inglehart, R., Moreno, A., Welzel, C., Kizilova, K., Diez-Medrano, J., Lagos, M., Norris, P., Ponarin, E., & Puranen, B. (Eds). (2022). *World Values Survey: Round seven–Countrypooled datafile (Version 5.0)*. JD Systems Institute & WVSA Secretariat. https://doi.org/10.14281/18241.20

Haidt, J. (2000). The positive emotion of elevation. *Prevention & Treatment, 3*(3), Article 3a. https://doi.org/10.1037/1522-3736.3.3.3a

Hamai, T. A., & Felitti, V. J. (2022). Adverse childhood experiences: Past, present, and future. In R. Geffner, J. W. White, L. K. Hamberger, A. Rosenbaum, V.-E. Vaughan-Eden, & V. I. Vieth (Eds), *Handbook of interpersonal violence and abuse across the lifespan* (pp. 305–320). Springer. https://doi.org/10.1007/978-3-319-89999-2_305

Hao, R. N. (2011). Critical compassionate pedagogy and the teacher's role in first-generation student success. *New Directions for Teaching and Learning, 2011*(127), 91–98. https://doi.org/10.1002/tl.466

Harms, P. D., & Credé, M. (2010). Emotional intelligence and transformational and transactional leadership: A metaanalysis. *Journal of Leadership and Organizational Studies, 17*(1), 5–17. https://doi.org/10.1177/1548051809350894

Hartley, C. A., & Phelps, E. A. (2010). Changing fear: The neurocircuitry of emotion regulation. *Neuropsychopharmacology, 35*(1), 136–146. https://doi.org/10.1038/npp.2009.121

Hartmann, M., Lenggenhager, B., & Stocker, K. (2023). Happiness feels light and sadness feels heavy: Introducing valencerelated bodily sensation maps of emotions. *Psychological Research, 87*(1), 59–83. https://doi.org/10.1007/s00426-022-01661-3

Hatfield, E., & Rapson, R. L. (1987). Passionate love/sexual desire: Can the same paradigm explain both? *Archives of Sexual Behavior, 16*(3), 259–278. https://doi.org/10.1007/BF01541613

Hatfield, E., & Rapson, R. L. (2006). Love and passion. In *Textbook of female sexual dysfunction* (pp. 93–97).

Hatfield, E., & Sprecher, S. (1986). Measuring passionate love in intimate relationships. *Journal of Adolescence, 9*(4), 383–410. https://doi.org/10.1016/S0140-1971(86)80043-4

Hatfield, E., & Walster, G. W. (1985). *A new look at love.* University Press of America.

Hebb, D. O. (1955). Drives and the C.N.S. (Conceptual Nervous System). *Psychological Review, 62,* 117–125.

Heinze, A., & Heinze, M. (1999). From pleasure to anhedonia: Forbidden desires and the construction of schizophrenia. *Theory & Psychology, 9*(1), 47–65. https://doi.org/10.1177/0959354399091003

Helliwell, J. F., Layard, R., Sachs, J. D., De Neve, J.-E., Aknin, L. B., & Wang, S. (Eds). (2024). *World Happiness Report 2024.* Wellbeing Research Centre, University of Oxford.

Hendrick, C., & Hendrick, S. (1986). A theory and method of love. *Journal of Personality and Social Psychology, 50*(2), 392–402. https://doi.org/10.1037/0022-3514.50.2.392

Herz, R. S. (2016). The role of odor-evoked memory in psychological and physiological health. *Brain Sciences, 6*(3), Article 22. https://doi.org/10.3390/brainsci6030022

Hess, U., Adams, R. B., Jr., & Kleck, R. E. (2007). Looking at you or looking elsewhere: The influence of head orientation on the signal value of emotional facial expressions. *Motivation and Emotion, 31*(2), 137–144. https://doi.org/10.1007/s11031-007-9057-x

Hill, Z., Spiegel, M., & Gennetian, L. A. (2020). Pride-based self-affirmations and parenting programs. *Frontiers in Psychology, 11,* Article 523639. https://doi.org/10.3389/fpsyg.2020.523639

Hirsch, J. K., & Sirois, F. M. (2016). Hope and fatigue in chronic illness: The role of perceived stress. *Journal of Health Psychology, 21*(4), 451–456. https://doi.org/10.1177/1359105314527142

Hirschberger, G. (2018). Collective trauma and the social construction of meaning. *Frontiers in Psychology, 9,* Article 1441. https://doi.org/10.3389/fpsyg.2018.01441

History. (2017, October 2). PTSD and shell shock. *History.* https://www.history.com/topics/inventions/history-of-ptsd-and-shell-shock

Hochschild, A. R. (1983). Emotion work, feeling rules, and social structure. *American Journal of Sociology, 85*(3), 551–575. https://doi.org/10.1086/227049

Hodgkins, A. (2022). Exploring early childhood practitioners' perceptions of empathy with children and families: Initial findings. *Educational Review, 76*(2), 223–241. https://doi.org/10.1080/00131911.2021.2023471

Hodzic, S., Scharfen, J., Ripoll, P., Holling, H., & Zenasni, F. (2018). How efficient are emotional intelligence trainings: A meta-analysis. *Emotion Review, 10*(2), 138–148. https://doi.org/10.1177/1754073917708613

Hoekstra, A. Y., & Wiedmann, T. O. (2014). Humanity's unsustainable environmental footprint. *Science, 344*(6188), 1114–1117. https://doi.org/10.1126/science.1248365

Hoffman, M. (2000). *Empathy and moral development.* Cambridge University Press.

Hoffman, M. (2012). Empathy, its arousal and prosocial functioning. In *Empathy and moral development* (pp. 129–167). Cambridge University Press.

Hoffmann, E. A. (2016). Emotions and labour at worker-owned businesses: Deep acting, surface acting, and genuine emotions. *The Sociological Quarterly, 57*(1), 152–173. https://doi.org/10.1111/tsq.12113

Hofmann, S. G., Sawyer, A. T., Witt, A. A., & Oh, D. (2010). The effect of mindfulness-based therapy on anxiety and depression: A meta-analytic review. *Journal of Consulting and Clinical Psychology, 78*(2), 169–183. https://doi.org/10.1037/a0018555

Hogeveen, J., & Grafman, J. (2021). Alexithymia. In *Handbook of Clinical Neurology* (Vol. 183, pp. 47–62). Elsevier. https://doi.org/10.1016/B978-0-12-822290-4.00004-9

Holbrook, C., Piazza, J. R., & Fessler, D. M. (2014). Further challenges to the "authentic"/"hubristic" model of pride: Conceptual clarifications and new evidence. *Emotion, 14*(1), 38–42.

Holding, A. C., Verner-Filion, J., Lalande, D., Schellenberg, B. J., & Vallerand, R. J. (2021). The roles of need satisfaction and passion in symptoms of behavioral addiction: The case of video gaming and gambling. *Motivation Science, 7*(3), 345–359. https://doi.org/10.1037/mot0000241

Holman, D., Chissick, C., & Totterdell, P. (2002). The effects of performance monitoring on emotional labour and well-being in call centres. *Motivation and Emotion, 26*(1), 57–81. https://doi.org/10.1023/A:1015194108376

Holmes, L. (2023). Sadness vs. clinical depression. *Verywell Mind.* https://www.verywellmind.com/sadness-is-not-depression-2330492

Hong, E., & Lee, Y. S. (2016). The mediating effect of emotional intelligence between emotional labour, job stress, burnout and nurses' turnover intention. *International Journal of Nursing Practice, 22*(6), 625–632. https://doi.org/10.1111/ijn.12493

Honkalampi, K., Hintikka, J., Tanskanen, A., Lehtonen, J., & Viinamäki, H. (2000). Depression is strongly associated with alexithymia in the general population. *Journal of Psychosomatic Research, 48*(1), 99–104. https://doi.org/10.1016/S0022-3999(99)00083-5

Horberg, E. J., Oveis, C., Keltner, D., & Cohen, A. B. (2009). Disgust and the moralization of purity. *Journal of Personality and Social Psychology, 97*(6), 963–976.

Hölzel, B. K., Brunsch, V., Gard, T., Greve, D. N., Koch, K., Sorg, C., Lazar, S. W., & Milad, M. R. (2016). Mindfulness-based stress reduction, fear conditioning, and the uncinate fasciculus: A pilot study. *Frontiers in Behavioral Neuroscience, 10*, 124. https://doi.org/10.3389/fnbeh.2016.00124

Hu, J., Yan, Y., Jing, F., & Nguyen, B. (2018). Awe, spirituality and conspicuous consumer behavior. *International Journal of Consumer Studies, 42*(6), 829–839. https://doi.org/10.1111/ijcs.12470

Huesmann, L. R. (1988). An information processing model for the development of aggression. *Aggressive Behavior, 14*(1), 13–24. https://doi.org/10.1002/1098-2337(1988)14:1<13::AID-AB2480140104>3.0.CO;2-J

Hülsheger, U. R., & Schewe, A. F. (2011). On the costs and benefits of emotional labor: A meta-analysis of three decades of research. *Journal of Occupational Health Psychology, 16*(3), 361–389. https://doi.org/10.1037/a0022876

Hutcherson, C. A., & Gross, J. J. (2011). The moral emotions: A social-functionalist account of anger, disgust, and contempt. *Journal of Personality and Social Psychology, 100*(4), 719–737. https://doi.org/10.1037/a0022408

Hutto, D. D., Robertson, I., & Kirchhoff, M. D. (2018). A new, better BET: Rescuing and revising basic emotion theory. *Frontiers in Psychology, 9*, 360717. https://doi.org/10.3389/fpsyg.2018.01217

Hwang, H. C., & Matsumoto, D. (2016). Emotional expression. In *The expression of emotion: Philosophical, psychological and legal perspectives* (pp. xx–xx). Cambridge University Press.

I

Ihm, E. D., Paloutzian, R. F., Van Elk, M., & Schooler, J. W. (2019). Awe as a meaning-making emotion. In *The evolution of religion, religiosity and theology* (pp. 138–153). https://doi.org/10.4324/9780429285608-9

Inbar, Y., Pizarro, D. A., Knobe, J., & Bloom, P. (2009). Disgust sensitivity predicts intuitive disapproval of gays. *Emotion, 9*(3), 435–439. https://doi.org/10.1037/a0015960

Ingenhoff, D., & Sommer, K. (2010). Trust in companies and in CEOs: A comparative study of the main influence. *Journal of Business Ethics, 95,* 339–355.

International Crisis Group. (2022). *Answering four hard questions about Russia's war in Ukraine.* International Crisis Group. http://www.jstor.org/stable/resrep45704

Inwood, E., & Ferrari, M. (2018). Mechanisms of change in the relationship between self-compassion, emotion regulation, and mental health: A systematic review. *Applied Psychology: Health and Well-Being, 10*(2), 215–235.

Irving, L. M., Snyder, C. R., Cheavens, J., Gravel, L., Hanke, J., Hilberg, P., & Nelson, N. (2004). The relationships between hope and outcomes at the pretreatment, beginning, and later phases of psychotherapy. *Journal of Psychotherapy Integration, 14*(4), 419. https://doi.org/10.1037/1053-0479.14.4.419

Isbell, F., Balvanera, P., Mori, A. S., He, J. S., Bullock, J. M., Regmi, G. R., Seabloom, E. W., Ferrier, S., Sala, O. E., Guerrero-Ramírez, N. R., Tavella, J., Larkin, D. J., Schmid, B., Outhwaite, C. L., Pramual, P., Borer, E. T., Loreau, M., Omotoriogun, T. C., Obura, D. O., Anderson, M., ... Palmer, M. S. (2023). Expert perspectives on global biodiversity loss and its drivers and impacts on people. *Frontiers in Ecology and the Environment, 21*(2), 94–103. https://doi.org/10.1002/fee.2536

Ishizaki, J., & Mimura, M. (2011). Dysthymia and apathy: Diagnosis and treatment. *Depression Research and Treatment, 2011*(7). https://doi.org/10.1155/2011/893905

Izard, C. E. (1992). Basic emotions, relations among emotions, and emotion-cognition relations. *Psychological Review, 99*(3), 561–565. https://doi.org/10.1037/0033-295X.99.3.561

Izard, C. E. (1993). Four systems for emotion activation: Cognitive and noncognitive processes. *Psychological Review, 100*(1), 68–90. https://doi.org/10.1037/0033-295X.100.1.68

J

Jackson, W. T., Taylor, R. E., Palmatier, A. D., Elliott, T. R., & Elliott, J. L. (1998). Negotiating the reality of visual impairment: Hope, coping, and functional ability. *Journal of Clinical Psychology in Medical Settings, 5*(2), 173–185. https://doi.org/10.1023/A:1026259115029

Jahanitabesh, A., Cardwell, B. A., & Halberstadt, J. (2019). Sadness and ruminative thinking independently depress people's moods. *International Journal of Psychology, 54*(3), 360–368. https://doi.org/10.1002/ijop.12466

Jamieson, J. P., Hangen, E. J., Lee, H. Y., & Yeager, D. S. (2018). Capitalizing on appraisal processes to improve affective responses to social stress. *Emotion Review, 10*(1), 30–39.

Jang, D., & Elfenbein, H. A. (2015). Emotion, perception and expression of. In J. D. Wright (Ed.), *International encyclopedia of the social & behavioral sciences* (2nd ed., pp. 483–489). Elsevier. https://doi.org/10.1016/B978-0-08-097086-8.25052-6

Jansz, J., & Timmers, M. (2002). Emotional dissonance: When the experience of an emotion jeopardizes an individual's identity. *Theory & Psychology, 12*(1), 79–95. https://doi.org/10.1177/0959354302121005

Jauniaux, J., Khatibi, A., Rainville, P., & Jackson, P. L. (2019). A meta-analysis of neuroimaging studies on pain empathy: Investigating the role of visual information and observers' perspective. *Social Cognitive and Affective Neuroscience, 14*(8), 789–813.

Jiang, L., Yin, J., Mei, D., Zhu, H., & Zhou, X. (2018). Awe weakens the desire for money. *Journal of Pacific Rim Psychology, 12*, e4. https://doi.org/10.1017/prp.2017.27

Jiao, L., & Luo, L. (2024). Dispositional awe negatively predicts corruption via the sense of connectedness. *PsyCh Journal*, 13(4), 608–615. https://doi.org/10.1002/pchj.737

Jones, S. L., & Shah, P. P. (2016). Diagnosing the locus of trust: A temporal perspective for trustor, trustee, and dyadic influences on perceived trustworthiness. *Journal of Applied Psychology*, 101(3), 392–414. https://doi.org/10.1037/apl0000041

Joseph, D. L., Jin, J., Newman, D. A., & O'Boyle, E. H. (2015). Why does self-reported emotional intelligence predict job performance? A meta-analytic investigation of mixed EI. *Journal of Applied Psychology*, 100(2), 298–342. https://doi.org/10.1037/a0037681

Joseph, D. L., & Newman, D. A. (2010). Emotional intelligence: An integrative meta-analysis and cascading model. *Journal of Applied Psychology*, 95(1), 54–78. https://doi.org/10.1037/a0017286

Joshi, M., Paul, P., Jean-Baptiste, C., Rahill, G. J., Odans, E., Salinas-Miranda, A., Heger, J., & Rice, C. (2023). Prevalence and correlates of suicidal ideation in a sample of urban Haiti residents. *International Journal of Mental Health*, 1–24. https://doi.org/10.1080/00207411.2023.2255435

Joye, Y., & Dewitte, S. (2016). Up speeds you down: Awe-evoking monumental buildings trigger behavioral and perceived freezing. *Journal of Environmental Psychology*, 47, 112–125. https://doi.org/10.1016/j.jenvp.2016.05.001

K

KabatZinn, J. (1994). Wherever you go, there you are: *Mindfulness meditation in everyday life*. Hyperion. *(Reprinted January 5, 2005, by Hachette Books; 304 pp.)*

KabatZinn, J. (2003). Mindfulness-based interventions in context: Past, present, and future. *Clinical Psychology: Science and Practice*, 10(2), 144–156. https://doi.org/10.1093/clipsy/bpg016

KabatZinn, J. (2005). Too early to tell: The potential impact and challenges – ethical and otherwise – inherent in the mainstreaming of Dharma in an increasingly dystopian world. *Mindfulness, 8*(5), 1125–1135. https://doi.org/10.1007/s12671-017-0758-2

Kansky, J. (2018). What's love got to do with it? Romantic relationships and wellbeing. In E. Diener, S. Oishi, L. Tay, & Z. Zhu (Eds), *Handbook of wellbeing* (pp. 1–24). Def Publishers.

Kapil, R. (2022, January 18). How protective factors can promote resilience. *Mental Health First Aid*. https://www.mentalhealthfirstaid.org/2022/01/how-protective-factors-can-promote-resilience/

Kaplan, B., Miller, E. G., & Iyer, E. S. (2023). Shades of awe: The role of awe in consumers' proenvironmental behavior. *Journal of Consumer Behaviour, 23*(2), 540–555. https://doi.org/10.1002/cb.2223

Kaplan, J. S., & Tolin, D. F. (2011). Exposure therapy for anxiety disorders: Theoretical mechanisms of exposure and treatment strategies. *Psychiatric Times, 28*(9), 33–37. (Publication No. 894207776) [Doctoral dissertation, ProQuest].

Karinen, A. K., Tybur, J. M., & de Vries, R. E. (2023). The disgust traits: Self–other agreement in pathogen, sexual, and moral disgust sensitivity and their independence from HEXACO personality. *Emotion, 23*(1), 75–85.

Kauhanen, J., Kaplan, G. A., Julkunen, J., Wilson, T. W., & Salonen, J. T. (1993). Social factors in alexithymia. *Comprehensive Psychiatry, 34*(5), 330–335. https://doi.org/10.1016/0010-440X(93)90019-Z

Kauppinen, A. (2017). Pride, achievement, and purpose. In J. A. Carter & E. C. Gordon (Eds), *The moral psychology of pride* (pp. 169–190). Roman & Littlefield International.

Kee, H. W., & Knox, R. E. (1970). Conceptual and methodological considerations in the study of trust and suspicion. *Journal of Conflict Resolution, 14*(3), 357–366. http://www.jstor.org/stable/173516

Keeling, J., & Fisher, C. (2012). Women's early relational experiences that lead to domestic violence. *Qualitative Health Research, 22*(11), 1559–1567. https://doi.org/10.1177/1049732312457076

Keltner, D., & Gross, J. J. (1999). Functionalist accounts of emotions. *Cognition and Emotion, 13*(5), 467–480. https://doi.org/10.1080/026999399379140

Keltner, D., & Haidt, J. (2003). Approaching awe: A moral, spiritual, and aesthetic emotion. *Cognition and Emotion, 17*(2), 297–314. https://doi.org/10.1080/02699930302297

Keltner, D., Haidt, J., & Shiota, M. N. (2006). Social functionalism and the evolution of emotions. In M. Schaller, J. A. Simpson, & D. T. Kenrick (Eds), *Evolution and social psychology* (pp. 115–142). Psychosocial Press.

Keltner, D., Oatley, K., & Jenkins, J. M. (2014). *Understanding emotions* (3rd ed.). Wiley.

Kessler, R. C., Aguilar-Gaxiola, S., Alonso, J., Benjet, C., Bromet, E. J., Cardoso, G., Degenhardt, L., De Girolamo, G., Dinolova, R. V., Ferry, F., Florescu, S., Gureje, O., Haro, J. M., Huang, Y., Karam, E. G., Kawakami, N., Lee, P., Lépine, J. P., Levinson, D., & Koenen, K. C. (2017). Trauma and PTSD in the WHO World Mental Health Surveys. *European Journal of Psychotraumatology, 8*(Suppl 5). https://doi.org/10.1080/20008198.2017.1353383

Khan, S. S., Hopkins, N., Reicher, S., Tewari, S., Srinivasan, N., & Stevenson, C. (2016). How collective participation impacts social identity: A longitudinal study from India. *Political Psychology, 37*(3), 309–325. https://doi.org/10.1111/pops.12260

Khatibi, A., Roy, M., Chen, J. I., Gill, L. N., Piché, M., & Rainville, P. (2023). Brain responses to the vicarious facilitation of pain by facial expressions of pain and fear. *Social Cognitive and Affective Neuroscience, 18*(1), nsac056.

Khoury, B., Sharma, M., Rush, S. E., & Fournier, C. (2015). Mindfulness-based stress reduction for healthy individuals: A metaanalysis. *Journal of Psychosomatic Research, 78*(6), 519–528. https://doi.org/10.1016/j.jpsychores.2015.03.009

Kim, J. J., Enrigh, R. D., & Wong, L. (2022). Compassionate love and dispositional forgiveness: Does compassionate love predict dispositional forgiveness? *Journal of Spirituality in Mental Health, 24*(1), 95–111.

Kim, S., Thibodeau, R., & Jorgensen, R. S. (2011). Shame, guilt, and depressive symptoms: A meta-analytic review. *Psychological Bulletin, 137*(1), 68.

Kim, Y., Nusbaum, H. C., & Yang, F. (2023). Going beyond ourselves: The role of selftranscendent experiences in wisdom. *Cognition and Emotion, 37*(1), 98–116. https://doi.org/10.1080/02699931.2022.2149473

Kirk, B. A., Schutte, N. S., & Hine, D. W. (2011). The effect of an expressive-writing intervention for employees on emotional self-efficacy, emotional intelligence, affect, and workplace incivility. *Journal of Applied Social Psychology, 41*(1), 179–195. https://doi.org/10.1111/j.1559-1816.2010.00708.x

Klebl, C., Dziobek, I., & Diessner, R. (2019). The role of elevation in moral judgment. *Journal of Moral Education, 49*(2), 158–176. https://doi.org/10.1080/03057240.2018.1550635

Klein, M. (1932). *The psychoanalysis of children.* (The International Psycho-Analytical Library, No. 22). Hogarth Press and the Institute of Psycho-Analysis.

Kli, M. (2018). Eros and Thanatos: A nondualistic interpretation: The dynamic of drives in personal and civilizational development from Freud to Marcuse. *The Psychoanalytic Review, 105*(1), 67–89.

Kliethermes, M., Drewry, K., & Wamser-Nanney, R. (2017). Trauma-focused cognitive behavioural therapy. In S. Gold (Ed.), *Evidence-based treatments for trauma related disorders in children and adolescents* (pp. 167–186). Springer. https://doi.org/10.1007/978-3-319-46138-0_8

Klopper, H. F., & Bezuidenhout, C. (2020). Crimes of a violent nature. In C. Bezuidenhout (Ed.), *A Southern African perspective on fundamental criminology* (2nd ed.). Pearson.

Koerner, M. M. (2013). Courage as identity work: Accounts of workplace courage. *Academy of Management Journal, 57*(1), 63–93. https://doi.org/10.5465/amj.2010.0641

Koh, A. H. Q., Tong, E. M. W., & Yuen, A. Y. L. (2019). The buffering effect of awe on negative affect towards lost possessions. *The Journal of Positive Psychology, 14*(2), 156–165. https://doi.org/10.1080/17439760.2017.1388431

Kollareth, D., Shirai, M., Helmy, M., & Russell, J. A. (2022). Deconstructing disgust as the emotion of violations of body and soul. *Emotion, 22*(8), 1919–1928. https://doi.org/10.1037/emo0000886

Kolnai, A. (2004). *On disgust*. Open Court Publishing Company. (Original work published 1929)

Konečni, V. J. (2005). The aesthetic trinity: Awe, being moved, thrills. *Bulletin of Psychology and the Arts, 5*(2), 27–44. https://doi.org/10.1037/e674862010-005

Konečni, V. J. (2008). Does music induce emotion? A theoretical and methodological analysis. *Psychology of Aesthetics, Creativity, and the Arts, 2*(2), 115–129. https://doi.org/10.1037/1931-3896.2.2.115

Konstan, D. (2005). The emotions of the ancient Greeks: A cross-cultural perspective. *Psychologia, 48*(4), 225–240. https://doi.org/10.2117/psysoc.2005.225

Koob, G. F., & Le Moal, M. (2011). *Neurobiology of addiction*. Academic Press.

Kotsou, I., Mikolajczak, M., Heeren, A., Grégoire, J., & Leys, C. (2019). Improving emotional intelligence: A systematic review of existing work and future challenges. *Emotion Review, 11*(2), 151–165. https://doi.org/10.1177/1754073917735902

Kowalska, M., & Wróbel, M. (2017). Basic emotions. In V. Zeigler-Hill & T. Shackelford (Eds), *Encyclopedia of personality and individual differences*. Springer. https://doi.org/10.1007/978-3-319-28099-8_495-1

Kragel, P. A., & LaBar, K. S. (2016). Decoding the nature of emotion in the brain. *Trends in Cognitive Sciences, 20*(6), 444–455. https://doi.org/10.1016/j.tics.2016.03.011

Kraiss, J. T., Ten Klooster, P. M., Moskowitz, J. T., & Bohlmeijer, E. T. (2020). The relationship between emotion regulation and well-being in patients with mental disorders: A meta-analysis. *Comprehensive Psychiatry, 102*, 152189. https://doi.org/10.1016/j.comppsych.2020.152189

Kristeller, J. L., & Johnson, T. (2005). Cultivating loving kindness: A two-stage model of the effects of meditation on empathy, compassion, and altruism. *Zygon®, 40*(2), 391–408. https://doi.org/10.1111/j.1467-9744.2005.00674.x

Kroc, J. B. (2008). Reason for hope [Distinguished Lecture Series]. In E. Noma (Ed.), *Lecture delivered at Jenny Craig Pavilion, University of San Diego, California*. University of San Diego Press. https://digital.sandiego.edu/cgi/viewcontent.cgi?article=1015&context=lecture_series

Krueger, F., Parasuraman, R., Iyengar, V., Thornburg, M., Weel, J., Lin, M., Clarke, E., McCabe, K., & Lipsky, R. H. (2012). Oxytocin receptor genetic variation promotes human trust behaviour. *Frontiers in Human Neuroscience, 6*, Article 4. https://doi.org/10.3389/fnhum.2012.00004

Kryazh, I., & Grankina-Sazonova, N. (2018). Mediating role of trust between emotional intelligence and positive functioning of personality. *Fundamental and Applied Researches in Practice of Leading Scientific Schools, 26*(2), 326–334. https://farplss.org/index.php/journal/article/view/356

Krys, K., Uchida, Y., Oishi, S., Diener, E., et al. (2023). Happiness maximization is a WEIRD way of living. *Perspectives on Psychological Science, 18*(5), 1–29. https://doi.org/10.1177/17456916231208367

Kubzansky, L. D., Epel, E. S., & Davidson, R. J. (2023). Prosociality should be a public health priority. *Nature Human Behavior, 7*, 2228–2230. https://doi.org/10.1038/s41562-023-01777-5

Kuhn, T. S. (1962). *The structure of scientific revolutions* (2nd ed.). University of Chicago Press.

Kujala, J., Lehtimäki, H., & Pucetaitė, R. (2016). Trust and distrust constructing unity and fragmentation of organisational culture. *Journal of Business Ethics, 139*, 701–716. https://doi.org/10.1007/s10551-015-2915-7

Kummar, A. S. (2018). Mindfulness and fear extinction: A brief review of its current neuro-psychological literature and possible implications for posttraumatic stress disorder. *Psychological Reports, 121*(5), 792–814. https://doi.org/10.1177/0033294118755094

Kwok, S. Y. C. L., Gu, M., & Kit, K. T. K. (2016). Positive psychology intervention to alleviate child depression and increase life satisfaction: A randomized clinical trial. *Research on Social Work Practice, 26*(4), 350–361. https://doi.org/10.1177/1049731516629799

L

Lachman, V. D. (2007). Moral courage: A virtue in need of development. *MedSurg Nursing, 16*(2), 131–133.

Ladson, D. (n.d.). Delayed reaction to trauma in an aging woman. *PubMed Central (PMC)*. https://www.ncbi.nlm.nih.gov/pmc/articles/PMC2921251/

Lanctôt, K. L., Agüera-Ortiz, L., Brodaty, H., Francis, P. T., Geda, Y. E., Ismail, Z., Marshall, G. A., Mortby, M. E., Onyike, C. U., & Padala, P. R. (2017). Apathy associated with neuro-cognitive disorders: Recent progress and future directions. *Alzheimer's & Dementia, 13*(1), 84–100. https://doi.org/10.1016/j.jalz.2016.05.008

Landry, A. P., Ihm, E., & Schooler, J. W. (2022). Filthy animals: Integrating the behavioral immune system and disgust into a model of prophylactic dehumanization. *Evolutionary Psychological Science, 8*(2), 120–133.

Lane, R. D. (2000). Levels of emotional awareness: Neurological, psychological, and social perspectives. In R. Bar-On & J. D. A. Parker (Eds), *The handbook of emotional intelligence* (pp. 171–191). Jossey-Bass.

Larsen, J. T., & McGraw, A. P. (2014). The case for mixed emotions. *Social and Personality Psychology Compass, 8*(6), 263–274. https://doi.org/10.1111/spc3.12108

Larsen, R. R., McLaren, S. A., Griffiths, S., & Jalava, J. (2024). Do psychopathic persons lack empathy? An exploratory systematic review of empathy assessment and emotion recognition studies in psychopathy checklist samples. *Psychology, Public Policy, and Law.* Advance online publication. https://doi.org/10.1037/law0000435

Lasiuk, G., & Hegadoren, K. (2006). Posttraumatic stress disorder part I: Historical development of the concept. *Perspectives in Psychiatric Care, 42*(1), 13–20. https://doi.org/10.1111/j.1744-6163.2006.00045.x

Lauharatanahirun, N., & Aimone, J. (2021). Trust and risk: Neuroeconomic foundations of trust based on social risk. In F. Krueger (Ed.), *The neurobiology of trust* (pp. 101–123). Cambridge University Press. https://doi.org/10.1017/9781108770880.008

Lazarus, R. S. (1991). *Emotion and adaptation.* Oxford University Press.

Lazarus, R. S. (1999). Hope: An emotion and a vital coping resource against despair. *Social Research, 66*(2), 653–678. https://www.jstor.org/stable/40971343

Le, M. T. (2023). Does brand love lead to brand addiction? *Journal of Marketing Analytics, 11*(1), 57–68. https://doi.org/10.1057/s41270-021-00151-6

Leach, E. (1973). Don't say "boo" to a goose. In A. Montagu (Ed.), *Man and aggression* (2nd ed.). Oxford University Press.

LeDoux, J. E. (2014). Coming to terms with fear. *Psychology and Cognitive Sciences, 111*(8), 2871–2878.

LeDoux, J. E. (2017). Semantics, surplus meaning and the science of fear. *Trends in Cognitive Sciences, 21*(5), 303–306.

Lee, J. I., Dirks, K. T., & Campagna, R. L. (2022). At the heart of trust: Understanding the integral relationship between emotion and trust. *Group & Organization Management, 48*(2), 546–580. https://doi.org/10.1177/10596011221118499

Lee, J. Y., Kim, S., & Kim, J. (2020). The impact of community disaster trauma: A focus on emerging research of PTSD and other mental health outcomes. *Chonnam Medical Journal, 56*(2), 99. https://doi.org/10.4068/cmj.2020.56.2.99

Le Heron, C., Holroyd, C. B., Salamone, J., & Husain, M. (2019). Brain mechanisms underlying apathy. *Journal of Neurology, Neurosurgery & Psychiatry, 90*(3), 302–312. https://doi.org/10.1136/jnnp-2018-318265

Lenggogeni, S., Ashton, A. S., & Scott, N. (2022). Humour: Coping with travel bans during the COVID-19 pandemic. *International Journal of Culture, Tourism and Hospitality Research, 17*(1), 222–237. https://doi.org/10.1108/IJCTHR-09-2020-0223

Levine, L., & Munsch, J. (2016). *Child development from infancy to adolescence: An active learning approach.* Sage.

Levy, M. L., Cummings, J. L., Fairbanks, L. A., Masterman, D., Miller, B. L., Craig, A. H., Paulsen, J. S., & Litvan, I. (1998). Apathy is not depression. *The Journal of Neuropsychiatry and Clinical Neurosciences, 10*(3), 314–319. https://doi.org/10.1176/jnp.10.3.314

Leweke, F., Leichsenring, F., Kruse, J., & Hermes, S. (2011). Is alexithymia associated with specific mental disorders? *Psychopathology, 45*(1), 22–28. https://doi.org/10.1159/000325170

Lewis, M. (2000). Self-conscious emotions: Embarrassment, pride, shame, and guilt. In M. Lewis & J. M. Haviland-Jones (Eds), *Handbook of emotions* (2nd ed., pp. 623–636). Guilford Press.

Lewis, M. (2010). Self-conscious emotions: Embarrassment, pride, shame, and guilt. In M. Lewis, J. M. Haviland-Jones, & B. L. Feldman Barrett (Eds), *Handbook of emotions* (3rd ed., pp. 742–756). Guilford Press.

Li, G., Liu, H., Qui, C., & Tang, W. (2022). Fear of COVID-19, prolonged smartphone use, sleep disturbances, and depression in the time of COVID-19: A nation-wide survey. *Frontiers in Psychiatry, 13*, 1–12. https://doi.org/10.3389/fpsyt.2022.971800

Li, J. J., Dou, K., Wang, Y. J., & Nie, Y. G. (2019). Why awe promotes prosocial behaviors? The mediating effects of future time perspective and self-transcendence meaning of life. *Frontiers in Psychology, 10*, 1140. https://doi.org/10.3389/fpsyg.2019.01140

Li, M., Gu, Y., Ma, Y., Liu, M., & Tang, Y. (2022). Positive emotions, hope, and life satisfaction in Chinese college students: How useful is the broaden-and-build model in studying well-being in victims of intimate partner violence? *Journal of Interpersonal Violence, 37*(13–14). https://doi.org/10.1177/08862605211005131

Lim, S. L., Sinaram, S., Ung, E., & Kua, E. H. (2007). The pursuit of thinness: An outcome study of anorexia nervosa. *Singapore Medical Journal, 48*(3), 222–226.

Lin, H. C., & Janice, J. (2020). Disengagement is as revealing as prosocial action for young children's responding to strangers in distress: How personal distress and empathic concern come into play. *International*

Journal of Behavioural Development, 44(6), 515–524. https://doi.
org/10.1177/0165025420912015

Lin, R., Chen, Y., Shen, Y., Xiong, X., Lin, N., & Lian, R. (2021). Dispositional
awe and online altruism: Testing a moderated mediating model. *Frontiers
in Psychology, 12*, 688591. https://doi.org/10.3389/fpsyg.2021.688591

Lindquist, K. A., Wager, T. D., Kober, H., Bliss-Moreau, E., & Barrett, L. F.
(2012). The brain basis of emotion: A meta-analytic review. *Behavioral and
Brain Sciences, 35*(3), 121–143. https://doi.org/10.1017/S0140525X11000446

Liuzza, M. (2020). The smell of prejudice: Disgust, sense of smell and social
attitudes. An evolutionary perspective. *Lebenswelt (Milano), 17*. https://doi.
org/10.54103/2240-9599/17058

Llamas-Díaz, D., Cabello, R., Megías-Robles, A., & Fernández-Berrocal, P.
(2022). Systematic review and meta-analysis: The association between
emotional intelligence and subjective well-being in adolescents. *Journal
of Adolescence, 94*(7), 925–938. https://doi.org/10.1002/jad.12075

Lockey, S. J. (2017). *The role of emotions and individual differences in the trust
repair process* [Doctoral dissertation, Durham University]. Durham
E-Theses Online. http://etheses.dur.ac.uk/12039/

Lohani, M., Payne, B. R., & Isaacowitz, D. M. (2018). Emotional coherence
in early and later adulthood during sadness reactivity and regulation.
Emotion, 18(6), 789–804. https://doi.org/10.1037/emo0000345

Lomas, T., & VanderWeele, T. J. (2023). The complex creation of happiness:
Multidimensional conditionality in the drivers of happy people and
societies. *The Journal of Positive Psychology, 18*(1), 15–33. https://doi.org/10.1
080/17439760.2021.1991453

Long, K. N., Kim, E. S., Chen, Y., Wilson, M. F., Worthington, E. L., Jr., &
VanderWeele, T. J. (2020). The role of hope in subsequent health
and well-being for older adults: An outcome-wide longitudinal

approach. *Global Epidemiology*, 2, 100018. https://doi.org/10.1016/j.
gloepi.2020.100018

Long, L. J. (2022). Hope and PTSD. *Current Opinion in Psychology*, 48, 101472.
https://doi.org/10.1016/j.copsyc.2022.101472

Lopes, P. N., Salovey, P., & Straus, R. (2003). Emotional intelligence,
personality, and the perceived quality of social relationships. *Personality
and Individual Differences*, 35(3), 641–658. https://doi.org/10.1016/S0191-
8869(02)00242-8

Lopez, S. J., Snyder, C. R., & Pedrotti, J. T. (2003). Hope: Many definitions,
many measures. In S. J. Lopez & C. R. Snyder (Eds), *Positive psychological
assessment: A handbook of models and measures* (pp. 91–106). American
Psychological Association.

Lorenz, K. (1966). *On aggression*. Harcourt Brace Jovanovich.

Lu, J., Potts, C. A., & Allen, R. S. (2021). Homeless people's trait mindfulness
and their resilience: A mediation test on the role of inner peace and hope.
Journal of Social Distress and Homelessness, 30(2), 155–163. https://doi.org/10
.1080/10530789.2020.1774847

Lu, Y., Lu, G., Li, J., Zhang, Z., & Xu, Y. (2021). Fully shared convolutional
neural networks. *Neural Computing and Applications*, 33, 8635–8648.
https://doi.org/10.1007/s00521-020-05618-8

Lucht, A., & van Schie, H. T. (2024). The evolutionary function of awe: A
review and integrated model of seven theoretical perspectives. *Emotion
Review*, 16(1), 46–63. https://doi.org/10.1177/17540739231197199

Luhmann, N. (1986). *Love as passion: The codification of intimacy*. Harvard
University Press.

Lumineau, F. (2015). How contracts influence trust and distrust. *Journal of
Management*, 43, 256–279. https://doi.org/10.1177/0149206314556656

Luntz, B. K., & Widom, C. S. (1994). Antisocial personality disorder in abused and neglected children grown up. *American Journal of Psychiatry, 151,* 670–674.

Luo, L., Yang, D., Tian, Y., Gao, W., Yang, J., & Yuan, J. (2022). Awe weakens the AIDS-related stigma: The mediation effects of connectedness and empathy. *Frontiers in Psychiatry, 13,* Article 1043101. https://doi. org/10.3389/fpsyt.2022.1043101

Lupoli, M. J., Zhang, M., Yin, Y., & Oveis, C. (2020). A conflict of values: When perceived compassion decreases trust. *Journal of Experimental Social Psychology, 91,* Article 104049. https://doi.org/10.1016/j.jesp.2020.104049

Luppino, O. I., Tenore, K., Mancini, F., & Mancini, A. (2023). The role of childhood experiences in the development of disgust sensitivity: A preliminary study on early moral memories. *Clinical Neuropsychiatry, 20*(2), 109–121.

Lüscher, C., Robbins, T. W., & Everitt, B. J. (2020). The transition to compulsion in addiction. *Nature Reviews Neuroscience, 21*(5), 247–263. https://doi.org/10.1038/s41583-020-0289-z

Lv, Y., Shi, J., Yu, F., & Zhang, C. (2023). The effect of awe on natural risk-taking preferences: The role of need for closure. *Current Psychology: Research & Reviews, 42*(5), 4181–4195. https://doi.org/10.1007/s12144-021-01758-9

Lyons, S. (2020). *Dissociation in children and teens.* Beacon House. https:// beaconhouse.org.uk/wp-content/uploads/2020/02/Dissociation-in-Children-Teens-Resource_compressed.pdf

Lyubomirsky, S., King, L., & Diener, E. (2005). The benefits of frequent positive affect: Does happiness lead to success? *Psychological Bulletin, 131*(6), 803–855. https://doi.org/10.1037/0033-2909.131.6.803

M

Ma, F., Wylie, B. E., Luo, X., He, Z., Xu, F., & Evans, A. D. (2018). Apologies repair children's trust: The mediating role of emotions. *Journal of Experimental Child Psychology, 176*, 1–12. https://doi.org/10.1016/j.jecp.2018.05.008

MacCann, C., Jiang, Y., Brown, L. E. R., Double, K. S., Bucich, M., & Minbashian, A. (2020). Emotional intelligence predicts academic performance: A metaanalysis. *Psychological Bulletin, 146*(2), 150–186. https://doi.org/10.1037/bul0000219

Mackenzie, J. L., & AlbaJuez, L. (Eds). (2019). *Emotion in Discourse* (Pragmatics & Beyond New Series; Vol. 302). John Benjamins Publishing Company. https://doi.org/10.1075/pbns.302

MagyarMoe, J. L., & Lopez, S. J. (2015). Strategies for accentuating hope. In S. Joseph (Ed.), *Positive psychology in practice: Promoting human flourishing in work, health, education, and everyday life* (pp. 483–505). John Wiley & Sons.

Mancilla, V. J., Peeri, N., Silzer, T., Basha, R., Felini, M., Jones, H. P., Phillips, N., Tao, M. H., Thyagarajan, S., & Vishwanatha, J. K. (2020). Understanding the interplay between health disparities and epigenomics. *Frontiers in Genetics, 11*, Article 903. https://doi.org/10.3389/fgene.2020.00903

Manfredi, P., & Taglietti, C. (2022). A psychodynamic contribution to the understanding of anger: The importance of diagnosis before treatment. *Research in Psychotherapy, 25*(2), 587. https://doi.org/10.4081/ripppo.2022.587

Mann, R. S. (1990). Differential diagnosis and classification of apathy. *American Journal of Psychiatry, 147*(1), 22–30. https://doi.org/10.1176/ajp.147.1.22

Marcuse, H. (1966). Repressive tolerance. In W. R. P. Wolf (Ed.), *A Critique of Pure Tolerance*. Beacon Press.

Marin, R. S., Firinciogullari, S., & Biedrzycki, R. C. (1994). Group differences in the relationship between apathy and depression. *The Journal of Nervous and Mental Disease, 182*(4), 235–239. https://doi.org/10.1097/00005053-199404000-00008

Marinova, S., Anand, S., & Park, H. (2025). Otheroriented emotional intelligence, OCBs, and job performance: A relational perspective. *Journal of Social Psychology*, 1–20. https://doi.org/10.1080/00224545.2024.2439944

Marshall, S. L., Parker, P. D., Ciarrochi, J., Sahdra, B., Jackson, C. J., & Heaven, P. C. L. (2015). Self-compassion protects against the negative effects of low selfesteem: A longitudinal study in a large adolescent sample. *Personality and Individual Differences, 74*, 116–121. https://doi.org/10.1016/j.paid.2014.09.013

Martínez-Sánchez, F., AtoGarcía, M., & OrtizSoria, B. (2003). Alexithymia – state or trait? *The Spanish Journal of Psychology, 6*(1), 51–59. https://doi.org/10.1017/S1138741600005205

Martino, J., Pegg, J., & Frates, E. P. (2015). The connection prescription: Using the power of social interactions and the deep desire for connectedness to empower health and wellness. *American Journal of Lifestyle Medicine, 11*(6), 466–475. https://doi.org/10.1177/1559827615608788

Martins, A., Ramalho, N. C., & Morin, E. M. (2010). A comprehensive meta-analysis of the relationship between emotional intelligence and health. *Personality and Individual Differences, 49*(6), 554–564. https://doi.org/10.1016/j.paid.2010.05.029

Marwaha, S., Goswami, M., & Vashist, B. (2017). Prevalence of principles of Piaget's theory among 4–7yearold children and their correlation with IQ. *Journal of Clinical and Diagnostic Research, 11*(8), ZC111–ZC115.

Masuda, M. (2003). Meta-analyses of love scales: Do various love scales measure the same psychological constructs? *Japanese Psychological Research, 45*(1), 25–37. https://doi.org/10.1111/1468-5884.00030

Matich, O. (2009). Poetics of disgust: To eat and die in Andrei Belyi's *Petersburg*. *Slavic Review, 68*(2), 284–307. https://doi.org/10.2307/27697959

Matthews, G., Zeidner, M., & Roberts, R. D. (2002). *Emotional intelligence: Science and myth*. MIT Press.

Matthiesen, N., Cavada-Hrepich, P., & Tanggaard, L. (2022). The trust imperative: Conceptualizing the dynamics of trust and distrust in parent–professional collaboration. *Educational Theory, 72*(2), 663–683. https://doi.org/10.1111/edth.12549

Mattingly, V., & Kraiger, K. (2019). Can emotional intelligence be trained? A metaanalytical investigation. *Human Resource Management Review, 29*(2), 140–155. https://doi.org/10.1016/j.hrmr.2018.03.002

Mauss, I. B., Bunge, S. A., & Gross, J. J. (2007). Automatic emotion regulation. *Social and Personality Psychology Compass, 1*(1), 146–167. https://doi.org/10.1111/j.1751-9004.2007.00005.x

Mayer, J. D., Caruso, D., & Salovey, P. (1999). Emotional intelligence meets traditional standards for an intelligence. *Intelligence, 27*(4), 267–298. https://doi.org/10.1016/S0160-2896(99)00016-1

Mayer, J. D., & Salovey, P. (1997). What is emotional intelligence? In P. Salovey & D. Sluyter (Eds), *Emotional development and emotional intelligence: Implications for educators* (pp. 3–31). Basic Books.

Mayer, J. D., Caruso, D., & Salovey, P. (2002). *Mayer–Salovey–Caruso Emotional Intelligence Test: User's manual*. MultiHealth Systems.

Mayer, J. D., Salovey, P., Caruso, D. R., & Sitarenios, G. (2001). Emotional intelligence as a standard intelligence. *Emotion, 1*(3), 232–242. https://doi.org/10.1037/1528-3542.1.3.232

Mayer, R. C., Davis, J. H., & Schoorman, F. D. (1995). An integrative model of organizational trust. *Academy of Management Review, 20*(3), 709–734. https://doi.org/10.2307/258792

McCarty, R. (2016). The fight-or-flight response: A cornerstone of stress research. In G. Fink (Ed.), *Stress: Concepts, cognition, emotion, and behaviour* (Handbook of Stress Series, Vol. 1, pp. 33–37). Academic Press. https://doi. org/10.1016/B978-0-12-800951-2.00004-2

McCullough, L. B., Coverdale, J., & Chervenak, F. A. (2022). John Gregory's medical ethics elucidates the concepts of compassion and empathy. *Medical Teacher, 44*(1), 45–49.

McGuire, J., Bastardoz, N., Hentrup, L. J., De Cremer, D., & Menges, J. I. (2024). The backdrop of leadership: How environmental awe influences charisma attributions. *Journal of Organizational Behavior.* Advance online publication. https://doi.org/10.1002/job.2849

McIntyre, L., & Rauch, J. (2021, June 25). A war on truth is raging: Not everyone recognizes we're in it. *The Washington Post.* https://www. washingtonpost.com/opinions/2021/06/25/war-truth-is-raging-not-everyone-recognizes-were-it/

Megías-Robles, A., Gutiérrez-Cobo, M. J., Gómez-Leal, R., Cabello, R., Gross, J. J., & Fernández-Berrocal, P. (2019). Emotionally intelligent people reappraise rather than suppress their emotions. *PLoS ONE, 14*(8), Article e0220688. https://doi.org/10.1371/journal.pone.0220688

Meloy, J. R. (1996). Stalking (obsessional following): A review of some preliminary studies. *Aggression and Violent Behavior, 1*(2), 147–162. https:// doi.org/10.1016/1359-1789(95)00013-5

Meloy, J. R. (1998). The psychology of stalking. In *The psychology of stalking* (pp. 1–23). Elsevier.

Meloy, J. R., & Fisher, H. (2005). Some thoughts on the neurobiology of stalking. *Journal of Forensic Sciences, 50*(6), 1472–1480. https://doi. org/10.1520/JFS2004508

Meng, L., & Wang, X. (2022). Awe in the workplace promotes prosocial behavior. *PsyCh Journal.* Advance online publication. https://doi. org/10.1002/pchj.593

Menschner, C., & Maul, A. (2016, April). Key ingredients for successful trauma-informed care implementation. Center for Health Care Strategies. https://www.samhsa.gov/sites/default/files/programs_campaigns/childrens_mental_health/atc-whitepaper-040616.pdf

MerriamWebster. (n.d.-a). Awe. In *Merriam-Webster.com dictionary*. Retrieved February 3, 2024, from https://www.merriam-webster.com/dictionary/awe

MerriamWebster. (n.d.-b). Emotion. In *Merriam-Webster.com dictionary*. Retrieved February 3, 2024, from https://www.merriam-webster.com/dictionary/emotion

Messerli, L., Semmer, N. K., & Tschan, F. (2016). Disentangling the components of surface acting in emotion work: Experiencing emotions may be as important as regulating them. *Journal of Applied Social Psychology, 46*(1), 46–64. https://doi.org/10.1111/jasp.12364

Meston, C. M., & Frohlich, P. F. (2003). Love at first fright: Partner salience moderates rollercoaster-induced excitation transfer. *Archives of Sexual Behavior, 32*, 537–544. https://doi.org/10.1023/A:1026182111034

Meyer, W. F., Moore, C., & Viljoen, H. G. (1993). *Persoonlikheidsteorieë – van Freud tot Frankl* [Personality theories – from Freud to Frankl]. Lexicon.

Miao, C., Humphrey, R. H., & Qian, S. (2017). A meta-analysis of emotional intelligence and work attitudes. *Journal of Occupational and Organizational Psychology, 90*(2), 177–202. https://doi.org/10.1111/joop.12167

Michl, L. C., McLaughlin, K. A., Shepherd, K., & Nolen-Hoeksema, S. (2013). Rumination as a mechanism linking stressful life events to symptoms of depression and anxiety: Longitudinal evidence in early adolescents and adults. *Journal of Abnormal Psychology, 122*(2), 339–352. https://doi.org/10.1037/a0031994

Michl, P., Meindl, T., Meister, F., Born, C., Engel, R. R., Reiser, M., & HennigFast, K. (2014). Neurobiological underpinnings of shame and guilt: A pilot fMRI study. *Social Cognitive and Affective Neuroscience, 9*(2), 150–157. https://doi.org/10.1093/scan/nss114

Midgley, Mary (1994). The End of Anthropocentrism? Royal Institute of Philosophy Supplement 36:103-112. https://doi.org/10.1017/s135824610000648

Miller, P. A., & Eisenberg, N. (1988). The relation of empathy to aggressive and externalizing/antisocial behavior. *Psychological Bulletin, 103*(3), 324–344. https://doi.org/10.1037/0033-2909.103.3.324

Miller, P. H. (2022). Developmental theories: Past, present, and future. *Developmental Review, 66*, Article 101049. https://doi.org/10.1016/j.dr.2022.101049

Miller, S. B. (2004). *Disgust: The gatekeeper emotion*. Taylor & Francis (Analytic Press).

Millon, T., Lerner, M. J., & Weiner, I. B. (Eds). (2003). *Handbook of Psychology: Volume 5, Personality and social psychology* (2nd ed.). John Wiley & Sons.

Milona, M., & Stockdale, K. (2018). A perceptual theory of hope. *Ergo: An Open Access Journal of Philosophy, 5*(8), 203–222. https://doi.org/10.3998/ergo.12405314.0005.008

Mobbs, D., Adolphs, R., Fanselow, M. S., Barrett, L. F., LeDoux, J. E., Ressler, K., & Tye, K. M. (2019). Viewpoints: Approaches to defining and investigating fear. *Nature Neuroscience, 22*(8), 1205–1216. https://doi.org/10.1038/s41593-019-0456-6

Mocanu, L. (2019). Traveling between our own fear and courage. *EIRP Proceedings, 14*(1), 203–210. Danubius University Press. https://proceedings.univdanubius.ro/index.php/eirp/article/view/1938/0

Modecki, K. L., Minchin, J., Harbaugh, A. G., Guerra, N. G., & Runions, K. C. (2014). Bullying prevalence across contexts: A meta-analysis measuring cyber and traditional bullying. *Journal of Adolescent Health, 55*(5), 602–611. https://doi.org/10.1016/j.jadohealth.2014.06.007

Moeller, R. W., Seehuus, M., & Peisch, V. (2020). Emotional intelligence, belongingness, and mental health in college students. *Frontiers in Psychology, 11*, Article 93. https://doi.org/10.3389/fpsyg.2020.00093

Moldes, O., & Ku, L. (2020). Materialistic cues make us miserable: A meta-analysis of the experimental evidence for the effects of materialism on individual and societal wellbeing. *Psychology & Marketing, 37*(10), 1396–1419. https://doi.org/10.1002/mar.21387

Monroy, M., & Keltner, D. (2023). Awe as a pathway to mental and physical health. *Perspectives on Psychological Science, 18*(2), 309–320. https://doi.org/10.1177/17456916221094856

Montagu, A. (1976). *The nature of human aggression*. Oxford University Press.

Moosavi, J., Resch, A., Sokolov, A. N., Fallgatter, A. J., & Pavlova, M. A. (2024). "The mirror of the soul?" Inferring sadness in the eyes. *Scientific Reports, 14*(1), Article 20063. https://doi.org/10.1038/s41598-024-68178-0

Mor, N., & Winquist, J. (2002). Self-focused attention and negative affect: A meta-analysis. *Psychological Bulletin, 128*(4), 638–662. https://doi.org/10.1037/0033-2909.128.4.638

Mordka, C. (2016). What are emotions? Structure and function of emotions. *Studia Humana, 5*(3), 29–44. https://doi.org/10.1515/sh-2016-0013

Morley, R. H. (2015). Violent criminality and self-compassion. *Aggression and Violent Behavior, 24*, 226–240. https://doi.org/10.1016/j.avb.2015.05.017

Mortillaro, M., & Dukes, D. (2018). Jumping for joy: The importance of the body and of dynamics in the expression and recognition of positive emotions. *Frontiers in Psychology, 9*, Article 763. https://doi.org/10.3389/fpsyg.2018.00763

Mosak, H. H., & Bluvshtein, M. (2019). Faith, hope, and love in psychotherapy. *The Journal of Individual Psychology, 75*(1), 75–88. https://doi.org/10.1353/jip.2019.0005

Moss-Pech, S. A., Southward, M. W., & Cheavens, J. S. (2020). Hope attenuates the negative impact of general psychological distress on goal progress. *Journal of Clinical Psychology, 77*(6), 1412–1427. https://doi.org/10.1002/jclp.23087

Mousourakis, G. (2007). Reason, passion and self-control: Understanding the moral basis of the provocation defence. *Law – Université de Sherbrooke Law Journal, 38*(1), 145–168. https://doi.org/10.17118/11143/11556

Mouton, A. R., & Montijo, M. N. (2017). Love, passion, and peak experience: A qualitative study on six continents. *The Journal of Positive Psychology, 12*(3), 263–280. https://doi.org/10.1080/17439760.2016.1225117

Moye, J., & Rouse, S. J. (2014). Posttraumatic stress in older adults: When medical diagnoses or treatments cause traumatic stress. *Clinics in Geriatric Medicine, 30*(3), 577–589. https://doi.org/10.1016/j.cger.2014.04.006

Mpako, A., & Ndoma, S. (2023, November 24). South Africans see genderbased violence as most important women's rights issue to address (*Afrobarometer Dispatch No. 738*). Afrobarometer; Institute for Justice and Reconciliation (IJR). https://www.afrobarometer.org/publication/ad738-south-africans-see-gender-based-violence-as-most-important-womens-rights-issue-to-address/

Mueller, A. Psycho-dynamic Psychology. (2023, October 6). Object relations theory explained [Video]. YouTube. https://www.bing.com/videos/riverview/relatedvideo?q=winnicott+object+relations+theory&mid=F933E7C3E94A2E E58807F933E7C3E94A2EE58807

Mullen, P. E. (1991). Jealousy: The pathology of passion. *The British Journal of Psychiatry, 158*(5), 593–601. https://doi.org/10.1192/bjp.158.5.593

Munoz, R. T., Brady, S., & Brown, V. (2017). The psychology of resilience: A model of the relationship of locus of control to hope among survivors of intimate partner violence. *Traumatology, 23*, 102–111. https://doi.org/10.1037/trm0000102

Muris, P. E. H. M. (2009). Fear and courage in children: Two sides of the same coin? *Journal of Child and Family Studies, 18*(4), 486–490. https://doi.org/10.1007/s10826-009-9271-0

N

Nakajima, R., Kinoshita, M., Okita, H., & Nakada, M. (2022). Posteriorprefrontal and medial orbitofrontal regions play crucial roles in happiness and sadness recognition. *NeuroImage: Clinical, 35,* Article 103072. https://doi.org/10.1016/j.nicl.2022.103072

Năstasă, L. E., Zanfirescu, Ș. A., Iliescu, D., & Farcaș, A. D. (2023). Improving emotional intelligence in adolescents: An experiential learning approach. *Current Psychology, 42,* 9119–9133. https://doi.org/10.1007/s12144-021-02132-5

National Council for Mental Wellbeing. (n.d.). How to manage trauma. *National Council for Mental Wellbeing.* https://www.thenationalcouncil.org/wp-content/uploads/2022/08/Trauma-infographic.pdf

National Sexual Violence Resource Center. (n.d.). Why do we have trauma? *National Sexual Violence Resource Center.* https://www.nsvrc.org/blogs/exploring-conversation-trauma-blog-series/why-do-we-have-trauma

Navarini, C., & De Monte, E. (2019). Fear as related to courage: An Aristotelian Thomistic redefinition of cognitive emotions. *Humana Mente: Journal of Philosophical Studies, 12*(35), 167–189.

Negami, H. R., & Ellard, C. G. (2023). How architecture evokes awe: Predicting awe through architectural features of building interiors. *Psychology of Aesthetics, Creativity, and the Arts, 17*(1), 3–15. https://doi.org/10.1037/aca0000394

Nélis, D., Kotsou, I., Quoidbach, J., Hansenne, M., Weytens, F., Dupuis, P., & Mikolajczak, M. (2011). Increasing emotional competence improves psychological and physical wellbeing, social relationships, and employability. *Emotion, 11*(2), 354–366. https://doi.org/10.1037/a0021554

Nemeroff, C. B. (2016). Paradise lost: The neurobiological and clinical consequences of child abuse and neglect. *Neuron, 89*(5), 892–909. https://doi.org/10.1016/j.neuron.2016.01.019

Nesse, R. M. (1990). Evolutionary explanations of emotions. *Human Nature, 1*(3), 261–289. https://doi.org/10.1007/BF02733986

Newland, B. L., & Aicher, T. J. (2023). Understanding runner's passion and addiction: A Kano method analysis. *Managing Sport and Leisure*, 1–20. https://doi.org/10.1080/23750472.2023.2219692

Newport Institute Staff. (2023, December 4). 5 ways childhood trauma impacts young adults. *Newport Institute*. https://www.newportinstitute.com/resources/treatment/childhood-trauma/

Nguyen, N. N., Takahashi, Y., & Nham, T. P. (2022). Relationship between emotional intelligence and narcissism: A metaanalysis. *Management Research Review, 45*(10), 1338–1353. https://doi.org/10.1016/j.paid.2021.110961

Niedenthal, P. M., Krauth-Gruber, S., & François, R. (2006). *Psychology of emotion: Interpersonal, experiential, and cognitive approaches*. Psychology Press/Taylor & Francis.

Niedenthal, P. M., Tangney, J. P., & Gavanski, I. (1994). "If only I weren't" versus "if only I hadn't": Distinguishing shame and guilt in counterfactual thinking. *Journal of Personality and Social Psychology, 67*(4), 585–595. https://doi.org/10.1037/0022-3514.67.4.585

Niemiec, R. M., & Lissing, J. (2016). Mindfulness-based strengths practice (MBSP) for enhancing wellbeing, managing problems, and boosting positive relationships. In I. Ivtzan & T. Lomas (Eds), *Mindfulness in positive psychology: The science of meditation and wellbeing* (pp. 15–36). Routledge/Taylor & Francis Group.

Nobis, L., & Husain, M. (2018). Apathy in Alzheimer's disease. *Current Opinion in Behavioral Sciences, 22,* 7–13. https://doi.org/10.1016/j.cobeha.2017.12.007

NolenHoeksema, S., Wisco, B. E., & Lyubomirsky, S. (2008). Rethinking rumination. *Perspectives on Psychological Science, 3*(5), 400–424.

Noordewier, M. K., & Gocłowska, M. A. (2024). Shared and unique features of epistemic emotions: Awe, surprise, curiosity, interest, confusion, and boredom. *Emotion, 24*(4), 1029–1048. https://doi.org/10.1037/emo0001314

Northrup, J. M., Vander Wal, E., Bonar, M., Fieberg, J., LaForge, M. P., Leclerc, M., Prokopenko, C. M., & Gerber, B. D. (2022). Conceptual and methodological advances in habitat-selection modeling: Guidelines for ecology and evolution. *Ecological Applications, 32*(1), Article e02470. https://doi.org/10.1002/eap.2470

Nye, J. (2021, May 4). Impulse-control and conduct disorders: A case study of videogame-related violence among adolescents. *Psychiatry Advisor.* https://www.psychiatryadvisor.com/home/conference-highlights/apa-2021/videogames-may-negatively-affect-children-and-adolescents-by-promoting-aggressive-behaviours/

O

O'bi, A., & Yang, F. (2024). Seeing awe: How children perceive awe-inspiring visual experiences. *Child Development, 95*(4), 1271–1286. https://doi.org/10.1111/cdev.14069

Obschonka, M. (2018, March 26). Research: The industrial revolution left psychological scars that can still be seen today. *Harvard Business Review.* https://hbr.org/2018/03/research-the-industrial-revolution-left-psychological-scars-that-can-still-be-seen-today

Obschonka, M., Stuetzer, M., Rentfrow, P. J., Shaw-Taylor, L., Satchell, M., Silbereisen, R. K., ... Gosling, S. D. (2018). In the shadow of coal: How large-scale industries contributed to present-day regional differences in personality and wellbeing. *Journal of Personality and Social Psychology*, 115(5), 903–927. https://doi.org/10.1037/pspp0000175

O'Byrne, K. K., Lopez, S. J., & Peterson, S. (2000, August). Building a theory of courage: A precursor to change? Paper presented at the 108th Annual Convention of the American Psychological Association, Washington, DC.

O'Donovan, A., Hughes, B. M., Slavich, G. M., Lynch, L., Cronin, M. T., O'Farrelly, C., & Malone, K. M. (2010). Clinical anxiety, cortisol and interleukin6: Evidence for specificity in emotion-biology relationships. *Brain, Behavior, and Immunity*, 24(7), 1074–1077. https://doi.org/10.1016/j.bbi.2010.03.003

Oh, H., Lee, D. G., & Cho, H. (2023). The differential roles of shame and guilt in the relationship between self-discrepancy and psychological maladjustment. *Frontiers in Psychology*, 14, Article 1215177. https://doi.org/10.3389/fpsyg.2023.1215177

Öhman, A. B. (2005). The role of the amygdala in human fear: Automatic detection of threat. *Psychoneuroendocrinology*, 30(10), 953–958. https://doi.org/10.1016/j.psyneuen.2005.03.019

Oishi, S., & Westgate, E. C. (2021). A psychologically rich life: Beyond happiness and meaning. *Psychological Review*. Advance online publication. https://doi.org/10.1037/rev0000317

O'Keefe, P. A., Horberg, E., Chen, P., & Savani, K. (2022). Should you pursue your passion as a career? Cultural differences in the emphasis on passion in career decisions. *Journal of Organizational Behavior*, 43(9), 1475–1495. https://doi.org/10.1002/job.2552

Olatunji, B. O., Berg, H. E., & Zhao, Z. (2017). Emotion regulation of fear and disgust: Different effects of reappraisal and suppression. *Cognition and Emotion*, 31(2), 403–410. https://doi.org/10.1080/02699931.2015.1110117

Olofinbiyi, S. A. (2022). Anti-immigrant violence and xenophobia in South Africa: Untreated malady and potential snag for national development. *Insight on Africa, 14*(2), 193–211. https://doi.org/10.1177/09750878211055950

Olsthoorn, P. (2007). Courage in the military: Physical and moral. *Journal of Military Ethics, 6*(4), 270–279. https://doi.org/10.1080/15027570701755471

Online Etymology Dictionary. (n.d.). Trauma | Etymology of trauma by etymonline. https://www.etymonline.com/word/trauma

Ornaghi, V., Conte, E., & Grazzani, I. (2020). Empathy in toddlers: The role of emotion regulation, language ability, and maternal emotion socialization style. *Frontiers in Psychology, 11*, Article 586862. https://doi.org/10.3389/fpsyg.2020.586862

Orth, U., Berking, M., & Burkardt, S. (2006). Self-conscious emotions and depression: Rumination explains why shame but not guilt is maladaptive. *Personality and Social Psychology Bulletin, 32*(12), 1608–1619. https://doi.org/10.1177/0146167206292958

Orth, U., Robins, R. W., & Soto, C. J. (2010). Tracking the trajectory of shame, guilt, and pride across the life span. *Journal of Personality and Social Psychology, 99*(6), 1061–1071. https://doi.org/10.1037/a0021342

Ortigue, S., Bianchi-Demicheli, F., Hamilton, A. F. de C., & Grafton, S. T. (2007). The neural basis of love as a subliminal prime: An event-related functional magnetic resonance imaging study. *Journal of Cognitive Neuroscience, 19*(7), 1218–1230. https://doi.org/10.1162/jocn.2007.19.7.1218

Ortony, A. (2022). Are all "basic emotions" emotions? A problem for the (basic) emotions construct. *Perspectives on Psychological Science, 17*(1), 41–61. https://doi.org/10.1177/1745691620985415

Ortony, A., Clore, G. L., & Collins, A. (2022). *The cognitive structure of emotions.* Cambridge University Press. https://doi.org/10.1017/9781009051958

Özel, Y., & Özkan, B. (2020). Psikiyatride Güncel Yaklaşımlar-Current Approaches in Psychiatry, 12(3), 352–367. https://doi.org/10.18863/pgy.652126

P

Pace, M. (2017). The strength of faith and trust. *International Journal for Philosophy of Religion, 81*(1–2), 135–150. https://doi.org/10.1007/s11153-016-9611-0

Pace, M. (2020). Trusting in order to inspire trustworthiness. *Synthese.* Advance online publication. https://doi.org/10.1007/s11229-020-02840-8

Palmer, B. R., Gignac, G., Ekermans, G., & Stough, C. (2008). A comprehensive framework for emotional intelligence. In R. J. Emmerling, V. K. Shanwal, & M. K. Mandal (Eds), *Emotional intelligence: Theoretical and cultural perspectives* (pp. 17–38). Nova Science Publishers.

Panzer, A., Viljoen, M., & Roos, J. L. (2007). The neurobiological basis of fear: A concise review. *South African Psychiatry, 10,* 71–75.

Papousek, I. (2018). Humor and well-being: A little less is quite enough. *Humor: International Journal of Humor Research, 31*(2), 311–327. https://doi.org/10.1515/humor-2016-011

Park, C. L. (2010). Making sense of the meaning literature: An integrative review of meaning making and its effects on adjustment to stressful life events. *Psychological Bulletin, 136*(2), 257–301. https://doi.org/10.1037/a0018301

Park, N., Peterson, C., & Seligman, M. E. P. (2005). Character strengths in fifty-four nations and the fifty U.S. states. *Journal of Positive Psychology, 1*(3), 118–129. https://doi.org/10.1080/17439760600619567

Parker, B. (2023, November 27). World's most dangerous countries for 2023 revealed: The world has become less peaceful over the last 15 years, report shows. *The Independent.* https://www.independent.co.uk/travel/news-and-advice/most-dangerous-countries-2023-b2454258.html

Pasyar, N., Jowkar, M., & Rambod, M. (2023). The predictive role of hope and social relational quality in disability acceptance among Iranian patients under hemodialysis. *BMC Nephrology, 24*(1), Article 101. https://doi.org/10.1186/s12882-023-03161-x

Patterson, S. L. (2016). The effect of emotional freedom technique on stress and anxiety in nursing students: A pilot study. *Nurse Education Today, 40,* 104–110. https://doi.org/10.1016/j.nedt.2016.02.003

Peh, C. X., Liu, J., Bishop, G. D., Chan, H. Y., Chua, S. M., Kua, E. H., & Mahendran, R. (2017). Emotion regulation and emotional distress: The mediating role of hope on reappraisal and anxiety/depression in newly diagnosed cancer patients. *Psycho-Oncology, 26*(8), 1191–1197. https://doi.org/10.1002/pon.4297

Pehlivan, T., & Güner, P. (2020). Compassionate care: Benefits, barriers and recommendations. *Journal of Psychiatric Nursing, 11*(2), 148–153. https://doi.org/10.14744/phd.2020.41599

Pekrun, R., & Linnenbrink-Garcia, L. (Eds). (2014). *International handbook of emotions in education.* Routledge.

Pena-Sarrionandia, A., Mikolajczak, M., & Gross, J. J. (2015). Integrating emotion regulation and emotional intelligence traditions: A meta-analysis. *Frontiers in Psychology, 6,* Article 160. https://doi.org/10.3389/fpsyg.2015.00160

Perez-Escoda, N., Filella, G., Alegre, A., & Bisquerra, R. (2012). Developing the emotional competence of teachers and pupils in school contexts. *Electronic Journal of Research in Educational Psychology, 10*(3), 1183–1208.

Peterson, C., & Seligman, M. E. P. (2004). *Character strengths and virtues: A handbook and classification.* Oxford University Press.

Peterson, S. (2018, May 25). Early childhood trauma. *The National Child Traumatic Stress Network.* https://www.nctsn.org/what-is-child-trauma/ trauma-types/early-childhood-trauma

Peterson, S. (2018a, May 25). Complex trauma. *The National Child Traumatic Stress Network.* https://www.nctsn.org/what-is-child-trauma/trauma-types/complex-trauma

Peterson, S. (2018b, May 25). Medical trauma. *The National Child Traumatic Stress Network.* https://www.nctsn.org/what-is-child-trauma/trauma-types/medical-trauma

Peterson, S. (2018c, June 11). Effects. *The National Child Traumatic Stress Network.* https://www.nctsn.org/what-is-child-trauma/trauma-types/ complex-trauma/effects

Petrides, K. V., & Furnham, A. (2000). On the dimensional structure of emotional intelligence. *Personality and Individual Differences, 29*(2), 313–320. https://doi.org/10.1016/S0191-8869(99)00195-6

Phillips, M. L., Senior, C., Fahy, T., & David, A. S. (1998). Disgust – The forgotten emotion in psychiatry. *The British Journal of Psychiatry, 172*(5), 373–375. https://doi.org/10.1192/bjp.172.5.373

Phillips, W. J., & Hine, D. W. (2021). Self-compassion, physical health, and health behaviour: A meta-analysis. *Health Psychology Review, 15*(1), 113–139. https://doi.org/10.1080/17437199.2019.1705872

Piaget, J. (1956). *The origins of intelligence in children.* International Universities Press.

Piaget, J. (1978). *Success and understanding.* Routledge & Kegan Paul.

Piff, P. K., Dietze, P., Feinberg, M., Stancato, D. M., & Keltner, D. (2015). Awe, the small self, and prosocial behavior. *Journal of Personality and Social Psychology, 108*(6), 883–899. https://doi.org/10.1037/pspi0000018

Piretti, L., Pappaianni, E., Garbin, C., Rumiati, R. I., Job, R., & Grecucci, A. (2023). The neural signatures of shame, embarrassment, and guilt: A voxel-based meta-analysis on functional neuro-imaging studies. *Brain Sciences, 13*(4), Article 559. https://doi.org/10.3390/brainsci13040559

Pirsoul, T., Parmentier, M., Sovet, L., & Nils, F. (2023). Emotional intelligence and career-related outcomes: A meta-analysis. *Human Resource Management Review, 33*, Article 100967. https://doi.org/10.1016/j.hrmr.2023.100967

Pittman, C. M., & Youngs, W. H. (2021). *Rewire your OCD brain: Powerful neuroscience-based skills to break free from obsessive thoughts and fears.* New Harbinger Publications.

Pleeging, E. (2022). Measuring hope: Validity of short versions of four popular hopelessness scales. *Quality & Quantity, 56*(6), 4437–4464. https://doi.org/10.1007/s11135-022-01316-w

Pocock, M., Jackson, D., & Bradbury-Jones, C. (2020). Intimate partner violence and the power of love: A qualitative systematic review. *Health Care for Women International, 41*(6), 621–646. https://doi.org/10.1080/0739 9332.2019.1621318

Polanco-Roman, L., Danies, A., & Anglin, D. M. (2016). Racial discrimination as race-based trauma, coping strategies, and dissociative symptoms among emerging adults. *Psychological Trauma: Theory, Research, Practice, and Policy, 8*(5), 609–617. https://doi.org/10.1037/tra0000125

Pollard, H. B., Shivakumar, C., Starr, J., Eidelman, O., Jacobowitz, D. M., Dalgard, C. L., Srivastava, M., Wilkerson, M. D., Stein, M. B., & Ursano, R. J. (2016). "Soldier's heart": A genetic basis for elevated cardiovascular disease risk associated with post-traumatic stress disorder. *Frontiers in Molecular Neuroscience, 9*, Article 87. https://doi.org/10.3389/fnmol.2016.00087

Poresky, R. H. (1990). The young children's empathy measure: Reliability, validity and effects of companion animal bonding. *Psychological Reports, 66*(3), 931–936. https://doi.org/10.2466/pr0.1990.66.3.931

Potgieter, J. C., & Botha, K. F. H. (2020). Functioning well: The eudaimonic perspective on well-being. In M. P. Wissing, J. C. Potgieter, T. Guse, I. P. Khumalo, & L. Nel (Eds), *Towards flourishing: Embracing well-being in diverse contexts* (2nd ed., pp. 58–98). Van Schaik.

Prade, C. (2022). Awe in childhood: Conjectures about a still unexplored research area. *Frontiers in Psychology, 13*, Article 791534. https://doi.org/10.3389/fpsyg.2022.791534

Prade, C., & Saroglou, V. (2016). Awe's effects on generosity and helping. *The Journal of Positive Psychology, 11*(5), 522–530. https://doi.org/10.1080/17439760.2015.1127992

Pury, C. L. S., & Hensel, A. D. (2010). Are courageous actions successful actions? *The Journal of Positive Psychology, 5*(1), 62–72. https://doi.org/10.1080/17439760903435224

Pury, C. L. S., & Kowalski, R. M. (2007). Human strengths, courageous actions, and general and personal courage. *The Journal of Positive Psychology, 2*(2), 120–128. https://doi.org/10.1080/17439760701228755

Putman, D. (2001). The emotions of courage. *Journal of Social Philosophy, 32*(4), 463–470. https://doi.org/10.1111/0047-2786.00108

Q

Quesnel, D., & Riecke, B. E. (2018). Are you awed yet? How virtual reality gives us awe and goose bumps. *Frontiers in Psychology, 9*, Article 2158. https://doi.org/10.3389/fpsyg.2018.02158

Quílez-Robres, A., Usán, P., Lozano-Blasco, R., & Salavera, C. (2023). Emotional intelligence and academic performance: A systematic review and meta-analysis. *Thinking Skills and Creativity, 49,* Article 101355. https://doi.org/10.1016/j.tsc.2023.101355

R

Rachman, S. J. (1984). Fear and courage. *Behaviour Therapy, 15*(1), 109–120. https://doi.org/10.1016/S0005-7894(84)80045-3

Radcliffe, E. S. (2015). Hume's psychology of the passions: The literature and future directions. *Journal of the History of Philosophy, 53*(4), 565–605. https://doi.org/10.1353/hph.2015.0069

Rai, A., VillarrealOtálora, T., Blackburn, J., & Choi, Y. J. (2020). Correlates of intimate partner stalking precipitated homicides in the United States. *Journal of Family Violence, 35*(7), 705–716. https://doi.org/10.1007/s10896-020-00137-5

Rankin, K., Andrews, S. E., & Sweeny, K. (2020). Awefull uncertainty: Easing discomfort during waiting periods. *The Journal of Positive Psychology, 15*(3), 338–347. https://doi.org/10.1080/17439760.2019.1615106

Rate, C. R., Clarke, J. A., Lindsay, D. R., & Sternberg, R. J. (2007). Implicit theories of courage. *Journal of Positive Psychology, 2*(2), 80–98. https://doi.org/10.1080/17439760701228755

Ratelle, C. F., Carbonneau, N., Vallerand, R. J., & Mageau, G. A. (2013). Passion in the romantic sphere: A look at relational outcomes. *Motivation and Emotion, 37,* 106–120. https://doi.org/10.1007/s11031-012-9286-5

Ratelle, C. F., Vallerand, R. J., Mageau, G. A., Rousseau, F. L., & Provencher, P. (2004). When passion leads to problematic outcomes: A look at gambling. *Journal of Gambling Studies, 20,* 105–119. https://doi.org/10.1023/B:JOGS.0000022304.96042.e6

Rauf, K., & Iqbal, N. (2024). Exploring the relationship between testanxiety, emotional intelligence and academic performance among university students. *Journal of Education and Educational Development, 11*(1), 119–141. https://doi.org/10.22555/joeed.v11i1.883

Raza, Z., Hussain, S. F., Foster, V. S., Wall, J., Coffey, P. J., Martin, J. F., & Gomes, R. S. (2023). Exposure to war and conflict: The individual and inherited epigenetic effects on health, with a focus on posttraumatic stress disorder. *Frontiers in Epidemiology, 3,* Article 1066158.

Reimann, M., Schilke, O., & Cook, K. S. (2017). Trust is heritable, whereas distrust is not. *Proceedings of the National Academy of Sciences, 114*(27), 7007–7012. https://doi.org/10.1073/pnas.1617132114

ReinermanJones, L., Sollins, B., Gallagher, S., & Janz, B. (2013). Neurophenomenology: An integrated approach to exploring awe and wonder. *South African Journal of Philosophy, 32*(4), 295–309. https://doi.org/ 10.1080/02580136.2013.867397

Reisenzein, R., Horstmann, G., & Schützwohl, A. (2019). The cognitiveevolutionary model of surprise: A review of the evidence. *Topics in Cognitive Science, 11*(1), 50–74. https://doi.org/10.1111/tops.12292

Reynaud, M., Karila, L., Blecha, L., & Benyamina, A. (2010). Is love passion an addictive disorder? *The American Journal of Drug and Alcohol Abuse, 36*(5), 261–267. https://doi.org/10.3109/00952990.2010.495183

Reynolds, C., & Askew, C. (2019). Effects of vicarious disgust learning on the development of fear, disgust, and attentional biases in children. *Emotion, 19*(7), 1268–1283. https://doi.org/10.1037/emo0000511

Richesin, M. T., & Baldwin, D. R. (2023). How awe shaped us: An evolutionary perspective. *Emotion Review, 15*(1), 17–27. https://doi. org/10.1177/17540739221136893

Ridley, C. A., Cate, R. M., Collins, D. M., Reesing, A. L., Lucero, A. A., Gilson, M. S., & Almeida, D. M. (2006). The ebb and flow of marital lust: A relational approach. *Journal of Sex Research, 43*(2), 144–153. https://doi. org/10.1080/00224490609552309

Riedl, R. (2021). Trust and digitalization: Review of behavioural and neuroscience evidence. In F. Krueger (Ed.), *The neurobiology of trust* (pp. 54–76). Cambridge University Press. https://doi.org/10.1017/9781108770880.00

Riess, H. (2017). The science of empathy. *Journal of Patient Experience, 4*(2), 74–77. https://doi.org/10.1177/2374373517701852

Rip, B., Vallerand, R. J., & Lafrenière, M. A. K. (2012). Passion for a cause, passion for a creed: On ideological passion, identity threat, and extremism. *Journal of Personality, 80*(3), 573–602. https://doi.org/10.1111/j.1467-6494.2011.00743.x

Ritter, K., Vater, A., Rüsch, N., Schröder-Abé, M., Schütz, A., Fydrich, T., Lammers, C., & Roepke, S. (2014). Shame in patients with narcissistic personality disorder. *Psychiatry Research, 215*(2), 429–437. https://doi.org/10.1016/j.psychres.2013.10.045

Rizvi, S. J., Pizzagalli, D. A., Sproule, B. A., & Kennedy, S. H. (2016). Assessing anhedonia in depression: Potentials and pitfalls. *Neuroscience & Biobehavioral Reviews, 65*, 21–35. https://doi.org/10.1016/j.neubiorev.2016.03.004

Roberts, R. D., Zeidner, M., & Matthews, G. (2001). Does emotional intelligence meet traditional standards for an intelligence? Some new data and conclusions. *Emotion, 1*(3), 196–231. https://doi.org/10.1037/1528-3542.1.3.196

Robins, R. W., & Schriber, R. A. (2009). The self-conscious emotions: How are they experienced, expressed, and assessed? *Social and Personality Psychology Compass, 3*(6), 887–898. https://doi.org/10.1111/j.1751-9004.2009.00217.x

Rosenman, S. (1938). Franklin D. Roosevelt, inaugural address, March 4, 1933. In *The public papers of Franklin D. Roosevelt, Volume Two: The Year of Crisis, 1933* (pp. 11–16). Random House.

Rottmann, J. (2014). Evolution, development, and the emergence of disgust. *Evolutionary Psychology*, 12(2), 417–433. https://doi.org/10.1177/147470491401200209

Rozin, P., & Haidt, J. (2013). The domains of disgust and their origins: Contrasting biological and cultural evolutionary accounts. *Trends in Cognitive Sciences*, 17(8), 367–368. https://doi.org/10.1016/j.tics.2013.06.005

Rubin, M., Neria, M., & Neria, Y. (2016). Fear, trauma, and posttraumatic stress disorder: Clinical, neurobiological, and cultural perspectives. In Y. Ataria, D. Gurevitz, H. Pedaya, & Y. Neria (Eds), *Interdisciplinary Handbook of Trauma and Culture* (pp. 303–313). Springer Cham.

Rudd, M., Vohs, K. D., & Aaker, J. (2012). Awe expands people's perception of time, alters decision making, and enhances wellbeing. *Psychological Science*, 23(10), 1130–1136. https://doi.org/10.1177/0956797612438731

Ruggeri, K., GarciaGarzon, E., Maguire, Á., et al. (2020). Wellbeing is more than happiness and life satisfaction: A multidimensional analysis of 21 countries. *Health and Quality of Life Outcomes*, 18, Article 192. https://doi.org/10.1186/s12955-020-01423-y

Rummel, R. J. (1977). *Understanding conflict and war: Vol. 3: Conflict in perspective*. Sage Publications.

Ryff, C. D. (2017). Eudaimonic wellbeing, inequality, and health: Recent findings and future directions. *International Review of Economics*, 64(2), 159–178. https://doi.org/10.1007/s12232-017-0277-4

S

Saadatmehr, S. R., Vedadhir, A., Sanagoo, A., & Jouybari, L. (2024). Raising patients' hope in despair: The culture of nursing care of burn pain—An ethnographic study. *Journal of Education and Health Promotion*, 12(1), Article 451. https://doi.org/10.4103/jehp.jehp_1807_22

Saarni, C. (2000). Emotional competence: A developmental perspective. In R. Bar-On & J. D. A. Parker (Eds), *The handbook of emotional intelligence* (pp. 68–91). JosseyBass.

Saboor, Z., Rahimi, P. T., & Mohammadzadeh, E. A. (2019). Effect of hope therapy on general selfefficacy among substance abusers. *Journal of Research in Health, 9*(4), 302–308. https://doi.org/10.29252/jrh.9.4.302

Saleem, F., Zhang, Y. Z., Gopinath, C., & Adeel, A. (2020). Impact of servant leadership on performance: The mediating role of affective and cognitive trust. *SAGE Open, 10*(1). https://doi.org/10.1177/2158244019900562

Salovey, P., Detweiler-Bedell, B. T., Detweiler-Bedell, J. B., & Mayer, J. D. (2008). Emotional intelligence. In M. Lewis, J. M. Haviland-Jones, & L. F. Barrett (Eds), *Handbook of emotions* (pp. 533–547). Guilford Press.

Salovey, P., & Mayer, J. D. (1990). Emotional intelligence. *Imagination, Cognition and Personality, 9*(3), 185–211. https://doi.org/10.2190/DUGGP24E52WK6CDG

Salovey, P., Mayer, J., Goldman, S., Turvey, C., & Palfai, T. (1995). Emotional attention, clarity, and repair: Exploring emotional intelligence using the Trait MetaMood Scale. In J. W. Pennebaker (Ed.), *Emotion, disclosure, and health* (pp. 125–154). American Psychological Association.

Saluja, S., Croy, I., Gruhl, A., Croy, A., Kanbadaty, M., Hellmann, A., & Stevenson, R. J. (2023). Facial disgust in response to touches, smells, and tastes. *Emotion.* Advance online publication. https://doi.org/10.1037/emo0001257

Samadiani, N., Huang, G., Hu, Y., & Li, X. (2021). Happy emotion recognition from unconstrained videos using 3D hybrid deep features. *IEEE Access, 9,* 35524–35538. https://doi.org/10.1109/ACCESS.2021.3061744

SAMHSA. (2023). Practical guide for implementing a traumainformed approach. https://store.samhsa.gov/sites/default/files/pep23-06-05-005.pdf

Sánchez-Álvarez, N., Extremera, N., & Fernández-Berrocal, P. (2016). The relation between emotional intelligence and subjective wellbeing: A metaanalytic investigation. *Journal of Positive Psychology*, 11(3), 276–285. https://doi.org/10.1080/17439760.2015.1058968

Sangha, S., Diehl, M. M., Bergstrom, H. C., & Drew, M. R. (2020). Know safety, no fear. *Neuroscience & Biobehavioral Reviews*, 108, 218–230. https://doi.org/10.1016/j.neubiorev.2019.11.012

Sarrionandia, A., Ramos-Díaz, E., & Fernández-Lasarte, O. (2018). Resilience as a mediator of emotional intelligence and perceived stress: A crosscountry study. *Frontiers in Psychology*, 9, Article 2653. https://doi.org/10.3389/fpsyg.2018.02653

Satpute, A. B., Nook, E. C., Narayanan, S., Shu, J., Weber, J., & Ochsner, K. N. (2016). Emotions in "Black and White" or shades of gray? How we think about emotion shapes our perception and neural representation of emotion. *Psychological Science*, 27(11), 1428–1442. https://doi.org/10.1177/0956797616661555

Sauter, D. A. (2017). The non-verbal communication of positive emotions: An emotion-family approach. *Emotion Review*, 9(3), 222–234. https://doi.org/10.1177/1754073916667236

Schaffer, V., Huckstepp, T., & Kannis-Dymand, L. (2023). Awe: A systematic review within a cognitive behavioural framework and proposed cognitive behavioural model of awe. *International Journal of Applied Positive Psychology*. https://doi.org/10.1007/s41042-023-00116-3

Scherer, K. R., Schorr, A., & Johnstone, T. (Eds). (2001). *Appraisal processes in emotion: Theory, methods, research*. Oxford University Press.

Schnall, S. (2011). Affect, mood and emotions. In S. Järvelä (Ed.), *Social and emotional aspects of learning* (pp. 59–63). Academic Press.

Schöggl, H., Kapfhammer, H. P., Arendasy, M., Sommer, M., & Schienle, A. (2014). Selfdisgust in mental disorders – Symptom-related or disorder-specific? *Comprehensive Psychiatry, 55*(4), 938–943. https://doi. org/10.1016/j.comppsych.2013.12.020

Schonert-Reichl, K. A., & Oberle, E. (2011). Teaching empathy to children: Theoretical and empirical considerations and implications for practice. In B. Weber & E. Marsal (Eds), *The politics of empathy: New interdisciplinary perspectives on an ancient phenomenon*. Lit Verlag.

Schonert-Reichl, K. A., Smith, V., Zaidman-Zait, A., & Hertzman, C. (2011). Promoting children's prosocial behaviours in school: Impact of the "Roots of Empathy" program on the social and emotional competence of schoolaged children. *School Mental Health, 4*(1), 1–21. https://doi. org/10.1007/s12310-011-9040-7

Schornick, Z., Ellis, N., Ray, E., Snyder, B. J., & Thomas, K. (2023). Hope that benefits others: A systematic literature review of hope theory and prosocial outcomes. *International Journal of Applied Positive Psychology, 8*, 1–25. https://doi.org/10.1007/s41042-022-00084-0

Schreiber, K., & Hausenblas, H. A. (2015). *The truth about exercise addiction: Understanding the dark side of thinspiration*. Lanham, MD: Rowman & Littlefield.

Schurtz, D. R., Blincoe, S., Smith, R. H., Powell, C. A. J., Combs, D. J. Y., & Kim, S. H. (2012). Exploring the social aspects of goose bumps and their role in awe and envy. *Motivation and Emotion, 36*(2), 205–217. https://doi. org/10.1007/s11031-011-9243-8

Schutte, N., & Malouff, J. M. (2014). *A Comprehensive Model of Emotional Intelligence*. Nova Science Publishers Inc., New York.

Schutte, N. S., Malouff, J. M., & Thorsteinsson, E. B. (2013). Increasing emotional intelligence through training: Current status and future directions. *The International Journal of Emotional Education, 5*(1), 56–72. https://www.um.edu.mt/library/oar/handle/123456789/6150

Schutte, N. S., Malouff, J. M., Thorsteinsson, E. B., Bhullar, N., & Rooke, S. E. (2007). A meta-analytic investigation of the relationship between emotional intelligence and health. *Personality and Individual Differences, 42*(6), 921–933. https://doi.org/10.1016/j.paid.2006.09.003

Scott, E. (2022, April 18). What is rumination? How rumination differs from emotional processing. *Verywell Mind.* https://www.verywellmind.com/repetitive-thoughts-emotional-processing-or-rumination-3144936

Scott, E. (2024, May 6). Avoidance coping and why it creates additional stress. *Verywell Mind.* https://www.verywellmind.com/avoidance-coping-and-stress-4137836 [Accessed: 05/06/2024].

Scott, K. L., Ferrise, E., Sheridan, S., & Zagenczyk, T. J. (2024). Workrelated resilience, engagement and wellbeing among music industry workers during the Covid19 pandemic: A multiwave model of mindfulness and hope. *Stress and Health, 40*(5), Article e3466.

Sebastian, C. L., & Ahmed, S. P. (2018). The neurobiology of emotion regulation. In *The Wiley Blackwell Handbook of Forensic Neuroscience* (pp. 125–143). John Wiley & Sons. https://doi.org/10.1002/9781118650868.ch6

Seligman, M. E., Abramson, L. Y., Semmel, A., & von Baeyer, C. (1979). Depressive attributional style. *Journal of Abnormal Psychology, 88*(3), 242–247. https://doi.org/10.1037/0021-843X.88.3.242

Seligman, M. E., Steen, T. A., Park, N., & Peterson, C. (2005). Positive psychology progress: Empirical validation of interventions. *American Psychologist, 60*(5), 410–421. https://www.researchgate.net/publication/7701091_Positive_Psychology_Progress_Empirical_Validation_of_Interventions

Shackman, A. J., & Wager, T. D. (2019). The emotional brain: Fundamental questions and strategies for future research. *Neuroscience Letters, 693*, 68–74. https://doi.org/10.1016/j.neulet.2018.10.012

Shafieioun, D., & Haq, H. (2023). Radicalization from a societal perspective. *Frontiers in Psychology*, 14, Article 1197282. https://doi.org/10.3389/fpsyg.2023.1197282

Shammi, P., & Stuss, D. T. (2003). The effects of normal aging on humor appreciation. *Journal of the International Neuropsychological Society*, 9(8), 855–863.

Sharman, L. S., Dingle, G. A., Vingerhoets, A. J. J. M., & Vanman, E. J. (2020). Using crying to cope: Physiological responses to stress following tears of sadness. *Emotion*, 20(7), 1279–1291. https://doi.org/10.1037/emo0000633

Sheldon, K. M., & Lyubomirsky, S. (2021). Revisiting the sustainable happiness model and pie chart: Can happiness be successfully pursued? *The Journal of Positive Psychology*, 16(2), 145–154. https://doi.org/10.1080/17439760.2019.1689421

Shelp, E. E. (1984). Courage: A neglected virtue in the patient-physician relationship. *Social Science & Medicine*, 18(4), 351–360.

Sherman, S. J., & Hoffmann, J. L. (2007). The psychology and law of voluntary manslaughter: What can psychology research teach us about the "heat of passion" defense? *Journal of Behavioral Decision Making*, 20(5), 499–519. https://doi.org/10.1002/bdm.573

Sherwood, L. (2015). Human physiology: From cells to systems. Boston, MA: Cengage Learning.

Shi, H., Yang, L., Zhao, L., Su, Z., Mao, X., Zhang, L., & Liu, C. (2017). Differences of heart rate variability between happiness and sadness emotion states: A pilot study. *Journal of Medical and Biological Engineering*, 37(4), 527–539. https://doi.org/10.1007/s40846-017-0271-5

Shi, M., Stey, A. M., & Tatebe, L. C. (2021). Recognizing and breaking the cycle of trauma and violence among resettled refugees. *Current Trauma Reports*, 7(4), 83–91. https://doi.org/10.1007/s40719-021-00217-x

Shinde, V. (2017). Happiness: Hedonic and eudaimonic. *Indian Journal of Positive Psychology, 8*(2), 169–173. https://doi.org/10.15614/ijpp/2017/v8i2/157136

Shiota, M. N., Campos, B., & Keltner, D. (2003). The faces of positive emotion: Prototype displays of awe, amusement, and pride. *Annals of the New York Academy of Sciences, 100*(1), 296–299.

Shiota, M. N., Campos, B., Oveis, C., Hertenstein, M. J., Simon-Thomas, E., & Keltner, D. (2017). Beyond happiness: Building a science of discrete positive emotions. *The American Psychologist, 72*(7), 617–643. https://doi.org/10.1037/a0040456

Shiota, M. N., Keltner, D., & John, O. P. (2006). Positive emotion dispositions differentially associated with Big Five personality and attachment style. *The Journal of Positive Psychology, 1*(2), 61–71. https://doi.org/10.1080/17439760500510833

Shiota, M. N., Keltner, D., & Mossman, A. (2007). The nature of awe: Elicitors, appraisals, and effects on self-concept. *Cognition and Emotion, 21*(5), 944–963. https://doi.org/10.1080/02699930600923668

Shiota, M. N., Thrash, T. M., Danvers, A. F., & Dombrowski, J. T. (2014). Transcending the self: Awe, elevation, and inspiration. In M. M. Tugade, M. N. Shiota, & L. D. Kirby (Eds), *Handbook of Positive Emotions* (pp. 362–377). New York, NY: The Guilford Press.

Shrira, A., Shmotkin, D., & Litwin, H. (2012). Potentially traumatic events at different points in the life span and mental health: Findings from SHAREIsrael. *American Journal of Orthopsychiatry, 82*(2), 251–259. https://doi.org/10.1111/j.1939-0025.2012.01149.x

Sigmundsson, H., Dybendal, B. H., & Grassini, S. (2022). Motion, relation, and passion in brain physiological and cognitive aging. *Brain Sciences, 12*(9), 1–9. https://doi.org/10.3390/brainsci12091122

Silva, B. A., Gross, C. T., & Graff, J. (2016). The neural circuits of innate fear: Detection, integration, action, and memorization. *Learning & Memory*, 23(10), 544–555. https://doi.org/10.1101/lm.042812.116

Silvia, P. J., Fayn, K., Nusbaum, E. C., & Beaty, R. E. (2015). Openness to experience and awe in response to nature and music: Personality and profound aesthetic experiences. *Psychology of Aesthetics, Creativity, and the Arts*, 9(4), 376–384. https://doi.org/10.1037/aca0000028

Šimić, G., Tkalčić, M., Vukić, V., Mulc, D., Španić, E., Šagud, M., Olucha-Bordonau, F. E., Vukšić, M., & Hof, P. R. (2021). Understanding emotions: Origins and roles of the amygdala. *Biomolecules*, 11(6), Article 823. https://doi.org/10.3390/biom11060082

Simon, P., & NaderGrosbois, N. (2021). Preschoolers' empathy profiles and their social adjustment. *Frontiers in Psychology*, 12, Article 782500. https://doi.org/10.3389/fpsyg.2021.782500

Simpson, J. A. (2007). Psychological foundations of trust. *Current Directions in Psychological Science*, 16(5), 264–268. https://doi.org/10.1111/j.1467-8721.2007.00517.x

Simpson, J. A., & Vieth, G. (2021). Trust and psychology: Psychological theories and principles underlying interpersonal trust. In F. Krueger (Ed.), *The neurobiology of trust* (pp. 15–35). Cambridge University Press.

Sims, K. E., & Meana, M. (2010). Why did passion wane? A qualitative study of married women's attributions for declines in sexual desire. *Journal of Sex & Marital Therapy*, 36(4), 360–380. https://doi.org/10.1080/009262 3X.2010.498727

Simson, J. (1982). Love: Addiction or road to selfrealization—a second look. *American Journal of Psychoanalysis*, 42(3), 253–263. https://doi.org/10.1007/BF01253492

Sin, J., Spain, D., Furuta, M., Murrells, T., & Norman, I. (2017). Psychological interventions for post-traumatic stress disorder (PTSD) in people with severe mental illness. *Cochrane Database of Systematic Reviews, 2017*(1). https://doi.org/10.1002/14651858.CD011464.pub2

Sin, N. L., & Lyubomirsky, S. (2009). Enhancing wellbeing and alleviating depressive symptoms with positive psychology interventions: A practice-friendly meta-analysis. *Journal of Clinical Psychology, 65*(5), 467–487. https://doi.org/10.1002/jclp.20593

Singer, T., & Klimecki, O. M. (2014). Empathy and compassion. *Current Biology, 24*(18), R875–R878. https://doi.org/10.1016/j.cub.2014.06.054

Singh, S., Kshtriya, S., & Valk, R. (2023). Health, hope, and harmony: A systematic review of the determinants of happiness across cultures and countries. *International Journal of Environmental Research and Public Health, 20*(3306), 1–24. https://doi.org/10.3390/ijerph20043306

Skarlicki, D. P., Hoegg, J., Aquino, K., & Nadisic, T. (2013). Does injustice affect your sense of taste and smell? The mediating role of moral disgust. *Journal of Experimental Social Psychology, 49*, 852–859. https://doi.org/10.1016/j.jesp.2013.04.011

Sliter, M., Kale, A., & Yuan, Z. (2014). Is humor the best medicine? The buffering effect of coping humor on traumatic stressors in firefighters. *Journal of Organizational Behavior, 35*(2), 257–272. https://doi.org/10.1002/job.1868

Smith, C. A., David, B., & Kirby, L. D. (2012). Emotion-eliciting appraisals of social situations. In J. P. Forgas (Ed.), *Affect in social thinking and behavior* (pp. 85–102). Psychology Press.

Smith, H., & Schneider, A. (2009). Critiquing models of emotions. *Sociological Methods & Research, 37*(4), 560–589. https://doi.org/10.1177/0049124109335790

Smith, R., Killgore, W. D. S., Alkozei, A., & Lane, R. D. (2018). A neuro-cognitive process model of emotional intelligence. *Biological Psychology, 139*, 131–151. https://doi.org/10.1016/j.biopsycho.2018.10.012

Smith, R. L. (2015). Adolescents' emotional engagement in friends' problems and joys: Associations of empathetic distress and empathetic joy with friendship quality, depression, and anxiety. *Journal of Adolescence*, 45(1), 103–111. https://doi.org/10.1016/j.adolescence.2015.05.011

Smith, T. W. (2016). *The book of human emotions: From ambiguphobia to umpty – 154 words from around the world for how we feel*. Little, Brown Spark.

Snyder, C. R. (2002). Hope theory: Rainbows in the mind. *Psychological Inquiry*, 13(4), 249–275. http://www.jstor.org/stable/1448867

Snyder, C. R., Harris, C., Anderson, J. R., Holleran, S. A., Irving, L. M., Sigmon, S. T., ... Harney, P. (1991). The will and the ways: Development and validation of an individualdifferences measure of hope. *Journal of Personality and Social Psychology*, 60(4), 570–585. https://doi.org/10.1037/0022-3514.60.4.570

Snyder, C. R., Rand, K. L., & Sigmon, D. R. (2002). Hope theory: A member of the positive psychology family. Unpublished manuscript. https://teachingpsychology.files.wordpress.com/2012/02/Hope-theory.pdf [Accessed: 01/06/2024].

Sober, E., & Wilson, D. S. (1998). *Unto others: The evolution and psychology of unselfish behavior*. Harvard University Press.

Song, J. Y., Klebl, C., & Bastian, B. (2023). Awe promotes moral expansiveness via the small-self. *Frontiers in Psychology*, 14, Article 1097627. https://doi.org/10.3389/fpsyg.2023.1097627

South African Concise Oxford Dictionary. (2002). *South African concise Oxford dictionary*. Oxford University Press.

Souza, G. G., Mendonçade-Souza, A. C., Barros, E. M., Coutinho, E. F., Oliveira, L., Mendlowicz, M. V., Figueira, I., & Volchan, E. (2007). Resilience and vagal tone predict cardiac recovery from acute social stress. *Stress*, 10(4), 368–374. https://doi.org/10.1080/10253890701419886

Spallone, P. (1998). New biology of violence: New geneticisms for old? *Body & Society*, 4(4), 47–65. https://doi.org/10.1177/1357034X98004004003

Spice, A., Viljoen, J. L., Douglas, K. S., & Hart, S. D. (2015). Remorse, psychopathology, and psychopathy among adolescent offenders. *Law and Human Behavior*, 39(5), 451. https://doi.org/10.1037/lhb0000155

Spinrad, T. L., & Gal, D. E. (2018). Fostering prosocial behaviour and empathy in young children. *Current Opinion in Psychology*, 20, 40–44. https://doi.org/10.1016/j.copsyc.2017.08.002

Spurr, J. M., & Stopa, L. (2002). Self-focused attention in social phobia and social anxiety. *Clinical Psychology Review*, 22(7), 947–975. https://doi.org/10.1016/S0272-7358(02)00107-1

Stafford, J. M. (1977). On distinguishing between love and lust. *Journal of Value Inquiry*, 11, 292–303. https://doi.org/10.1007/BF00142092

Stamkou, E., Brummelman, E., Dunham, R., Nikolic, M., & Keltner, D. (2023). Awe sparks prosociality in children. *Psychological Science*, 34(4), 455–467. https://doi.org/10.1177/09567976221150616

Starkstein, S. E., & Leentjens, A. F. (2008). The nosological position of apathy in clinical practice. *Journal of Neurology, Neurosurgery & Psychiatry*, 79(10), 1088–1092. https://doi.org/10.1136/jnnp.2007.136895

Statharakos, N., Alvares, A. J., Papadopoulou, E., & Statharakou, A. (2022). Psychology of emotions. In H. T. Hashim & A. Alexiou (Eds), *The psychology of anger* (pp. 21–50). Springer.

Steffen, L. E., Cheavens, J. S., Vowles, K. E., Gabbard, J., Nguyen, H., Gan, G., Edelman, M. J., & Smith, B. W. (2020). Hope-related goal cognitions and daily experiences of fatigue, pain, and functional concern among lung cancer patients. *Supportive Care in Cancer*, 28, 827–835. https://doi.org/10.1007/s00520-019-04878-y

Steimer, T. (2001). The biology of fear and anxiety-related behaviours. *Dialogues in Clinical Neuroscience, 4*(3), 231–249.

Steinberg, V. L. (2005). A heat of passion offense: Emotions and bias in "trans panic" mitigation claims. *Boston College Third World Law Journal, 25,* 499–530.

Steinvik, H. R., Duffy, A. L., & Zimmer-Gembeck, M. J. (2013). Bystanders' responses to witnessing cyberbullying: The role of empathic distress, empathic anger, and compassion. *International Journal of Bullying Prevention.* https://doi.org/10.1007/s42380-023-00164-y

Stellar, J. E., Gordon, A., Anderson, C. L., Piff, P. K., McNeil, G. D., & Keltner, D. (2018). Awe and humility. *Journal of Personality and Social Psychology, 114*(2), 258–269. https://doi.org/10.1037/pspi0000109

Stellar, J. E., Gordon, A. M., Piff, P. K., Cordaro, D., Anderson, C. L., Bai, Y., Maruskin, L. A., & Keltner, D. (2017). Self-transcendent emotions and their social functions: Compassion, gratitude, and awe bind us to others through prosociality. *Emotion Review, 9*(3), 200–207. https://doi.org/10.1177/1754073916684557

Stellar, J. E., John-Henderson, N., Anderson, C. L., Gordon, A. M., McNeil, G. D., & Keltner, D. (2015). Positive affect and markers of inflammation: Discrete positive emotions predict lower levels of inflammatory cytokines. *Emotion, 15*(2), 129–133. https://doi.org/10.1037/emo0000033

Sternberg, R. J. (1985). Implicit theories of intelligence, creativity, and wisdom. *Journal of Personality and Social Psychology, 49*(3), 607–627.

Sternberg, R. J. (1986). A triangular theory of love. *Psychological Review, 93*(2), 119–135. https://doi.org/10.1037/0033-295X.93.2.119

Sternberg, R. J. (1997). Construct validation of a triangular love scale. *European Journal of Social Psychology, 27*(3), 313–335. https://doi.org/10.1002/(SICI)1099-0992(199705)27:3<313::AID-EJSP824>3.0.CO;2-4

Sternberg, R. J., & Sternberg, K. (2018). *The new psychology of love*. Cambridge University Press. https://doi.org/10.1017/9781108658225

StLouis, A. C., Rapaport, M., Chénard Poirier, L., Vallerand, R. J., & Dandeneau, S. (2021). On emotion regulation strategies and wellbeing: The role of passion. *Journal of Happiness Studies, 22*, 1791–1818. https://doi.org/10.1007/s10902-020-00296-8

Strauss, C., Lever, T. B., Gua, J., Kuyken, W., Baer, R., Jones, F., & Cavanagh, K. (2014). What is compassion and how can we measure it? A review of definitions and measures. *Clinical Psychology Review, 47*, 15–27.

Straussner, S. L. A., & Calnan, A. J. (2014). Trauma through the life cycle: A review of current literature. *Clinical Social Work Journal, 42*(4), 323–335. https://doi.org/10.1007/s10615-014-0496-z

Straussner, S. L. A., & Phillips, N. K. (2003). Understanding mass violence: A social work perspective. National Center for Industrial Information. http://ci.nii.ac.jp/ncid/BA78794959

Strohminger, N., Lewis, R., & Meyer, D. (2011). Divergent effects of different positive emotions on moral judgment. *Cognition, 119*(2), 295–300.

Strongman, K. T. (2003). *The psychology of emotion: From everyday life to theory* (5th ed.). Wiley.

Stuewig, J., & Tangney, J. P. (2007). Shame and guilt in antisocial and risky behaviors. In J. L. Tracy, R. W. Robins, & J. P. Tangney (Eds), *The self-conscious emotions: Theory and research* (pp. 371–388). Guilford Publications.

Stuss, D. T., Van Reekum, R., & Murphy, K. J. (2000). Differentiation of states and causes of apathy. In J. C. Borod (Ed.), *The neuropsychology of emotion* (pp. 340–364). Oxford University Press.

Substance Abuse and Mental Health Services Administration. (2023, October 3). Recognizing and treating child traumatic stress. SAMHSA.

https://www.samhsa.gov/child-trauma/recognizing-and-treating-child-traumatic-stress#signs

Sugianto, M. (2020). The birth of compassion. *Budapest International Research and Critics Institute Journal, 3*(2), 777–790. https://doi.org/10.33258/birci.v3i2.890

Summers, J. S. (2015). What is wrong with addiction. *Philosophy, Psychiatry, & Psychology, 22*(1), 25–40. https://doi.org/10.1353/ppp.2015.0011

Sun, H., Tan, Q., Fan, G., & Tsui, Q. (2014). Different effects of rumination on depression: Key role of hope. *International Journal of Mental Health Systems, 8*, Article 53, 1–5. https://doi.org/10.1186/1752-4458-8-53

Sun, Z., Hou, Y., Song, L., Wang, K., & Yuan, M. (2023). The buffering effect of awe on negative emotions in self-threatening situations. *Behavioral Sciences, 13*(1), Article 44. https://doi.org/10.3390/bs13010044

Sung, B., & Yih, J. (2016). Does interest broaden or narrow attentional scope? *Cognition & Emotion, 30*(8), 1485–1494. https://doi.org/10.1080/02699931.2015.1071241

Sussman, S. (2010). Love addiction: Definition, etiology, treatment. *Sexual Addiction & Compulsivity, 17*(1), 31–45. https://doi.org/10.1080/10720161003604095

Szabo, A., de la Vega, R., Kovácsik, R., Almendros, L. J., Ruíz-Barquín, R., Demetrovics, Z., Boros, S., & Köteles, F. (2022). Dimensions of passion and their relationship to the risk of exercise addiction: Cultural and gender differences. *Addictive Behaviors Reports, 16*, Article 100451. https://doi.org/10.1016/j.abrep.2022.100451

Szőcs, H., Sandheden, L., Horváth, Z., & Vizin, G. (2022). The mediating role of state shame, guilt, and pride in the relationship between self-compassion and prolonged grief. *European Journal of Psychiatry, 65*(1), 179–180. https://doi.org/10.1192/j.eurpsy.2022.65.1.179

Szmukler, G. (2013). Anorexia nervosa as a "passion"—or an "addiction". *Philosophy, Psychiatry, & Psychology, 20*(4), 371–374. https://doi.org/10.1353/ppp.2013.0053

Szymańska, M. (2023). The relationship between the harmonious passion development and the human integral development: Educational perspective in brief. *Horyzonty Wychowania, 22*(63), 33–42.

T

Tabibnia, G., & Radecki, D. (2018). Resilience training that can change the brain. *Consulting Psychology Journal: Practice and Research, 70*(1), 59–88. https://doi.org/10.1037/cpb0000110

Tajima-Pozo, K., Bayón, C., Díaz-Marsá, M., & Carrasco, J. L. (2015). Correlation between personality traits and testosterone concentrations in a healthy population. *Indian Journal of Psychological Medicine, 37*(3), 317–321. https://doi.org/10.4103/0253-7176.162945

Takano, R., & Nomura, M. (2023). A closer look at the time course of bodily responses to awe experiences. *Scientific Reports, 13*(1), Article 22506. https://doi.org/10.1038/s41598-023-49681-2

Takayanagi, Y., & Onaka, T. (2021). Roles of oxytocin in stress responses, allostasis, and resilience. *International Journal of Molecular Sciences, 23*(1), Article 150. https://doi.org/10.3390/ijms23010150

Tanay, M. A. L., Roberts, J., & Ream, E. (2013). Humour in adult cancer care: A concept analysis. *Journal of Advanced Nursing, 69*(9), 2131–2140. https://doi.org/10.1111/jan.12059

Tangney, J. P. (1995). Recent advances in the empirical study of shame and guilt. *American Behavioral Scientist, 38*(8), 1132–1145. https://doi.org/10.1177/0002764295038008008

Tangney, J. P. (1999). The self-conscious emotions: Shame, guilt, embarrassment, and pride. In T. Dalgleish & M. J. Power (Eds), *Handbook of cognition and emotion* (pp. 541–568). John Wiley & Sons.

Tangney, J. P., Miller, R. S., Flicker, L., & Barlow, D. H. (1996). Are shame, guilt, and embarrassment distinct emotions? *Journal of Personality and Social Psychology, 70*(6), 1256–1269. https://doi.org/10.1037/0022-3514.70.6.1256

Tangney, J. P., Stuewig, J., Mashek, D., Kendall, S., Goodman, K., & Taylor, C. (2003). Moral emotions and psychopathy: Inmates' shame, guilt, and empathy. In J. P. Tangney (Chair), *Symposium conducted at the 111th Annual Convention of the American Psychological Association.* American Psychological Association.

Tangney, J. P., Youman, K., & Stuewig, J. (2009). Proneness to shame and proneness to guilt. In M. R. Leary & R. H. Hoyle (Eds), *Handbook of individual differences in social behavior* (pp. 192–209). Guilford Press.

Tao, D., He, Z., Lin, Y., Lui, C., & Tao, Q. (2021). Where does fear originate in the brain? A coordinate-based meta-analysis of explicit and implicit fear processing. *NeuroImage, 227*, Article 117634. https://doi.org/10.1016/j.neuroimage.2020.117634

Tarasiuk, J. C., Ciorciari, J., & Stough, C. (2009). Understanding the neurobiology and emotional intelligence: A review. In C. Stough, D. H. Saklofske, & J. A. D. Parker (Eds), *Assessing emotional intelligence: Theory, research, and applications* (pp. 307–320). Springer.

Tarlaci, S. (2012). The brain in love: Has neuroscience stolen the secret of love? *NeuroQuantology, 10*(4), 581–588. https://doi.org/10.14704/nq.2012.10.4.581

Taylor, A., Hodgson, D., Gee, M., & Collins, K. (2017). Compassion in healthcare: A concept analysis. *Journal of Radiotherapy in Practice, 16*(4), 350–360. https://doi.org/10.1017/S1460396917000290

TenHouten, W. (2023). The emotions of hope: From optimism to sanguinity, from pessimism to despair. *The American Sociologist, 54*(1), 76–100. https://doi.org/10.1007/s12108-022-09544-1

Terrizzi, J. A., & Shook, N. J. (2020). On the origin of shame: Does shame emerge from an evolved disease-avoidance architecture? *Frontiers in Behavioral Neuroscience, 14*, Article 19. https://doi.org/10.3389/fnbeh.2020.00019

The Cambridge Handbook of Personal Relationships Editorial Group. (2018). *The Cambridge handbook of personal relationships* (2nd ed). Cambridge University Press.

The Jewish Federations of North America. (n.d.). Aging and trauma. https://cdn.fedweb.org/fed-42/2/AgingAndTrauma_FactSheet_CenterOnAgingAndTrauma_2fdbr.pdf

Thomas, K., Dowd, C., & Broman-Fulks, J. (2017). Systematic desensitization. In *Systematic exploratory interview* (pp. 5355–5356). https://doi.org/10.1007/978-3-319-28099-8_952-1

Thomas, K., Namntu, M., & Ebert, S. (2023). Virtuous hope: Moral exemplars, hope theory, and the centrality of adversity and support. *International Journal of Applied Positive Psychology, 8*(1), 169–194. https://doi.org/10.1007/s41042-022-00083-1

Thompson, J. (2023). Police wellbeing interventions: Using awe narratives to promote resilience. *Journal of Community Safety and Wellbeing, 8*(4), 197–204. https://doi.org/10.35502/jcswb.337

Thomson, A. L., & Siegel, J. T. (2017). Elevation: A review of scholarship on a moral and other-praising emotion. *The Journal of Positive Psychology, 12*(6), 628–638. https://doi.org/10.1080/17439760.2016.1269184

Thorndike, E. L. (1920). Intelligence and its uses. *Harper's Magazine, 140*(835), 227–235.

Timoney, L. R., & Holder, M. D. (2013). Definition of alexithymia. In *Emotional processing deficits and happiness: Assessing the measurement, correlates, and wellbeing of people with alexithymia* (pp. 1–6). Springer.

Ting, E. Y., Yang, A. C., & Tsai, S. J. (2020). Role of interleukin6 in depressive disorder. *International Journal of Molecular Sciences, 21*(6), 2194. https://doi.org/10.3390/ijms21062194

Tinoco-Gonzalez, D., Fullana, M. A., Torrents-Rodas, D., Vervliet, B., Blasco, M. J., Farré, M., & Torrubia, R. (2015). Conditioned fear acquisition and generalization in generalized anxiety disorder. *Behaviour Therapy, 46*(5), 627–639.

Titova, L., & Sheldon, K. M. (2022). Happiness comes from trying to make others feel good, rather than oneself. *The Journal of Positive Psychology, 17*(3), 341–355. https://doi.org/10.1080/17439760.2021.1897867

Titus, C. S., & Scrofani, P. (2012). Psychology of love. *Journal of Psychology and Christianity, 31*(2), 118–129.

Totan, T., Özer, A., & Özmen, O. (2017). The role of hope, life satisfaction, and motivation in bullying among adolescents. *International Online Journal of Educational Sciences, 9*(2), 1–12. https://doi.org/10.15345/iojes.2017.02.008

Tracy, J. L., Cheng, J. T., Robins, R. W., & Trzesniewski, K. H. (2009). Authentic and hubristic pride: The affective core of selfesteem and narcissism. *Self and Identity, 8*(2–3), 196–213. https://doi.org/10.1080/15298860802505053

Tracy, J. L., & Randles, D. (2011). Four models of basic emotions: A review of Ekman and Cordaro, Izard, Levenson, and Panksepp and Watt. *Emotion Review, 3*(4), 397–405. https://doi.org/10.1177/1754073911410747

Tracy, J. L., & Robins, R. W. (2004). Putting the self into self-conscious emotions: A theoretical model. *Psychological Inquiry, 15*(2), 103–125. https://doi.org/10.1207/s15327965pli1502_01

Tracy, J. L., & Robins, R. W. (2007a). Emerging insights into the nature and function of pride. *Current Directions in Psychological Science, 16*(3), 147–150. https://doi.org/10.1111/j.1467-8721.2007.00491.x

Tracy, J. L., & Robins, R. W. (2007b). The psychological structure of pride: A tale of two facets. *Journal of Personality and Social Psychology, 92*(3), 506–525. https://doi.org/10.1037/0022-3514.92.3.506

Tracy, J. L., & Robins, R. W. (2007c). The self in self-conscious emotions: A cognitive appraisal approach. In J. L. Tracy, R. W. Robins, & J. P. Tangney (Eds), *The selfconscious emotions: Theory and research.* Guilford Press.

Trzmielewska, W. D., Rak, T., & Wrześniowski, S. (2022). Does hope in mind influence people's problemsolving performance? *Polish Psychological Bulletin, 53*(1), 22–30. https://doi.org/10.24425/ppb.2022.140478

Tsai, J. L. (2021). Why does passion matter more in individualistic cultures? *Proceedings of the National Academy of Sciences, 118*(14), e2102055118. https://doi.org/10.1073/pnas.2102055118

Turner, R., & Lloyd-Walker, B. (2008). Emotional intelligence (EI) capabilities training: Can it develop EI in project teams? *International Journal of Managing Projects in Business, 1*(4), 512–534. https://doi.org/10.1108/17538370810906237

Tybur, J. M., Lieberman, D., & Griskevicius, V. (2009). Microbes, mating, and morality: Individual differences in three functional domains of disgust. *Journal of Personality and Social Psychology, 97*(1), 103–122. https://doi.org/10.1037/a0015474. PMID: 19586243.

Tybur, J. M., Lieberman, D., Kurzban, R., & DeScioli, P. (2013). Disgust: Evolved function and structure. *Psychological Review, 120*(1), 65–84. https://doi.org/10.1037/a0030778

U

Ulrich, R. S. (1983). Aesthetic and affective response to natural environment. In I. Altman & J. F. Wohlwill (Eds), *Behavior and the natural environment* (Vol. 6, pp. 85–125). Springer. https://doi.org/10.1007/978-1-4613-3539-9_4

University of York. (2015, March 31). *The evolution of our emotional intelligence.* https://www.york.ac.uk/research/themes/cave-art-empathy/

V

Vaccaro, A. G., Wu, H., Iyer, R., Shakthivel, S., Christie, N. C., Damasio, A., & Kaplan, J. (2024). Neural patterns associated with mixed valence feelings differ in consistency and predictability throughout the brain. *Cerebral Cortex, 34*(4). https://doi.org/10.1093/cercor/bhae122

Valabdass, S. N., Subramaney, U., & Edge, A. (2021). Characteristics of persons accused of intimate partner homicide amongst forensic psychiatric observations. *South African Journal of Psychiatry, 27,* Article 1675. https://doi.org/10.4102/sajpsychiatry.v27i0.1675

Valdesolo, P., Shtulman, A., & Baron, A. S. (2017). Science is awe-some: The emotional antecedents of science learning. *Emotion Review, 9*(3), 215–221. https://doi.org/10.1177/1754073916673212

Vallerand, R. J. (2008). On the psychology of passion: In search of what makes people's lives most worth living. *Canadian Psychology / Psychologie Canadienne, 49*(1), 1–13. https://doi.org/10.1037/0708-5591.49.1.1

Vallerand, R. J. (2012). The role of passion in sustainable psychological well-being. *Psychology of Well-Being: Theory, Research and Practice, 2,* Article 1. https://doi.org/10.1186/2211-1522-2-1

Vallerand, R. J., Blanchard, C., Mageau, G. A., Koestner, R., Ratelle, C., Léonard, M., Gagné, M., & Marsolais, J. (2003). Les passions de l'âme:

On obsessive and harmonious passion. *Journal of Personality and Social Psychology, 85*(4), 756–767. https://doi.org/10.1037/0022-3514.85.4.756

Vallerand, R. J., Mageau, G. A., Elliot, A. J., Dumais, A., Demers, M.-A., & Rousseau, F. (2008). Passion and performance attainment in sport. *Psychology of Sport and Exercise, 9*(3), 373–392. https://doi.org/10.1016/j.psychsport.2007.05.003

Vallerand, R. J., Paquette, V., & Richard, C. (2022). The role of passion in psychological and cardiovascular responses: Extending the field of passion and positive psychology in new directions. *Frontiers in Psychology, 12*, Article 744629. https://doi.org/10.3389/fpsyg.2021.744629

Vallerand, R. J., Salvy, S. J., Mageau, G. A., Elliot, A. J., Denis, P. L., Grouzet, F. M., & Blanchard, C. (2007). On the role of passion in performance. *Journal of Personality, 75*(3), 505–534. https://doi.org/10.1111/j.1467-6494.2007.00447.x

Van Cappellen, P., & Rimé, B. (2014). Positive emotions and self-transcendence. In V. Saroglou (Ed.), *Religion, personality, and social behavior* (pp. 123–145). Psychology Press.

Van Cappellen, P., & Saroglou, V. (2012). Awe activates religious and spiritual feelings and behavioral intentions. *Psychology of Religion and Spirituality, 4*(3), 223–236. https://doi.org/10.1037/a0025986

Vanderbilt, K. E., Liu, D., & Heyman, G. D. (2011). The development of distrust. *Child Development, 82*(5), 1372–1380. https://doi.org/10.1111/j.1467-8624.2011.01629.x

Van der Eijk, F., & Columbus, S. (2023). Expressions of moral disgust reflect both disgust and anger. *Cognition and Emotion, 37*(3), 499–514. https://doi.org/10.1080/02699931.2023.2183179

Van der Kolk, B. (2000). Posttraumatic stress disorder and the nature of trauma. *Dialogues in Clinical Neuroscience, 2*(1), 7–22. https://doi.org/10.31887/dcns.2000.2.1/bvdkolk

Van der Westhuizen, M. M., & Bezuidenhout, C. (2020). Criminological theories. In C. Bezuidenhout (Ed.), *A Southern African perspective on fundamental criminology* (2nd ed.). Pearson.

Van Elk, M., Arciniegas Gomez, M. A., van der Zwaag, W., van Schie, H. T., & Sauter, D. (2019). The neural correlates of the awe experience: Reduced default mode network activity during feelings of awe. *Human Brain Mapping, 40*(12), 3561–3574. https://doi.org/10.1002/hbm.24616

Van Elk, M., Karinen, A., Specker, E., Stamkou, E., & Baas, M. (2016). 'Standing in awe': The effects of awe on body perception and the relation with absorption. *Collabra, 2*(1), Article 4. https://doi.org/10.1525/collabra.36

Van Kleef, G. A., & Côté, S. (2022). The social effects of emotions. *Annual Review of Psychology, 73*, 629–658. https://doi.org/10.1146/annurev-psych-020821-010855

Van Kleef, G. A., & Lelieveld, G. J. (2022). Moving the self and others to do good: The emotional underpinnings of prosocial behavior. *Current Opinion in Psychology, 44*, 80–88. https://doi.org/10.1016/j.copsyc.2021.08.029

Van Lange, P. A. M. (2015). Generalized trust: Four lessons from genetics and culture. *Current Directions in Psychological Science, 24*(1), 71–76. https://doi.org/10.1177/0963721414552473

Van Leeuwen, E. J. C., Cohen, E., Collier-Baker, E., Rapold, C. J., Schafer, M., Schutte, S., & Haun, D. B. N. (2018). The development of human social learning across seven societies. *Nature Communications, 9*, Article 2076. https://doi.org/10.1038/s41467-018-04468-2

Van Limpt-Broers, H. A. T., Postma, M., & Louwerse, M. M. (2020). Creating ambassadors of planet Earth: The overview effect in K12 education. *Frontiers in Psychology, 11*, Article 540996. https://doi.org/10.3389/fpsyg.2020.540996

Van Reekum, R., Stuss, D. T., & Ostrander, L. (2005). Apathy: Why care? *The Journal of Neuropsychiatry and Clinical Neurosciences, 17*(1), 7–19. https://doi. org/10.1176/jnp.17.1.7

Van Steelandt, K., Van Mechelen, I., & Nezlek, J. B. (2005). The co-occurrence of emotions in daily life: A multilevel approach. *Journal of Research in Personality, 39*(3), 325–335. https://doi.org/10.1016/j.jrp.2004.05.006

Van Zomeren, M., Pauls, I. L., & Cohen-Chen, S. (2019). Is hope good for motivating collective action in the context of climate change? Differentiating hope emotion- and problem-focused coping functions. *Global Environmental Change, 58*, Article 101915. https://doi.org/10.1016/j. gloenvcha.2019.04.003

Ventura, L. (2024, January 1). *World's most peaceful country 2023. Global Peace Index*. Global Finance. https://gfmag.com/data/most-peaceful-countries/

Verduyn, P., Delvaux, E., Van Coillie, H., Tuerlinckx, F., & Van Mechelen, I. (2009). Predicting the duration of emotional experience: Two experience sampling studies. *Emotion, 9*(1), 83–91. https://doi.org/10.1037/a0014610

Verduyn, P., & Lavrijsen, S. (2015). Which emotions last longest and why: The role of event importance and rumination. *Motivation and Emotion, 39*(1), 119–127. https://doi.org/10.1007/s11031-014-9445-y

Veteran Affairs. (n.d.). *Common reactions*. U.S. Department of Veterans Affairs. https://www.ptsd.va.gov/understand/isitptsd/common_ reactions.asp

Vieth, V. I. (2005). Unto the third generation. *Journal of Aggression, Maltreatment & Trauma, 12*(3–4), 5–54. https://doi.org/10.1300/ J146v12n03_02

Violence Policy Center. (2017). *The relationship between community violence and trauma*. https://vpc.org/studies/trauma17.pdf

Voorend, C. G., van Buren, M., Berkhout-Byrne, N. C., Kerckhoffs, A. P., van Oevelen, M., Gussekloo, J., Richard, E., Bos, W. J. W., & Mooijaart, S. P. (2024). Apathy symptoms, physical and cognitive function, health-related quality of life, and mortality in older patients with CKD: A longitudinal observational study. *American Journal of Kidney Diseases*, 83(2), 162–172.e161. https://doi.org/10.1053/j.ajkd.2023.07.021

W

Wager, K. B., & Kiel, E. J. (2019). The influence of parenting and temperament on empathy development in toddlers. *Journal of Family Psychology*, 33(4), 391–400. https://doi.org/10.1037/fam0000511

Walker, K. D. (2006). Fostering hope: A leader's first and last task. *Journal of Educational Administration*, 44(6), 540–569. https://doi.org/10.1108/09578230610704783

Walsh, C. (2020, February 4). *What the nose knows*. The Harvard Gazette. https://news.harvard.edu/gazette/story/2020/02/how-scent-emotion-and-memory-are-intertwined-and-exploited/ [Accessed: 04/11/2023].

Walton, S. (2004). *A natural history of human emotions*. Grove Press.

Wang, L., Zhang, G., Chen, J., Lu, X., & Song, F. (2022). The territory effect: How awe reduces territoriality and enhances sharing intention. *Journal of Business Research*, 148, 1–11. https://doi.org/10.1016/j.jbusres.2022.04.014

Wang, L., Zhang, G., Shi, P., Lu, X., & Song, F. (2019). Influence of awe on green consumption: The mediating effect of psychological ownership. *Frontiers in Psychology*, 10, 2484. https://doi.org/10.3389/fpsyg.2019.02484

WebMD Editorial Contributors. (2021, April 18). *What is emotional dysregulation?* WebMD. https://www.webmd.com/mental-health/what-is-emotional-dysregulation

Wechsler, D. (1943). Non-intellective factors in general intelligence. *Journal of Abnormal and Social Psychology*, 38(1), 101–103. https://doi.org/10.1037/h0060613

Wells, R., Rehman, U. S., & Sutherland, S. (2016). Alexithymia and social support in romantic relationships. *Personality and Individual Differences*, 90, 371–376. https://doi.org/10.1016/j.paid.2015.11.029

Wen, G., Niu, C., Zhang, Y., & Santtila, P. (2023). Bidirectional relationship between sexual arousal and (sex-related) disgust. *PLOS ONE*, 18(5), e0285596. https://doi.org/10.1371/journal.pone.0285596

Wernli, D., Böttcher, L., Vanackere, F., Kaspiarovich, Y., Masood, M., & Levrat, N. (2023). Understanding and governing global systemic crises in the 21st century: A complexity perspective. *Global Policy*, 14(2), 207–228. https://doi.org/10.1111/1758-5899.13192

Westphal, M. (2011). Kierkegaard on faith, reason, and passion. *Faith and Philosophy*, 28(1), 82–92. https://doi.org/10.5840/faithphil201128118

Whelan, E., Laato, S., Islam, A. N., & Billieux, J. (2021). A casino in my pocket: Gratifications associated with obsessive and harmonious passion for mobile gambling. *PLOS ONE*, 16(2), e0246432. https://doi.org/10.1371/journal.pone.0246432

Wickramaratne, P. J., Yangchen, T., Lepow, L., Patra, B. G., Glicksburg, B., Talati, A., Adekkanattu, P., Ryu, E., Biernacka, J. M., Charney, A., Mann, J. J., Pathak, J., Olfson, M., & Weissman, M. M. (2022). Social connectedness as a determinant of mental health: A scoping review. *PLOS ONE*, 17(10), e0275004. https://doi.org/10.1371/journal.pone.0275004

Williams, L. A., & DeSteno, D. (2009). Pride: Adaptive social emotion or seventh sin? *Psychological Science*, 20(3), 284–288. https://doi.org/10.1111/j.1467-9280.2009.02295.x

Winer, E. S., Nadorff, M. R., Ellis, T. E., Allen, J. G., Herrera, S., & Salem, T. (2014). Anhedonia predicts suicidal ideation in a large psychiatric inpatient sample. *Psychiatry Research*, 218(1–2), 124–128. https://doi.org/10.1016/j.psychres.2014.04.016

Winnicott, D. W. (1965). *The maturational processes and the facilitating environment*. International Universities Press.

Wissing, M. P., Potgieter, J. C., Guse, T., Khumalo, I. P., & Nel, L. (Eds). (2020). *Towards flourishing: Embracing well-being in diverse contexts* (2nd ed.). Van Schaik.

Wlodarczyk, A., Zumeta, L., Basabe, N., Rimé, B., & Páez, D. (2021). Religious and secular collective gatherings, perceived emotional synchrony and self-transcendent emotions: Two longitudinal studies. *Current Psychology*, 42(3), 4754–4771. https://doi.org/10.1007/s12144-021-01826-0

Wolf, Z., Giardino, E., Osborne, P., & Ambrose, M. (1994). Dimensions of nurse caring. *Image: Journal of Nursing Scholarship*, 26, 107–111. https://doi.org/10.1111/j.1547-5069.1994.tb00925.x

Wood, A. M., Froh, J. J., & Geraghty, A. W. (2010). Gratitude and well-being: A review and theoretical integration. *Clinical Psychology Review*, 30(7), 890–905. https://doi.org/10.1016/j.cpr.2010.03.005

Woodard, C. R. (2004). Hardiness and the concept of courage. *Consulting Psychology Journal: Practice and Research*, 56(3), 173–185. https://doi.org/10.1037/1065-9293.56.3.173

Woodard, C. R., & Pury, C. L. S. (2007). The construct of courage: Categorization and measurement. *Consulting Psychology Journal: Practice and Research*, 59(2), 135–147. https://doi.org/10.1037/1065-9293.59.2.135

Worden, J. W. (2018). *Grief counseling and grief therapy: A handbook for the mental health practitioner* (5th ed.). Springer Publishing Company. https://doi.org/10.1891/978082613475

World Health Organization. (2021). *Health promotion glossary of terms 2021* (Licence: CC BY-NC-SA 3.0 IGO). https://www.who.int/publications/i/item/9789240038349

Wrangham, R. W. (2018). Two types of aggression in human evolution. *Proceedings of the National Academy of Sciences*, 115(2), 245–253. https://doi.org/10.1073/pnas.1713611115

Wrigley, A. (2019). Hope, dying and solidarity. *Ethical Theory and Moral Practice*, 22, 187–204. https://doi.org/10.1007/s10677-019-09985-7

X

Xie, J. (2024). Emotional mastery: A comprehensive guide to understanding, processing, and transforming emotions for personal growth. *International Journal of Social Sciences and Public Administration*, 2(1), 129–138. https://doi.org/10.62051/ijsspa.v2n1.17

Xu, N., Zhao, S., Xue, H., Fu, W., Liu, L., Zhang, T., Huang, R., & Zhang, N. (2017). Associations of perceived social support and positive psychological resources with fatigue symptom in patients with rheumatoid arthritis. *PLOS ONE*, 12(3), e0173293. https://doi.org/10.1371/journal.pone.0173293

Xu, S., & Hu, Y. (2023). Nature-inspired awe toward tourists' environmentally responsible behavior intention. *Tourism Review*. Advance online publication. https://doi.org/10.1108/TR-12-2022-0617

Y

Yaden, D. B., Haidt, J., Hood, R. W., Vago, D. R., & Newberg, A. B. (2017). The varieties of self-transcendent experience. *Review of General Psychology*, 21(2), 143–160. https://doi.org/10.1037/gpr0000102

Yaden, D. B., Iwry, J., Slack, K. J., Eichstaedt, J. C., Zhao, Y., Vaillant, G. E., & Newberg, A. B. (2016). The overview effect: Awe and self-transcendent experience in space flight. *Psychology of Consciousness: Theory, Research, and Practice*, 3(1), 1–11. https://doi.org/10.1037/cns0000086

Yaden, D. B., Kaufman, S. B., Hyde, E., Chirico, A., Gaggioli, A., Zhang, J. W., & Keltner, D. (2019). The development of the Awe Experience Scale

(AWE-S): A multifactorial measure for a complex emotion. *The Journal of Positive Psychology, 14*(4), 474–488. https://doi.org/10.1080/17439760.2018 .1484940

Yehuda, R., & Lehrner, A. (2018). Intergenerational transmission of trauma effects: Putative role of epigenetic mechanisms. *World Psychiatry, 17*(3), 243–257. https://doi.org/10.1002/wps.20568

Yin, M., & Lee, E. J. (2023). Planet Earth calling: Unveiling the brain's response to awe and driving eco-friendly consumption. *Frontiers in Neuroscience, 17,* 1251685. https://doi.org/10.3389/fnins.2023.1251685

Young, S., & McGrath, R. (2021). Character strengths as predictors of trust and cooperation in economic decision-making. *Journal of Trust Research, 10,* 1–21. https://doi.org/10.1080/21515581.2021.1922911

Young, S. N. (2008). The neurobiology of human social behaviour: An important but neglected topic. *Journal of Psychiatry & Neuroscience, 33*(5), 391–392. https://www.ncbi.nlm.nih.gov/pmc/articles/PMC2527724/

Youssef, N. A. (2022). Potential societal and cultural implications of transgenerational epigenetic methylation of trauma and PTSD: Pathology or resilience? *The Yale Journal of Biology and Medicine, 95*(1), 171–174. https://pubmed.ncbi.nlm.nih.gov/35370497/

Ypsilanti, A., Robson, A., Lazuras, L., Powell, P., & Overton, P. (2020). Self-disgust, loneliness and mental health outcomes in older adults: An eye-tracking study. *Journal of Affective Disorders, 266,* 646–654. https://doi.org/10.1016/j.jad.2020.01.108

Yu, C. K.-C. (2013). Lust, pornography, and erotic dreams. *Dreaming, 23*(3), 175–193. https://doi.org/10.1037/a0032660

Yuan, W., Chang, J., Jiang, F., & Jiang, T. (2025). Be kinder to yourself: Awe promotes self-compassion via self-transcendence. *Emotion.* Advance online publication. https://doi.org/10.1037/emo0001495

Yuksel-Sokmen, O. (2008). The balance of power, ego & aggression: Deprivation leads to delinquency. *Undergraduate Research Journal for the Human Sciences, 7*. CUNY John Jay College of Criminal Justice. https://publications.kon.org/urc/v7/yuksel-sokmen-3.html

Z

Zackheim, L. (2007). Alexithymia: The expanding realm of research. *Journal of Psychosomatic Research, 63*(4), 345–347. https://doi.org/10.1016/j.jpsychores.2007.08.011

Zaid, S. M., Hutagalung, F. D., Abd Hamid, H. S. B., & others. (2025). The power of emotion regulation: How managing sadness influences depression and anxiety? *BMC Psychology, 13*(1), Article 38. https://doi.org/10.1186/s40359-025-02354-3

Zak, P. J. (2017, January). The neuroscience of trust: Management behaviours that foster employee engagement. *Harvard Business Review*. https://hbr.org/2017/01/the-neuroscience-of-trust

Zelenski, J. (2020). *Positive psychology: The science of well-being*. SAGE.

Zelenski, J. M., & Larsen, R. J. (2000). The distribution of basic emotions in everyday life: A state and trait perspective from experience sampling data. *Journal of Research in Personality, 34*(2), 178–197. https://doi.org/10.1006/jrpe.1999.2275

Zhang, B., & Lin, R. (2023). Dispositional awe and self-worth in Chinese undergraduates: The suppressing effects of self-concept clarity and small self. *International Journal of Environmental Research and Public Health, 20*(13), 6296. https://doi.org/10.3390/ijerph20136296

Zhang, H., Li, J., Sun, B., & Wei, Q. (2023). Effects of childhood maltreatment on self-compassion: A systematic review and meta-analysis. *Trauma, Violence, & Abuse, 24*(2), 873–885. https://doi.org/10.1177/15248380211043825

Zhang, M. (2021). Assessing two dimensions of interpersonal trust: Other-focused trust and propensity to trust. *Frontiers in Psychology*, 12, 654735. https://doi.org/10.3389/fpsyg.2021.654735

Zhang, S., Shi, R., Liu, X., & Miao, D. (2014). Passion for a leisure activity, presence of meaning, and search for meaning: The mediating role of emotion. *Social Indicators Research*, 115, 1123–1135. https://doi.org/10.1007/s11205-013-0260-8

Zhao, H., Zhang, H., Xu, Y., He, W., & Lu, J. (2019). Why are people high in dispositional awe happier? The roles of meaning in life and materialism. *Frontiers in Psychology*, 10, 1208. https://doi.org/10.3389/fpsyg.2019.01208

Zheng, W., Ailin, Y., Fang, P., & Peng, K. (2021). Cultural differences in mixed emotions: The role of dialectical thinking. *Frontiers in Psychology*, 11, Article 538793. https://doi.org/10.3389/fpsyg.2020.538793

Zhou, J., Lang, Y., Wang, Z., Gao, C., Lv, J., Zheng, Y., Gu, X., Yan, L., Chen, Y., Zhang, X., Zhao, X., Luo, W., Chen, Y., Jiang, Y., Li, R., & Zeng, X. (2023). A meta-analysis and systematic review of the effect of loving-kindness and compassion meditations on negative interpersonal attitudes. *Current Psychology*, 42(31), 27813–27827. https://doi.org/10.1007/s12144-022-03866-6

Zhu, A. Q., Kivork, C., Vu, L., Chivukula, M., Piechniczek-Buczek, J., Qiu, W. Q., & Mwamburi, M. (2017). The association between hope and mortality in homebound elders. *International Journal of Geriatric Psychiatry*, 32(12), e150–e156. https://doi.org/10.1002/gps.4676

Zillmann, D. (1983). Arousal and aggression. In R. G. Geen & E. I. Donnerstein (Eds), *Aggression: Theoretical and empirical reviews* (Vol. 1, pp. 75–102). Academic Press.

Zovkic, I. B., & Sweatt, J. D. (2013). Epigenetic mechanisms in learned fear: Implications for PTSD. *Neuropsychopharmacology*, 38(1), 77–93. https://doi.org/10.1038/npp.2012.177

Zuchetto, M. A., Schoeller, S. D., Tholl, A. D., Lima, D. K. S., Neves da Silva Bampi, L., & Ross, C. M. (2020). The meaning of hope for individuals with spinal cord injury in Brazil. *British Journal of Nursing, 29*(9), 526–532. https://doi.org/10.12968/bjon.2020.29.9.526

Zuckerman, B., & Tronick, E. (2020). Origins of empathy and caring: Pediatric implications. *Journal of Developmental & Behavioral Pediatrics, 41*(8), 644–645. https://doi.org/10.1097/DBP.0000000000000839

CONTRIBUTING AUTHORS

Prof. Christiaan Bezuidenhout holds a DPhil in Criminology from the University of Pretoria, and an MSc in Criminology and Criminal Justice from the University of Oxford. He is affiliated to the Department of Social Work and Criminology, University of Pretoria, where he teaches psychocriminology, criminal justice and contemporary criminology at undergraduate and postgraduate level as a full professor. Psychocriminology, criminal justice (policing) and youth misbehaviour are some of his research foci. He has completed a cross-cultural study with an American colleague, focusing on the legal and policing dilemmas of trafficking in humans, and he holds a research rating from the National Research Foundation in South Africa. Further, he was awarded the 2019/2020 University of Pretoria Institutional Community Engagement Award. He has assisted the South African government in the development of different crime prevention initiatives; he serves on the South African Police Service Tertiary Institutions Cluster for Training and Research, and does court work as an expert witness and he was the president of the Criminological Society of Africa (CRIMSA) from 2015–2017. [https://orcid.org/0000-0002-2357-3974] Email: cb@up.ac.za

Dr Linda Bosman is a specialist in early childhood education at Stellenbosch University's Faculty of Education. She is involved in undergraduate and postgraduate teaching and supervises master's and doctoral-level students with various research topics in early childhood. Her scholarly interests centre on child-empowering approaches that uphold children's participation rights, voice, and agency in practice and research. She currently holds the position of president of the South African Research Association for Early Childhood Education (SARAECE). [https://orcid.org/0000-0002-7304-793X] Email: lindabosman@sun.ac.za

Prof. Lobna Chérif holds the position of Chair in Resilience at the Royal Military College of Canada and serves as a Professor in the Department of Military Psychology and Leadership. She is also the founding Director of the Resilience Plus Program, whose objective is to enhance naval officer cadets and leaders' performance through the development and implementation of evidence-based leadership and resilience training and interventions. Her current research delves into character strengths, resilience, and accomplishment, exploring their practical applications. [https://orcid.org/0000-0003-1803-3938] Email: lobna.cherif@rmc.ca

Dr Tyler I. Counsil has amassed over a decade of diverse experience as a forensic scientist, medico-legal death investigator, and postsecondary education instructor and administrator. He uses this expertise in the realm of child abuse investigation and prevention as Zero Abuse Project's Child Advocacy Studies (CAST) Director, overseeing the only evidence-based child maltreatment prevention and response curriculum available for higher education today. Dr Counsil also trains child protection professionals on evidence collection, forensic testing, and child death investigation best practices while simultaneously working to bring the CAST program to new academic institutions and programmes of study. [https://orcid.org/0000-0003-1051-5967] Email: tyler@zeroabuseproject.org

Dr Elsa Etokabeka is a postdoctoral research fellow at Stellenbosch University. A PhD graduate from the University of Pretoria, her study centred on exploring how structured play facilitates executive functions. Prior to obtaining her PhD, she worked as a part-time lecturer, academic supporter, and research assistant. Her research interests include developing executive functions, socio-emotional skills, and improving early childhood learning. In her spare time, she runs Guided Postgrad on Instagram, an online platform that provides research support. [https://orcid.org/0000-0003-1110-2283] Email: elsa.marlyse@gmail.com

Ms Judite Ferreira-Prevost qualified as a teacher and an educational psychologist. After working in private practice for several years, and lecturing at the University of Pretoria, she was appointed Head of the Academic Quality Enhancement Unit at SANTS Private Higher Education Institution. Her work now focuses on quality assurance, assessment, and student affairs in a distance education context, serving students from various sectors of society in South Africa. She has helped develop programme materials for teacher training and development, including those related to inclusive education, life skills, and early childhood education. [https://orcid.org/0000-0001-8767-8954] Email: judite@sants.co.za

Prof. Mathieu Gagnon is an associate professor of psychology at the Royal Military College of Canada in Kingston, Ontario. He was trained as an experimental psychologist and his main research interest centers on emotions. Specifically, he studies how we conceptualize emotions and recognize them in people's faces. His past work has focused on a variety of phenomena including smile interpretation, moral disgust and confusions between fear and surprise. His most recent work focuses on the emotion of awe in both the normal population and specific subgroups (e.g., individuals who grew up with high international mobility). [https://orcid.org/0000-0003-3982-6478] Email: mathieu.gagnon@rmc.ca

Prof. Gina Görgens-Ekermans is an Associate Professor at the Department of Industrial Psychology at Stellenbosch University. Gina attained her PhD from Swinburne University of Technology, in Melbourne, Australia. She is a Chartered HR Practitioner with South African Board of Personnel Practice (SABPP). She is also a National Research Foundation (NRF) C2 rated researcher. Up to date, she has supervised more than 40 master's students, and 3 PhD students to completion. Following from her PhD, which focused on Emotional Intelligence from a cross-cultural perspective, she regularly publishes in national and international journals on research themes pertaining to psychological resources and occupational health, wellbeing and organisational effectiveness. Her research has a strong cross-cultural focus. [https://orcid.org/0000-0002-9742-6889] Email: ekermans@sun.ac.za

Ms Melissa Greenberg holds a Juris Doctor and has been called to the bars of Ontario and California. She has practised civil, family, and criminal law, including legal aid and per diem crown work. Her extensive pro bono advocacy covers a range of issues such as school board closures, antisemitism, defamation, employment, and administrative law. Additionally, she serves on equity and interfaith committees. Melissa earned her undergraduate degree in Criminology and Psychology from the University of Toronto, which sparked her interest in researching and writing academically for the Psychology Department at the Royal Military College of Canada, focusing on Positive Psychology. Email: melissa@mdg18.com

Dr Yolandi-Eloïse Fontaine (née **Janse van Rensburg**) served as an officer in the South African National Defence Force over the period 2000 to 2014. She resigned from the South African Military Health Service, where she worked as an industrial psychologist, to pursue her dream of obtaining a PhD. She received a Joint PhD degree from both Ghent University, Belgium, and the University of Cape Town in 2019. Her collaborative work in Roots of Human Experiences reflects a commitment to interdisciplinary dialogue, compassion, and emotional literacy for all readers—whether in the classroom or everyday life. Her research interests include topics related to positive psychology, emotions- and personality in the work environment. [https://orcid.org/0000-0002-2821-5797] Email: yolandij@sun.ac.za

Ms Palesa Luzipo is a military officer, a registered Industrial/Organizational Psychologist and a lecturer (Head of the Department of IOP [Mil]) at the Faculty of Military Science, Stellenbosch University. She holds a master's degree in Industrial Psychology. Her research interests include military psychology, positive psychology, adaptive psychology, military leadership, wellbeing, training and development, and spirituality in the workplace. [https://orcid.org/0000-0001-7392-7462] Email: palesal@sun.ac.za

Ms Lindiwe Masole is an Industrial/Organisational Psychologist and Lecturer at the Faculty of Military Science, Military Academy, Stellenbosch University, with more than eight years of teaching experience. She is particularly interested in wellness in the workplace. [https://orcid.org/0009-0009-1263-4602] Email: lindim@sun.ac.za

Prof. Melanie Moen is an Associate Professor in the Department of Educational Psychology at Stellenbosch University. Melanie completed her

PhD in Educational Psychology and is a registered psychologist. Her research focus areas are family murder, youth violence and childhood adversity. She has published articles in national and international journals as well as a mono scholarly book titled *Portraits of Pain: Children who kill family members*. She supervises master's and PhD students with their various research topics. She has experience in working with parents and children in private practice, as well as in the education system. She is a C2-rated researcher with the South African National Research Foundation. [https://orcid.org/0000-0001-9075-6642] Email: melaniem@sun.ac.za

Dr Sifiso Shabangu is a clinical psychologist who has worked in public service at a psychiatric hospital, and in private practice. He is currently a post-doctoral research fellow at Stellenbosch University in the Department of Educational Psychology, under the mentorship of Professor Melanie Moen. His research interests are in family murder, violence against children, adolescent mental health, corrections, resilience, and the role of socio-cultural practices within these spaces. [https://orcid.org/0000-0002-3335-1021] Email: sifisombhele1@gmail.com

www.ingramcontent.com/pod-product-compliance
Lightning Source LLC
Chambersburg PA
CBHW080642270326
41928CB00017B/3162